T0305383

THE INSTITUTIONAL FOUNDATION
OF ECONOMIC DEVELOPMENT

The Institutional Foundation of Economic Development

Shiping Tang

PRINCETON UNIVERSITY PRESS

PRINCETON AND OXFORD

Published by Princeton University Press
41 William Street, Princeton, New Jersey 08540
99 Banbury Road, Oxford OX2 6JX

press.princeton.edu

Library of Congress Cataloging-in-Publication Data

Names: Tang, Shiping, 1967– author.
Title: The institutional foundation of economic development / Shiping Tang.
Description: Princeton, NJ : Princeton University Press, [2022] | Includes
    bibliographical references and index.
Identifiers: LCCN 2021059949 (print) | LCCN 2021059950 (ebook) |
    ISBN 9780691235561 (hardback) | ISBN 9780691235578 (paperback) |
    ISBN 9780691235585 (ebook)
Subjects: LCSH: Economic development. | Institutional economics. |
    Political stability—Economic aspects.
Classification: LCC HD82 .T3155 2022 (print) | LCC HD82 (ebook) |
    DDC 338.9—dc23/eng/20220131
LC record available at https://lccn.loc.gov/2021059949
LC ebook record available at https://lccn.loc.gov/2021059950

British Library Cataloging-in-Publication Data is available

Editorial: Bridget Flannery-McCoy and Alena Chekanov
Production Editorial: Jaden Young and Ellen Foos
Jacket/Cover Design: Karl Spurzem
Production: Lauren Reese
Publicity: Kate Hensley and Charlotte Coyne
Copyeditor: Jennifer McClain

This book has been composed in Adobe Text and Gotham

10 9 8 7 6 5 4 3 2 1

To the memory of my grandma (1902–1999)

To my parents and my parents-in-law,
wishing them many happy years ahead.

CONTENTS

Figures

Tables

ABBREVIATIONS

CCGR Cross-country growth regressions

EADS East Asian developmental state

ELF Ethnolinguistic fractionalization

FE Fixed effects (regression model)

GDP Gross domestic product

GDPpc GDP per capita

GMM Generalized method of moments

IFED Institutional foundation of economic development

LAC Latin America and the Caribbean

LDCs Least developed countries

NCE Neoclassical economics

NCT Niche construction theory

NDT New development triangle (state capacity, institutions, and policies)

NIE New institutional economics

OLS Ordinary least squares

OTA Obedience to authority

QOG Quality of governance

RE Random effects (regression model)

SEP Social evolution paradigm

SNC Social niche construction

SSA Sub-Saharan Africa

SVI Selection-variation-inheritance (as the central mechanism of social evolution)

TFP Total factor productivity

VSI Variation-selection-inheritance (as the central mechanism of biological evolution)

As far as I can tell, there are only two fundamental and enduring topics in the whole of social sciences: conflict and cooperation (or, war and peace in lay terms), and economic development or long-run growth (which can also be referred to as the rise and fall of nations). Economic development is the more pressing one now, because the world has gradually evolved into a more peaceful system (Tang 2013).

Born in 1967, I grew up in a tiny, mountainous, and poor village of about a dozen households in Hunan Province in southern China. My mother is my grandparents' only surviving child, and my grandfather passed away in 1960 during the Great Famine, before my mother got married in 1965. Not too long after the beginning of the Cultural Revolution in early 1968, my father, who was a high school teacher of Chinese, was jailed as a counterrevolutionary when I was just 14 months old. My father remained in jail from 1968 to 1974. Thus, for six long years, my mother and grandmother brought me up through their sheer stamina and hard labor. Back then, however, I had no idea what poverty was, only remembering that my family could consume meat only once in a great while. I began to do some light farm work when I was only four.

I started primary school in 1972 when I was five years old. As I moved from my village to the county capital for junior high and then high school, and finally to a provincial capital—Wuhan of Hubei Province—for college in 1981, I became aware of the different levels of income enjoyed by different people. But overall, China was a very poor country until 2000. Indeed, in 1984 I was shocked to discover that some villages in the southern part of Shan-Xi Province were even poorer than my village, which I thought was already extremely poor.

Like most young Chinese students of my generation, I used to believe firmly that science and technology were the most direct and vital engines of economic development. Therefore, when I enrolled in college, I chose a natural science major, geology, as an undergraduate and then molecular biology as an MA student. Yet, the shocks I experienced after moving from inland China to the coastal city of Shenzhen (a Special Economic Zone just across from Hong Kong), as well as from watching the collapse of the socialist countries of Central and Eastern Europe on live TV, gave me a greater awareness of the profound economic, political, and social changes unfolding in China and beyond. Perhaps I was already preparing myself for my preordained shift to social sciences even back then.

I studied molecular biology in the United States from 1990 to 1997 and then switched to social sciences from 1997 to 1999. I came back to China in 1999, and in early 2006 I moved to Singapore and worked there from 2006 to 2009. For the past 20-plus years, I have also traveled to several other countries. All these travels and periods of foreign residence have made me more aware of the extreme poverty endured by most people in developing countries but also the much higher living standard enjoyed by most common folks in developed countries. Within the United States, I also witnessed glaring inequality and racial discrimination firsthand in Detroit, Michigan. More relevant for this project, I began wondering why my salary in China, the United States, and Singapore has varied so enormously. These are all problems of economic development. Perhaps I had been thinking about economic development all along, however subconsciously, even when I was thinking about conflict and cooperation.

I began to take the puzzle of economic development more seriously when I was posted as a midlevel government official in Ningxia Hui Autonomous Region in northwestern China from 2002 to 2003. Ningxia hosted three counties, Xi-ji, Hai-yuan, and Gu-yuan, that were collectively known as one of the poorest regions not only in China but in the world. During my year-long stay in Ningxia, I had the opportunity to travel extensively throughout the region. I visited villages, factories, and schools and talked to peasants, workers, teachers, students, and officials. Everywhere I went, I saw that people wanted to better their lives but often felt that not much could be done by themselves.

During that time, I began to think that if a country is poor, it must be the state's responsibility, and the state must act through policies and institutions. I also came to appreciate the profound effect of the "simple" reform initiated by the late Deng Xiaoping. By rejecting the Confucian and socialist mantra that only self-sacrifice makes a community prosperous, Deng Xiaoping was merely going back to the teaching of Adam Smith ([1776] 1981): a country can only prosper if it lets its people make money for their self-interest. With such a simple move, Deng Xiaoping had unleashed the potential of the Chinese people and made possible the "China miracle" over the past four decades or so.

This book is the product of my rather long journey of puzzling over economic development, starting from that tiny village in Hunan, China. Along the way, I have incurred enormous intellectual and spiritual debt.

In Berkeley, Hong-yung Lee introduced institutions and economic development to me in his course on the post–World War II political economy of East Asia in 1998. Besides the works of Douglass North and Mancur Olson Jr., Hong-yung also highlighted the political economy of the East Asian developmental state. Furthermore, I learned something about the critical role of industrial policy from the courses taught by Laura Tyson and John Zysman.

This project formally started at the Institute of Asia-Pacific Studies (IAPS), part of the Chinese Academy of Social Sciences (CASS), after I returned from Ningxia in 2003. I have been extremely fortunate to have worked under the directorship of Professor Yunling Zhang, whose generosity, encouragement, and support made my various academic ventures possible.

Perhaps most critically for this project, I was able to secure that yearlong stint as a local official in Ningxia during my days with IAPS. It was during that year that my thinking about the institutional foundation of economic development began to crystallize and come together. As assistant director in the Bureau of International Trade (before it merged with another bureau to form the Bureau of Commerce) in Ningxia, I had the responsibility of attracting foreign and domestic investment to Ninxia and promoting Ninxia's exports. Equally important, I also participated in poverty alleviation programs for poor rural families and local schools, trying to promote economic growth at both the meso- and micro levels, even if only marginally. I learned a great deal about economic development on the job, and many key lessons might not have been possible by merely reading textbooks, playing with models, and running regressions.

I took this project with me to various places as I moved around. At the East Asian Institute at the National University of Singapore, then under the directorship of the great historian Wang Gungwu, I drafted the first outline of this volume. Life took an interesting turn, however, and I ended up writing a different book. After discovering that there was no general theory of institutional change despite the voluminous literature on the subject, I wrote a book titled *A General Theory of Institutional Change* (Tang 2011b).

The Institutional Foundation of Economic Development was put on the back burner while I was teaching at the S. Rajaratnam School of International Studies of Nanyang Technological University (2006–2009). During that period, I was mostly working on conflict and cooperation and published two volumes on international relations (Tang 2010, 2013). Only after coming to Fudan University in 2009 was I able to pick up the project again.

Three giants, Adam Smith, Arthur Lewis, and Albert Hirschman, laid much of the foundation for my understanding of economic development. While building upon the work of many learned economists, however, my project also departs from mainstream developmental economics decisively at its starting point: I drew from a very diverse body of literature—from anthropology, to political science, to sociology. I believe that if one wants to solve the puzzle of economic development, one cannot only think within the boundary of economics; one must bring insights from all the fields of social science.

Put differently, economic development is not an economic puzzle, but a political puzzle first, an economic puzzle second, and perhaps a sociological puzzle third. Economic development should not be the exclusive domain of economics and economists. After all, neither David Hume—the first serious economist ahead of Adam Smith, according to Walt Whitman Rostow—nor Smith was an economist by training as there was no formal discipline of economics back then.

As a social scientist who has never been formally trained as an economist, I have never been bound by the straitjacket of mainstream economics. In fact, I think the field of mainstream economics may be inherently incapable of solving the puzzle of economic development due to its neglect of contributions from other fields of the social sciences and its obsession with technical details (either in modeling or in econometric exercises) that leaves out deductive theorization without models and qualitative evidence from historical cases. Formal modeling often prevents us from incorporating enough variables and contexts. Obsession with "clean" causal identification dictates that many questions of great importance are ignored or pushed aside due to a lack of data that allow for "clean" causal inferences.

Thus, in order to understand economic development more adequately, we need a more eclectic and pragmatic approach. While I do value deduction more, I also include induction; and while I do employ formal modeling, I also use deductive theorization without formal modeling. In my work, I present econometric evidence whenever possible and wherever appropriate, yet I also draw from powerful qualitative evidence. The proper yardstick for scientific progress cannot be a singular measure, but should be a reasonable combination of theorization, hypothesis, and evidence.

Among contemporary institutional development economists (besides the usual suspects, such as Douglass North and his followers), I drew more inspiration from Mancur Olson Jr. and Dani Rodrik; both of them possess a style similar to that of Hirschman. Although both Olson and Rodrik are mainstream (i.e., neoclassical) development economists, they are also open-minded or unorthodox enough to think beyond the boxes of neoclassical economics and rational choice, despite Rodrik's (2007, 3) insistence otherwise.

Before his untimely death, Olson had examined two different types of economies—developing countries and developed countries—most prominently in his *Rise and Decline of Nations* (1982) and "Big Bills Left on the Sidewalk" (1996). He had also inquired into the political economy of two types of political regimes, most visibly in his "Dictatorship, Democracy, and Development" (1993) and "The Economics of Autocracy and Majority Rule" (McGuire and Olson 1996). Unfortunately, Olson was unable to bring these two themes together even in his last book, *Power and Prosperity* (2000), partly because he was still too much under the spell of neoclassical economics (despite his deep interest in political power and his scathing attack against the universality of the Coase theorem; see Dixit and Olson 2000) and partly because he had always been fond of "stark and simplifying propositions," or big theories centered on one or two big variables or mechanisms. Needless to say, with both traits in place, his big theories cannot carry us very far (Keefer 2000; McLean 2000; Wintrobe 2001; Rose-Ackerman 2003).

Rodrik has always taken a more eclectic approach toward economic development. Despite valuing the utilities of models, he does not insist that only models can lead to theories. Rodrik (2003b, 10) has also rightly stressed that "a claim based on case studies that does not find support from cross-country regressions requires closer scrutiny. By the same token, any cross-national empirical regularity that cannot be meaningfully verified on the basis of country studies should be regarded as suspect." In other words, we often need both kinds of evidence to arrive at an adequate understanding about how development works.

Among contemporary Chinese economists, I have learned most from Justin Yifu Lin. While I like his earlier work on institutions (Lin 1989, 1995; Lin and Nugent 1995) more than his "new structural economics," which singles out development strategy (Lin 2003, 2009, 2012b, 2012c), his passionate search for different perspectives on development has always been an inspiration. I also thank Justin for hosting a conference on development economics in 2017 at which I was able to present some of the ideas contained herein, albeit in rough forms.

In the broader social sciences, including economics, I have learned a great deal from the works of Pranab Bardhan, Ha-Joon Chang, Jared Diamond, Stanley Engerman, Stephan Haggard, Yukon Huang, Geoffrey Hodgson, Charles Jones, Michael Miller, Barry Naughton, Richard Nelson, Arkebe Oqubay, Michael Ross, Kenneth L. Sokoloff, Rory Truex, Andrew Walder, Yong Wang, and Yi Wen. Many of them have kindly provided comments for various parts of this book. My apologies to other scholars I have forgotten to acknowledge here.

As previously mentioned, I started this project when I was still with IAPS of CASS. I also drafted parts of the manuscript when visiting the East Asia Institute at the National University of Singapore and the School of Global Policy at the University of California, San Diego. Much of the writing has been done at Fudan University, my home institution, over the past decade or so.

Many former and current colleagues and students have also provided intellectual discussion and spiritual support over the years: Cheng Gao, Zhan Hu, Zhengqian Huang, Chen Liu, Min Tang, Rui Tang, Chengcheng Ye, Yuyang Zhang, Jianglin Zhao, Litao Zhao, Yu Zheng, Xiaobing Zhou, and Qing Zhu. I have been very fortunate to work with some wonderful coauthors as well: Suo Chen (chapter 4), Rui Tang (chapter 6), and Chengcheng Ye (chapter 4).

Yue Tian deserves special credit for her outstanding assistance in checking references and compiling the indexes. Her editorial skills and meticulousness have been essential.

I thank Mingjiong Jiang and Wei Shao for being kind enough to keep their "boutique" coffee shop open for the past decade so that I had a place to read and think while sipping good coffee. Alas, that was a lot of coffee.

Three special friends, Tao Cui, Hongmei Li, and Yu Zhang, have helped me carry on in hard times, with their unflinching faith in me, coupled with support, encouragement, and understanding. Leslie Fong, Jin Han, and Xin Yan—friends as well as mentors—have taught me things that I could not possibly learn by reading books.

Special thanks are due to audiences at the School of International Development of China Agricultural University, Fudan University, the Institute of World Economics and Politics of CASS, the East Asian Institute of National University of Singapore, a Peking University–Fudan University joint workshop, Ren-min University, Peking University, Shanghai Jiao-tong University, and Tsing-hua University, where I have presented various parts of the project.

At Princeton University Press, things got started in 2015 with a coffee chat. For whatever reason, Eric Crahan took an early interest in my work, and I thank him for his initial blind confidence. Bridget Flannery-McCoy then shouldered the burden of actually guiding the project and provided patient direction before the manuscript was ready (with several passed deadlines, inevitably). During Bridget's maternity leave, Alena Chekanov shepherded the project over the finish line with great enthusiasm. Jennifer McClain copyedited the manuscript with meticulosity and precision. Additionally, two anonymous reviewers have provided critical support for the project. All of them have made this project a blissful experience in its final stage. In fact, among the five books I have published, this book has been the easiest sailing.

A very crude version of chapter 2 was published as working paper no. 156 (2005) by the East Asian Institute of the National University of Singapore under the title "What Do Institutions Do Exactly? Toward an Understanding of the Institutional Foundation of Economic Growth." An earlier and shorter version of chapter 3 was published in the *Journal of Economic Issues* (2010). An earlier version of chapter 6, coauthored with Rui Tang, was published in *Kyklos* (2018). I thank Taylor & Francis and Wiley & Sons for allowing me to reuse these previously published materials.

My deepest gratitude goes to my extended family. My parents not only endowed me with the stamina to tough it out but also tolerated me for spending so little time with them over the years. My wife, Lin Wang, and my parents-in-law have shouldered much of the burden of raising my son, Xiaoyu, who has grown up with my books. So far, he has had the same reaction to yet another book published by his father: "Wooh, another book!"

Finally, I dedicate this book to my grandma, my parents, and my parents-in-law. My grandma and my mom raised me in that tiny village when my dad was away. Unfortunately, my grandma passed away in 1999: she survived the turbulent years of modern China but enjoyed little of the fruits of China's development. I wish she could still be with us today. My parents and parents-in-law can now reap some of the benefits of China's development after too having endured much hardship. I wish all of them a very long life and many happy years ahead.

THE INSTITUTIONAL FOUNDATION
OF ECONOMIC DEVELOPMENT

Introduction

INSTITUTIONS MATTER?

Economic development, or long-run economic growth, is one of the most central questions in the social sciences, and arguably the most pressing challenge for developing countries. Robert Lucas Jr. (1988, 5) did not overstate it by much: "Once one starts to think about them [i.e., the vast differences in income and welfare across time and space, underpinned by their histories of economic development], it is hard to think about anything else."

Today, the notion that institutions matter for economic development is widely accepted (North 1990; Olson 2000; Acemoglu, Johnson, and Robinson 2005a; World Bank 1997, 2002, 2005, 2017). In fact, other than neoclassical economics (NCE) and endogenous growth theory, the new institutional economics (NIE) is the other mainstream approach toward development.[1]

Institutions can be understood as instruments for allocating production factors to different sectors or shifting an economy from one state to another. In Adam Smith's ([1776] 1981, 10) penetrating words, "*[The wealth of nations] must be regulated by two different circumstances; first, the skill, dexterity, and judgment with which its labor is generally applied; and secondly, the proportion between the number of those who are employed in useful labor, and that of those who are not so employed*" (emphasis added). Thus, with an institutional component within a toy model, Tang and Gao (2020) have shown that many folds of differences in growth rates can materialize once the population growth rate reaches around 0.5%–1%, simply because institutions can channel production factors into very different production processes. One state channels production factors mostly to welfare-improving productive processes, whereas another state channels mostly to welfare-reducing ones. As a result, the income gap between them gradually becomes enormous after several decades. The model therefore makes it clear that the most critical role for institutions is to allocate production factors (i.e., land, labor, capital, technology), including talent (Murphy et al. 1991), to different production processes, and the outcomes of these production processes then determine the overall welfare.

Thus, it was perhaps no accident that although Adam Smith and Karl Marx disagreed on fundamental things, they agreed on one particular point: at least since the emergence of capitalism, institutions (with capitalism as an overarching institutional system) have been a critical force, if not the primary mover, behind development.

But what exactly is the institutional foundation of economic development, or IFED? Despite much ink spilled, social scientists, including (institutional) economists, have not provided a systematic statement on what constitutes IFED. North and his followers may believe that it is mostly property rights and constraining the executive (or the state) with parliament or democracy as an "open access order" (e.g., North et al. 2009; see also Olson 2000) or an "inclusive (economic and political) institutional system" (e.g., Acemoglu and Robinson 2012). This answer, however, is simplistic and tautological (Boldrin et al. 2013). Others may hold that it is "development clusters" (Besley and Persson 2011). This answer smacks of all-good-things-go-together: it is like pointing to a fresco of prosperity to the least developed countries (LDCs) and telling them, "Just get there!" As such, they are of little help to policymakers and their advisers in developing countries for engineering development (Jennings 2013; Bardhan 2016; see chapter 1 for details).[2]

A key shortcoming of the above-mentioned works is that they have taken a mostly inductive approach, either by extrapolating from the British (or Western European) experience or by identifying correlations between institutional factors and indicators of economic performance. As such, they cannot possibly offer a systematic statement of IFED.

This book thus tackles the puzzle with a mostly deductive approach. Starting with the metaphor of "Big Bills Left on the Sidewalk" (Olson 1996), I ask the question, What institutions will *encourage* and *enable* an individual to pick up those "big bills" *in a socially productive way* (i.e., welfare-improving) and discourage and prevent an individual from picking up those big bills *in a socially unproductive if not destructive way* (i.e., welfare-decreasing)? Hence, I focus on the *functions* performed by institutions rather than the *forms* of institutions (on this key understanding, see Chang 2007b, 17–21), explicitly admitting that the same function can be performed by different forms (and combinations) of institutions.

Here, it is important to note that "socially productive" is different from "Pareto-improving." Most critically, socially productive initiatives may well reduce the welfare of some members within a society even though collectively the overall welfare of the society improves because those initiatives increase the welfare of more members within a society. In other words, an initiative is socially productive as long as it increases the overall welfare of the society. For instance, land reform is often considered a socially productive initiative in most LDCs, and yet it almost certainly reduces the welfare of large landlords, at least in the short run. The deep reason for staking the seemingly "collectivist" stance is that (almost) all institutions are made and backed by power and have distributional effects (Tang 2011b).[3]

Through logical deduction, I then contend that for an individual to pick up those big bills in a socially productive way, "four big things" must be in place: *possibility, incentive, capability,* and *opportunity.* I further contend that these four big things must be understood interactively rather than independently. Thus, NIE's overselling of incentives following North (1990, 3), often in conjunction with restraining the executive, is at least too simplistic, if not misleading, because incentives can be for unproductive activities as well as productive activities (e.g., Baumol 1990; see chapter 1 for details).[4]

Assuming the four big things are to be underpinned by IFED, then IFED must contain at least six major dimensions, namely, (political) hierarchy, property rights, social mobility, good redistribution (as empowering), liberty for protecting innovation, and equality of opportunity.[5] To elaborate on the six dimensions, I draw insights from the economics literature on economic development but also from the literature on economic (and political) development in comparative politics, sociology (e.g., the sociology of development), social psychology, and political theory.

Combining growth modeling, econometrics, and in-depth case studies, I then provide evidence that countries with the right combination of institutions at the right stage of development have indeed managed to grow robustly for a significant period of time and transform their economies. As such, in order to achieve economic development, states should get key dimensions within IFED *roughly* right for their particular stages of development. I also argue for an evolutionary and pragmatic, rather than a static and dogmatic, understanding about IFED: different stages of economic development need different combinations of specific institutions within the six dimensions of IFED.

I, however, explicitly recognize that economic development is a challenge without any institutional panacea (e.g., property rights plus democracy), contrary to what North and his followers have explicitly or implicitly preached (e.g., North 1990; North et al. 2009; Acemoglu and Robinson 2012). In short, I reject "institutional determinism" as just another one of those "X-theories" of economic development (Adelman 2001; see also below).

In fact, IFED is only one component of the "new development triangle" (NDT), which contains state capacity and socioeconomic policy in addition to IFED (cf. Besley and Persson 2011; Aghion and Roulet 2014; Bardhan 2016). Essentially, for a state to achieve economic development, it has to become a "developmental state" underpinned by NDT, by working with what it has rather than with what is ideal.

Before going any further, four caveats regarding terms are in order. First, this book addresses the question of economic development or economic growth in the long run, rather than economic growth per se. Economic development is more than economic growth (Myrdal 1974). The former implies not just growth over a significant period of time but also progressive changes in the structure of an economy (see Herrendorf et al. 2014 for a review). More concretely, economic development means that an economy has climbed up the technological ladder: growth of income from oil or gas (e.g., Saudi Arabia, Venezuela) does not mean development. Our discussion here is about development,[6] although for simplicity I often use development and growth interchangeably.

Second, when referring to institutions, I adopt North's (1990, 3) definition: institutions are formal or informal rules, not organizations (or "institutes"), because organizations are agents rather than rules for agents.[7] Although organizations are underpinned by institutions and they are often makers and enforcers of institutions (e.g., in the case of states), organizations are not institutions. Hence, the state is a highly complex organization but not an institution. Of course, a state must use or deploy institutions and policies and rely on suborganizations within it (e.g., bureaucracies) to rule and govern.

Also, although economic and sociopolitical policies are also rules, following many others (Easterly 2005; Rodrik 2007; Lin and Nugent 1995; Lin 2009) I use "institutions" to denote rules that cast a long shadow on how an economy operates and "policies" to denote measures or rules that are mostly designed to address short- to medium-term fluctuations (e.g., interest rate changes, fiscal stimuli), while admitting that the boundary between institutions and rules is not always clear-cut. Indeed, I address the interplay of institutions, state capacity, and socioeconomic policy in chapter 8.

I, however, explicitly reject two critical elements associated with North's definition. When North (1990, 3) followed his definition of institutions with the sentence "[Institutions] structure incentives in human exchange," and then centered his whole theory of institutions and institutional change on transaction costs (North 1990, esp. ch. 4), he sowed the seeds for NIE's overselling of both incentives and transaction costs. More critically, his focus on incentives and transaction costs almost inevitably leads to a functionalism theory of institutions that cannot possibly explain the making and persistence of welfare-reducing institutions. Institutions do far more than reducing uncertainties, structuring incentives, and regulating transaction costs: because institutions are made and backed by power, the foremost role of institutions is to allocate and (re)distribute resources and payoffs (for a detailed critique, see Tang 2011b).[8] Moreover, institutions not only constrain but also enable agents: there is duality associated with institutions as part of the social (and power) structure (Tang 2011b, esp. 56–60; see also Giddens 1976, 1979, 1984; Foucault 2000; Sewell 1992).

Third, *even though I am a firm institutionalist, this volume does not argue that only institutions matter.* As becomes clear below and especially in chapter 8, I actually admit that both state capacities and (development) policies also matter a great deal, and together with institutions they form a (new) development triangle (NDT). The purpose of this book is to map out the exact dimensions of IFED only because a systematic statement on IFED has yet to exist. Moreover, a systematic statement on IFED contributes to a more integrated and evolutionary understanding of economic development (see chapters 7 and 8).[9]

Finally, although my project is mostly a deductive project with empirical evidence, I cannot possibly provide supporting evidence for all my theoretical conjectures. What I do is provide enough evidence to suggest that the theory developed here is plausible and hence point to new directions for future inquiries.

The rest of this introduction unfolds as follows. Section I briefly identifies key shortcomings within the existing literature on institutions and development, and section II then foreshadows what this volume is and is not about. Section III lays out the structure of the book, with a brief summary of each chapter.

I. Searching for the (Prime) Movers behind Development

Ever since Kaldor (1961), it has been a cliché to begin any discussion of economic development with "stylized facts" (e.g., Pritchett 2003, 126–28; Jones and Romer 2010; Jones 2015; see also Jones 1997; Hall and Jones 1999; Pritchett 1997, 2000; Easterly and Levine 2001). While different authors may differ in their exact listing of facts, one is common to all of them: there remain large per capita income and total factor productivity (TFP) differences across countries. What, then, accounts for this "divergence, big time"?

An immediate answer to this puzzle is obviously that some countries have managed to grow robustly for a significant period of time and become rich, whereas most countries have failed to do so despite some episodes of robust growth. This has indeed been the case. As shown in table I.1, with reliable data (1970–2015), only 43 countries have managed to grow their per capita GDP at a rate of 4% or more over a period of two decades or more.

So the puzzle of "divergence, big time" becomes, *Why* have some countries managed to grow robustly for a significant period of time and become rich, whereas most countries have failed to do so despite some (shorter) episodes of robust growth?

The first factors we can exclude are the usual suspects: labor, capital, and technology, or production factors. As noted by both Abramovitz (1956) and Solow (1957), measured input of production factors can only account for 13%–14% of the growth. In other words, the "big three" of capital, labor, and technology (or knowledge), either treated exogenously or endogenously (Solow 1956; Swan 1956; Romer 1989, 1990; Grossman and Helpman 1991; Jones 2001, 2005), cannot account for this significant disparity (Jones and Romer 2010, 237; see also Pritchett 2003; Subramanian and Roy 2003).[10]

In light of this fact, several alternative "primary movers" have been put forward for explaining the divergence.[11] Five have been most prominent: biology, geography, culture, (developmental) strategies and policies,[12] and institutions.

We can readily reject biology: economic development is not genetic or biological (Tang 2020). Contrary to Ashraf and Galor (2013), there is no plausible (direct and indirect) link between the genetic or biological makeup of the human population and complex social outcomes such as economic development. Indeed, the supposedly robust regression results in Ashraf and Galor (2013) suggesting genetic diversity is linked to development are

TABLE I.1. The "Lucky" Few: Countries with at Least 10 Years of ≥4% Growth in GDPpc

Only 10 years (then stagnated)	Only 20 years	Only 30 years	Only 40 years	50 years or more
Argentina	Albania	Bhutan	Iraq	Botswana
Bulgaria	Algeria	Chile	Ireland	China
Burundi	Angola	Cyprus	Malaysia	Korea, South
Cameroon	Bangladesh	Equatorial Guinea	Portugal	Oman
Chad	Brazil	India	Sri Lanka	Singapore
Costa Rica	Cambodia	Indonesia		Thailand
Cote d'Ivoire	Congo, Rep.	Lao PDR		
Ecuador	Cuba	Mauritius		
Egypt, Arab Rep.	Dominican Republic	Mozambique		
Eritrea	Ethiopia	Vietnam		
Fiji	Gabon			
Ghana	Greece			
Guyana	Lebanon			
Hungary	Lesotho			
Iran, Islamic Rep.	Mongolia			
Israel	Poland			
Jordan	Rwanda			
Kenya	Spain			
Malawi	Sudan			
Mauritius	Swaziland			
Mexico	Syrian Arab Republic			
Morocco	Trinidad and Tobago			
Nigeria				
Pakistan				
Papua New Guinea				
Peru				
Panama				
Paraguay				
Romania				
Sierra Leone				
Togo				
Tunisia				
Turkey				
Uganda				
Uruguay				
Venezuela, RB				
Zambia				
Zimbabwe				

Note: Of course, countries with more than 20 years of ≥4% growth of GDPpc must also have been countries with more than 10 years of ≥4% growth of GDPpc. Likewise, countries with more than 30 years of ≥4% growth of GDPpc must also have been countries with more than 20 years of ≥4% growth of GDPpc.

not robust at all: they vanish after controlling for a single dummy variable, the Eurasian advantage (Tang 2016a; see Diamond 1997). Ashraf and Galor's (2013) thesis is untenable, if not pseudoscientific. The same criticism applies to Gregory Clark's (2007) fuzzier biological thesis that the Industrial Revolution had been mostly driven by bourgeoisies having more offspring than nonbourgeoisies (for earlier critiques, see Allen 2008; Mokyr 2017, 22–24).

Geography has been a real primary mover, at least before AD 1500. In his majestic *Guns, Germs and Steel* (1997), Jared Diamond provides a sweeping account for the puzzle of economic development before 1500: Why had all the earliest civilizations emerged from the Eurasia supercontinent, but not from Africa, the Americas, Oceania, or Antarctica? The reason was simple: the Eurasia supercontinent possessed immense advantages in terms of biodiversity for the development of settled agriculture. Thus, at least before 1500, geography had dominated the fate of human societies, more or less (see also Tang 2016a).

After 1500, however, institutions (and policies) became more significant. Today, one can plausibly argue that institutions are the more critical force for determining economic performance. Of course, this does not mean that geography is no longer important (Easterly and Levine 2003; Sachs 2003). In fact, other than Australia, Canada, New Zealand, the United States, and oil-producing countries, most of the richest countries are still from the Eurasia supercontinent. Thus, contrary to Acemoglu and Robinson (2012, ch. 2), just because institutions are more critical today, it does not mean that geography no longer matters. Likewise, contrary to Easterly and Levine (2003) and Sachs (2003), just because geography has cast a long shadow on development, it does not mean that institutions are unimportant. Both stands reflect a nonevolutionary approach to understanding human society (Tang 2020).

Geography can shape economic development through at least four channels. The first channel is the most direct: geography shapes development by providing the biodiversity foundation for settled agriculture (Diamond 1997). The second is also quite direct: geography impacts the diffusion of technology and institutions (Diamond 1997). The third and fourth are indirect. On one hand, geography can shape institutions directly and then indirectly impact development (Engerman and Sokoloff 2012). On the other hand, geography can shape culture, which can in turn shape institutions, which in turn shapes development. Hence, the relationship between geography, institutions, and development is interactive, nonlinear, systematic, and both direct and indirect, rather than linear or either-or (Nugent and

Robinson 2010; Engerman and Sokoloff 2012; see also Herbst 2000; Garcia-Jimeno and Robinson 2011; Williamson 2012).

After briefly addressing biology and geography, I now discuss culture and strategies in some detail before taking on institutions in the rest of the book.

A. CULTURE MATTERS, BUT ONLY VIA INSTITUTIONS (AND STRATEGIES)

Culture has been suggested as a second primary mover, beginning with Weber's (1958) "Protestant ethic," followed by the "achievement motive" by McClelland et al. (1976), and then more loosely as "cultural beliefs" or "cultural values" by Greif (1994), Granato et al. (1996), Landes (1998, 2000), Harrison and Huntington (2000), McCloskey (2006), and Mokyr (2014, 2017). Unfortunately, none of these earlier theses have received any systematic and convincing empirical support. Rather, most of these works were based on a selective reading of economic history in a few cases (e.g., Britain versus China and India; for a pithy critique, see Tilly 1999). Moreover, they cannot answer these embarrassing questions: (1) If one's theory is static (i.e., a culture is conducive or unconducive to development), how can one know that culture has been the lone decisive factor out of a universe of factors? (2) If one's theory is dynamic (i.e., one uses cultural changes to explain changes in economic fortune) and yet culture is supposed to change slowly, then why does culture change?

More recently, with econometrics, cultural traits have been found to affect both individual decisions (Tabellini 2008, 2010; Guiso et al. 2009) and macroeconomic outcomes (Barro and McCleary 2003; Guiso et al. 2006, 2009, 2016; Gorodnichenko and Roland 2017; for a review, see Alesina and Giuliano 2015). These studies, however, still suffer from some serious deficiencies.[13]

First of all, while it is sound to code "values" as cultural, it is not so to code "beliefs" as cultural because beliefs can change quite readily whereas culture is supposed to be sticky. Second, almost all recent empirical studies on culture and development have been based on the World Values Survey (Inglehart et al. 2000) or some other self-reported surveys; all of them have been shown to be quite problematic, with serious measurement biases (Jackman and Miller 1996a, 1996b; Clarke et al. 1999), even though few economists seem to be aware of the criticism directed against them. Third, many econometric results in these more recent studies have been seriously questioned (Herrmann-Pillath 2010). Fourth, while cultural traits may impact individual behaviors at the micro level, whether they can account for macro outcomes, such as "divergence, big time," is doubtful. Indeed, few recent empirical studies on culture and development have proposed and tested plausible mechanisms that can link cultural traits or values with macroeconomic outcomes.

Fifth, and most critically, as the great sociologist Norbert Elias ([1939] 1994) argued long ago, many supposedly cultural values or traits (especially, trust as social capital, self-control, obedience) are sediments of institutional outcomes in the long run (see also Mokyr 2014). Certainly, the level of trust (generalized or not) and obedience cannot but be a sediment of institutional history rather than cultural (cf. Putnam 1993). Likewise, the prioritization of interests (or profit) over honor (or passion) (as the capitalist spirit) too has been an institutional outcome in *the long duress* (Elias [1939] 1994; Hirschman 1977) The only trait in the literature that is essentially cultural might be individualism versus collectivism (Gorodnichenko and Roland 2017), but even this trait may have been the residue of the institutional past of these societies. Hence, while there is a plausible link from culture to economic outcomes via institutions, the opposite direction (i.e., from institutions to economic outcomes, sometimes but not always via culture) is not only more plausible but also potentially far more powerful (Alesina and Giuliano 2015). At the very least, institutions have a more powerful impact on development outcomes than culture and social norms (cf. Greif 2006), even though culture and institutions work together (Keefer and Knack 2005).

Finally, these new waves of econometric studies of culture and development have the same difficulties in answering the two challenging questions faced by earlier cultural theories.

B. DEVELOPMENT STRATEGIES AND POLICIES REQUIRE INSTITUTIONS

After rejecting biology, culture, and geography (to a less extent) as the prime movers for modern economic development, we are left with two critical ingredients: (developmental) strategies and policies versus institutions.

As I argue in detail in chapter 8, these two ingredients are complementary rather than competing: they are the primary instruments that a state deploys in shaping economic development. Moreover, both can be understood as instruments for shifting or reallocating production factors to different sectors

(Tang and Gao 2020). As a result, I contend that institutions, policies, and state capacity form the new development triangle (NDT).

The focus on developmental strategies and policies has a long pedigree, dating back at least to Lewis (1955), Myrdal (1957), and Hirschman (1958). Justin Yifu Lin (2009, 2012b, 2012c) has been the most vocal proponent recently. Staking a "new structural economics" (NSE) school, Lin and his collaborators have argued that the key to successful development must lie with whether an economy has followed a developmental strategy of defying or following its (latent) comparative advantages: a comparative advantage defying strategy usually focuses on heavy industry and import substitution, whereas a comparative advantage following one starts with light industries that aim for export. Countries following the former have generally failed (exemplified by numerous newly independent countries after WWII), whereas those following the latter have succeeded (exemplified primarily by a few East Asian countries).[14]

I share Lin's conviction that mainstream NIE's singular focus on the long-run impact of institutions and state capacities is potentially misleading and inevitably leads to dreadful pessimism. Because many institutions are difficult to change and state capacities are slow to build, emphasizing the shackles of institutions and state capacities implies that LDCs have no real chance of moving out of their poverty trap (Lin 2012c). Once we realize that policies, especially industrial policies,[15] are also instruments for shifting an economy from one state to another state, we arrive at a more hopeful stance: states can indeed jump-start growth with some pushes and then try to sustain their growth momentum with institutional changes and new state capacities (see also Rodrik 2007; World Bank 2008). *Thus, despite the fact that I am a firm institutionalist, the purpose of this volume is not to argue that only institutions matter.*

Ultimately, however, I insist that institutions are more fundamental (for similar arguments, see Rodrik 2007 and Bardhan 2016), because there are a few key weaknesses in insisting that strategies and policies are the primary movers behind development in the long run.

First of all, when trying to slight the role of institutions, Lin has focused on only meta-institutions, such as political regime type and power structure (e.g., 2009, 14). This is misleading. Take post-1978 China and post-1989 Vietnam, Lin's two primary supporting cases, for example. While the regime type of both countries did not change and the overall power structure did not change, at least two key institutional changes were instrumental in igniting and sustaining their reform. (1) Before their open and reform policies, these two countries were mostly planned economies. When they launched their reforms, however, both allowed the market to play a much more prominent role. (2) Both countries reopened the channel of upward social mobility via education by supporting higher education. These two reforms were institutional changes that put incentives in both the material market and the positional market back in place (see chapters 2 and 3). Thus, although the role of important shifts in strategies and policies should be appreciated, it is difficult to imagine that these two countries could have succeeded as they have so far without these two key institutional changes, even if they employed a comparative advantage following strategy.

Second, although a developmental strategy can be long term, policies (including industrial policies) within the strategy must constantly adjust to changing situations. In contrast, institutions are generally more stable or more difficult to change (North 1990; Lin 1989; Lin and Nugent 1995). Moreover, whereas policies may operate as external shocks for jump-starting growth, institutions are necessary for sustaining the momentum (Rodrik 2007). In this sense, institutions are again more fundamental.

Third, and perhaps most critically, *all strategies and policies require some institutions to operate.* When Lin (2009) rightly identified the state as the most critical actor in development, as many institutionalists have done (e.g., Lewis 1955, 376; North 1981; Aghion and Roulet 2014), he was in fact admitting a more central role for institutions since states must be underpinned by institutions (see also Haggard 1990, ch. 1). Thus, in numerous pages within his new manifesto for NSE, Lin (2009, 2012c) had to admit critical roles for institutions.[16]

Finally, even if we admit that leaders (and their close associates) play instrumental roles in shaping developmental strategies and policies (and they do), they can only do so with the help of organizations that are underpinned by institutions. Even an omnipotent leader has to rely on an able bureaucracy, and such a bureaucracy can only be built with meritocracy that promotes upward social mobility for able technocrats (see chapter 3). In fact, all the good things that sound developmental strategies and (industrial) policies can bring to an economy depend on a state with a decent threshold of state capacity!

Here, North's (1990, 113–16) brief discussion regarding the role of ideas and ideologies in shaping the different outcomes of Britain and Spain during the seventeenth century is especially illuminating. The Count-Duke of Olivares (in power, 1621–1640) was keenly aware of the right directions and even procedures for reforming and restoring Spain. Unfortunately, he was severely constrained by Spain's morbid institutions, and his efforts to save Spain eventually pushed the country into disaster (Elliott [1963] 2002, ch. 9; 1989, ch. 10). In short, "ideas and ideologies [and development strategies] matter, [but] institutions play a major role in determining just how much they matter" (North 1990, 111).

II. How This Book Approaches Institutions

Following Smith, Marx, and many others, this book is unabashedly institutional toward the puzzle of development. But then, what is the institutional foundation of economic development (IFED)? There have been many courageous attacks of this puzzle. This book draws and builds upon all of them, but also differs from them quite significantly.

I first reject the simple dichotomy of "extractive versus inclusive," "market augmenting versus market depressing," or "natural state versus open access order" (e.g., Olson 2000; North et al. 2009; Acemoglu and Robinson 2012). These dichotomies are simply too blunt to be helpful. Worse, explanations based on them are often tautological (see chapter 1 for details).

We must also go beyond the orthodoxy of strong but limited states (e.g., North and Weingast 1989; Acemoglu and Robinson 2012), because it hinders our understanding of the role of states and institutions in economic development (Aghion and Roulet 2014; Bardhan 2016, esp. 866–74). After all, unless a state can extract effectively, it cannot build anything, including institutions (Elias [1939] 1994; Tilly 1990).

Fundamentally, despite economics' claim to deduction, North, Olson, and their followers were inducing and extrapolating from the British experience without admitting it. By the same logic, we therefore have to reject the purely inductive exercises based on regressions without theorization. Growth regressions can only produce a laundry list of institutional (and cultural) factors that at best are correlated with development,[17] but they cannot tell us the institutional causes of development (Rodrik 1999; Pritchett 2000). We need to guide growth regressions and any other empirical exercises with rigorous theorization. Moreover, observational data will always limit the kind of techniques we can deploy to obtain reliable causal inference.

My approach here is thus foremost a deductive approach. By a deductive approach, however, I do not mean modeling alone (and there are models within this project). A model is one way of developing theoretical insights, but it is not the only way. Economists confuse themselves by taking mathematical models as the only method of theorization. In most cases, a model is too simplified to solve a task like the systemic foundation of economic growth, whereas a model that is too complex (even if it is tractable) is not easily accessible to most policymakers and hence of little practical value.

For supporting evidence, I combine both statistics and in-depth case studies: we need them both. Furthermore, because there is so much heterogeneity across countries, it is not so useful to pool all countries with data in econometric exercises. To be consistent with my overall concern and theorization, therefore, I perform regressions with only developing countries.[18]

The institutionalist approach adopted here is also historically systematic or, more precisely, evolutionary. It is systematic in the sense that I emphasize that IFED is a system, consisting of multiple dimensions. As such, I reject such blunt approaches that label growth-promoting institutions as "inclusive" or "market augmenting" and growth-retarding institutions as "extractive," "excluding," or "market restricting." I also reject idealizing the British experience as the only path toward economic development.

My approach is historically systematic in the sense that development is not only a complex system but, more importantly, an evolutionary system. In fact, any thoroughly institutional approach, whether it is about development or other social outcomes, must be evolutionary because institutional change is a thoroughly evolutionary process and hence all institutions are the product of social evolution (Tang 2011b, 2020). Development itself, plus social and political developments, and even international developments (e.g., war, financial crisis from other places) can change or even transform a social system, thus changing the overall environment for development. When this is the case, it is imperative for us to adopt an evolutionary approach toward development. For understanding changes, an evolutionary approach promises greater payoffs than any nonevolutionary one (Tang 2020).

Hence, just because state capacity, internal peace, and prosperity tend to cluster with each other (Besley and Persson 2011), it does not mean that Britain and other European countries struck gold in one stroke (Jones 2003; Greif 2006; Mokyr 2008; McNeill [1963] 1991). The Northian imagination of economic history can hardly be helpful in the real world (Ankarloo 2002). Certainly, even in the modern age, the East Asian miracle was not necessarily the product of an "inclusive regime" (Pritchett 2003). When this is the case, if one follows the Northian message, developing countries would be at a loss as to where to start (Rodrik 2005).

Finally, three critical caveats are in order. First, adopting a mostly institutionalist approach does not discount the role of individuals in development. What I do reject is the atomic and utterly micro approach espoused by Banerjee and Duflo's (2011) *Poor Economics*. Their approach toward development is fundamentally flawed and presents an overly optimistic or even "romantic" picture of economic development (Karnani 2009; Ravallion 2012). They fail to grasp that different individuals' capabilities, visions, and even ways of calculating have a history and hence an institutional root (Sen 2000; Graham 2015). Put it bluntly, the poor do not make calculations and decisions in an institutional vacuum. In fact, Banerjee and Duflo (2011, 234–35) came close to admitting this depressing fact when they lamented: "The poor often lack critical pieces of information and believe things that are not true . . . some markets are missing for the poor, or . . . the poor face unfavorable prices in them."

Also, by heavily relying on randomized controlled trials (RCTs) or experimental methods (for critique of RCTs, see Cartwright 2010; Deaton 2010; Deaton and Cartwright 2018), Banerjee and Duflo and their followers can only limit their inquiries to how people make a decision within the present (micro) situation while neglecting the possibility that these people have limited possibilities, incentives, capabilities, and opportunities precisely because they have been handicapped by the larger institutional environment of their country (Ravallion 2012; Reddy 2012). As such, Banerjee and Duflo not only risk making governance and the state disappear (if we just let people choose and decide!) but also falling and staying in the trap of atomic individualism that has been proved false and harmful but that is so enshrined by many economists (Karnani 2009).[19]

Institutions and individual decisions are not incompatible with each other. In fact, the key to development is not to pit individuals against states or markets against states. Rather, it is to make states, by building better institutions, serve the people (individuals) better.

Second, adopting a mostly institutionalist approach does not mean that land, capital, labor, human capital, and technology are unimportant. Here, Abramovitz (1986), North (1990), and Nelson and Pack (1999) got it right: While land, capital, labor, and technology provide the upper bound or full potential for development, institutions provide the actual limitation on what a country can achieve, given fixed production inputs. Thus, the key is for countries to build capacities so that their people and organizations can absorb first and then invent new technologies as a result. Indeed, as

I have emphasized elsewhere (Tang 2005), if there is something called the "national learning capacity," institutions mostly determine it—directly (e.g., via investing in R&D) or indirectly (e.g., via investing in education).

Third, and most critically, adopting a mostly institutionalist approach does not mean that politics is irrelevant (Sangmpam 2007). Indeed, it is exactly the opposite. Because institutions are rules and making and enforcing rules require political power most of the time (Evans 2007; Mahoney and Thelen 2010; Tang 2011b), an institutionalist approach makes politics a central force in shaping economic performance, especially in the long run. In chapter 8, I bring (or return) politics to the center of our discussion of state capacity, institutions, and socioeconomic policies. For now, taking an institutionalist approach means assuming that institutions, once in place, have a life of their own in shaping development, and I leave the politics behind institutional changes for now.

III. Structure of the Book

In chapter 1, "Laying the Groundwork: What Do We Know about IFED?," I provide an in-depth and systematic critique of the existing literature on institutions and economic development, thus paving the way for the systematic statement on IFED to be advanced in chapter 2. I identify key defects in the existing literature and defend the approach taken in this book.

In chapter 2, "A Systematic Statement of IFED," I start with the metaphor of "big bills left on the sidewalk," and I ask the question, What institutions will encourage and enable an individual to pick up those "big bills"? Through logical deduction, induction, and drawing insights from the existing literature on economic development and beyond, I contend that for an individual to be able to pick up those big bills, four "big things" must be in place: *possibility, incentive, capability,* and *opportunity*.

I then ask the question, What institutions underpin the four big things? I arrive at a rigorous theoretical framework contending that IFED has six major dimensions, namely, (political) hierarchy, property rights, social mobility, good redistribution (as empowering), liberty for protecting innovation, and equality of opportunity. Hierarchy and liberty (protected by democracy), which can be understood as having a dialectical relationship when it comes to maintaining stability and promoting welfare-enhancing change, underpins possibility. The channel of property rights and the channel of social mobility underpin incentives in the material market and the positional market. Good redistribution underpins empowering underserved individuals with capabilities so that they can achieve gains in the material market and the positional market: individuals should not be handicapped from picking up those big bills. Finally, equality of opportunity underpins opportunities for marginalized individuals in the sense that they will not be prevented from picking up those big bills in the material market and the positional market, usually by other individuals in more advantaged positions.

I then briefly discuss the two dimensions that have been well studied and supported: political hierarchy for order and (political and economic) stability, and property rights for the material market. I also briefly address a third dimension, equality of opportunity, due to the difficulty of measuring it and hence a lack of available data for rigorous empirical exercises, either qualitative or quantitative. The chapter then highlights the other three channels that are still subject to debate, paving the way for chapters 3–6 that provide original theoretical exposition and more systematic evidence for them.

Before going further, however, I present a brief digression on the subject of inequality, with a more detailed discussion to be advanced elsewhere.

"Excursion: Three Inequalities" briefly outlines three inequalities and discusses the importance of distinguishing between them as critical for understanding them. The three inequalities—inequality of capability (innate and acquired), inequality of opportunity, and factual (material and positional) inequality—can only be addressed with different institutions and means. Inequality of capability should be addressed by good redistribution. Inequality of opportunity should be addressed by affirmative action, broadly understood. Finally, factual inequality, an extremely complex social outcome with both biological and historical roots, can only be addressed by a combination of institutions and individual efforts.

Chapter 3, "The Positional Market and Development: Social Mobility as an Incentive," contends that in addition to the material market, there is also a positional market in human society. The channel of social mobility—the institutional system that regulates individuals' and groups' performances in the positional market—is a critical dimension within IFED because it underpins the incentive structures in the positional market. As such, understanding the interaction between the incentive structures in the material market and those in the positional market sheds new light on economic history and some of the ongoing "natural experiments" in economic development today. Most importantly, understanding the relationship between the positional market and economic growth makes it clear that states should strive to eliminate institutional discrimination because it is not only morally unjust but also economically costly. An earlier version of this chapter was published in the *Journal of Economic Issues* (2010).

Chapter 4, "Redistribution and Development: Good Redistribution as Empowerment" (with Shuo Chen and Chengcheng Ye), argues that good redistribution is about empowering marginalized individuals with capabilities so that they can achieve gains in the material market and the positional market. In other words, good redistribution is to address the inequality of capability among individuals and groups within a society.

We use public investment in basic education, a measure that has long been identified as one of the most beneficial redistributive measures, to substantiate our argument. Consistent with our overall position that good redistribution is about empowering underserved individuals with capabilities, we reason that the crucial constraint shaping a household's decision to invest in human capital is the share rather than the amount of public investment in basic education. We construct a model that explicitly shows the share of public investment out of the total cost of basic education and a household's budget as the two central factors that shape a household's decision about investing in human capital. Our model yields the critical insight that the larger the share of public investment out of the total cost of basic education is, the less overall burden a household has to shoulder for investing in its human capital and the more a household is incentivized to invest in its human capital. Our model also yields other interesting insights. We then present empirical evidence that demonstrates the operation of the central mechanism and the effect upon households' decisions of the two central factors identified in our model, taking advantage of some unique data opportunities provided by China's reform in funding basic education.

Chapter 5, "Hierarchy, Liberty, and Innovation: A New Institutional Theory and Qualitative Evidence," advances a new theory that identifies democracy's unique advantage in prompting economic development. Bringing together the classic defense of liberty and democracy, the political economy of hierarchy, endogenous growth theory, and the new institutional economics on growth, I contend that *the channel of liberty-to-innovation is the most critical channel in which democracy holds a unique advantage over autocracy in promoting growth, especially during the stage of growth via innovation.* Because all human societies are hierarchical, and hierarchy facilitates growth by bringing stability and order yet harms innovation and growth by demanding obedience to authority, an economy must strike a balance between maintaining stability and facilitating innovation. Democracy achieves this balance by protecting liberty, whereas autocracy sacrifices innovation for stability. Democracy thus does hold a unique advantage in promoting growth over autocracy, but this advantage is far more subtle and (fragile) than what North and his followers have argued: it is indirect, channel-specific, and conditional.

I then present evidence from three historical cases, demonstrating that although key scientific breakthroughs can indeed pop up under autocracies, democracy is a necessary, though insufficient, condition for protecting major scientific breakthroughs that may challenge religious and political orthodoxies.

Chapter 6, "Democracy's Unique Advantage in Promoting Development: Quantitative Evidence" (coauthored with Rui Tang), continues the discussion on democracy and growth. The theory advanced in chapter 5 argues that the channel of liberty-to-innovation is the most critical channel in which democracy holds a unique advantage over autocracy in promoting growth, especially during the stage of growth via innovation. My theory thus predicts that democracy holds a positive but indirect effect upon growth via the channel of liberty-to-innovation, conditioned by the level of economic development. This means that there is a threshold above which democracy begins to have a conditional positive effect on growth. Chapter 6 presents quantitative evidence for this key hypothesis. An earlier version of chapter 6 was published in *Kyklos* (2018).

Together, chapters 5 and 6 propose an indirect and conditional effect of democracy on economic development and provide systematic evidence for my theory. Our theory and empirical evidence promise to integrate and reconcile many seemingly unrelated and often contradictory theories and evidence regarding regimes and growth, including providing a possible explanation for the inconclusive results from regressing an overall regime score against the rate of economic growth or the change in level of GDP per capita.

Turning to chapters 7–9, I present a wide and holistic understanding of economic development. Chapter 7, "Development as a Social Evolutionary Process," advances two principal arguments. First and foremost, because different institutional arrangements interact with each other, "the efficiency of a particular institutional arrangement cannot be assessed without referring to the other related institutional arrangements in that society" (Lin 1989, 3). Many existing studies have neglected this interaction and its impact. As such, their interpretations of economic history, some of which may have become conventional wisdom, are open to question. Second, because economic development also transforms the social and political system of a society, different stages of economic development need different combinations of institutions. As such, we must adopt an evolutionary approach to IFED and economic development itself rather than simplistic and dogmatic notions of protecting property rights and constraining the executive. There is no simplistic dichotomy of inclusive versus extractive institutions as championed by North et al. (2009) and Acemoglu and Robinson (2011).

Chapter 8, "The New Development Triangle: State Capacity, Institutional Foundation, and Socioeconomic Policy," argues that once we admit that institutions matter for economic development, it becomes inevitable that the state is a key player in engineering and sustaining, or hindering, economic growth (Olson 1993, 2000; North et al. 2009; Besley and Persson 2011; Bardhan 2016), because the state has been the most powerful actor in erecting and enforcing institutions. This in turn means that development requires a state with adequate state capacity. As Andrew Schrank (2015, 36), put it pithily: *"An effective state is all but indispensable to late development"* (emphasis added). In addition, we also need sound economic policy, including industrial policy (e.g., Oqubay 2015; Lee 2013a, 2013b; Lin 2012b; Stiglitz and Lin 2013), in the short to medium run to maintain growth momentum because policies in the short to medium run are surely going to impact long-run economic performance. Together, they point to a "new development triangle" (NDT) consisting of state capacity, institutions, and economic policy. While this development triangle is only a framework for further research, it clarifies and indeed dissolves several unproductive debates that pit institutions against state capacity and state intervention with economic policy, including industrial policies (Aghion and Roulet 2014; Bardhan 2016; Maloney and Nayyar 2018).

In the conclusion to the book, "Laying the Foundation for Development," I argue that for developing countries the ultimate question for economic development can be put as this: How can a state become and then remain a "developmental state"? Unfortunately, this challenge has no simple institutional or policy panacea, and this is the primary reason why economic development has been so rare and difficult to sustain. Time and time again, the illusion of having found a solution by some economists and development consultants has been shattered. Without an easy answer, then, how can developing countries lay a broad foundation for economic development? Bringing my discussion together, I conclude with some practical principles for laying such a foundation without any pretense of a panacea.

1

Laying the Groundwork

WHAT DO WE KNOW ABOUT IFED?

I. What Institutions Matter?

The notion that institutions matter for economic development is now a cliché, judging by the voluminous literature on institutions and development (for selective reviews, see Williamson 2000; Acemoglu et al. 2005a, 2005b; Shirley 2005; Chang 2011; Jennings 2013; MacLeod 2013; Ogilvie and Carus 2014; Bardhan 2016; Lloyd and Lee 2018). What is the institutional foundation for economic development (IFED), then? Embarrassingly, we know remarkably little about the exact or even rough dimensions of development-prompting institutions. Sure, we can always list property rights, regime type, and so on. But that's about it.

One may think that North et al.'s *Violence and Social Orders* (2009) or Acemoglu and Robinson's *Why Nations Fail* (2012) has solved the puzzle about IFED. This is far from the case. Their simplistic dichotomy of inclusive/open—versus extractive/closed–order institutions is tautological and hence of little theoretical value or practical guidance for developing countries (Chang 2011; Sachs 2012; Boldrin et al. 2013; Bardhan 2016, 871–74). Moreover, neither North et al. (2009) nor Acemoglu and Robinson (2012) has provided any systematic evidence for their grand narratives (e.g., North et al. 2013). The same criticism applies to Mancur Olson's (2000) "market-augmenting" institutions or government (McLean 2000).

For instance, only a relatively equal distribution of property (with rights) is conducive to growth, whereas rigid property rights protection for the rich few is counterproductive for development (Engerman and Sokoloff 2012). Hence, a single-minded emphasis on property rights (e.g., North 1981; North and Weingast 1989; Acemoglu et al. 2001; Acemoglu and Robinson 2012) is misleading (Chang 2011). Indeed, before an economy can become inclusive, a state has to use (often violent) power to extract resources from landowners for redistribution. Moreover, autocracies with a socialist ideology might have done more redistribution than democracies (Albertus 2015).

Despite having done a better job than *Violence and Social Orders* and *Why Nations Fail*, Besley and Persson's *Pillars of Prosperity* (2011) suffers from the defect of "all good things have to go together" for development (Chang 2011; Bardhan 2016, 871–74). Yet, as countless in-depth case studies on East Asian developmental states (EADS) have shown (Amsden 1989; Wade 1990; Haggard 1990; Evans 1995; for a recent review, see Haggard 2015), if all good things have to go together, we could not possibly have witnessed the robust growth patterns in East Asia and now in some African countries that have been emulating EADS, such as Ethiopia and Nigeria (e.g., Oqubay 2015).

In sum, despite a voluminous literature on institutions and development, no NIE theorists have explicitly specified just what constitutes IFED (Aron 2000; Bardhan 2016). Only fragmented discussions of one or two (sub) dimensions of IFED exist. What has gone wrong?

This chapter identifies four critical causes behind our failure to grasp IFED more systematically. By doing so, I lay part of the foundation for moving toward a systemic understanding of IFED.

II. The Causes of Our Ignorance about IFED

Existing literature on institutions and development suffers from four major shortcomings, with each of them containing more specific subcomponents. This section details these shortcomings, with selected illustrations from the literature.

A. QUESTIONABLE CONCEPTUALIZATION AND MEASUREMENT

Early on, Aron (2000, 100) lamented that "the growth literature does not subscribe to one overarching definition of economic, political, and social institutions, their processes of change, and their likely channels of influence. . . .

Economists often rely on several of these types of indicators to capture the features of institutions, although each has a potentially different channel of impact on growth." In fact, the problem of questionable conceptualization and measurement with the existing literature on institutions and development goes much deeper than what Aron has noticed (see also Rodrik 2007, ch. 6).

To begin with, leading NIE theorists seem to be extremely fond of blunt concepts, from market-augmenting (vs. market-hindering?) government (Olson 2000), to open versus closed (access) order (North et al. 2009) and inclusive versus extractive institutions (Acemoglu and Robinson 2012). Unfortunately, these blunt concepts are theoretically tautological because, by definition, they explain development and stagnation (Ogilvie and Carus 2014). In fact, although Ogilvie and Carus (2014) have rightly criticized North et al. (2009) and Acemoglu and Robinson (2012), their own "generalized versus particularized" institutions are no better than their competitors.

Take Acemoglu and Robinson's definition of inclusive versus extractive political institutions, for example. They define "political institutions that are sufficiently centralized and pluralistic as inclusive political institutions. When either of these conditions falls, we will refer to the institutions as extractive political institutions" (2012, 74–75). Judged by any minimal standard of social science, this is sloppy conceptualization because it is simply inoperable.[1]

Acemoglu and Robinson's definition of inclusive versus extractive economic institutions is even worse: "Inclusive economic institutions are those that allow and encourage participating by the great mass of people in economic activities that make best use of their talents and skills and that enable individuals to make the choices they wish. To be inclusive, economic institutions must feature secure private property, an unbiased system of law, and a provision of public services that provides a level playing field in which people can exchange and contract; it must also permit the entry of new business and allow people to choose their careers" (2012, 74–75). While this definition of inclusive economic institutions seems more specific than their definition of inclusive political institutions, it packs all the good things into one blunt concept. Unsurprisingly, their discussion is plainly tautological (Boldrin et al. 2013) and contradictory (Bardhan 2016, 871–74). Certainly, Acemoglu and Robinson (2012) had no valid measurement for inclusive or extractive institutions, either political or economic (Wen 2015, 2–4, 194, fn. 29).

Consequently, these concepts are practically unhelpful. To put it bluntly, telling LDCs that they need a market-augmenting government, open access order, or inclusive order/institutions is no better than telling LDCs, "You guys need to develop!" What they really need to know is what specific institutions a government should erect in order to augment the market or make the system more inclusive. More depressingly, pooling all the good things together means that no LDCs can develop because it is impossible for them to obtain all the good institutions with one stroke (or "big bang").

The debate on whether political regime type (e.g., democracy and autocracy) matters for economic development has suffered from similar shortcomings (e.g., Olson 1993; North et al. 2009; Acemoglu and Robinson 2012; Acemoglu et al. 2019). Because regimes are meta-institutions (Rodrik 2007, 166–83), regime type is simply too crude for understanding how a regime impacts growth. Rather, we need a more fine-grained understanding about how a regime contingently impacts growth via specific channels (see chapter 5 for details).

Finally, North et al.'s (2009; see also North et al. 2013) notion of limited access order versus open access order is laughable in terms of conceptualization (Sartori 1970, 1984; Collier and Mahon 1993; Goertz 2005). When North et al. (2009, 2013) delineate limited access order into three states— fragile, basic (i.e., quite stable), and mature (i.e., very stable)—and then contrast them with open access order, their classification scheme has two dimensions rather than one: control of political violence (or internal political stability) and access. Hence, when one combines the two dimensions, all possible combinations should be exhausted, for a total of six (figure 1.1). Yet, North et al. (2013, 14) had only four combinations: fragile, basic, mature limited access, and then open access.

When the conceptual framework is faulty, one can only twist and then squeeze facts into the conceptual holes. Hence, North et al. (2013, 14) had a serious problem by putting India, postapartheid South Africa, and China all into the category of mature limited access order." And by putting all the rich democracies into the category of open access order, they merely retell the Northian Whiggish fairy tale one more time under another disguise (see below for details).

The same criticism applies to Besley and Persson's (2011, 2014) scheme (figure 1.2), which actually bears strong similarities to that of North et al. (2009, 2013) and Acemoglu and Robinson (2012).

Access\Control of violence	Fragile	Basic	Mature
Limited	Limited\Fragile	Limited\Basic	Limited\Mature
Open	Open\Fragile	Open\Basic	Open\Mature

FIGURE 1.1. Order and Access: What North et al. (2013) Ought to Have.

Access\Control of violence	Weak	Strong
Special-interest	Special-interest\Weak	Special-interest\Strong
Common-interest	Common-interest\Weak	Common-interest\Strong

FIGURE 1.2. Order and Access: What Besley and Persson (2011, 2014) Ought to Have.

B. LACK OF RIGOROUS THEORIZATION

1. Inductive Rather Than Deductive

As a discipline that prides itself on being more deductive (via modeling) and hence more scientific than other branches of social science, the NIE literature has been mostly inductive and only marginally deductive, when examined closely.

The old institutional economics (OIE) literature has been almost exclusively inductive. Adam Smith famously listed three essential (institutional) elements for development, namely, "peace, easy taxes, and a tolerable administration of justice" (quoted in Hanley 2014). Similarly, Commons (1924) identified the court and the law. Likewise, Lewis (1955, 57) articulated three roles for institutions in development, arguing that "institutions promote or restrict growth according to the *protection* they accord to effort, according to the *opportunities* they provide for specialization, and according to the *freedom of maneuver* they permit" (emphasis added). Later on, Lewis listed "nine ways in which governments may bring about economic stagnation or decline" (408–15), by apparently mixing institutions with policies.

Although NIE has long claimed to have moved beyond OIE, when it comes to identifying the institutional elements for development, NIE has done no better. To begin with, mostly extrapolating from the British experience, North and his followers have primarily focused on property rights and transaction costs. Elinor Ostrom's (1986) inductive exercise did a bit better. Starting from a public choice perspective, she identified seven types of rules, without restricting herself to IFED. They were rules governing position, boundary, scope, authority, aggregation (in decision making), information, and payoff. She, however, did not provide any rationale for the seven types.

Sen (2000, 17–20) differentiates two types of freedom provided by institutions: process freedom (freedom of action and decisions) and actual opportunity. His process freedom corresponds to possibility in my framework, and his actual opportunity to my capability and equality of opportunity. Unfortunately, Sen then went on to enlist five types of freedom: political, economic facilitative, social opportunities, transparency guarantee, and protection security. By doing so, he might have stretched the concept of freedom beyond recognition without providing any sound rationale for doing so.

Rodrik (2007, 15–17), following "an unabashedly inductive approach," first listed 20 rules of good behavior for promoting economic growth, which he named the "augmented Washington Consensus." Here, he mixed institutions with policies. Later on, Rodrik (ch. 5) identified five types of institutions for growth: property rights, regulatory institutions, institutions for macroeconomic stabilization, institutions for social insurance, and institutions of conflict management. In this case, he apparently conflated institutions (as rules) with organizations.

Other important institutions that impact development as identified by the more historical NIE include institutions governing transaction costs (Coase 1937, 1960), property rights or incentive structure underpinned by exemption from expropriation by the state and individuals (North and Thomas 1973; North and Weingast 1989; Olson 1993, 1996), regime type (Olson 1993; North et al. 2009, 2014; Acemoglu and Robinson 2012; Acemoglu et al. 2019), political and social stability (Olson 1993), the market (Smith [1776] 1981), social mobility (Lewis 1955, 84–90, 107–13), liberty (Polanyi 1941; Hayek 1960; Popper [1945] 1966; Sen 2000), and distributive politics (Olson 1982; Alesina and Rodrik 1994).

The contributions in the edited volumes by Rodrik (2003a) and Helpman (2008) are excellent narratives on specific issues within a particular country or across countries. Unfortunately, they do not add to a coherent picture. Indeed, each chapter in the two volumes decides what institutions are and what institutions are important for understanding growth. Some chapters are on short-term policies whereas others are on medium- to long-run policies and institutions. The result is that different chapters wander far and away in different directions. Without rigorous deductive theorization, even in-depth case studies cannot shed much light on what IFED is, other than identifying some specific dimensions (see also World Bank 2002; Costa and Lamoreaux 2011).

The voluminous cross-country growth regressions (CCGR) literature with institutions as independent variables has fared even worse. The first wave of CCGR literature, mostly pre-2001, primarily contains kitchen-sink regressions (Ray 2003). Although CCGR, following the seminal article by Acemoglu et al. (2001), has paid more attention to causal inference and endogeneity, theorization within CCGR remains thin. The CCGR literature is more or less about crunching data, and it lacks a coherent framework specifying just what constitutes IFED and how institutions impact development (Rodrik 2007, 15; Ciccone and Jarociński 2010).

Finally, NIE's focus on property rights, constraint on executives, and credible commitment exemplifies a symptom of NIE's overall inductivism: it was singularly inspired by the British experience (North 1981; North and Weingast 1989; North et al. 2009; Acemoglu et al. 2001, 2002, 2003, 2005a, 2005b; Weingast 2005). The induction behind this is simple: property rights must be the key because Britain became the first industrialized society by institutionalizing property rights. Yet, property rights, constraint on executives, and credible commitment are not everything, and certainly not a panacea for development (Bardhan 2005b, ch. 1; 2016).

When the British experience is taken as the key for development, NIE theorists often had to squeeze historical facts into the shoes of property rights and credible commitment. For instance, staying with only property rights, Acemoglu et al. (2003) cannot square the facts with their narratives on Botswana. Botswana (1965–1998) had an average annual growth rate of 7.7% while Mauritius (1965–1980) grew at a rate of 3.8% and (1980–1998) 5.4%. During the same period, Singapore's average annual growth rate was 6.4% while South Korea's was 6.6%. But Botswana had a lot of diamonds, which accounted for about a third of GDP, whereas Mauritius, Singapore, and South Korea were all resource poor. During the same period, Botswana had little growth in its manufacturing sector whereas Mauritius, Singapore, and South Korea had rapidly built up their manufacturing capacities. In fact, Acemoglu et al. (2003) even had to squeeze political stability (e.g., precolonial arrangements) into property rights (for a critique, see Poteete 2009). Rodrik (2007, 185–86) was thus correct in deriding Acemoglu et al.'s (2001) Northian obsession with property rights, constraint on executives, and credible commitment as "no theory" and "property-rights reductionism" (see also Ankarloo 2002; Bardhan 2005a; Chang 2007b, 21–25, 2011; Evans 2007).

In sum, the existing literature on institutions and development has been mostly inductive. As such, it cannot provide us with a systematic statement on IFED. We need to start with a more deductive exercise and then strike a balance between deduction and induction in order to integrate our knowledge about IFED.

2. Form Rather Than Function

The same (institutional) function can be performed by different forms of institutions. Thus, although China has had no legally binding private property rights since 1949, and only came to have formal rules on this in 2002–2003, it has been able to grow with informal property rights and collective property rights (Montinola et al. 1995; Che and Qian 1998; Chang 2007b, 21–25; Xu 2011). Similarly, although China overall lacks grassroots democracy and hence formal accountability from below, Chinese villages have relied on informal institutions and social capital to enforce accountability on officials in providing public goods (Tsai 2007). Likewise, just having the procedural form of a democratic regime does not necessarily mean that a country is democratic.

Meanwhile, institutions that are adequate for certain functions may not be so for other functions. Thus, while Botswana had all the right institutions for economic development according to Acemoglu et al. (2003), it fared much worse in combating the HIV/AIDS epidemic than many other African countries that were much poorer than Botswana (Kiiza 2007; see also Evans 2007, 46–48).

Hence, function is just as important, if not more so, than form. Unfortunately, existing NIE literature on institutions and development has been more about form than function.

The first manifestation of putting form ahead of function has been an attempt to bracket economic institutions from political and social ones, and to suggest that political and social institutions cannot have the same level of impact on economic development (Chang 2007b, esp. 17–21; Sangmpam 2007). Trying to bracket political institutions from economic institutions may be useful for some purposes, but is unhelpful most of the time because most economic institutions have been made by politics (rather than political institutions directly), and politics mediates the effect of political institutions (Tang 2011b).

In fact, any effort to clearly bracket political institutions from economic institutions when it comes to development distorts reality (Kurtz 2013, 30–32). Unsurprisingly, such efforts get easily bogged down and become self-contradictory (cf. Acemoglu et al. 2008 vs. Acemoglu and Robinson

2012, esp. 81–87). After all, the dimension of "an unbiased system of law" in Acemoglu and Robinson's (2012, 74–75) definition of "inclusive economic institutions" is evidently more political than economic.

The second symptom has been that most NIE theorists have focused on one function while neglecting others. Most prominently, NIE has almost zeroed in on institutions constraining power. Indeed, North (1981, 201–2) defined institutions as "a set of rules, compliance procedures, and moral and ethical behavioral norms designed to constrain the behavior of individuals in the interests of maximizing the wealth or utility of principle." By 1990, North had abandoned the efficiency definition, but he still defined institutions simply as "the humanly devised constraints that shape human interaction: a major role of institutions is to "define and limit the set of choices of individuals" (1990, 3–6).

Yet, North himself admitted that institutions also enable by facilitating individuals' choices. For instance, North (1990, 3–6) wrote that institutions also reduce uncertainty by providing a stable (not necessarily efficient) structure to everyday life or human interactions. Similarly, Lin (1989, 3, 7) defined institutions as "human devices designed to cope with uncertainty and to increase individual utility," and added that "rules and norms are needed for collective actions." Hence, institutions both enable (plus empower) and constrain. In other words, there is a duality of institutions (for a detailed discussion, see Tang 2011b).

As becomes clear in the chapters below, another key function of institutions is to enable and empower. Indeed, for development, what activities institutions actually constrain matters, but so do what activities they enable and what individuals they empower. If institutions constrain unproductive activities and enable productive activities, an economy flourishes. In contrast, if institutions constrain productive activities but enable unproductive activities, then an economy suffers. The same logic applies to empowerment. Adam Smith, on the very first page of his *Wealth of Nations*, put it forcefully: *"[The wealth of nations] must be regulated by two different circumstances; first, the skill, dexterity, and judgment with which its labor is generally applied; and secondly, the proportion between the number of those who are employed in useful labor, and that of those who are not so employed"* ([1776] 1981, 10, emphasis added; see also Baumol 1990; Kremer 1993).

3. Emergent Outcomes as Institutions

Due to sloppy theorization and conceptualization, many indicators have been proposed as measurements of institutions or institutional quality. Yet, more often than not, these indicators do not measure institutions or institutional quality but instead (sometimes extremely) complex social out-comes. As such, they are ill suited for understanding what institutions impact development and how they impact it. Three indicators have been the most prominent.

Ever since the publication of the first batch of Worldwide Governance Indicators (WGI), efforts have been made to show that better governance contributes to better economic development. Yet, (the quality of) gover-nance is an outcome of long-run historical development, behind which state formation, state building, institutional changes, and economic development itself have all played critical roles across time and space. As a result, (the quality of) governance cannot be deployed as independent variables when the dependent variable is development (for details, see chapter 8; see also Kurtz and Schrank 2007).[2]

Similar drawbacks have bedeviled attempts to link factual inequality with development. Empirical efforts to link factual inequality (often measured by the Gini index or other related indicators) with development, however, have produced only inconclusive results (e.g., Persson and Tabellini 1994; Perotti 1996; Knack and Keefer 1997; Li and Zou 1998; Barro 2000, 2008; Forbes 2000; Sylwester 2000; Atkinson and Bourguignon 2000; Stevans 2012; for earlier reviews, see Bénabou 1996; Aghion et al. 1999; esp. 1617–21; Banerjee and Duflo 2003; Kanbur 2000; Piketty 2000; Boix 2009, 2010; Voitchovsky 2009; Kahhat 2011).

A key cause behind this fact is that factual inequality is the result of a long, evolutionary process with many factors involved—including development, technological change, and redistribution policies (Diamond 1997; Lundberg and Squire 2003; Galor and Moav 2004; Boix 2010; Piketty 2014). At the same time, development itself is a complex social outcome shaped by redis-tributive policies, democratization, democracy consolidation, economic volatility, and political stability. When this is the case, it is no surprise that a firm relationship between factual inequality and development cannot be found (cf. Boix 2009).

Moreover, the thesis that greater factual inequality is bad for develop-ment is explicitly or implicitly underpinned by the assumption that greater factual inequality often leads to social and political instability, which in turn discourages investment (Voitchovsky 2009). Yet, as Bollen and Jackman (1985, 1995) perceptively pointed out, factual inequality does not necessarily lead to social instability because factual inequality is not automatically *injus-tice*: unless a large portion of the population perceives factual inequality as unjust, it does not necessarily lead to social and political instability (Cramer

2003).[3] In fact, as Gimpelson and Treisman (2018) have demonstrated, the public often got factual inequality wrong. Moreover, the relationship between factual inequality and investment in the economy may be nonlinear and nonmonotonic (Voitchovsky 2009).

C. THE MODERN WHIGGISH MYTH: NORTH AND HIS FOLLOWERS

From their selective reading of the British (or Western European) experience, North and his disciples have promulgated a modern Whiggish myth for development by idealizing the British experience (e.g., North and Thomas 1973; Levi 1988; North and Weingast 1989; Weingast 1997, 2005; North et al. 2009; Acemoglu et al. 2001; Besley and Persson 2011; Acemoglu and Robinson 2012).[4] This myth has four key components, and each of them unravels under closer scrutiny (Chang 2002, 2007b, 2011; Evans 2004, 2007; O'Brien 2007; Bardhan 2016, 871–74; Narizny 2019).

The first component is that the Glorious Revolution was all about constraining the executive and enforcing secure property rights with credible commitments via parliamentary democracy. This reading, however, is mostly based on selective misreading into historical evidence (for a recent critique and detailed references, see Narizny 2019).

First of all, "contrary to the received wisdom, the [British] state that arose after 1688 did not so much increase protection for existing property rights but reordered them, in many cases dismantling or discarding preexisting feudal or customary property rights in favor of property rights that were suitable for investment in commercial agriculture or for exploiting land for industrial purposes" (Johnson and Koyama 2017, 4). In other words, if preexisting property rights had been retained, Britain might not have had the Industrial Revolution at all! (See also Epstein 2000; O'Brien 2007; Ogilvie and Carus 2014, esp. 418–27.)

The second component is that what Britain (and other Western European countries) had done in the seventeenth to nineteenth centuries must be replicated. Morris and Adelman (1989, 1417) stated such a Whiggish mantra most blatantly: "Favorable impacts of government policies on the structure of development can be expected only where political institutions limit elite control of assets, land institutions spread a surplus over subsistence widely, and domestic education and skills are well diffused." While the two authors identified three dimensions in IFED (property rights, redistribution of land, and distribution in education), they forgot the simple historical fact that the three could not have been accomplished in one stroke. More critically, for today's LDCs, how to obtain the three dimensions may pose an entirely different challenge from what Britain faced back then. When this is the case, their call for replicating the British experience is irresponsible extrapolation, as Chang (2007b, 21–25) and Evans (2004, 2007) have pointed out.

The third component of this modern Whiggish myth is that all the good things associated with developed countries today must have been associated with good things in historical times. As North et al. (2009, 2) put it: "Although evidence from the past few decades is mixed, over the past two centuries, political and economic development appear to have gone hand in hand." Translation: *Development and democracy go hand in hand*.

In particular, the Northian NIE explicitly assumed that a state that is capable of predatory actions has always existed and hence it must be constrained (Levi 1988; North and Weingast 1989). Yet, a state that can extract institutionally is no piece of cake: in order to extract, you must have an army, a bureaucracy, and true sovereignty over your subjects.

As Epstein (2000) demonstrated, the predatory state, which by implication is strong enough to extract extensively, came very late in medieval Europe (AD 1300–1700). In historical times, many states are extremely weak. Thus, "evidence of state depredation is in fact either negative or inclusive, and suggests instead that *the main political regime barrier to premodern development arose from the state's inability to enforce a unified, nondiscriminatory fiscal and legal regime. . . . Limitations to, rather than excesses of, state sovereignty are what restrained the rise of competitive markets.*" He continued, "*Most pre-modern states failed to meet modern definitions of state authority. . . . Jurisdictional fragmentation, which gave rise to multiple coordination failures, rather than autocratic rule was arguably the main source of the institutional inefficiency of 'absolutism' before the nineteenth century. . . . The major source of economic inefficiency in societies with fragmented sovereignty was the limited extension of the state's . . . powers over competing jurisdictional rights*" (Epstein 2000, 8, 14–16, 36, emphasis added; Elias [1939] 1994; Tilly 1990; Dincecco 2010, 2011; Bardhan 2016; Johnson and Koyama 2017). At this stage, states were almost constrained entirely, and development becomes difficult if not impossible.

Before a state can plunder its subjects, it must have enough subjects and be powerful enough to plunder. NIE's mistake was to assume that both the state and the state with strong state capacity had always existed and thus the top priority should always be to limit state power. Nothing could be further from the truth. Before one can try to limit a state's power, there must be some state power to begin with.

The fourth component is that the political regime matters critically for development simply because the first industrialized state was a constitutional monarchy (or democracy) and almost all developed countries today are democracies, either implicitly or explicitly (e.g., North et al. 2009; Acemoglu and Robinson 2012; Besley and Persson 2011; cf. Engerman and Sokoloff 2012). As becomes clear in chapters 5 and 6, however, a focus on the nature of the political regime is misplaced: a regime's effect on growth is channel specific, indirect, and conditional.

Indeed, even a cursory look at autocracies indicates that not all autocracies are alike. This is true not only when it comes to oppression but also with regard to economic performance. East Asian "dragons" (Singapore, South Korea, Taiwan) and "tigers" (Indonesia, Malaysia, Thailand) were all autocracies when their economies took off and remained so well after. And there have been other successful autocracies as well, such as Chile and Portugal (1935–1970). In this sense, China, Cambodia, Ethiopia, and Vietnam all have been more recent embodiments of an autocratic developmental state. When NIE theorists, such as Acemoglu, North, and Olson, insist that only democracies can achieve economic development, they can only declare these cases to be anomalies (North et al. 2009, 2013).

In fact, Acemoglu and Robinson (2012) and others had only this to say regarding China today and many East Asian developmental states (EADS) earlier: they must have been anomalies. Acemoglu and Robinson (2012) cannot admit that China, like many EADS, had done many things right given its conditions! Indeed, they have ignored this cluster of growth almost entirely, despite citing Amsden (1989) and Wade (1990).[5] Yet, for understanding development, ignoring this cluster of success outside Western Europe cannot be justified (Fogel 2011).

Because of these shortcomings, the Northian Whiggish fairy tale has been met with dismissal from specialists. As Allen (2009, 4–5) and McCloskey (2010, chs. 33–36, esp. 310–24) noted, numerous societies developed secure property rights long before the Glorious Revolution (see also Coffman et al. 2013). In fact, judging from records, the Qing Empire had better-protected property rights than Britain prior to the Glorious Revolution (Pomeranz 2000). IFED is much more than constraining the state and structuring incentives.

This being the case, North and his followers could only gloss over the inherent tension between the two key pillars of their ideal "inclusive institutions" or "open access order"—a sufficiently strong (and centralized) state and a sufficiently constrained state (Bardhan 2016, 871–74)—often by twisting historical facts (Ankarloo 2002).

Epistemically and more fundamentally, extrapolating from the British experience (i.e., from the Glorious Revolution to the Industrial Revolution) is not so straightforward, if not entirely invalid (Bardhan 2016, 886). As a one-time and single "miracle," there is nothing inevitable about the path from the Glorious Revolution to the Industrial Revolution (O'Brien 2000; Pomeranz 2000; Goldstone 2000, 2002; Allen 2009). As a result, the Industrial Revolution (and the "great divergence" it led to) cannot possibly have a definitive explanation; it can only have "possible stories." And this is precisely why there have been so many different theories or explanations that emphasize different factors and mechanisms (e.g., North and Thomas 1973; North and Weingast 1989; Jones 2003; Landes 1998; Acemoglu et al. 2001; Clark 2007; Allen 2009; Tang 2010; Mokyr 2017). When stagnation had been the norm in the rest of the world before 1500–1700, accounting for a miracle can be superficially difficult but actually easy: or, something or everything (in hindsight) must have gone right!

Finally, the Whiggish myth is another embodiment of functionalism. For North and his followers, welfare-improving (i.e., good) institutions exist because they reduce uncertainty and transaction costs, whereas welfare-reducing (i.e., bad) institutions exist mostly because of a lock-in effect and positive feedback as path dependence (e.g., North 1990, 6–10; cf. 16). Yet, there is a far more straightforward and powerful explanation for welfare-reducing institutions: institutions are made and backed by power (for details, see Tang 2011b).

D. A NONEVOLUTIONARY UNDERSTANDING OF INSTITUTIONAL CHANGE AND DEVELOPMENT

Finally, existing discussions on institutions and development, whether in economics, politics, or sociology, have largely staked a linear, static, and unsystematic stance rather than an evolutionary approach toward the role of institutions in development (for an earlier discussion, see Chang 2011, 480–82). In short, the extant literature does not admit the possibility that different stages of development require different combinations because institutions and development coevolve with each other. As such, IFED cannot be built on a tabula rasa. Rather, all institutions are products of social evolution, and development must operate mostly within existing institutions with limited social engineering.

For instance, Acemoglu and Robinson (2012) dismissed the possibility that geography had been and continued to be a critical factor in shaping the economic history before AD 1500 (Diamond 1997; see also Sachs 2012; Wen 2015, 2–4). Luo and Wen (2016) documented that "non-institutional factors (e.g., environmental diseases) predominantly explain the cross-country income variations among agrarian countries, while institutional factors largely account for the income differences across industrialized economies. Moreover, it is the stage of economic development (or the absence/presence of industrialization) that explains a country's quality of institutions rather than vice versa." (See also Foa 2017.)

Meanwhile, North and his many collaborators or followers have largely relied on changes in the incentive structure for explaining the rise of the West, based almost exclusively on the British case. As noted above, their reading of economic history regarding the rise of the West has been simplistic, to say the least (Epstein 2000, ch. 1; Ankarloo 2002; Chang 2011).

Indeed, the brief historical narratives on France and Spain by North and Thomas (1973, ch. 10) themselves clearly pointed to the fact that before enforcing property rights, France and Spain, from the fifteenth to seventeenth centuries, had other more pressing tasks at hand—from surviving the Hundred Years' War, to fending off and eliminating potential domestic rivals, monopolizing coercive power, and eventually, monopolizing extraction (i.e., taxation), to name just a few (see also Elias [1939] 1994; Tilly 1990). By all counts, on these fronts, France and Spain were quite successful. The only key error that they had committed might have been dividing rather than unifying their states into a single market.[6]

Another key cause behind NIE's nonevolutionary approach toward IFED has been its NIE roots. The revival of institutional economics was not achieved by OIE's followers but by economic historians who have bought into NCE (e.g., Acemoglu, North, Ostrom, and Williamson), via Coase (1937, 1960). In short, NIE is an offshoot of NCE: NIE accepts neoclassical doctrines and merely "seeks to extend the range of applicability of neoclassical theory" (Furubotn and Richter 1991, 1). Rodrik (2007, 3) was similarly unequivocal: "NCE is not just a powerful discipline for organizing our thoughts on economic affairs, but *the only sensible* way of thinking about them!" (emphasis added). (See also North 1981, 1990.)

Fundamentally, NCE is a functionalist approach and hence inherently incapable of understanding institutional change: its explanation for institutional change is essentially tautological, as all functionalist explanations have been. For NIE theorists, institutions are either a means to reduce uncertainty and transaction costs (e.g., Coase 1937, 1960; North 1981, 1990) or a means to advance collective interests (Ostrom 1990). In short, institutions are public goods, and hence most institutional changes are all for the better. As such, NIE simply cannot explain how so many bad institutions come to exist and are sustained without relying on ad hoc assumptions. NIE fails to admit that institutions are not necessarily welfare-improving public goods, but instead are private goods that reflect the preferences and advantages in terms of power held by the powerful (for a detailed critique, see Tang 2011b).[7]

Thus, for North and his NIE disciples, the Glorious Revolution settlement was a negotiated compromise between Whigs and Tories. Such an interpretation could not be further from the truth. "The (Glorious) Revolution settlement was not a negotiated compromise between Whigs and Tories, nor was it a clever solution to a coordination problem. *Rather, it was imposed on Tories by the Dutch and Whigs*" (Narizny 2019, 10, emphasis added).

III. Concluding Remarks: Toward a Systematic Statement of IFED

In short, no systematic statement on IFED exists. The lack of a systematic understanding of IFED has some really unpleasant consequences both for research and for policymaking. On one hand, much of the empirical work on the relationship between institutions and economic performance suffers from "a range of serious problems with data, methodology, and identification" (Aron 2000, 100; see also Temple 1999; Rodrik 2007, ch. 6), and the accumulation of knowledge from this literature has been less than satisfactory.

Empirically, without a proper understanding of IFED, we cannot measure institutions' contributions to development with great confidence (Aron 2000; Glaeser et al. 2004; Nelson and Sampat 2001; Temple 1999). Without knowing what exactly constitutes IFED, the CCGR literature could not possibly subscribe to one overarching definition of economic, political, and social institutions. Consequently, different studies in this literature often do not engage each other, and knowledge accumulation from this literature has been less than satisfactory (Aron 2000). Meanwhile, most case studies with the "comparative institutional approach" centered on how the state manages the economy with macroeconomic policies and ignored the more foundational aspects of the "developmental state." The later literature, therefore, has yet to really connect with the larger NIE literature. If institutions are fundamental determinants of long-term economic performance, the more fundamental and interesting question must be, What makes a developmental state? Or, what exactly are the institutional arrangements that make a state a "developmental state"?

Policywise, without a proper understanding of IFED, telling LDCs or transitional economies to "get the institutions right" is meaningless. Because a proper understanding of IFED is missing, the advice given to LDCs by NIE economists has often focused on one or two aspects of IFED (e.g., property rights) while ignoring the rest. Indeed, after noting that many attempts at institutional reform in LDCs have faltered, Andrews (2013) singled out two causes behind the failures; namely, (1) the social contexts in which (designed) institutions operate are not taken into account and (2) the reforms are overspecified and oversimplified solutions. Yet there is a distinct third possibility: we simply do not know enough about the IFED (Easterly 2005).

Hence, we badly need a systematic statement on just what IFED is. Such a statement should integrate and organize our fragmented existing understanding of the institutions that underpin growth. To achieve such a goal, we need to avoid the four shortcomings within the existing discussions on institutions and development.

So, why is it now high time for a systemic understanding of IFED? The most critical reason is that we have accumulated a large body of knowledge from which a more systemic understanding of IFED can be advanced, thanks to two important developments. The CCGR literature has accumulated a vast number of regressions that explicitly or implicitly try to assess the impact of institutional arrangements on development. Meanwhile, the "comparative institutional approach" literature has also marshaled many cases studies showing that some states were able to achieve development whereas other states were unable to do so. And these two bodies of literature complement each other: while growth regressions are good at screening potential leads about institutional arrangements that affect growth, case studies are good at analyzing whether and how these institutional arrangements influence growth in greater detail (Temple 1999; Aron 2000; Rodrik 2007). What we need now is a deductive framework that integrates these insights into a coherent statement.

The next chapter takes on this challenge by advancing a systematic statement on IFED.

2

A Systematic Statement of IFED

This chapter takes a crucial first step toward a systemic understanding about what constitutes the institutional foundation of economic development (IFED). Taking a more deductive approach, I contend that institutions (and policies) shape development by governing four immediate drivers of individual actions: possibility (freedom), incentive, capability, and opportunity. In turn, these four drivers are regulated by six dimensions, and these six dimensions together make up IFED.

I start with a simple and famous metaphor ("big bills on the sidewalk") and then deduce the critical dimensions of IFED. I show that a more deductive approach overcomes the fragmented state of the existing literature on IFED and integrates existing findings, but it also points to important gaps in our understanding of IFED.

The chapter is structured as follows. Section I spells out the four fundamental roles that institutions play in development, starting with the metaphor of "big bills on the sidewalk." Section II briefly elaborates on the specific dimensions of IFED, foretelling the empirical chapters to come. A brief conclusion follows.

I. What Do Institutions Do Exactly?

The critique of NIE in chapter 1 suggests that orthodox NIE cannot lead us to a systemic understanding of IFED. Instead, adopting a more deductive approach, I argue that the proper question for a systemic understanding of

IFED must be as follows: When it comes to development, what formal (and informal) rules can make individuals' and organizations' socially productive initiatives more likely while making socially destructive initiatives less likely?

To answer this question, I start with one of NIE's cleverest attacks against the largely institution-free NCE: the metaphor of an assistant professor versus a full professor looking at some big bills left on the sidewalk (Olson 1996; see also Rodrik 2007, 4).

In Olson's words, if there are many big bills left on the sidewalk (as it appears so), why haven't they been collected? Reciting the NIE gospel that institutions are all about incentives, Olson (1996, 6) had a quick answer: there were no incentives.

Yet, Olson gave himself away even before his answer, stating that "he (the assistant professor) *was held back* by his senior colleague" (1996, 3, emphasis added). Right here lies a clue toward a systemic understanding of IFED. The key is to push the metaphor as far as we can to deduce the necessary condition(s) for individuals to pick up those big bills.

If we take the poor assistant professor as just any individual and the imposing full professor as the state or an individual with a gun, then besides the possibility of lacking incentives (e.g., the bills are fake), at least one additional possibility becomes evident: those big bills were left on the sidewalk because an external force, either an organization (e.g., the state) or an individual, prevented the poor assistant professor from picking them up.

We can push the metaphor even further: the poor assistant professor was unable to pick up those big bills because he was physically unable to do so. In other words, some individuals cannot pick up the bills because they lack certain capabilities.

Moreover, the poor assistant professor may be holding back because some institutions (as rules) have been dictating that only the more senior full professor has the right to pick up the big bills. We can easily push the notion of privileged access to opportunity to race, ethnicity, gender, age, holding property, and so on. This implies that equality of opportunity is also of critical importance. This possibility also means that the assistant professor has great incentives to become a full professor in the positional market.

Finally, the metaphor implicitly assumes that the two faculty members were walking down the sidewalk on a peaceful morning or afternoon. But what if they were in a gang battleground or even a war zone? In this case, even if they had all the capability, incentive, and opportunity, they would not have the possibility of picking up those big bills (cf. Olson 1993).

TABLE 2.1. The Four Immediate Drivers and the Six Dimensions

Drivers	Institutional dimensions
Possibility	1. Hierarchy for order and stability 2. Liberty for protecting innovation (as possibilities)
Incentive	1. Property rights and beyond: for incentives in the material market 2. The channels of social mobility: for incentives in the positional market
Capability	Redistribution that impacts capabilities, directly and indirectly
Opportunity	Equality of opportunity, or affirmative action for employment and bidding

Altogether, at the very least, we need possibility, capability, incentive, and (equality of) opportunity for those big bills on the sidewalk to be picked up by individuals. Moreover, here we have implicitly assumed that picking up the bills on the sidewalk is a productive exercise. For the sake of development, we also need individuals to engage in productive rather than unproductive or even destructive activities or entrepreneurships (Baumol 1990).

Hence, institutions underpin four immediate drivers of productive activities when it comes to development, and *incentives* is only one of them. The other three roles are to govern individuals' and organizations' *possibility*, *capability*, and *opportunity* for taking productive initiatives. *Without incentives, individuals will not make an effort even if they have possibility and capability. Without possibility and capability, however, individuals cannot make an effort even if there are incentives offered. Without equality of opportunity, some individuals will be excluded from taking initiatives.* By single-mindedly focusing on institutions' role of governing (material) incentives, NIE has been neglecting the other three functions or roles of institutions almost completely.

From the four immediate drivers of individual actions or initiatives, we can then deduce that six dimensions of institutions should underpin the four drivers, and these six dimensions form IFED (table 2.1). In other words, according to our framework, six dimensions of institutions shape economic development by impacting four drivers of individuals' actions and initiatives, which are the ultimate drivers of economic development.

Our framework subsumes all the major components within IFED that had been identified inductively by various authors earlier (see chapter 1). Our framework is thus not only more parsimonious but also sufficiently fine grained. For instance, components previously lumped together under protection, opportunity, and freedom by Lewis (1955) are now differentiated into possibility, opportunity, and incentives: his freedom (and protection) corresponds to possibility in our framework, and his opportunity correlates with both opportunity and incentives in our framework. Similarly, our framework makes it clear that grasping that the key goal of redistribution is to enhance the capabilities of disadvantaged individuals is far more useful than renaming capabilities as another type of freedom, as Sen (2000) has done.

II. IFED: Outline of a Systematic Statement

This section elaborates the six major dimensions of IFED in greater detail, paying more attention to the dimensions that have been relatively underexplored or unexplored while adding only essential but underappreciated points for those dimensions that have been treated more extensively. Of course, each dimension consists of many specific institutional arrangements.

A. INSTITUTIONS GOVERNING POSSIBILITY: HIERARCHY FOR ORDER AND STABILITY

Without hierarchies, there can be only two outcomes for a group of individuals: social disorder or an egalitarian social order.[1]

If disorder reigns, individuals have to fend for themselves. Here, Hobbes ([1651] 1985, 186) was not too far off when he wrote: "[Under anarchy in which every man is against every man,] there is no place for industry; because the fruit thereof is uncertain, and consequently no culture of the earth; no navigation, nor use of the commodities that may be imported by sea; no commodious building; no instruments for moving, and removing such things as require much force; no knowledge of the face of the earth, no account of time; no arts; no letters; no society; and which is worst of all, continual fear, and danger of violent death; and the life of man, solitary, poor, nasty, brutish, and short." In other words, without order and stability, human society will be a "nasty and brutish" place and any socially productive initiatives will be extremely difficult, if not totally impossible (Olson 1993; McGuire and Olson 1996).[2]

Order can exist without hierarchy. In fact, many early human communities were egalitarian societies, and order in these societies is mostly maintained by leveling (Boehm 1999; Miller and Cook 1998, 72–82). Yet, leveling is inherently inimical for growth because it not only works against and hence discourages accumulation of surplus (as capital) but also limits the effectiveness of provision of public goods (e.g., irrigation). Unsurprisingly, egalitarian societies tend to be small and have only very simple social structures. As a result, egalitarian societies are feeble against external threats (Keeley 1996; see also Tang 2013 for detailed citations).

Compared to disorder and egalitarian order, hierarchical order is more conducive to growth, ceteris paribus, even though predatory chiefs and kings can certainly retard growth. In Olson's (1993) memorable phrasing, "stationary bandits" are much better than "roving bandits."

Since humans are not angels, an essential dimension of IFED is to prevent individuals from taking socially destructive initiatives (e.g., stealing, robbery, killing) through "order and stability" so that they will be more willing to consider socially productive initiatives. Fundamentally, order and stability is about "releasing this (human) talent and controlling it for larger social purposes" (Moore 1966, 386). By gradually monopolizing and limiting violence, hierarchy slowly but decisively reduces the risk and cost of taking socially productive initiatives and increases the risk and cost of taking socially unproductive ones, thus making development possible.[3]

The rise of political hierarchy also makes more complex social organizations (e.g., bureaucracy) possible. Arrow (1974, 16) did not overstate this: "Truly among man's innovations, the use of organization to accomplish his ends is among both his greatest and his earliest." The growing complexity of organization makes it a major force behind human progress.

Finally, the scope of order determines the size of the potential market. With a larger market, division of labor becomes more profitable and fine grained, which in turn contributes to development (Smith [1776] 1981). The emergence of political hierarchy in the form of chiefdoms and then protostates, therefore, was a watershed event in human history and a crucial step toward sustained development (Service 1975; Earle 1997; Diamond 1997; Tang 2016b).

Thus, it was perhaps no coincidence that modern (capitalist) development materialized only after order and stability were established over larger and larger expanses of territory. As Elias ([1939] 1994) wrote so forcefully, in France, the "civilizing process" was essentially to use force and then "culture" to eliminate private violence and especially knightly warfare. Likewise, in England, "*The Tudor discipline, with its stern prohibition of livery and maintenance, its administrative jurisdiction and tireless bureaucracy, had put down private warfare with a heavy hand, and, by drawing the teeth of feudalism, had made the command of money more important than the command of men*"

TABLE 2.2. Political Stability and Economic Growth Rate: Five African Countries

Country	Period	GDP growth rate	Political stability score
Democratic Republic of Congo	1999–2003	−1.0	−2.28
	2004–2008	6.1	−2.19
Ethiopia	1998–2000	2.59	−0.86
	2002–2006	7.31	−1.41
Cote d'Ivoire	2002–2011	0.66	−1.79
	2012–2016	9.26	−1.02
Angola	1998–2002	2.1	−1.98
	2003–2007	15.5	−0.83
Sierra Leone	1997–2001	−1.3	−1.85
	2002–2006	10.4	−0.61

Sources: GDP growth rate compiled from World Development Indicators (WDI); political stability score from Worldwide Governance Indicators (WGI). Updated March 06, 2022.

Note: The more negative a country's political stability score is, the more political instability the country had. According to the data, Ethiopia was the only exception: it experienced more robust economic growth from 2002 to 2006 when its political instability increased.

(Tawney 1912, 188–89, emphasis added). In both cases, monopolizing violence with violence had been a critical, if not an indispensable, instrument for rulers' expanding the modern market economy (see also Mann 1986, 1993; Tilly 1990; Epstein 2000).

Unsurprisingly, since Alesina et al. (1996), political instability, ranging from labor strikes and government collapse to coup, riot, and especially armed conflict such as civil war, has been found to be consistently and negatively associated with economic growth (e.g., Collier et al. 2003; Kang and Meernik 2005; Bates 2008; Jong-A-Pin 2009; Skaperdas 2011; Gates et al. 2012; Aisen and Veiga 2013; Costalli et al. 2017).

Tables 2.2–2.4 present our own results from more updated data (see also Tang and Tang 2018). Table 2.2 shows that after the cessation of civil wars, economic recovery has been common and quite rapid in sub-Saharan Africa. Tables 2.3 and 2.4 show that political stability is always positively and robustly associated with economic growth. According to our own estimation, with a sample of 80 countries, an increase of 1,000 points in political instability as measured by Databanks International (2011) is associated with a 0.22%–0.32% decrease in a country's growth rate of GDP per capita. With a sample of 113 countries, an increase of 1,000 points in political instability

TABLE 2.3. Political Stability Contributes to Development (80 Economies)

(Dependent variable: GDP per capita growth rate)

	(1) FE	(2) FE	(3) FE	(4) FE	(5) RE	(6) RE
Stability	0.000311***	0.000319***	0.000246***	0.000246***	0.000217***	0.000216***
	(6.92e-05)	(6.89e-05)	(6.01e-05)	(5.96e-05)	(5.75e-05)	(5.70e-05)
GDPpc		−0.814	−1.121**	−2.373***	−0.847**	−1.163***
		(0.547)	(0.522)	(0.635)	(0.340)	(0.351)
GDP deflator			−0.00111***	−0.00111***	−0.00112***	−0.00112***
			(0.000243)	(0.000250)	(0.000238)	(0.000241)
GCF			0.221***	0.224***	0.206***	0.209***
			(0.0255)	(0.0257)	(0.0231)	(0.0231)
Population growth			−0.323	−0.225	−0.322	−0.281
			(0.255)	(0.251)	(0.216)	(0.221)
Time trend				0.420***		0.174
				(0.147)		(0.120)
East Asia					1.552***	1.581***
					(0.513)	(0.520)
SSA					−0.489	−0.608
					(0.373)	(0.391)
LAC					0.232	0.261
					(0.385)	(0.385)
Landlocked					0.274	0.164
					(0.375)	(0.389)
Tropical					−0.679*	−0.779**
					(0.367)	(0.362)
ELF6					0.634	0.516
					(0.600)	(0.605)
Constant	−5.928***	−3.661	−5.029**	−2.580	−4.770***	−4.218**
	(1.735)	(2.249)	(2.219)	(2.319)	(1.786)	(1.790)
Observations	3,068	3,031	2,948	2,948	2,948	2,948
R-squared	0.012	0.014	0.089	0.093	0.508	0.489
No. of countries	80	79	79	79	79	79

Note: Robust standard errors in parentheses; *** p < 0.01, ** p < 0.05, * p < 0.1. GCF: Growth capital formation. The result holds when using three- or five-year average of GDP growth rate as dependent variables (for details, see Tang and Tang 2018).

TABLE 2.4. Positive Effect of Political Stability on Growth (113 Economies)

(Dependent variable: GDP per capita growth rate)

	(1) FE	(2) FE	(3) FE	(4) FE	(5) RE	(6) RE
Stability	0.000449***	0.000409***	0.000297***	0.000295***	0.000230***	0.000227***
	(8.47e-05)	(8.04e-05)	(6.10e-05)	(6.09e-05)	(6.05e-05)	(6.02e-05)
GDPpc		−0.0296	−0.660	−1.265	−0.395	−0.659*
		(0.529)	(0.582)	(0.899)	(0.345)	(0.374)
GDP deflator			−0.00114***	−0.00114***	−0.00111***	−0.00111***
			(0.000243)	(0.000247)	(0.000227)	(0.000229)
GCF			0.196***	0.197***	0.178***	0.179***
			(0.0296)	(0.0287)	(0.0219)	(0.0214)
Population growth			−0.554**	−0.508*	−0.445**	−0.407**
			(0.246)	(0.261)	(0.200)	(0.207)
Time trend				0.217		0.160
				(0.176)		(0.113)
East Asia					0.792	0.842
					(0.697)	(0.699)
SSA					−0.826**	−0.913**
					(0.409)	(0.416)
LAC					−0.506	−0.422
					(0.451)	(0.439)
Landlocked					0.000136	−0.0851
					(0.382)	(0.392)
Tropical					0.0669	−0.0593
					(0.419)	(0.422)
ELF6					0.223	0.131
					(0.619)	(0.618)
Constant	2.438***	2.465	0.996	2.116	0.543	0.951
	(0.0886)	(1.594)	(2.148)	(2.631)	(1.470)	(1.471)
Observations	4,045	3,986	3,805	3,805	3,805	3,805
R-squared	0.014	0.012	0.088	0.089	0.464	0.469
No. of countries	113	112	112	112	112	112

Robust standard errors in parentheses; *** p < 0.01, ** p < 0.05, * p < 0.1. GCF: Growth capital formation. The result holds when using three- or five-year average of GDP growth rate as dependent variables (for details, see Tang and Tang 2018).

is associated with a 0.23%–0.45% decrease in a country's growth rate of GDP per capita.

B. INSTITUTIONS GOVERNING POSSIBILITY: LIBERTY

The second dimension of IFED that governs the possibility of agents' actions is civil and political liberty, in the broadest sense. I develop the thesis that institutions governing liberty are a critical part of IFED more fully in chapters 4 and 5. Here, I merely underscore one critical point.

Individuals were "absolutely free" before the emergence of hierarchy. After hierarchy was established, however, this was no longer so: now individuals' actions were governed by formal (and informal) rules. It is here that liberty comes into the picture. If humans are not angels, what about the state? If the state is not an angel, can we do anything about it? Because the state can impose limits on individual actions that are socially destructive, it can also impose limits on individual actions that are socially productive. Can anything be done about this latter possibility?

The institutions that govern liberty are designed precisely to limit the state's freedom in imposing limits on individual actions that are socially productive (Polanyi 1941, 439; Lewis 1955, 57). Hence, there is a dialectic relationship between liberty and the rise of hierarchy: it makes no sense to talk about liberty when there is no hierarchy, and liberty becomes necessary (and possible to define) only after the coming of hierarchy.

So how does liberty impact development? Briefly, development, especially development on the technological frontier, must be powered by both technological and institutional innovations. Yet, innovation requires the freedom to try out new things and new ideas. As such, development via innovation does pose some risk for stability (Mokyr 1992; Acemoglu and Robinson 2006). Because states may value stability over innovation, therefore, states may well stifle innovation.

With liberty, individual initiative—the ultimate engine of development— is preserved. Therefore, when it comes to development, the foremost value of liberty is not to prevent the state from confiscating individuals' property (cf. North and Weingast 1989), *but to prevent the state from limiting individuals' initiatives that are socially productive* because they may be perceived as destabilizing and even threatening by the state and its ruling class. After all, while all liberal democracies have secure property rights, not all states with secure property rights are liberal democracies (Friedman 1962, 10). Here lies the unique value of democracy for development: democracy protects liberty, and hence innovation, better than autocracy.

C. INSTITUTIONS GOVERNING MATERIAL INCENTIVE:
PROPERTY RIGHTS AND BEYOND

The material market is a marvel for presenting potential profits to individuals. Without the market, there will be no profit to be made, thus no incentives beyond subsistence. Moreover, without the market, division of labor not only will be unprofitable but will also lead to starvation and stagnation rather than prosperity and growth. In contrast, with profit to be made, the market sustains the ever-increasing division of labor, and the ever-increasing division of labor then comes back to drive the ever-expanding market (Smith [1776] 1981, chs. 1–3). The contrast between North and South Korea, former East Germany and West Germany, and prereform and postreform China and Vietnam unequivocally proves the necessity of the material market for sustaining development.

Hence, institutions governing the incentives in the material market— most prominently among them, secure property rights and contract enforcement—must be a key dimension of IFED (North 1981; North and Thomas 1973; North and Weingast 1989; Acemoglu and Robinson 2012; Ogilvie and Carus 2014). Unfortunately, the Northian NIE literature has overemphasized the necessity of constraining the state and underemphasized the necessity of constraining individuals (see the critique of NIE in chapter 1). Certainly, incentives in the material market are regulated by institutions far beyond secure property rights and contract enforcement (Rodrik 2007, ch. 6; Poteete 2009; Evans 1995, 2007; Haggard 2018).

D. INSTITUTIONS GOVERNING POSITIONAL INCENTIVE:
THE CHANNEL OF SOCIAL MOBILITY

In every society (and organization, for that matter), in addition to the all-too-familiar material market, there is another market: the positional market. Similar to the material market, incentives are also necessary in the positional market for powering individual effort and hence development (Lewis 1955, 84–90; Malthus [1798] 1951, 254; Marshall [1920] 1982, 176– 77; Hirsch 1977; Frank 1985).[4] Indeed, considering that the accumulation of knowledge and technological progress have been the most critical engines behind development and that many scientists may not be so interested in material gains (Marshall 1982 [1920], 4–5; see also Merton 1973; Rosenberg and Birdzell 1986, 243; Stephan 1996), the notion that institutions governing incentives in the positional market is part of IFED becomes unavoidable.

Institutions that govern incentives in the positional market create the channel of social mobility. While positional inequality provides incentives for individuals in the positional market, it is the channel of social mobility that truly sustains or stifles individual effort: individuals' efforts cannot be sustained unless they can see somebody around them really achieve a higher status. As Gellner (1983, 24–25) put it succinctly, there must be some illusion of actual social mobility and that illusion must have some basis in reality.

As Schumpeter ([1943] 2003, 14–20) alluded to but did not explicate, according to Marx's image of capitalism, there is no possibility for upward social mobility for the proletariat unless through social revolt or revolution. Moreover, according to Marx, even capitalists can only move down rather than up, saving the few monopolists. Thus, if capitalism does not provide any upward social mobility, Marx's prophecy will come true! This counterfactual exercise attests to the channel of social mobility as a critical dimension of IFED.

E. INSTITUTIONS GOVERNING CAPABILITY: GOOD REDISTRIBUTION AS EMPOWERING

One caveat is in order. There is no doubt that institutions governing capability can also indirectly impact individuals' incentives: By influencing individuals' capabilities, they in turn influence individuals' calculations of undertaking initiatives. When individuals possess greater capability, they have more incentives for undertaking more difficult initiatives with higher potential returns. Yet, it is conceptually critical and operationally useful to differentiate institutions governing capability from those governing incentives.

Past debates on redistribution have pitted the socialist impulse and the libertarian counterattack (e.g., Rawls 1999 versus Nozick 1974). Both camps, however, have missed the real issue.

The defect of the socialist impulse is obvious. For those with a socialist agenda, redistribution is fundamentally an issue of social justice, and the purpose of redistribution is to engineer factual social equality as an ultimate goal (at least as proclaimed). Factual equality, however, is simply unattainable. Worse, factual equality may well kill incentive, and in the end the whole economy would suffer and everyone would be worse off. As Kant put it, "Inequality among men is a rich source of much that is evil, but also of everything that is good" (quoted in Dahrendorf 1968, 152; see also Olson 1983, 217).

The defect of libertarian thinking is less obvious (although perhaps morally more repugnant). Maintaining that a minimal (if not ultraminimal) state is all that we need (Nozick 1974), libertarians assert that *any* attempt to redistribute would unravel the incentive structure of a society, and the whole society would again get less than it potentially could.

To resolve this dispute, it is critical to make one thing clear: there are actually *two* related issues involved here, and previous debates have tended to conflate the two. The first is about the purpose of redistribution and the second about the question of how much redistribution. Without addressing the first question, the second question cannot be properly considered (e.g., Olson 1983), and it will have to be, as it has been, fought on the ideological battlefield.

In light of the larger question, if we start with our inquiry into IFED, the first question about redistribution's role in development can be rephrased as follows: How can redistribution help people take socially productive initiatives without undermining the incentives for individual effort (Bénabou 2002)? Libertarians have largely dismissed the possibility of achieving such a balance, whereas socialists and mainstream economists have yet to adequately explore this possibility. Libertarians' position, however, is ideologically motivated and wrong.

To address this question properly, we need to admit that the accumulation of knowledge (i.e., learning) is the most critical engine of development and that the growth of the economy is fundamentally the growth of knowledge (Romer 1990; Jones 2005). Moreover, because learning depends on the human brain, the population is the ultimate resource of growth (Simon 1981): without adequate population growth, there would be no economic progress (Becker et al. 1999; Galor and Weil 2000; Jones 2001; Kremer 1993). With the first question about redistribution rephrased and the perspective that the growth of knowledge is the most critical engine of development and the growth of knowledge ultimately depends on all individuals, it becomes clear that the right purpose of redistribution must be twofold.

First, redistribution is to preserve the possibility that a Newton, Einstein, or Mozart may be among those disadvantaged individuals, and we surely do not want to lose them before they have contributed to human progress (Phelps 1968, 511–12). This can be done through basic food support and health care, so that these geniuses do not have to die prematurely or become mentally or physically impaired due to hunger, famine, and malnutrition.

Second, redistribution is to help those geniuses realize their true potential by giving them an initial push so that they can move up and contribute more. In modern society, this is usually done through publicly funded mass education. Marshall's fundamental insight is worth quoting fully here: "*There is no extravagance more prejudicial to the growth of national wealth than that wasteful negligence which allows genius that happens to be born of lowly parentage to expend itself in lowly work"* ([1982] 1920, 176–77, emphasis added; see also 179–80).

Pulling the two points together, the right purpose of redistribution for development then becomes providing those disadvantaged with the necessary basic life support and initial investment in human capital so that they can grow up despite poverty and contribute to social welfare afterward (e.g., Rawls 1999, 86–93; Sen 2000, 21). In other words, a good distribution policy furthers individuals' capabilities without jeopardizing their incentives for socially productive activities, whereas a bad distribution policy reduces the incentives for individuals without contributing to the development of individual capability, or worse, makes the disadvantaged even worse off. Redistribution designed according to these principles benefits, rather than harms, the whole society. Of course, because redistribution is enormously complex and is deeply intertwined with politics, redistribution in any given society often falls somewhere between the two poles.

Several growth models have shown that redistribution can indeed be capability enhancing and thus growth enhancing (e.g., Aghion et al. 1999; Glomm and Ravikumar 1992; Saint-Paul and Verdier 1993; Chou and Talman 1996). This is so because individual initiative often requires a fair amount of investment of physical capital (which is more influenced by inheritance than intelligence), yet the distribution of talent is mostly biological: good redistribution provides those disadvantaged individuals or groups with indispensable initial physical capital for investing in health care and education so that they can be in a position to undertake initiatives later. In other words, good redistribution empowers individuals so that they can pursue their dreams.

In modern history, publicly funded mass education, especially primary education, has been the primary means of good redistribution because it greatly improves disadvantaged individuals' capabilities and their chances of further success without jeopardizing incentives for individual initiative. Indeed, Marshall explicitly advocated for the expansion of publicly funded mass education following this logic: "It will be profitable as a mere investment. . . . For by this means many, who would have died unknown, are enabled to get the start needed for bringing out their latent abilities" ([1920] 1982, 179; see also 176–77) Along the same logic, Romer (1990, S95–99) argued that to facilitate development, the best policy is not to subsidize physical capital but to subsidize the accumulation of human capital.

Moreover, because publicly funded mass education facilitates social mobility, it may actually enhance incentives in the positional market. In turn, this increase in social mobility limits poor people's desire for unproductive redistribution schemes, as demonstrated by several models and empirical work (Bénabou and Ok 2001; Bénabou and Tirole 2006; Alesina and La Ferrara 2005). Hence, good redistribution can actually propel a society into a virtuous cycle: stronger belief in one's own chance of moving up leads to higher motivation and less demand for unproductive redistribution.

Many empirical studies have found publicly funded mass education to be strongly associated with development (Barro 1991; Acemoglu and Robinson 2000; Lindert 2003). In contrast, an elitist education system (e.g., more money for higher education than for primary education), which can be seen as an institutional arrangement reinforcing the distribution pattern, is fundamentally bad for growth (Lindert 2003). Chapter 4 presents our own evidence.

F. INSTITUTIONS GOVERNING OPPORTUNITY: (IN)EQUALITY OF OPPORTUNITY

Even if there are plenty of big bills on the sidewalk, only some individuals have access to the opportunity to pick up those big bills. In order to have all individuals participate in productive activities, they need a level playing field. Hence, institutions governing opportunities constitute the sixth dimension of IFED.

Let's begin with a familiar story. One white American and one African American in post–civil rights America sent identical resumes for job applications. Yet, the resume bearing a possible African American name got fewer callbacks than the resume with an implicitly white name (Lodder, McFarland, and White 2003; Bertrand and Mullainathan 2004).

Essentially, inequality of opportunity prevents some individuals from participating and hence competing in the material market and the positional market to contribute to development. As a result, both markets remain far from the ideal state of complete competition and fail to reach a better outcome (Sowell 2018, ch. 2). In contrast, meritocratic and open recruitment from the whole population improves the quality of not just bureaucracy but almost everything (Evans and Rauch 1999; Rauch and Evans 2000). As a result, a society becomes better off (see also Lewis's discussion on social mobility and slavery: 1955, 84–90, 107–13). Hence, to promote development, institutions governing opportunity should level the playing field in both markets and beyond, from employment to promotions, bidding for contracts, and competition in politics.

Due to the lack of systematic data on inequality of opportunity (Sowell 2004), I won't be able to present systematic evidence for this dimension of IFED that governs opportunity. Most studies on discrimination in the labor market or workplace have been about explaining the causes and persistence of discrimination rather than about understanding discrimination's overall economic impact (e.g., Becker 1971). And even when they have focused on the effects of discrimination, they have been mostly about actual wage and employment gaps at the micro level rather than about anything related to development at the macro level or even a firm's productivity (for reviews, see Loury 1998; Land and Lehmann 2012).

Here, I can only mention two relevant studies. In a study on how political violence against African Americans had impacted their innovation, measured in filed patents from 1870 to 1940, Cook (2014) found that "valuable patents decline in response to major riots and segregation laws." Apparently, violence against African Americans must have taken critical opportunities from them (see also Sowell 2018, ch. 2).[5] In a very recent study, examining the effect of India's quota system that allocates more access to education and hiring opportunities in government to "other backward classes" (OBCs), Lee (2021) contended that India's quota system has indeed benefited individuals from the OBC castes. Yet, in light of the daunting complexities of India's affirmative action programs and especially the fact that OBCs may account for more than half of India's population (Sowell 2004, 24), Lee's results should be taken cautiously.

III. Concluding Remarks

By moving beyond the mostly inductive and unsystematic approach shared by both NIE and CCGR literature toward IFED, this chapter provides a concise yet systematic statement of IFED and thus takes a crucial step toward a more adequate understanding of what constitutes IFED. In chapters 3–6, I turn to a more detailed discussion of the dimensions of IFED. I skip three of the dimensions due to their status as conventional wisdom (i.e., hierarchy, incentives in the material market) or a lack of systematic quality data (i.e., equality of opportunity). Instead, I focus on the three dimensions that contribute new theoretical insight and/or new empirical evidence with systematic data and adequate historical underpinnings.

First, however, we take an excursion.

Excursion: Three Inequalities

Inequality has been a central concern of humankind since the days of Plato, Aristotle, Confucius, and Mencius, and our interest in it has continued unabated. In the past couple of decades, it seems that every year has brought a significant contribution regarding inequality into the marketplace of ideas (e.g., Tilly 1998; Dworkin 2000; Sen 1992, 2000; Haggard and Kaufman 2012; Cederman et al. 2013; Piketty 2014; Boix 2015) and still more studies that touch upon various aspects of inequality and issues related to it (e.g., Mann 1986, 1993; Acemoglu and Robinson 2012; Sowell 2018).

Pulling together discussions scattered in the literature, but without exhausting all the possible conceptual and normative difficulties, there are only three broad inequalities or equalities (for key conceptual expositions, see Rae 1981; Arneson 1989, 1999; Sen 1992, esp. ch. 1, 79–84; Rawls 1999; and Dworkin 2000, esp. part I; for a brief summary, see Roemer 2009). The first is factual inequality, denoted here as inequality 1. The second is inequality of capability, denoted as inequality 2. The third is inequality of opportunity, in terms of access to opportunity, which can also be described as an unfair or unlevel playing field, denoted as inequality 3. Inequality of rights can be subsumed under inequality of opportunity.

Among the three inequalities, inequality 1 has attracted the most attention from the general public and the scholarly community (e.g., the Gini coefficient). When people talk about inequality, they are mostly talking about inequality 1. Inequality 2 has received much less attention, with Sen (2000) being one of the most important expositions. Inequality 3 has also attracted much attention from the general public, though it is actually quite different from the other two inequalities. Inequality of opportunity is really about the institutional system of a society that regulates the social mobility of individuals (see chapter 4; see also Tang 2010), rather than inequality per se as conventionally understood (cf. Roemer 1998).

Unfortunately, some earlier discussions of inequality have failed to differentiate the three inequalities, thus leading to even more profound confusion. Most prominently, although Rawls had explicitly differentiated the three inequalities, his notion of "primary goods" pooled "rights, liberties, and opportunities, and income and wealth" together (Rawls 1999, 54–56, 78–81). Rawls (54) also asserted that "health and vigor, intelligence and imagination, are natural goods" without grasping that these so-called natural goods are actually impacted by economic, political, and social factors. Similarly, despite rightly defending capability as a critical concern, Sen (2000) has essentially lumped together all three inequalities.

Even this scheme of three inequalities, however, is not fine grained enough. More critically, the (theoretical, hence possibly empirical) logic of the relationships among the three inequalities has not been adequately grasped. As such, our theoretical debates, empirical efforts, and policies directed at factual inequality and other related issues (such as redistribution policies, affirmative action, and poverty reduction) have been mostly muddled and inconsistent.

This excursion seeks to fill this critical lacuna, at least partly. I argue that we need to differentiate forms or kinds of inequality with an even more fine-grained scheme and then propose such a scheme. Only with a more fine-grained framework can we adequately understand the possible logical relationships of the different inequalities. Moreover, only by adequately grasping the logical relationships can we understand the causes behind the lack of consistent results and empirical progress. Only after such progression can we forge a more solid normative stance toward inequalities based on sound empirics and then design sound policy responses for addressing different inequalities.

A caveat is in order. Although inequalities among groups within a state or inequalities among states are also of critical interest (e.g., Gellner 1983; Jones 1997; Pritchett 1997; Stewart 2008; Cederman et al. 2013), I focus here on inequality among individuals or families within a state. If within a country a group (or the individuals of a group) as a whole holds a significant advantage over another group in the form of inequality 1, this mostly reflects inequality of opportunity (inequality 3) over a long period of time. Following the same logic, inequalities among countries also reflect the outcome of historical evolution over a long period of time, including conquest, colonialism, and exploitation (e.g., Frank 1967; Mann 1986, 1993; Diamond 1997; Wallerstein [1989] 2011). Because I cannot devote adequate space to it, I merely emphasize that inequality in all forms is an outcome derived from long historical processes and embedded in a network of power, institutions, and path dependence (Diamond 1997; Tilly 1998; Boix 2015).

The rest of this excursion is structured as follows. Section I provides a more fine-grained classification of the three inequalities, section II addresses the complex logic of the relationships between them, and section III wraps up our excursion with a brief conclusion. A full discussion of how to address these inequalities demands much more detailed discussion, which is outside the scope of this book.

I. Three Inequalities and Their Subforms

This section provides a more fine-grained classification of the three inequalities (summarized in table E.1). With this more delineated framework, the next section goes on to clarify the complex logic of the relationships between the three inequalities.

A. INEQUALITY 1: FACTUAL INEQUALITY, HORIZONTAL AND VERTICAL

Although inequality 1 is often known as "economic inequality," this understanding is too narrow. Certainly, nonmaterial inequality in individuals' social capital or social resources should be counted as part of inequality 1 (Dworkin 2000, ch. 2), although nonmaterial inequality is more difficult to measure. Thus, an individual who was born into a low-income family but nonetheless has a relative who has already climbed up the social ladder, and hence obtained some political and social capital, would have a greater chance of getting a good job than an individual from a similar background who does not have a relative with political or social capital.[1] More accurately, therefore, inequality 1 should be understood as factual inequality.

Inequality 1 can be divided into two subforms: horizontal (i.e., intragenerational) and vertical (i.e., intergenerational). Inequality 1/H is the distribution of wealth, income, and other material and nonmaterial resources within a population, whereas inequality 1/V is the unchanging pattern of distribution of wealth, income, and other material and nonmaterial resources (i.e., social and political capital) through generations.

Inequality 1/H and inequality 1/V interact with each other. On the one hand, inequality 1/V reinforces inequality 1/H materially as well as

TABLE E.1. Three Kinds of Inequality and Their Determinants

Explanation and determinants	Factual/actual inequality (inequality 1)	Inequality of capability (inequality 2)	Inequality of opportunity (inequality 3)
Meaning	The distribution of wealth, income (earnings), and other material and nonmaterial resources (such as status) within a population.	Difference in capabilities (esp. physical talent, intellectual talent, level of education, skills).	Inequality of opportunity is not really "inequality," as conventionally understood, but institutional discrimination.
	Besides material inequality, inequality in social resources, both horizontal and vertical, is part of inequality 1. This covers things such as social and political capital. This inequality is strongly transmittable but difficult to measure.		
Subdimensions	Inequality 1 can be divided into two subforms: horizontal (intragenerational) and vertical (intergenerational).	There are at least three sources or types of inequality 2: biological (natal/postnatal), developmental, and education/training.	Inequality 3 can be divided into two phases: inequality of opportunity before an individual enters the labor market, and inequality of opportunity when and after an individual enters the labor market.
Proximate determinants	-Inheritance of wealth	-Genetic inheritance	Ideas for institutions and political power that makes and supports institutions
	-Individuals' capacities	-Natal and postnatal development (i.e., "nurture")	
	-Work ethic (motivation, persistence)	-Schooling/training	
	-Opportunities (which are partially determined by institutions)		
	-Pure luck (i.e., winning a lottery)		

Deeper determinants	- Determinants of individuals' capacities (see inequality 2) - Determinants of opportunities (see inequality 3) - Redistributive policies that address material inequality - The dynamics of different economic growth regimes (e.g., agricultural, industrial)	- Household endowments, both material and intellectual (e.g., more endowment leads to more investment in schooling and training) - Public support for basic health care and education - On-the-job training provided by employers	- Existing power structure of a society, which may be subject to change via social protest, social movements, rebellions, and revolutions. - Historical path dependence (from political to economic and social) in institutional change
Possible good redistribution policies or measures (immediate measures only)	- Land reform (redistribution to the poor) - Progressive tax - Inheritance tax	- Basic food support for the poor and (temporary) unemployment support - Publicly funded basic health care - Publicly funded primary to secondary education (for developing countries) - Publicly funded primary to college education (for developed countries)	Not applicable: Because inequality of opportunity is underpinned by institutions, changes in inequality of opportunity are really institutional changes rather than redistributive policies per se, strictly speaking.
Political doctrines that advocate for or against	- For: (material) egalitarianism, strictly defined - For: political liberalism (e.g., Rawls; Dworkin)? - Against: libertarianism (e.g., Hayek, Nozick)?	- For: the capability approach (e.g., Sen) - For (implicitly): the "human capital" approach toward economic growth (e.g., Schultz, Becker) - Against: racism and biological determinism	- For: political liberalism (e.g., Rawls; Dworkin) - Against: libertarianism?

psychologically and developmentally (Aize and Currie 2014; Autor 2014). On the other hand, past inequality 1/H reinforces existing inequality 1/H within an individual's lifetime and underpins future inequality 1/V (Piketty 2014).

Most of the literature focuses on the causes and impacts of inequality 1/H, inequality 1/V, or both, especially how these two subforms interact. Yet, the most critical point about inequality 1 (both horizontal and vertical) is that it is an extremely complex social outcome underpinned not only by inequality 2 and inequality 3 (e.g., Piketty 2014; Boix 2015; Dorsch and Maarek 2019) but also by other macro factors, such as technological change and demographic change (Galor and Weil 2000; Galor and Moav 2004; Galor 2011), as well as micro factors, such as individuals' family backgrounds, decisions, luck, determination, capabilities, and numerous small and large decisions along the way.

B. INEQUALITY 2: CAPABILITIES, BIOLOGICAL/ DEVELOPMENTAL AND EDUCATIONAL

Inequality 2 denotes the uneven distribution of capabilities for performing different functions and tasks (cf. Sen 1992, 2000). Simply because of biological (i.e., more than genetic) differences among individuals as dictated by human biology, there are no two identical individuals—even identical twins are different.

There are at least three sources or types of inequality 2: biological, developmental (natal/postnatal), and education/training. For simplicity, I group biological and developmental into one type, inequality 2/BD. By education and training (inequality 2/ET), I mean that individuals gain capabilities not only from formal and informal education but also from formal and informal training. Inequality 2/BD comes before inequality 2/ET, and hence the former impacts the latter more extensively than the other way around.

C. INEQUALITY 3: ACCESS TO OPPORTUNITY VIA INSTITUTIONAL AND NONINSTITUTIONAL DISCRIMINATION

Inequality 3 can be divided into two phases (Roemer 1998; cf. Rawls 1999, 57–58, 86–92). The first is inequality of opportunity before an individual enters the labor market, first in terms of access to adequate physical and mental nourishment and development and then in terms of access to education and training. This is termed inequality 3/A. The second is inequality of opportunity when an individual enters the labor market and thereafter (i.e., hiring and career advancements after hiring). This is termed inequality 3/B and is perhaps more commonly known as fair play or meritocracy or a level playing

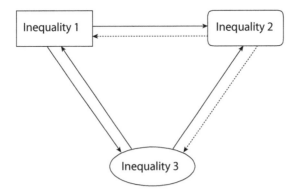

FIGURE E.1. The Relationships of the Three Inequalities. Solid arrows denote more powerful impact; dashed arrows represent less powerful impact.

field in the labor market. Hence, Becker's ([1964] 1993) work on human capital is mostly about inequality 3/A (before entering the labor market), whereas his work on discrimination is mostly about inequality 3/B (after entering the labor market) (Becker [1957] 1971). Inequality 3/A comes before inequality 3/B; the former impacts the latter, not the other way around.

Inequality 3 decisively underpins individuals' performance (or fortune) in both the material market and the positional market. The sources of inequality 3 can be roughly divided into two: institutional and noninstitutional discrimination in terms of individuals' access to opportunity, both before and after entering the labor market. Obviously, institutional discrimination is more detrimental to individuals' development of capabilities and access to career opportunities than noninstitutional discrimination.

Ideally, both inequality 3/A and inequality 3/B should be eliminated. Yet, both real personal discrimination and irrational decisions on individuals' access to basic health care/education and the labor market are hard to reduce and impossible to eradicate (Schelling 1971; Sowell 2018). Also, both inequality 3/A and inequality 3/B are constrained by geography: individuals in certain geographical locations do not have easy access to certain education and employment opportunities. Hence, even with fair play, the presence of a meritocracy, and a level playing field, de facto equality 3 is an impossibility.

II. Connections among the Three Inequalities and Their Implications

The three inequalities interact with each other, both intra- and intergenerationally. Moreover, each of the three inequalities is underpinned by multiple proximate and deeper determinants, and these determinants also interact with each other, both intra- and intergenerationally. Indeed, one can argue that it is the interaction of these determinants that really drives the interaction of the three inequalities. Because earlier discussions on inequality have generally failed to grasp these two critical facts, much confusion has resulted. This section takes a critical first step toward a better understanding.

Inequality 3 is the most institutional among the three inequalities. Because power underpins institutions (Tang 2011b), inequality 3 more decisively reflects the past and present distribution of power and is the most political and hence fundamental among the three. Inequality 3 impinges directly on inequality 1 and inequality 2 and indirectly on inequality 1 via inequality 2. Hence, inequality 3 is a key source of both inequality 1 and inequality 2. As such, inequality 3—rather than inequality 1 and inequality 2—should be the major focus of public policy debate.

Inequality 2 directly affects inequality 1. Inequality 2, however, has little impact on inequality 3, at least in the short run. If inequality 2 is to impact inequality 3, individuals must change a society's power structure and institutional system first.

Meanwhile, both inequality 1/H and inequality 1/V affect inequality 2, especially individuals' different developmental and educational attainments that cannot be attributed to purely biological factors. Moreover, inequality 1 and inequality 3 interact with each other to further reinforce inequality 2, especially inequality 2/ET, which in turn reinforces inequality 1. As a result, inequality 1 impacts both inequality 2 and inequality 3 directly and indirectly, interactively and noninteractively, and hence profoundly, extensively, and surreptitiously (e.g., Aizer and Currie 2014; Chetty et al. 2018; Hertel and Groh-Samberg 2019).

Finally, inequality 1 is one of the most complex social outcomes. It is immediately determined by inheritance of wealth and social capital, individuals' capacities, work ethics (e.g., motivation, persistence), opportunities (which are partially determined by institutions), pure luck (i.e., winning a huge lottery), and redistributive measures (or lack of them). Yet, behind these immediate determinants lie deeper determinants, including populational stratification, which impacts individuals' wealth and capabilities, and power and institutional structures that determine access to opportunities. Additional deeper determinants include the dynamics of different economic growth regimes (e.g., labor intensive/low technology, human capital–intensive/high technology; see Galor and Weil 2000; Galor and Moav 2004) and the cumulative effect of redistributive measures—or lack of them—in history. These factors go so far back that some of them can be traced all the way to the rise of hierarchy in human history (Diamond 1997; Boix 2010, 2015).

Pulling things together (summarized in figure E.1), several useful preliminary points can be made. First, putting the issue of endogeneity aside, assessing the impact of inequality 2/BD or inequality 2/ET on inequality 1 within an individual's life span is relatively straightforward. Similarly, within an individual's life span, the impact of inequality 1/H on inequality 2/BD and inequality 2/ET can be more readily established than the other way around. Putting these two aspects together, however, it becomes obvious that establishing a causal relationship between inequality 1 and inequality 2 across generations will be extremely difficult, if not impossible. Second, adding inequality 3 to the picture, it becomes evident that uncovering the immediate and deep causes of inequality 1 will be quite challenging. Third, assessing inequality 3's overall impact on inequality 1 and inequality 2 is also likely to be difficult, mostly due to data availability and quality—simply measuring inequality 3 has proved to be a challenge (for a review, see Roemer and Trannoy 2015). Fourth, because inequality 1 is an outcome, efforts to establish a causal relationship between inequality 1 and economic development is bound to be inconclusive (Voitchovsky 2009).

Hence, it may be more fruitful to first establish the impact of inequality 2 and inequality 3 on inequality 1 than to uncover the proximate or other confounding factors behind inequality 1, simply because such factors will be so numerous that establishing a connection between them and inequality 1 is unlikely to be very meaningful (e.g., Acemoglu et al. 2008; Boix 2015; Haggard and Kaufman 2012; Dorsch and Maarek 2019).

III. Concluding Remarks

Given the complex, interconnected relationships of the three inequalities, how to address these inequalities is beyond the scope of this brief excursion. Table E.1 summarizes some possible measures that have been alluded to in the existing literature. Instead, by providing a more valid conceptual framework that explicitly differentiates the three inequalities and spells out their complex relationships, the central purpose of this excursion is to encourage more productive research on how to address the three inequalities.

3

The Positional Market and Development

SOCIAL MOBILITY AS AN INCENTIVE

If no man could hope to rise or fear to fall in society; if industry did not bring its own reward, and indolence its punishment, we could not hope to see the animated activity in bettering our own condition, which now forms the master-spring of public prosperity.
—THOMAS MALTHUS ([1798] 1951, 254)

Progress is most rapid in those parts of the country in which the greatest proportions of the leaders of industry are the sons of working men.
—ALFRED MARSHALL ([1920] 1982, 176)

Economic growth is usually associated with a high degree of vertical mobility, upward and downward.
—ARTHUR LEWIS (1955, 84)

Adam Smith, the founding father of modern economics, recognized that vying for social status or "vanity" drives human behavior (Smith [1759] 1979, 50–54). As economics and sociology parted ways, however, economists have focused almost exclusively on material interests. Meanwhile, although social mobility, defined as individuals' or groups' movements within the stratified society, has been a principal subject of modern sociology, sociologists have been primarily interested in understanding the evolution of social stratification, the social and political consequences of social mobility, and the impact of economic development on social mobility. Most sociologists have thought little about the possibility that social mobility may actually influence economic development.[1]

By rediscovering, developing, and synthesizing often implicit insights that have been scattered in classical economics (e.g., Smith [1759] 1979, 50–54, 57; Malthus [1798] 1951, 254; Marshall [1920] 1982, 176–77), sociology (e.g., Tocqueville [1835] 2004, 362–66; Brown 1973; Hirsch 1977; Gellner 1983, 24–25; Goldthorpe 1985; Breen 1997), classical institutional economics (e.g., Veblen [1899] 1967; Lewis 1955, 84–90, 107–13; Hirschman 1973), and new institutional economics (e.g., Fershtman and Weiss 1993; Fershtman et al. 1996; Bénabou and Ok 2001), this chapter seeks to explicitly link the drive for social status and social mobility with economic growth.

Specifically, I argue that there are two distinctive markets in human society. In addition to the more recognized material market, there is also a positional market. I further contend that the channel of social mobility—the institutional system that regulates the performance of individuals and groups in the positional market—is a critical dimension of the overall institutional foundation of economic development (IFED). The channel of social mobility influences economic development by underpinning the incentive structure in the positional market, just as the channel of property rights influences economic development by underpinning the incentive structure in the material market. More concretely, the channel of social mobility influences economic development by regulating a critical motive of individual effort: vying for upward social mobility.

The rest of this chapter is structured as follows. Section I demarcates the material market and the positional market by tracing the emergence of the two markets in the course of social evolution. Section II introduces the differentiation of positions from position-symbolizing material goods, thus further differentiating the two markets and clarifying several areas of confusion. Section III outlines the core hypotheses linking positional incentives with economic development. Section IV employs the presence or lack of incentives in the material market and the positional market to delineate human societies into four "ideal types." Section V examines three historical cases to substantiate the thesis that positional incentives do influence economic development, *independently* from material incentives. Building on section V, section VI advances a more systematic understanding of the impact of positional incentives on economic development. Sections VII and VIII draw theoretical and empirical implications, respectively, and section IX concludes.

I. The Origin of Material and Positional Inequality and Markets

A fundamental assumption of this chapter is that there are two distinctive markets in human society: in addition to the more recognized material market, there is also a positional market. Although the two markets interact with each other to shape human behavior, they are also fundamentally different (for a summary, see table 3.1).

Foremost, in the material market, individuals compete for material gains (or profit). In the positional market, individuals compete for positions and the real and/or perceived social status, power, and prestige that are associated with those positions. Second, whereas the material market is horizontal, the positional market is vertical. Third, whereas the supply of material goods—including position-symbolizing material goods—is potentially unlimited, the supply of higher (thus better) positions at the upper tier of social hierarchies is inherently limited. Fourth, whereas all types of agents, including individuals, can supply material goods, only hierarchical organizations (e.g., states) can supply positions.

Yet, can we really differentiate the positional market from the material market? In other words, how can we be sure that it has been individuals' drive for social positions rather than their drive for material gains that has been driving a particular behavior?

Since the days of ancient Greece and China, moral philosophers have recognized that both material gains and positional gains drive human behavior and have been speculating on the origins of these two drivers of human behavior. Although they correctly recognized that the two different drivers were fundamentally driven by inequality in human society, they tended to conflate the two inequalities (i.e., positional versus material). Worse, they tended to believe that the rise of material inequality via the rise of private property led to positional inequality (e.g., Dahrendorf 1968, 157–63). Elman Service (1971, 150) might not have been far off when he attributed this "tendency in modern thought to see exploitation, wealth expropriation, and

TABLE 3.1. Material Market versus Positional Market

	Material market	Positional market
Characteristics	A horizontal market in which individuals compete for wealth or profit.	A hierarchical (vertical) market in which individuals compete for positions.
Goods	Material goods, with potentially unlimited supply. Position-symbolizing material goods are a specific type of material goods.	Positions, with inherently limited supply because top positions are always limited.
Supply of goods versus demand of goods	The supply and the demand of goods come from all possible agents (individuals, corporations, states).	Positions are supplied only by hierarchical organizations (e.g., states). Position-symbolizing material goods are supplied by all possible agents.
		Demand for both types of goods comes from all possible agents, other than the state. The state is exclusively a supplier of positions.
Ultimate source of incentives	The need for survival and material inequality.	Positional inequality.
Can the market exist independently from inequality?	Yes. In principle, the material market can exist without material inequality.	No. Without (positional) inequality, there will be no positional market.
The key institutional system that structures incentives in the market	The channel of property rights and contract enforcement.	The channel of social mobility.

greed as causes of the rise of authority, classes, and the state" to Marx's and Marxism's profound influence over the social sciences.

These earlier treatises could not get the origins of the two inequalities right, partly because they were not aided by modern anthropology. With the aid of modern anthropology, we can now reconstruct the origins of the two inequalities and the two markets. Two principal conclusions can now be drawn firmly. First, *positional inequality arose independently from and earlier than material inequality*. Second, *the positional market arose independently from and earlier than the material market*.[2]

The positional market emerges *simultaneously* with positional inequality, and the positional market and positional inequality are almost synonymous: a positional market exists wherever there is positional inequality.[3] In other words, the positional market cannot exist independently from positional inequality. In contrast, the material market can operate independently from material inequality, and material inequality arises *independently* from the material market. Moreover, as becomes clear below, material inequality arose *after and from* positional inequality.

At the first stage of human society—the stage of bands/tribes as foraging (i.e., hunting and gathering) societies—there already exists primitive positional inequality, thus also a primitive positional market because every band/tribe has a leader. These leaders occupy their positions almost exclusively based on personal capabilities and charisma. Occupation of the leadership position is thus "ephemeral and context-specific" (Johnson and Earle 1987, 31). Meanwhile, there is no material inequality in bands/tribes: they are egalitarian societies, and production outputs are redistributed in an egalitarian fashion within the entire community. As such, occupying the leadership position in a band/tribe is *almost inevitably* materially costly: leaders hold these positions mostly because they can provide more resources (e.g., food) to the community (Service 1971, 131–32; 1975, 49–56, 73–74).

At the band/tribe stage, a primitive material market based on gift exchanging exists as a primitive division of labor or specialization emerges, but this primitive material market comes after the primitive positional inequality or market. This is so because more developed division of labor based on specialization of skills emerges long after the primitive positional inequality. Moreover, within egalitarian societies, there is little sense of private property rights: all material goods belong to the community. Most importantly, material inequality cannot exist within egalitarian societies, not merely by definition: intentional "leveling" within egalitarian communities prevents the rise of material inequality (Miller and Cook 1998 and references cited there).

At the stage of chiefdom, occupation of the leadership position no longer depends on individual charisma or merit: it becomes hereditary (Service 1971, 139–40; 1975, 290–97; Johnson and Earle 1987, chs. 9 and 10; Earle 1997). In the chiefdom stage, positional inequality becomes institutionalized, and an institutionalized positional market as political hierarchy begins to exist. Anthropologists explain the transition from a mostly egalitarian band/ tribe to a hierarchical chiefdom as an outcome that was driven by a combination of population growth, scarcity of resources, settled agriculture, and external threat (e.g., Service 1971, 1975; Johnson and Earle 1987; Diamond 1997; Earle 1997).

This emergence of institutionalized positional inequality would have a profound impact on the course of social evolution, and any other inequality evolved after it cannot be understood without taking into consideration the role of power and social conflict (Lenski 1966, 104–5; Dahrendorf 1968; Service 1975, 8).

Foremost, *occupation of the leadership position becomes materially reward-ing.*[4] At the initial stage of semichiefdom, the chief may still observe material egalitarianism by pooling and then distributing production outputs evenly within the community. As times goes by, however, chiefs can usurp, embezzle, and then distribute resources to benefit themselves, their families, and eventually their kin, under the cover of providing religious service and public goods. This eventually leads to material inequality between the chiefs and their families and kin on the one side, and the rest of the community on the other (Service 1975, 290–97; Johnson and Earle 1987, chs. 9 and 10). Over the course of human history, the emergence of material inequality has been a direct product of the rise of institutionalized positional inequality within the community.

Moreover, precisely because occupation of the leadership position is now materially rewarding, a primary concern of the chiefs is to perpetuate their occupation of the position and make sure that the position remains occupied by their children or close kin (Service 1971, 145–47; 1975, 72–80). Happily, the chiefs have many tools to do this. Most importantly, they can use patronage to buy loyalty and thus strengthen their rule (Johnson and Earle 1987, chs. 9 and 10; see also Miller and Cook 1998, 88–90). Hence, once an institutionalized hierarchy is established, it becomes self-enforcing.

An institutionalized material market that is based on exchange of goods must have some sense of "private" property rights. In other words, for an institutionalized material market to exist, at least some production outputs can no longer be pooled and then redistributed evenly within the community. Within egalitarian societies, a sense of private property rights is weak. A strong sense of private property comes into existence only with the emergence of institutionalized political hierarchy: private property rights can only be enforced by institutionalized political power, and institutionalized political power can only be provided by a centralized political authority. As such, institutionalized material markets also emerge after institutionalized positional markets during the course of social evolution.

To summarize, in the course of social evolution, the positional market arose independently from and earlier than the material market, and material inequality emerged after the emergence of institutionalized positional inequality. The two markets are therefore distinct, although they have interacted with each other to shape human behavior and human society. Moreover, the material market, since its very beginning, has evolved in the shadow of the positional market or in the shadow of political power.

II. A Key Differentiation

Before I proceed further, a key differentiation must be introduced.

Positions should be clearly differentiated from "positional goods," as defined by Hirsch (1977) and then populated by Frank (1985). Although positions can be understood as a special type of positional goods, most of the positional goods as defined by Hirsch and Frank should be more fittingly called *position-symbolizing material goods*.

The positional market of a particular society is the total sum of all social hierarchies within that society. *In the positional market, the real positional goods are positions, not position-symbolizing material goods.* Individuals *compete* for positions, and they *consume* position-symbolizing material goods to show off or associate themselves with certain positions or status.[5] More often than not, individuals overconsume position-symbolizing material goods, resulting in wasteful "conspicuous consumption," as Veblen ([1899] 1967) put it.

As noted above, only hierarchical organizations (or social hierarchies) can supply positions. Quite evidently, among the various social hierarchies, the state has been the largest and thus the most important supplier of positions. In contrast, position-symbolizing material goods, just like regular material goods, can be supplied by all kinds of agents (states, individuals, corporations). Of course, all individuals are (potential and actual) consumers of positions and material goods (see table 3.1).

With this differentiation, it becomes clear that there have been two schools looking at two different but interrelated aspects of the positional market.

The first school was pioneered by Veblen ([1899] 1967) and further developed by Duesenberry (1949), Liebenstein (1950), Hirsch (1977), Frank (1985, 1997, 2005), Knell (1999), and Ng (1997) in economics, and by Collins (1979) in sociology. The French sociologist Pierre Bourdieu's work on distinction and taste also bears a strong resemblance to Veblen's work (Bourdieu 1984; see also Trigg 2001).[6] This school focuses on the usually negative impact of overconsumption (i.e., "conspicuous consumption" or "keeping up with the Joneses") of positional goods on welfare and growth. This school has generated quite an extensive literature, although most mainstream economists have chosen to ignore it, as noted by Frank (1997, 2005), Ng (1997), and Mason (2000).

A second school focuses on the potential (both positive and negative) impact of positional competition on economic development. In economics, this school has been prominently represented by Smith ([1759] 1979, 50–54, 57), Malthus ([1798] 1951, 254), Marshall ([1920] 1982, 176–77), Lewis (1955, 84–90, 107–13), Hirschman (1973), Bénabou and Ok (2001), and Fershtman and his colleagues (Fershtman and Weiss 1993; Fershtman et al. 1996). In sociology, this school also has a long and venerable lineage, represented by Tocqueville ([1835] 2004, 362–66), Brown (1973), Gellner (1983, 24–25), Goldthorpe (1985), and Breen (1997). Although these authors did not always explicitly differentiate the positional market from the material market (e.g., Malthus; Gellner), there is a core thesis that unifies this second school: although positional competition is zero sum for any two given individuals within a given social hierarchy, it can improve the welfare of the larger society *if the incentive structure in the positional market is properly structured*. Compared to the first school, the literature from the second school has been less extensive.

Apparently, the two schools are not incompatible. Indeed, how to strike a balance between providing individuals with the necessary incentives for positional competition that contributes to collective welfare on the one hand and limiting their competitive consumption of positional goods on the other hand is an important challenge for welfare economics and institutional economics (Frank 1989, 1997, 2005; Ng 1997).[7] Ultimately, one cannot— *and perhaps should not*—completely eliminate human desires to show off because doing so would also greatly weaken the incentives for positional competition.

III. Hypotheses on Incentives in the Positional Market and Growth

The channel of social mobility is the institutional system that regulates individuals' and groups' performance (i.e., rise and fall) in the positional market, and it regulates individuals' and groups' social mobility within a continuum between complete social immobility on the one end and "adequate" social mobility on the other end. An individual's or a group's real social mobility is the outcome from the interaction between that individual's or group's endowment and effort on the one hand and the channel of social mobility on the other hand.

The channel of social mobility is an institutional system that consists of many interrelated institutional arrangements. Intuitively, in terms of its impact on economic development, institutional arrangements fall into two ideal types: growth promoting and growth retarding. Due to incomplete knowledge and other (i.e., political) reasons (see below), human societies inevitably install some institutional arrangements in the channel of social mobility that are growth promoting and some that are growth retarding. As such, most societies' channels of social mobility are inevitably a mixture of growth-promoting arrangements and growth-retarding arrangements.

To fully understand the impact of institutional arrangements on economic development, two key notions need to be emphasized. First, production is the ultimate foundation of economic development, and learning (or the accumulation of knowledge) is the most critical engine of economic development (Jones 2005). In fact, because production is a process of utilizing, testing, and producing knowledge, production and learning are essentially inseparable (Smith [1776] 1981, ch. 1). Second, knowledge can be true and productive (e.g., Newtonian mechanics), false and unproductive (e.g., Lysenkoist genetics), or even evil and destructive (e.g., knowledge for producing poisonous gas), just as entrepreneurship can be productive, unproductive, or destructive (Baumol 1990). In other words, *knowledge has a quality dimension, in addition to a quantity dimension* (Tang and Gao 2020).[8]

For simplicity, we can assume that a growth-promoting institutional arrangement rewards individuals who contribute constructively to social welfare. At the same time, it denies rewards to individuals who do not contribute to social welfare and punishes those individuals who jeopardize social welfare. In contrast, a growth-retarding arrangement does just the opposite.

A growth-retarding institutional arrangement in the channel of social mobility thus means that some individuals or groups are denied the opportunity to advance their social positions even though they contribute to the welfare of a society. In other words, some barriers against those individuals' or groups' upward mobility must exist within the positional market. As such, a growth-retarding institutional arrangement in the channel of social mobility is essentially a form of discrimination; I call it *institutional discrimination*.[9] Institutional discrimination can range from the most extreme forms (i.e., ethnic cleansing, slavery) to racial, gender, and age discrimination.[10]

The presence of institutional discrimination must also mean that there are privileged individuals or groups versus discriminated individuals or groups. Only privileged individuals or groups have the incentives and the capabilities to erect and enforce an institutional arrangement or system that can prevent the discriminated individuals and groups from rising while simultaneously preventing themselves from falling in the positional market.

With the preceding discussion, we can now state the core thesis: adequate positional incentives for productive individual effort and knowledge promote economic development, whereas inadequate positional incentives for productive individual effort and knowledge depress economic development. Before I substantiate the core thesis, however, we need to understand the interaction between the two markets.

IV. Four Ideal Types of Society

Because there are both a material market and a positional market in human society, it is natural to assume that the two markets often provide different levels of incentives for individual effort that contributes to economic development. Because the incentive structures in the two markets do interact with each other to shape the allocation of individual effort in society and individuals can leverage gains in one market upon gains in the other market,[11] individuals can be expected to allocate their talent between the two markets according to the different levels of incentives in the two markets. Building on the theory of "allocation of talent" (Baumol 1990; Murphy et al. 1991), we can then come up with a general understanding about how different pairings of incentives for individual effort influence individuals' allocation of their talent and how this allocation affects the overall society's economic development and political stability.

Different combinations of the presence or lack of "adequate" incentives for individual effort that are ultimately conducive to economic development in the material market and the positional market delineate various human societies into four "ideal types," shown in the simple 2×2 matrix of figure 3.1.[12]

The lower right quadrant represents a society that offers inadequate incentives in both markets (type I). In such a society, wealth and positions are fixed by birth. Official ideologies in such a society not only sanction the fixed social hierarchy and discourage individuals from pursuing upward mobility but also idolize economic hardship and discourage individuals from pursuing wealth (usually by promising some kind of happy afterlife). In these societies, advances in either market often can only be achieved by usurpation with violent means. Most traditional societies belong to this category (Gellner 1983, 9–11), with slavery in the antebellum American South and apartheid in

	Incentives in the positional market	
Incentives in the material market	Adequate\Adequate (IV)	Adequate\Inadequate (III)
	Inadequate\Adequate (II)	Inadequate\Inadequate (I)

FIGURE 3.1. Incentives in the Two Markets and Human Societies.

South Africa being two prominent examples in more recent time. Primitive egalitarian societies represent a special kind of this type I society.

The lower left quadrant represents a society that offers adequate incentives in the positional market but inadequate incentives in the material market (type II). In such a society, the channel of social mobility is relatively open, mostly because the state bureaucracy is largely meritocratic. At the same time, material benefits in such a society are usually, if not exclusively, allocated according to individuals' social positions in the state bureaucracy. As a result, most individuals devote their talent first to advancing in the positional market and then use their social position to seek gains in the material market. In such a society, individual effort is mostly unproductive or even destructive for economic growth, because individuals are more concerned with dividing up the economic pie rather than enlarging it. Examples of this type of society include the Roman Empire, Imperial China, and most nonmarket economies in modern times (e.g., North Korea and Cuba today, China and Vietnam before their economic reform, the former Soviet Union and its satellite states).

The upper right quadrant of figure 3.1 represents a society that offers adequate incentives in the material market but inadequate incentives in the positional market (type III). Such a society produces a class with wealth but without power and prestige. Eventually, this class has to choose between two options: a "voice" option that demands power in the society and an "exit" option that leaves the society (Hirschman 1970). The Glorious Revolution was a case in which the class with wealth chose to exercise the voice option; on the other hand, human and physical capital flight from many developing countries to developed countries partly reflects the fact that those with human and physical capital, unable to advance in the positional market and unwilling to risk using the voice option, choose the exit option.

The upper left quadrant represents the (ideal) modern industrial society that offers adequate incentives for individuals in both markets (type IV). In modern industrial society, both position and wealth are temporary, and individuals have to endeavor constantly in order to gain and maintain them.

In modern industrial society, position and wealth reinforce each other, and individual efforts in the two markets also reinforce each other. Such an incentive structure strongly favors economic development.

If we take the path toward modernization as a one-way street, we can paint a rough picture about how the two markets interact with each other and how their interactions shape the evolution of human society.

Human societies at the stage of band and tribe are materially egalitarian but somewhat positionally hierarchical. In these societies, occupying the leadership position is often materially punishing rather than rewarding. Moreover, producing too much materially often brings moral castigation and even physical punishment (including death) because of others' "leveling" efforts. Band and tribe thus represent a primitive form of type I society—there is little positional incentive and little material incentive beyond subsistence. Such an incentive structure strongly discourages accumulation and innovation (Miller and Cook 1998, 72–82). Not surprisingly, economic development in such societies tends to be extremely slow, if there is any growth at all.

The channel of social mobility becomes necessary only after the coming of the hierarchical society. This is so not only because there is no positional inequality (or stratification) before that, but also because barriers to social mobility can only exist in a hierarchical structure: a hierarchical society, by definition, demands a certain (often, significant) degree of domination, and only a privileged, elite group can have both the incentives and the resources to enforce rules in the channel of social mobility (Tumin 1953, 389; Wrong 1959, 774, 782). Moreover, after human societies moved out of the tribal stage, occupying a leadership position became materially rewarding (often very). As such, incentives in the positional market began to grow, individuals began to desire (others') higher social positions, and positional competition became more intense. Because the emergence of positional inequality (and thus the positional market) inoculated more incentives for individuals and transformed a type I traditional society into a type II traditional society, it was a major step toward the making of civilization (Diamond 1997, ch. 14; see also Miller and Cook 1998).[13]

For most of our history, however, while most individuals certainly wanted to take up the good positions, those positions were not designed for them: they were designed by and for those who were powerful enough to ensure that only members of their own group could occupy those positions. In this sense, incentives for individual effort in a positional market had long existed, and the problem for most of our history has been that most individual efforts were not being rewarded in the positional market: there have always been political barriers that prevent individual effort from being rewarded in the positional market. Those who are powerful (and consequently rich) normally construct a society's institutions to exclude others for fear of being politically replaced (Acemoglu and Robinson 2006). Indeed, the more powerful and rewarding the positions, the more incentives and the more resources their owners have to protect their privileged positions (Tumin 1953, 389; Wrong 1959, 774, 782). This explains why, for much of our history, general upward social mobility could only be achieved through violent means.

Traditional societies can also evolve into type III societies. Today's China may represent a form of type III society.[14] After its opening up and reform, the Chinese state institutionalized strong incentives in the material market (Nee 2000), yet retained powerful barriers in the positional market. In China, the domination of the state apparatus by the Communist Party means that many elite administrative positions are off limits to nonparty members and loyalists (Bian et al. 2001; Walder 1995; Walder et al. 2000). In these societies, the political elite also hold significant, if not enormous, advantage in the material market, and business elites often have to buy into (corrupted) power. As such, both communism and capitalism inevitably become infected by "cronyism" (Dickson 2008b).

Contrary to traditional societies, where hereditary power and status determines wealth, power and status are more temporary in (ideal) modern industrial societies. Moreover, in modern societies, wealth usually determines power and status rather than the other way around (Gellner 1983, 24–25; Pagano 2003). Hence, in order to maintain power and status in modern industrial societies, one constantly has to accumulate wealth through investing in physical and human capital. As a result, the incentive structure in modern industrial society strongly favors productive entrepreneurship over unproductive entrepreneurship (Pagano 2003) and thus strongly favors growth. Indeed, it is only in modern industrial societies that incentives are present for individuals in both markets. The modern industrial society, by opening the opportunity for advances in both markets, has been able to make individuals' efforts in the two markets reinforce each other. By doing so, the modern industrial society has been able to turn an individual's effort into a "perpetual growth society," and it has remained so ever since (Gellner 1983).

In that sense, a major challenge for premodern societies on their path toward modernization is how to reshape the incentive structures in the two markets. To achieve modernization (through economic development), providing adequate incentives in the material market or the positional market alone is not enough: a state must provide adequate incentives in both markets. Surely, secure property rights for slaveholders did not help the overall economy in the pre–Civil War American South, nor it did help many Latin American economies (Engerman and Sokoloff 1997). To achieve modernization, a society therefore has to move from a state in which incentives in one or both markets are lacking to a state in which adequate incentives are provided in both markets, so that individual efforts that contribute to social welfare are rewarded not only materially but also positionally.

V. Three Historical Cases

This section contains three case studies. The first two studies add a new twist to the interpretations of two important empirical cases in economic history to substantiate the thesis developed above. In both cases, institutions that underpin material incentives were relatively weak, and therefore we can better isolate the impact of institutions that underpin positional incentives. Moreover, the two cases deliver contrasting implications The first case illustrates the idea that rewarding the "right" group of individuals in the positional market facilitates economic development. The second case illustrates that punishing the "right" group of individuals and rewarding the "wrong" group of individuals in the positional market depresses economic development. Together, these two cases present a nuanced picture about the role of positional incentives in economic development: while meritocracy and the rate of social mobility is of paramount importance, the kind of individual effort and knowledge that the positional market rewards, denies, and punishes also matters a great deal.

The third study recalls Alexis Tocqueville's ([1835] 2004) classic observation on slavery in America. Tocqueville's penetrating words on the effect of slavery as an extreme form of institutional discrimination serve as a powerful indictment against institutional discrimination and social immobility.

A. BRITAIN'S TRANSITION TO THE INDUSTRIAL REVOLUTION

Before the sixteenth century, England was just like every other traditional society in terms of its channel of social mobility. Both the state and the church enacted laws discouraging and prohibiting social mobility, while schools and churches taught the norm of accepting one's "God-given" place in the social hierarchy. Social mobility for lower classes was possible only by entering the church or by serving on the manor of a sponsoring lord (Herlihy 1973).

The situation began to change under the reign of Elizabeth I (1558–1603). By then, the state began to acquiesce upward social mobility to merchants, first through business and then by becoming aristocracy through land purchasing (Tawney 1941, 18; Brown 1973, 61–63). By the middle years of James I (1603–1625), business had become "a plateau from which more prestigious position can be reached" (Brown 1976, 60), and "it was an age of unprecedented opportunities for those already endowed with skills, capital, or entrepreneurship" (Mendels 1976, 209).

The increasing upward mobility of the merchant class (especially the Atlantic traders) gradually led to increased representation of the merchant class in the British parliament. From 1509 to 1558, among the 36 members of the House of Commons from the city of London, 26 of them were merchants. This pattern gradually diffused to other cities and eventually resulted in a substantial presence of merchant interests in the House of Commons. In 1584, merchant interests were still marginal in the House of Commons: other than the merchants that were sent from the city of London over a span of 50 years, there were few merchants in the House of Commons. By 1640, however, Atlantic traders alone regularly occupied 50 to 70 of the 550 seats of the Long Parliament. This increasing representation of merchants in the House of Commons undoubtedly played an instrumental role in a series of institutional reforms that finally laid the institutional foundation of an industrial capitalist society, including the Glorious Revolution (Acemoglu et al. 2005b; Zhang and Gao 2004).

By allowing upward social mobility for its merchant class, Britain was able to sustain its economic development *before* the Glorious Revolution. "The remarkable fluidity of English social stratification in the first two phases of industrialization undoubtedly contributed to the flourishing of industrial enterprise through individual initiatives" (Mendels 1976, 213). "Without these changes in patterns of mobility, . . . it is unlikely that the rapid expansion of industrial capitalism between 1540 and 1640 would have occurred" (Brown 1973, 63).[15]

Indeed, robust economic development was achieved in this period in which institutions' governing incentives in the material market were present but relatively weak. From 1558 to 1688, robust property rights was generally lacking in Britain just like in any other traditional society. The Statute of Monopolies as a major step toward protecting innovation and the Glorious Revolution as the defining moment of constitutional monarchy, the two events singled out by North and his coauthors as the decisive steps toward robust property rights protection (North and Thomas 1973, North and Weingast 1989), did not come until 1624 and 1688, respectively, long after the merchant class had achieved significant upward social mobility. During the same period, however, incentives in the positional market (for the merchant class) gradually strengthened. The merchants were able to leverage their gains in the material market to attain upward social mobility in the positional market, thus sustaining their individual efforts despite inadequate incentives in the material market. Moreover, the fact that merchants had tried to achieve upward social mobility in order to protect their material gains does not invalidate our thesis. In fact, it greatly strengthens our thesis: they clearly understood that gains in political power under a hierarchy facilitates further gains in wealth.

In terms of the four types of society in figure 3.1, pre-1688 Britain represented a specific kind of type II society. Although institutions that underpinned material incentives were relatively weak, there were enough incentives in the positional market for individuals (i.e., merchants) to power economic development. Merchants were able to leverage their material wealth into upward social mobility in the positional market. Rewarding the right group of individuals that contributed positively to economic development was indeed able to power economic development, somewhat independently from material incentives.

B. IMPERIAL CHINA AGAINST SCIENCE

One of the most perplexing puzzles in economic history is the Needham puzzle: Imperial China had failed to develop modern science, despite being a world technological leader until at least the Northern Song dynasty (AD 960–1127).[16] While Imperial China's failure to develop modern science was due to a peculiar combination of institutional and cultural factors (Lin 1995; Mokyr 1990, ch. 9; Needham 1969), an immediate cause behind that outcome was institutional discrimination. Only this time, the institutional discrimination was directed against those who pursued scientific and technological knowledge.

In the Western Han dynasty (202 BC to AD 8) under the reign of Emperor Wu (141–87 BC), Dong Zhong-shu (a special adviser to the emperor) made a modified Confucianism the official ideology of Imperial China. A critical modification that Dong introduced to the original Confucian teaching was that *ge-wu*—that is, seeking knowledge for its own sake by studying nature according to *The Great Learning* [*Da-xue*], was de-emphasized. From then on, *ge-wu* became part of the necessary self-cultivation effort toward becoming a state bureaucrat (i.e., a mandarin). Because governing the state did not seem to require much scientific and technological knowledge, only moral integrity and wisdom, classics (and history) became the only legitimate fountain of knowledge for the Chinese elite. With the simultaneous introduction of a state examination system for mandarins (commonly known as *ke-ju*), studying classics became the only path for upward social mobility for educated Chinese (Ho 1962, 92).

Furthermore, fearing the "replacement effect" (Acemoglu and Robinson 2006), Chinese mandarins—who became mandarins only because of their mastery of the classics and thus were a class without scientific and technological knowledge (Balazs 1964, 9)—erected an institutional system that prevented scientists and artisans from gaining upward social mobility. Under the system, scientists and artisans were far more likely to be ridiculed or even punished for "playing with exotic techniques" (*qi-ji-yin-qiao*) than to be encouraged and rewarded for their ingenuity by the state (Needham 1969, 31).

This institutional discrimination against science and technology was so pervasive and profound that it was alive and well even in the Tang dynasty (AD 618–907), widely believed to be the most open and cosmopolitan dynasty in Chinese history. In AD 645, a local official in Northern China successfully built a greenhouse (by burning charcoal inside a room) and grew fresh vegetables and fruits during the winter. When the official presented those fresh vegetables and fruits to Emperor Tai-zong—widely believed to the most open-minded emperor in Chinese history—the official was instantly reprimanded and demoted for the crime of trying to please the emperor with exotic techniques! (See Si-ma [1085] 1935, vol. 198.)

Of course, the fact that Si-ma Guang, a high mandarin trained in the institutionalized Confucianism tradition in the Northern Song dynasty (which immediately followed the Tang dynasty), recorded this event not as an indictment of Tai-zong's blunder but rather as a testament to Tai-zong's integrity and wisdom further attests to the power of the institutionalized Confucianism tradition.

Overall, under the incentive structures in Imperial China, studying classics became extremely profitable and studying science and technology became extremely unprofitable (Wang 1985). Consequently, consistent with the theory of allocation of talent, the Chinese society steadily allocated less and less talent to the pursuit of scientific and technological knowledge. Almost all of its best and brightest were eventually drawn into the unproductive but profitable enterprise of studying classics, and very few gifted Chinese devoted their time to pursuing scientific and technological knowledge in Imperial China (Lin 1995, 284–85). Under such an institutional system, it is no wonder that Imperial China could not develop modern science.

In terms of the four types of society in figure 3.1, Imperial China also represented a specific kind of type II society. As in most other premodern societies, material incentives were also weak in Imperial China. Positional incentives, however, were relatively strong, when compared to most other traditional societies. Unfortunately, contrary to pre-1688 Britain, where the incentive structure in the positional market rewarded productive kinds of individual effort, the incentive structure in the positional market in Imperial China rewarded unproductive kinds of knowledge (i.e., classics) and discriminated against productive kinds (i.e., science and technology). As a result, science and technology as a vital engine of economic development were depressed.

C. SLAVERY IN THE ANTEBELLUM SOUTH

Slavery, an extreme form of social immobility (second only to ethnic cleansing), had been with human beings for a long time. It was the young Alexis Tocqueville, however, who first shed light on slavery's impact on economic development in his *Democracy in America*.

Tocqueville, strolling along the Ohio River separating the state of Ohio (founded in 1787) to his right and the state of Kentucky (founded 1775) to his left, could not but be profoundly impressed by the difference between the two. He first, however, observed: "Undulating lands extend upon both shores of the Ohio, whose soil affords inexhaustible treasures to the laborer; on their bank the air is equally wholesome and the climate mild. . . . *These two states differ only in a single respect: Kentucky has admitted slavery, but the state of Ohio has prohibited the existence of slaves within its borders*" (Tocqueville [1835] 2004, 419, emphasis added).

The state of Ohio and the state of Kentucky, therefore, constituted a "natural experiment" because the two states shared many attributes (the same climate, the same fertile land, the same predominating Anglo-Saxon culture, and the same Constitution, thus the larger institutional environment) with only one significant difference: Ohio prohibited slavery while Kentucky did not. And the experiment produced dramatic results.

Tocqueville went on: "Upon the left bank of the stream the population is rare; from time to time one descries a troop of slaves loitering in the half-desert fields; the primeval forest reappears at every turn; society seems to be asleep, man to be idle, and nature alone offers a scene of activity and life. From the right bank, on the contrary, a confused hum is heard, which proclaims afar the presence of industry; the fields are covered with abundant harvests; the elegance of the dwelling announces the taste and activity of the laborers; and a man appears to be in the enjoyment of that wealth and contentment which is the reward of labor." And he continued: "Upon the left bank of the Ohio labor is confounded with the idea of slavery, while upon the right bank it is identified with that of prosperity and improvement; on the one side it is degraded, on the other it is honored. On the former territory no white laborers can be found, for they would be afraid of assimilating themselves to the Negroes; all the work is done by slavers; on the later no one is idle, for the white population extend their activity and intelligence to every kind of employment. Thus the men whose task it is to cultivate the rich soil of Kentucky are ignorant and apathetic, while those who are active and enlightened either do nothing or pass over into Ohio, where they may work without shame" (Tocqueville [1835] 2004, 419–20). In sum, by the time Tocqueville came to visit America, the contrast between Ohio and Kentucky was already stark. What differences a single dimension of institutional arrangements had made!

Writing more than a century after Tocqueville, Lewis not only connected slavery with a "lack of vertical mobility" (Lewis 1955, 108)[17] but also put slavery's impact on economic development in more economic and institutional terms. Most prominently, Lewis (1955, 84–90, 107–13) put both vertical mobility and slavery explicitly under the heading of "economic institutions" (see also Fogel and Engerman 1974). Combining Lewis's discussion on vertical mobility and slavery with Tocqueville's writing, we can detect several primary channels through which social immobility adversely influences economic development.[18]

VI. How Does the Channel of Social Mobility Impact Development?

The preceding discussion suggests that the channel of social mobility affects economic development primarily by regulating incentives in the positional market. Since it is easier to discuss the impact of the channel of social mobility on economic development by focusing on the negative impact of institutional discrimination on growth, below I mostly focus on how institutional discrimination negatively influences economic development—by systemically discouraging the productive effort of individuals and groups and thus blunting their potential contribution to growth—by building upon and extending beyond Lewis (1955, 84–90, 107–13).

First, institutional discrimination reduces the incentives to work of both the discriminated group and the privileged group. Because institutional discrimination means low probability of upward social mobility, thus less incentive in the positional market for the discriminated group, individuals of the discriminated group have less motivation to strive. At the same time, because institutional discrimination also means less competition in the positional market (and quite often in the material market as well) for the privileged group, individuals of the privileged group can afford to labor less. Institutional discrimination thus reduces the whole population's incentives to work, as Tocqueville ([1835] 2004, 362–63) so astutely observed in the antebellum American South (see also Lewis 1955, 107–8).

Second, institutional discrimination also means that members of the discriminated group cannot attain high social positions, thus they have less physical capital to invest in education for their children. Worse, because institutional discrimination often pushes families and individuals of the discriminated group into engaging in wasteful "compensatory consumption" (Caplovitz 1967), they further drain their already limited capital that can be invested in productive learning and entrepreneurship.[19]

Third, because social status is important for individuals' motivations and decisions on things such as going to college, getting out of the ghetto, and even educational attainment (Akerlof 1997; Akerlof and Kranton 2000; Feinstein 2004), institutional discrimination also means that children of the discriminated group have less incentive to learn. Hence, institutional discrimination does not merely influence one generation's incentives to learn; it influences the incentives to learn and the amount of physical capital to invest in learning, one generation after another, through a self-reinforcing vicious cycle.

Fourth, because economic development fundamentally depends on the growth of knowledge, the population is a nation's "ultimate resource." A large population means not only a larger market (thus larger returns for innovation) but also a larger talent pool for producing knowledge (Jones 2005; Kremer 1993; Phelps 1968; Simon 1981). Institutional discrimination, however, inevitably leads to underutilization of a nation's talent pool. Under institutional discrimination, members of the discriminated group go underdiscovered or undiscovered, thus being "wasted in misery and agony" and undercontributing to economic development (Marshall [1920] 1982, 176; Lewis 1955, 108, 410). Moreover, because individuals of the privileged group also have less incentive to produce and learn under institutional discrimination, their potential is also underutilized. Thus, institutional discrimination is essentially like "halving a nation's population" (Phelps 1968, 511–12), and it cannot but be bad for growth.

Fifth, and more profoundly, institutional discrimination leads to institutions and culture that reproduce and strengthen the existing social order. Institutionally, the privileged group erects barriers to upward social mobility against the discriminated group because the former deems any encroachment upon its privileges by the latter as vitally threatening: the fear of the replacement effect through redistribution of wealth and power looms large in the privileged group's calculation (Acemoglu and Robinson 2006; Engerman and Sokoloff 1997, 272–74; Sokoloff and Engerman 2000, 221–23). Culturewise, a society with institutional discrimination is very much like the traditional society depicted by Granato and his colleagues: "Social norms encourage one to accept one's social position in this life. Aspirations toward social mobility are sternly repressed. Such value systems help to maintain social solidarity but discourage economic accumulation" (Granato et al. 1996, 609–10; see also Gellner 1983, 9–11).

Sixth, the channel of social mobility also affects economic development by regulating the level of social division, tension, and instability and, in turn, the likelihood of cooperation and coordination inside a society. Institutional discrimination widens the divisions between the privileged group and the discriminated group. It also inflicts injustice upon the discriminated group. As a result, discontent and animosity against the privileged group inevitably arises within the discriminated group, and social tension inevitably develops between the two groups (Tocqueville [1835] 2004, 412–42; Lewis 1955, 107–13). Social tension and divisions in turn make social cooperation and coordination, which is critical for sustaining economic development, more difficult (Alesina et al. 2003; Rodrik 1999, 2000). Worse yet, grievances resulting from social immobility may directly contribute to political instability (for evidence, see Houle 2019), which in turn has been shown to be consistently and negatively associated with economic development (see tables 2.3 and 2.4).

Finally, precisely because injustice causes social division, tension, and instability, a society with institutional discrimination, especially the extreme kinds like slavery and apartheid, often has to spend significant amounts of resources to control the discriminated group, thus leaving fewer resources for investing in stimulating economic development. Under institutional discrimination, therefore, part of the population inevitably goes into the unproductive and often destructive business of enforcing the unjust institutional system. The result is an even smaller population for productive effort: institutional discrimination is worse than "halving a nation's population."

VII. Theoretical Implications

By rediscovering and extending the fundamental insight that positional incentives also drive human behavior, the preceding discussion suggests that the channel of social mobility, which underpins the incentive structure in the positional market, constitutes a critical dimension of IFED. Our recognition that the channel of social mobility is a critical dimension of IFED sheds important new light on the relationship between (positional) inequality, positional incentives, redistribution, and economic development.

First, while material and positional inequality drives an individual's effort, it alone cannot sustain that effort in the long run. Specifically, in the positional market, the channel of social mobility works together with positional inequality to regulate individual effort. When inequality is coupled with a relatively open channel of social mobility, individual effort can be easily sustained. In contrast, when inequality is coupled with a relatively closed channel of social mobility, individual effort is stymied. As Gellner (1983, 24–25) put it forcefully, "men can tolerate terrible inequalities . . . [but] that illusion (or reality) of social mobility is essential, and it cannot persist without at least a measure of reality." Hence, in order to sustain individuals' efforts in economic development (especially in the early stage in which inequality tends to increase rapidly), the state must maintain people's tendency to believe in the possibility of upward mobility and thus their tolerance for some inequality in the early phase of economic development (the "tunnel effect") before the tunnel effect wears off and a sense of injustice and the demand for unproductive redistribution starts to sink in (Hirschman 1973, esp. 550–53).[20]

Thus, only by recognizing the channel of social mobility as a dimension of the institutional foundation of economic development can we understand the assertions that "progress is most rapid in those parts of the country in which the greatest proportions of the leaders of industry are the sons of working men" (Marshall [1920] 1982, 176) and "economic growth is usually associated with a high degree of vertical mobility, upward and downward" (Lewis 1955, 84, also 88–89; see also Granato et al. 1996, 609–10).

Second, several studies point to an important link between individuals' beliefs in their prospects for upward social mobility (i.e., the POUM hypothesis, or "belief in a just world") and their preferences for redistribution: those who believe in a "just world" are less likely to demand redistribution (e.g., Bénabou and Ok 2001; Bénabou and Tirole 2006; Alesina and La Ferrara 2005). Taking together the discussion here and the notion that redistributive politics is usually bad for economic growth (Alesina and Rodrik 1994), we ask whether good redistributive measures contribute to economic development partly by facilitating the upward social mobility of the disadvantaged, thus sustaining their belief in a just world and their efforts to contribute to social welfare while simultaneously reducing their demand for unproductive redistribution. In Hirschman's words (1973), good redistribution measures help sustain the tunnel effect that is necessary for sustaining economic development.

Third, the new understanding about how the interaction between the channel of social mobility and redistribution affects economic development allows us to better understand the role of the expansion of publicly funded mass education, especially primary education, during the course of economic development.[21] In cross-country growth regressions, expansion of publicly funded primary education has been found to be a strong predictor of economic development for developing economies and for developed economies at their early stages of economic development (Lindert 2003). Because the difficulty of borrowing to send children to school under imperfect capital market affects the poor more (Aghion et al. 1999, 1621–24), public investment in primary education is a means of redistribution that enhances poor children's capabilities and opportunities (see chapter 4). Public investment in primary education provides poor children with the investment in human capital that gives them the initial push in the channel of social mobility and thereafter moves them into more productive positions.

Indeed, Marshall advocated for the expansion of mass education (especially primary education) explicitly on the grounds of furthering social mobility for the children of the disadvantaged: "No change would conduce so much to a rapid increase of material wealth as in improvement in our schools, especially those of the middle grades, provided it be combined with an extensive system of scholarships, which will enable the clever son of a working man to rise gradually from school to school till he has the best theoretical and practical education which the age can give." "*There is no extravagance more prejudicial to the growth of national wealth than that waste-ful negligence which allows genius that happens to be born of lowly parentage to expend itself in lowly work*" (Marshall [1920] 1982, 176, 179–80, emphasis added) Who knows, you may just find a future Beethoven, Einstein, Mozart, or Newton among those poor kids (Phelps 1968)!

Expansion of publicly funded primary education thus contributes to economic development not only because it directly diffuses knowledge but also because it is "a major commitment [or more precisely, a great facilitator] to greater upward social mobility" (Easterlin 1981, 14). In other words, expansion of publicly funded primary education facilitates economic development by strengthening incentives for individual effort in the positional market.

In contrast, during the early stage of economic development, public underinvestment in primary education effectively means an elitist bias in the educational system or a form of institutional discrimination against children from low-income families (Lindert 2003, 325). Hence, public underinvestment in primary education must be bad for growth, as Marshall ([1920] 1982, 176–80) astutely pointed out (see also chapter 4).

Fourth, once we recognize the channel of social mobility as a critical dimension of IFED and the growth of knowledge as the central driving force behind economic development, we can also better appreciate the role of science and technology in driving growth, especially modern economic development. Because modern industrial society has made scientists a social class of high status and prestige (although with relatively low pay), it has been able to sustain scientists' search for knowledge. As such, the scientific community has consistently attracted some of the best and brightest in the society, *despite its relatively low pay*. Most scientists may well make more in the corporate world, but they choose to stay in academia to hunt for fame and a place in history, and to enjoy the high social status (Fershtman and Weiss 1993; Fershtman et al. 1996) that accompanies their profession. Marshall was perhaps speaking for himself and for most of us too: "Those who do most to advance the boundaries of knowledge seldom care much about the possession of wealth for its own sake" ([1920] 1982, 4).

Finally, understanding the channel of social mobility as a critical dimension of IFED also allows us to better understand some earlier theoretical contributions on positional markets and economic development. Let me briefly emphasize two issues here.

First, once we recognize the channel of social mobility as a critical dimension of IFED and the growth of knowledge as the central driving force behind economic development, it becomes evident that Hirsch's thesis (1977, ch. 3) that overcompetition in the positional economy through "overeducation" must necessarily be bad for growth needs to be qualified. Because the growth of human civilization ultimately depends on the growth of productive knowledge, there is no such thing as "overeducation" when the knowledge being taught is productive. Only when education in unproductive knowledge confers social positions and symbolizes the status of "cultivated men" (Weber 1978, 1001–2), as in the case of Imperial China described above and the learning of classics in American higher education scathingly attacked by Veblen ([1899] 1967), will education—over or not—be inimical to growth.

Second, once we recognize that institutional discrimination systemati-cally undermines individuals' incentives to produce, it becomes apparent that Gary Becker's ([1957] 1971) economics of discrimination is utterly incomplete, despite being a powerful insight and providing part of the microfoundation for the central thesis developed here. By focusing only on discrimination's direct material cost (e.g., return for white capital and black labor) while largely neglecting the impact of discrimination on incentives in the positional market and its wider effects upon economic development, Becker has vastly underestimated the macroeconomic cost of discrimination.

VIII. Empirical Implications

Recognizing that the channel of social mobility is a critical dimension of IFED can also shed new light on some more recent and ongoing "natural experiments" in growth.

In the 1960s, many pundits predicted that East Asia's prospects for eco-nomic development would be less bright than that of resource-rich Latin America. The contrasting pattern of development between East Asia and Latin America after World War II thus poses a fundamental puzzle for eco-nomics and economists.

The neoclassical thesis that the East Asian miracle has been largely driven by physical input or accumulation of human capital through learning by doing provides us with a clue but not the real answer (e.g., Lucas 1993; Young 1995). If physical input and accumulation of human capital has caused the East Asian miracle, why has it not done so in other parts of the world, such as Latin America? Moreover, why hasn't the miracle occurred in all East Asian countries, but instead has been largely restricted only to some? In light of the thesis developed above, one of the major reasons behind the contrasting pattern of development between East Asia and Latin America might have been the differences in their channels of social mobility.

In East Asia in general, and in East Asian states that were more influenced by Confucian teaching especially, a Confucian teaching–based *ke-ju* system that allows and encourages social mobility through higher learning and meritocracy has long existed.[22] Hence, in these East Asian states, an institutional system that encourages upward social mobility through meritocracy was already in place before their economic takeoff, although the system had encouraged unproductive kinds of learning (i.e., studying classics) before the coming of the West. Once these states accepted the new religion of science and technology, it was easy for them to marry their meritocratic channel of social mobility with science and technology (i.e., achievements in science as merit). A direct result of this marriage has been that these Confucian East Asian states have been able to produce not only many scientists and engineers but also a whole new "class" in the society—the "technocrats." These technocrats have been instrumental in formulating industrial policies for the East Asian "development state" and engineering the East Asian miracle (Amsden 1989; Wade 1990).

In contrast, in many Latin American countries, power and privilege has long been monopolized by a rather closed elite class: these countries represent a kind of type III society with adequate material incentives but inadequate positional incentives. For the elite in these countries, preventing the replacement effect or minimizing political change by blocking the channel of social mobility holds priority over facilitating economic development. Hence, institutional arrangements in Latin American countries have generally emphasized class, nobility, and earlier entry (Sokoloff and Engerman 2000, 223–28). These institutional arrangements discourage social mobility and persist even today (Lovell and Wood 1998).

Two sets of evidence stand out. Whereas bureaucracy in East Asia is the most meritocratic among developing countries, bureaucracy in Latin America is the second least meritocratic after sub-Saharan Africa (Evans and Rauch 1999, 757). Whereas East Asian states usually allocate more resources to primary education, Latin American states have consistently allocated more resources to higher education than to primary education, indicating a strong elitist bias (Lindert 2003).

As a result, the tunnel effect that is necessary for sustaining economic development has rarely persisted, while demand for redistribution has emerged from time to time in many Latin American states (Hirschman 1973) and Latin America seems to have been locked into a trap of persistent low social mobility, high inequality, social upheaval, and low economic growth or growth collapse (Anderson 2000, 2001; Rodrik 1999). One can certainly wonder whether the recent left turn of many Latin American states at least partly reflects some sort of demand for redistribution.

Differences in the channel of social mobility may also partly account for another "natural experiment" inside East Asia: the contrasting path between South Korea and the Philippines. In 1960, South Korea and the Philippines stood roughly on the same footing in terms of their level of economic development, with the Philippines being far better endowed than South Korea in terms of natural resources. After 30 years, however, the contrast of the two countries could not be starker. South Korea is now a developed country, while the Philippines lags behind countries like Thailand in terms of economic development. Once again, part of the cause might have been that, whereas the South Korean society encourages upward social mobility through personal merit, the Philippines, like its Iberian parents, emphasizes class, status, and nobility. Again, one piece of evidence is that bureaucracy in the Philippines has been the least meritocratic in East Asia, whereas the bureaucracy in South Korea has been the second most meritocratic (Evans and Rauch 1999, 763).

India's economic backwardness can also be partly explained by a similar logic. Discrimination based on caste, tribe, class, and ethnicity run rampant in India, and this discrimination discourages individual effort. Moreover, there has also been a strong elitist bias in India's education policy (Lindert 2003, 338).

Finally, acknowledging social mobility's impact on economic growth also allows us to better understand some recent Chinese experience. Immediately after the founding of the People's Republic of China, the Chinese Communist Party (CCP) abolished private business, and businessmen were institutionally discriminated against. After the launching of the open and reform policy, however, China's channel of social mobility began to open for its business elite. Culturally, to get rich was no longer despised but glorious. Institutionally, under Jiang Zeming, the CCP promulgated the doctrine of the "three represents" (*sange daibiao*) to encourage the new rich to join the party and become part of the power elite in society (Fewsmith 2003; Dickson 2008a),[23] although mostly on the margin. Essentially, the party was trying to achieve what Britain had achieved in the sixteenth and seventeenth centuries: to allow its new business elite to gain limited but legitimate political power through upward social mobility so that they exercise the option of voice without violence, rather than the option of exit, or worse, voice with violence.[24]

IX. Concluding Remarks

For too long, most sociologists have not seriously considered the possibility that social mobility may actually influence economic growth. Meanwhile, economists have focused almost exclusively on material incentives, ignoring Smith's fundamental insight that vanity also drives human behavior. By bringing many fragmented discussions scattered in the literature into a more coherent framework, I advance the idea that the channel of social mobility—the institutional system that underpins the incentive structure in the positional market—is a critical dimension of IFED. The channel of social mobility structures incentives in the positional market, just as property rights structures incentives in the material market. Understanding the interaction between the incentive structures in the two markets of human society thus helps us better understand economic history.

The discussion here points to an important direction for future research. We should pay more attention to the different institutional arrangements that underpin social mobility (i.e., what it rewards, denies, and punishes) rather than to the rate of social mobility per se. More specifically, if we can measure the quality of those institutional arrangements, we can then more rigorously examine the relationship between the channel of social mobility and economic growth with cross-country growth regressions.

At an even more fundamental level, admitting that human behavior is driven not just by material gain demands key modifications to the whole neoclassical economics approach. Although some behavioral economists (e.g., Akerlof 2002, 2007; Akerlof and Kranton 2000; Akerlof and Schiller 2008; Thaler 2001) have (re)discovered that human behavior is driven by more than material gain, most economists have stayed with the neoclassical economics model. Yet, neoclassical economics is incompatible with a non-materialist approach toward human behavior.[25] Fundamentally, a large portion of human behavior is socially (and thus also historically) constructed, and this social construction includes not only material interests but also emotional and ideational influences. Thus, economics cannot start with a neoclassical economics baseline: economics is doomed to be a hopeless enterprise if it continues to assume atomistic individuals without a society (for a more detailed discussion, see Tang 2010). Echoing Thaler (2001) and Akerlof and Shiller (2008) but going even further, economics has to move away from *Homo economics* to the real *Homo sapiens* in real human societies. We need a more sociological approach toward economics, or better yet, an approach that brings sociology and economics together, in the spirit of Veblen's institutional economics.

Finally, the discussion here has an important and straightforward policy message for promoting economic growth. Because institutional discrimination is both morally unjust and economically costly, states should eliminate all forms of institutional discrimination. On this front, "interest is reconciled with morality" (Tocqueville [1835] 2004, 423).

4

Redistribution and Development

GOOD REDISTRIBUTION AS EMPOWERMENT

> The preservation of the means of knowledge among the lowest ranks is of more importance to the public than all the property of all the rich men in the country. . . . Let every sluice of knowledge be opened and set-a-flowing.
> —JOHN ADAMS, *A DISSERTATION ON THE CANON AND FEUDAL LAW* (1765)

> There is no extravagance more prejudicial to the growth of national wealth than that wasteful negligence which allows genius that happens to be born of lowly parentage to expend itself in lowly work.
> —ALFRED MARSHALL, *PRINCIPLES OF ECONOMICS* ([1920] 1982, 176)

Besides land redistribution to the poor and basic health care for all, public investment in basic education has long been identified as one of the most beneficial redistributive public policies because it greatly improves disadvantaged individuals' capabilities and their chances of further success.[1] Thus, John Adams was way ahead of his time when he made the above statement in 1765.

Using the exact same logic as Adams, Thomas Jefferson (1779) proposed the "Bill for a More General Diffusion of Knowledge," advocating

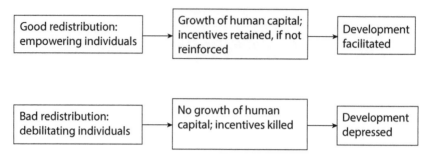

FIGURE 4.1. Redistribution and Development.

the establishment of free basic public education in the commonwealth of Virginia. Similarly, Alfred Marshall ([1920] 1982, 179) asserted that "it will be profitable as a mere investment, to give the masses of the people much greater opportunities than they can generally avail themselves of. For by this means many, who would have died unknown, are enabled to get the start needed for bringing out their latent abilities" (see also 176–80). More recently, examining the broader relationship between public spending and growth, Lindert (2004, 87, 84) concurred: "Of all the kinds of public spending [considered in his book], expenditures on public schooling are the most positively productive in the sense of raising national product per capita," and "primary public education [is] the kind of education that involves the greatest shift of resources from upper income groups to the poor" (see also Aghion et al. 1999, esp. 1621–28).

The underlying mechanism behind this insight is that public investment in basic education (as a means of good distribution) reduces the financial burden of low-income households in investing in their children's human capital (for recent reviews, see Heckman and Mosso 2014; Raudenbush and Eschmann 2015; see also Aghion et al. 1999, esp. 1621–28; Lindert 2004, 84–87; and the citations in section I). Figure 4.1 schematically captures this mechanism.

Establishing the underlying mechanism in empirical exercises, however, has been hampered by possible confounding variables and competing mechanisms, such as students' performance in school—which is in turn underpinned by students' endowment, effort, and other household-level variables—and broader socioeconomic factors.

We aim to establish the underlying mechanism more unambiguously. We reason that a key cause of the inability of existing studies to clearly establish the underlying mechanism in empirical exercises has been that they have focused on the *absolute amount of public support* for basic education. Instead, we believe that the focus should be on the (*relative*) *share of public investment out of the total cost* of basic education. Thus, our model explicitly delineates the share of public investment out of the total cost of basic education and a household's budget as the two central factors in shaping households' decisions to invest in human capital. By doing so, our model yields new insights into how households respond to different levels of public support and then make decisions about investing in basic education.

Although our new model builds on existing contributions, our model distinguishes itself on two critical fronts. First, it explicitly models a household's decision to invest in education under different regimes of public support for primary education as institutional arrangements. In contrast, most existing models either address a household's decisions about education without an institutional dimension or explore institutional regimes of education without a household's decisions (e.g., Becker [1964] 1993; Glomm and Ravikumar 1993; Galor and Moav 2000, 2004; Checchi 2005, chs. 2–5).[2] Second, our model explicitly focuses on the ratio between private investment for education and public support for education; models without public support for education thus become a special situation of our model (see below).

We then derive hypotheses for subsequent empirical exercises. Next, we present empirical evidence that demonstrates the operation of the central mechanism and the effect upon households' decisions about the two central factors, taking advantage of some unique data opportunities provided by China's reform in funding basic education in the mid-2000s. Using a nationwide panel dataset at the county level, we show that when public investment in basic education is inadequate, low-income households face strong financial constraints in investing in their children's primary education. Our exercises yield important policy implications for funding public education in developing countries and point to interesting directions for future research.

To the best of our knowledge, we are the first to construct a model that explicitly examines the share of public investment out of the total cost of basic education and household budgets as the two central factors in shaping households' decisions about investing in human capital. We are also the first to employ a nationwide panel dataset at the county level to study the impact of public investment on basic education in China. Our results complement most existing studies that rely on survey data from only a very limited number of counties or localities (see section III).

The rest of this chapter is structured as follows. Section I provides a brief literature review. Section II presents our model of household decision making regarding investing in basic education and derives hypotheses for empirical investigations. Section III provides empirical evidence. Section IV draws implications and concludes.

I. Literature Review

Existing studies on investment in human capital for the most part can be classified into four different bodies of literature. The first body of literature is the classic micro approach pioneered by Mincer (1958), which seeks to measure the returns from investment in human capital. The second focuses on the shifting role of human capital and families' decisions about investment in human capital with macro outcomes, such as technological change, inequality, and economic development (reviewed in Galor 2011). The third takes particular institutional arrangements regarding education, including public school versus private school, voucher systems, and funding for higher education, as the outcomes to be explained (reviewed in Glomm et al. 2011). Finally, the fourth body of literature takes particular institutional arrangements regarding education, such as public investment, school differentiation (tracking), and standardization, as the independent variables and seeks to understand how these institutional arrangements shape educational attainment, economic inequality, and social mobility (reviewed in Raudenbush and Eschmann 2015; Heckman and Mosso 2014; and Van de Werfhorst and Mijs 2010).

Our study falls under the fourth category. Theoretically, we focus on the relationship between public support and households' decisions about investing in basic education. Unlike most existing studies that model the absolute amount of public support for basic education, however, we explicitly model the share of public investment out of the total cost of basic education and household budgets as the two central factors shaping households' decisions to invest in human capital. We hold that while the absolute cost of basic education varies both temporally and spatially (e.g., due to inflation and geographic variations of labor cost and income), the degree of public support measured as the share of public investment out of the total cost of basic education and household budgets constrains households consistently. As such, the share of public investment out of the total cost of basic education is the more binding factor in shaping households' decisions to foster their children's education and thus should be the key yardstick for making proper public education policy.

Empirically, we also focus on developing countries (Glewwe 2002; Glewwe and Kremer 2006; Glewwe et al. 2011; Glewwe and Muralidharan

2015). After all, developing countries have fewer financial resources and thus have to allocate their public investment in education more wisely. Unfortunately, data that captures cross-country differences in education policy has been spotty and uneven at best, especially for developing countries (reviewed in Hansuek and Woessmann 2011). Within the literature on education in developing countries, a new trend, therefore, is to deploy high-quality subnational data that can help us identify the impact of different educational policies more explicitly.

As the largest developing country to undergo a massive transformation, China and its educational system have received sustained attention (reviewed in Hannum et al. 2008 and Knightet al. 2013). With more and better data from improved statistical compilation and various surveys, education in China has now been subjected to an array of empirical studies with more sophisticated econometric approaches. Taking advantage of some unique data opportunities provided by China's reforms in funding basic education, we also employ subnational data from China to support our theoretical contribution. Here, we single out several recent contributions that are most relevant and contrast our contribution against them.[3]

Zhao and Glewwe (2010), Yi et al. (2012), Chyi and Zhou (2014), Shi et al. (2015), and Shi (2016) are quite similar. All these studies are purely empirical exercises that use student-level and household survey data from rural areas in some of the least developed provinces in China to study the determining factors of children's educational attainment. Both Zhao and Glewwe (2010) and Shi (2016) use survey data from one province (Gansu). Yi et al. (2012) use survey data from four counties in two provinces (Shanxi and Shaanxi). Shi et al. (2015) combine data from eight surveys in four provinces (Shanxi, Shaanxi, Hebei, and Zhejiang). Chyi and Zhou (2014) use data from the China Health and Nutrition Survey, which covers 54 counties in eight provinces. The core findings of these studies are quite similar: poverty (or budgetary constraints) and parents' educational attainment (which may also partly capture budgetary constraints) are two of the most critical determinants that limit children's educational attainment in rural areas. For our purpose here, however, none of these studies attempt to directly match differences in local public investments in basic education with outcomes of educational attainment because they rely on survey data.

Yang et al. (2014) do address the impacts of educational policy on high school attainment in rural China by combining student and household survey data with county-level data on public investment in junior high school. Their focus on outcomes at the high school level complements our focus on the primary school level. Their key finding that increasing public invest-ment in junior high school increases high school attainment by students in rural areas while reducing the impact of household wealth on students' attainment is consistent with our finding. Yet, Yang et al. (2014) still rely on survey datasets, and this fact inevitably limits their capacity to match county-level policies with student and household-level data. Also, they employ only one indicator to measure education-related policies at the county level. In contrast, we use a battery of indicators.

Our contribution builds on and complements these studies. First and foremost, we explicitly model how households decide whether to continue investing in human capital under different educational policies (measured as the share of public investment out of the total cost of basic education) and then derive specific hypotheses that guide our subsequent empirical exercises. We believe such a model is especially important for understanding how different institutional arrangements on education shape investment in human capital under duress in mostly developing countries. Our model also explicitly predicts that other factors that impact the opportunity cost of stay-ing in school, such as the rate of technological change and the availability of low-skill jobs, may also increase dropout rates. Indeed, as becomes clear in section V, our model provides possible explanations for some of the results that may seem to contradict conventional wisdom from two recent studies (Chyi and Zhou 2014; Shi 2016).

Second, we aim to identify the redistribution effect of education-related policy more explicitly, taking cues from Lindert's (2004) influential work on "elitist bias" in educational policy at the cross-national level. Just as Lindert's indicators for elitist bias in educational policy measure both the absolute amount of public spending on education and the relative contri-bution of public money and private money to education, our indicators also measure both the absolute amount of public spending on education and the relative contribution of public and private money to education. We show that these indicators provide important leverage for measuring local governments' or officials' preferences in investing in basic education. Con-sistent with Lindert's cross-country results, we also find that elitist bias in educational policy leads to negative social outcomes at the subnational level: inadequate public support for basic education as an elitist institutional arrangement harms the accumulation of human capital. To the best of our knowledge, we are the first to adopt Lindert's indicators for elitist bias in subnational studies.

Finally, all the studies mentioned above use survey data. Survey data has the strength of being fine grained on socioeconomic status, but it also has weaknesses, such as self-reporting biases, measurement errors, and attrition of subjects. In contrast, by combining annual educational statistics data at the county level with the 1% population census data conducted in 2005, we are able to develop a nationwide panel dataset that provides us with important inference leverage over survey data. Our empirical exercises thus complement the studies that are based on survey data.

II. Public Basic Education as Good Redistribution: A New Model

As noted above, the underlying mechanism behind the redistributive benefit of public investment in basic education has been suggested to be that public investment in basic education reduces the financial burden of low-income households in investing in their children's educational development. Most models on households' decisions about investing in education, however, do not model this central mechanism explicitly enough. Most existing models focus on the absolute amount of public support for primary education. By doing so, these models are unable to gauge whether the key constraint is the relative burden rather than the absolute cost imposed upon households by the cost of basic education in a given temporal and spatial condition.

Critically drawing on existing models (e.g., Aghion et al. 1999; Checchi 2005; Glomm et al. 2011), this section constructs a model that explores this central mechanism distinctly. More concretely, our model makes the share of public investment out of the total cost of basic education and a household's budget the two central factors in shaping households' decisions to invest in human capital. By doing so, models with full public support or without any public support for education (i.e., purely private) become a special situation of our model.

A. MACROINSTITUTIONAL ASSUMPTIONS AND SETUP OF THE MODEL

To simplify our model, we start with two key macroinstitutional simplifications. First, because we are interested in the consequences rather than the causes of education policies, we assume that households have no say in such policies (as noted in section III below, this assumption holds almost completely in an autocracy like China). Second, following Aghion et al. (1999, 1621–28), we also assume that the credit market for private investment in education is absolutely imperfect (i.e., households cannot obtain loans for investing in education). These extreme simplifications allow us to demonstrate the implications of our model more forcefully. In addition, we only consider formal education (i.e., schooling), not other types of education, such as on-the-job training and apprenticeships.

With these two basic assumptions in place, we now set up the model as follows.

1. Each household lives for two periods. In period zero, each household has a wealth endowment, W_0, that is randomly distributed. This wealth endowment serves as the budgetary constraint for each household. Formally,

$$W_0 = K_0 + C_0 + E_{pr} + S_0 \tag{1}$$

where W_0 stands for wealth endowment, K_0 for capital to be deployed in production, C_0 for consumption, E_{pr} for the household's private investment in its education, and S_0 for anything left as savings.

2. Each household has an amount of human capital H_0 that is also randomly distributed.

3. A household's talent is randomly distributed.

4. In period zero, a household decides
   (a) To produce with its human capital $H_0 > 0$ and its capital $K_0 > 0$, according to a simple Cobb-Douglas production function,

   $$Y_0 = f(H_0^\alpha K_0^{1-\alpha}), \text{ where } 0 < \alpha < 1 \tag{2}$$

   (b) To invest $E_{pr} \geq 0$ amount of money for the education of its household members, so that the household's human capital in the next period is a function of its private investment in education and the amount of public support for education (E_{pu}) in period zero, plus a depreciated portion of its human capital in period zero as captured by βH_0. Formally,

   $$H_1 = f(E_{pr} + E_{pu}) + \beta H_0 \tag{3}$$

   Note that having the depreciated portion of human capital from period zero (i.e., βH_0, with $0 < \beta < 1$), as part of the human capital in the next period captures the fact that one's knowledge gradually becomes obsolete without continuous education and training because knowledge progresses and the human brain decays. Intuitively, the larger β is (i.e., the more slowly knowledge depreciates or the lower the rate of knowledge/technology progress is), the less incentive a household has to invest in education, and vice versa.

To further simplify the solution of our model (see appendix to chapter 4 at the end of the book), we also assume $f(E_{pr}+E_{pu}) = \gamma[(E_{pr}+E_{pu})]$, with γ being a constant, which can be understood to be an indicator of the raw intelligence of the members in a household.

(c) To consume $C_0 > 0$.

(d) To save $S_0 \geq 0$ for next period, if there is anything left after K_0, E_{pr}, and C_0.

5. In the next period, a household produces with its new human capital H_1 and again, according to a simple Cobb-Douglas production function,

$$Y_1 = f(H_1^\alpha K_1^{1-\alpha}) \tag{4}$$

where $K_1 = S_0 + Y_0$, and $S_0 = W_0 - K_0 - C_0 - E_{pr}$. Because we are only interested in how a household decides its investment in education in period zero and how its decision impacts its output in period one, we do not consider a household's consumption or savings in period one.

B. BUDGETARY CONSTRAINTS AND THE ROLE OF PUBLIC SPENDING IN EDUCATION

The key budgetary constraint in our model is that providing any level of formal education requires some amount of investment. As such, every household must decide whether to pay for education beyond a certain level or to put the possible investment for education into production now as capital.

For every year of formal education, there is a fixed cost E, and

$$E = E_{pr} + E_{pu} \tag{5}$$

where E_{pr} is the private investment in education per household, and E_{pu} is the public investment in education per child or household. E, of course, is subject to change due to inflation.

Each household contributes to p share of the total cost of t years (between zero and $t=12$, for example) of formal basic education, whereas the state contributes the rest, that is, $(1-p)$. Let ΣE denote the sum total of the cost for t years of education. Formally,

$$\frac{\Sigma E_{\mathrm{pr}}}{\Sigma E} + \frac{\Sigma E_{\mathrm{pu}}}{\Sigma E} = 1 \qquad (6)$$

$$\text{with } 0 < p = \frac{\Sigma E_{\mathrm{pr}}}{\Sigma E} \leq 1, \quad \text{and} \quad 0 \leq 1 - p = \frac{\Sigma E_{\mathrm{pu}}}{\Sigma E} < 1$$

p thus captures the fact that a household must shoulder some burden of its needed investment in education. More critically, $1-p$ captures the redistributive effort of publicly funded mass education, and by allowing $1-p$ to be zero, we capture the fact that the state may not shoulder any burden of a household's needed investment in education.[4]

C. EQUILIBRIUM SOLUTIONS OF THE MODEL

Equilibrium solutions of the model are determined by a household's utility maximization decision under different levels of public support for basic education (captured as the share of public investment out of the total cost of basic education) and a household's budgetary constraints.

Because the ultimate source of a household's welfare is determined by $Y_0 + Y_1$, the key utility maximization is to maximize $Y_0 + Y_1$, with both Y_0 and Y_1 being determined by a household's decision to produce, consume, save, and invest in human capital. Under this setup, the decision to invest in human capital in the period zero exerts its effect on production in the next period, when the amount of human capital accumulated in period zero becomes part of the human capital in the next period.

The key budgetary constraint, as noted above, is that providing any level of formal education requires an amount of investment. As such, every household must decide whether to invest in education up to a certain level or to put the possible investment for education into production as capital. Let $T (\geq 0)$ denote $K_0 + E_{\mathrm{pr}} = W_0 - C_0 - S_0$ as the budgetary constraint after consumption and savings in period zero. Let E_{min} denote the minimal total investment required for obtaining a certain level of education. Then $E_{\mathrm{min}} - E_{\mathrm{pu}}$ denotes the minimal private investment required for obtaining a certain level of education by a household.

The model has two basic scenarios. The first basic scenario is $T < E_{\mathrm{min}} - E_{\mathrm{pu}}$. In this scenario, a household cannot afford to provide any (formal) schooling for its members.

The second basic scenario is $T \geq E_{min} - E_{pu}$. In this scenario, the minimal budget support of a household is larger than the minimum total investment required for education, minus the public support for education. Under this scenario, a household has to optimize its investment in education (and hence in production too). Let E_{pr}^{*} denote the optimal level of private investment in education. This basic scenario has two subscenarios.

The first subscenario is $E_{pr}^{*} + E_{pu} > E_{min}$. Under this subscenario, the minimal level of investment for education is low enough that a household can afford schooling. Yet, a household may voluntarily withhold its members from schooling if the household deems the return from production after some schooling is actually lower than the return from investing the capital in production without schooling. As Rosen (1983) noted, "rational agents pursue investment (in education) up to the point where the marginal rate of return equals the opportunity cost of funds." A typical example of this subscenario is when schools merely teach superstition and religious doctrines, and hence the knowledge taught in schools is of little practical value for actual production. A real-world example of this subscenario is that many Chinese students from rural areas drop out of vocational high schools because such schools are often of very low quality (Shi et al. 2015).

The second subscenario is $E_{pr}^{*} + E_{pu} \leq E_{min}$. Under this sub-scenario, a household may deem the return from production after some schooling higher than the return from investing the capital in production without schooling because education or knowledge is of real practical value (e.g., knowledge taught is mathematics, physics, chemistry, and biology, rather than superstitions and religious doctrines). Yet, due to budgetary constraints, a household can only invest in schooling to a certain level under this sub-scenario, depending on the share of public investment out of the total cost of education up to a certain level. Under such a set-up, it is straightforward to obtain the solutions for the two sub-scenarios of the second basic scenario (i.e., $T \geq E_{min} - E_{pu}$; see appendix to chapter 4 at the end of the book for detailed proofs).

The solutions capture key stylized facts about households' decisions to invest in basic education under different shares of public investment out of the total cost of basic education. These facts are consistent with earlier insights on human capital, rate of technological change, wealth accumulation, and public support for basic education as advanced by others (e.g., Checchi 2005), including the following:

(1) The smaller β is—which means a greater rate of technological change—the greater the household's incentives to invest in human

capital are, and vice versa. By the same token, the more initial human capital a household possesses, the fewer incentives it has to invest in further education of its members.[5]

(2) The more wealth a household has from period zero and the more output (or new wealth) a household produces in period zero (as captured by $K_1 = S_0 + Y_0$, and $S_0 = W_0 - K_0 - C_0 - E_{pr}$), the greater a household's incentives and capabilities are to invest in its human capital.

(3) The higher γ is (i.e., the higher the raw intelligence of a household), the lower the cost that a household has to shoulder for investing in its human capital and the greater a household's incentives are to invest in its human capital.

(4) Finally, and most critically, the larger the share of public investment out of the total cost of basic education (per household) (i.e., E_{pu} is high), the less overall burden a household has to shoulder for investing in its human capital and the more numerous a household's incentives to invest in its human capital. In contrast, with inadequate public investment for primary education (i.e., E_{pu} is low), even though every household wants to invest more in its human capital, poor households may nonetheless be unable to continue the investment, due to a lack of available capital. Adequate public support for basic education is thus crucial, if not indispensable, for adequate accumulation of human capital within a society, especially for developing countries. More specifically:

(a) Adequate public support for basic education allows poor households to increase their human capital and is thus capability enhancing. Put differently, in a nonelitist education system, more low-income families will have access to basic education, and the pool of human capital within an economy increases faster (Lindert 2004).[6]

(b) In contrast, inadequate public support for basic education prevents poor families from investing in their human capital. In other words, in an elitist education system (i.e., higher education gets more subsidies), few low-income households will be able to adequately invest in their human capital.

These two outcomes can be depicted graphically. When public support for basic education is adequate (i.e., the share of public investment in education out of the total cost of basic education is sufficiently high), households tend to invest more in their human capital, sometimes beyond the level of basic education (figure 4.2-A). In contrast, when public investment in basic

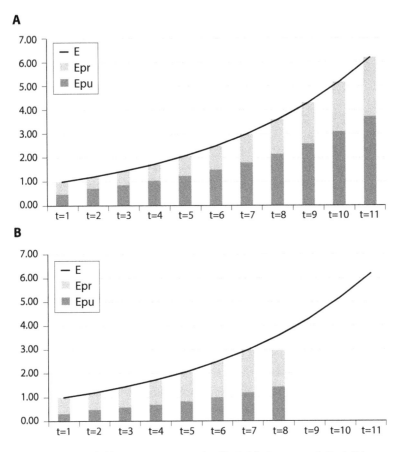

A

B

FIGURE 4.2. Household Decisions as Determined by Public Investment in Basic Education. (A) When public investment is adequate, the household completes its investment in basic education. (B) When public investment is inadequate, the household terminates its investment in basic education before basic education is completed. In China (like many other developing countries), basic education (primary and junior high) amounts to nine years (six years for primary and three years for junior high). Thus, when a household invests in more than nine years of basic education, it means that public policy has worked in supporting basic education (A). In contrast, when a household invests in less than nine years of basic education, it means that the public policy has failed to adequately support basic education (B). Epr: Private investment in basic education. Epu: Public investment in basic education. E: Total investment in basic education. See the model in the text and the appendix to chapter 4 at the end of the book.

education is nonexistent or inadequate (i.e., the share of public investment in education out of the total cost of basic education is sufficiently low), families rationally terminate their investment in human capital even before the basic education is complete (figure 4.2-B).

III. Empirical Evidence

In this section, we provide evidence for the two principal empirical predictions derived from our model by utilizing education data from China at the county level. We believe this data provides us with some key advantages for identifying the impact of public investment in basic education on households' decisions to invest in human capital.

First of all, China is a large country with enormous variations across local administrative units (for our exercise here, counties). Since the opening and reform started in 1978, China has become decentralized to the extent that some have even dubbed China a de facto "fiscal federalist" state (Montinola et al. 1995). More concretely, local governments have been given much leeway for determining where and how much to invest in public goods, including basic education. This in turn has led to significant variations in public investment in basic education across regions, due to a combination of the differences in local leaders' (and the populace's) preferences for investing in education and local socioeconomic factors, such as the level of economic development.

Second, China is an autocracy. As such, people have virtually no say on public spending from the county level and above. Differences in local public support for basic education thus mostly reflect the preferences of local leaders and local socioeconomic factors. This fact greatly limits the possible endogeneity between public demand and public spending (including public support for basic education), thus allowing us to identify the causal effects of public support for basic education on household investment in human capital with more clarity.

Third, land reform is perhaps an equally, if not more, critical means of redistribution than publicly funded basic education (Besley and Burgess 2000). Moreover, land inequality can impact educational inequality (Galor et al. 2009). In post-1949 China, land reform has been thorough and has eliminated a key source of inequality that could have impacted educational inequality. This again helps us isolate the effect of public investment in basic education on households' decisions to invest in human capital. This is even truer when employing county-level data from China because a county usually denotes a more rural area where land is often the most critical form of capital.

Fourth, all counties in China operate under essentially the same macroinstitutional system. As a result, differences in public support for basic education at the county level mostly reflect local differences. Moreover, counties in China are not responsible for investing in college-level education. Both facts allow one to draw more unambiguous inferences from econometric results.

Our empirical exercises focus on the stage of primary education. We believe such a step is critical for isolating the effect of public investment in basic education on households' decisions to invest in their children's education. As a child grows older, the opportunity cost of staying in school without the possibility of getting into a decent college increases as the number of years the child spends in school increases. Unsurprisingly, after primary school, academic performance carries more weight in a student's decision of whether to stay in school (for evidence from China with survey data, see Yi et al. 2012; Yang et al. 2014; Shi et al. 2015). As such, if we focus on education as a whole (i.e., from primary all the way through tertiary education), or even on junior high school and high school, we face more challenges in isolating the impact of public investment in primary education on households' decisions to invest in their children's education. In contrast, because children's contributions to their household's welfare are minimal if not negligible during their primary school years if they were to drop out of primary school, the most critical factor must be their household's financial constraints, which are partly underpinned by the level of public investment in primary education.

A. CHINA'S REFORMS IN FUNDING BASIC EDUCATION

China's reforms in funding primary and secondary education from 2000 to 2007 provide us with some unique opportunities to use panel data to isolate the effect of public investment in primary education on households' decisions to invest in their children's education, especially in rural areas from the country's less developed central and western regions.[7]

China officially began its policy of mandatory nine-year education—six years of primary school and three years of junior high school, or from grade one to nine—in 1986. But up until 2000, this policy existed only on paper because the central government did not commit serious resources to it. Instead, the central government mostly asked local governments and households to shoulder most of the burden of schooling, and the results were quite dismal, especially in rural areas in the central and western part of the country. In 2001, the central government finally decided to commit serious resources to funding basic education, especially in rural areas in the country's central and western regions. In 2001, the central government set an upward limit on tuition and demanded that local governments and schools stop collecting fees from students in "underdeveloped counties" (*pingkun xian*). This policy was expanded to cover the whole country in 2005. That same year the central government also decided to provide free textbooks, eliminate tuition and fees, and even provide subsidies for boarding and school meals for rural schools in underdeveloped counties, with the central government shouldering most of the cost. In September 2006, this policy, now known as *liangmian yibu*, was expanded to cover the whole central and western region.[8]

In 2000, the central government also started the process of gradually reducing agricultural taxes and fees borne by peasants, eventually culminating in the elimination of all agricultural taxes and fees by 2006. This policy, which dramatically reduced the financial burden of rural households, provides another key advantage to our empirical exercise. If we can still link rural student enrollment in primary schools to the financial burden for rural households when it has been greatly reduced, we should have established the impact of public investment in education upon households' decisions to invest in human capital more clearly.

All these policies have been implemented in several waves, both temporally and spatially. Moreover, local governments have implemented these policies with different levels of effort and resources, reflecting local governments' preferences and budgetary constraints. As a result, there are greater temporal and spatial variations in local policies, which results in the existence of localities that facilitate our task of identifying the effect of public investment in primary education on households' decisions to invest in their children's education. For these reasons, we believe that data on public support for basic education at the county level in China provides us with important leverage for identifying the causal effects of public support for basic education on households' decisions more conclusively. Although county-level data is still aggregate data and hence does not allow us to capture the exact decisions of individual households, the data is fine grained enough for our purpose of showing that different educational policies do impact households' decisions to invest in education.

B. DATA AND VARIABLES

Our county-level data is from all 30 provincial-level administrative units in China. The total number of counties is close to 2,800, which is larger than the number of countries in any possible cross-country dataset. This data is from the years 2000–2009 and includes the years in which all the key policies on funding education were promulgated and gradually implemented. The data has been compiled according to a standard procedure and reported annually with relatively few missing data points. This data provides us with anywhere from 15,000 to 22,000 observations (see the descriptive statistics in table 4.2).

1. Dependent Variable: Enrollment Rate for Primary School (ERPS)

Ideally, the rate of human capital accumulation should be measured as the rate of student graduation from primary, junior high, and high school. Yet, data points on graduation rates are not available. We thus use gross enroll- ment rates for primary school (ERPS) within a particular county as the key dependent variable that captures the rate of human capital accumulation. ERPS is calculated as the ratio between the number of actually enrolled stu- dents in primary schools within a county divided by the number of children who are due to enter primary school within the county. The number of actu- ally enrolled students is taken from the *Statistical Yearbook of Prefecture and County Level* (SYPCL) from 2000 to 2009.

The number of students who are due to enter primary school within the county is estimated from the national census of 2005 (1% population scale). This census has the county as the basic administrative unit. Moreover, within the census, every household reports the actual age of its members, thus allowing us to estimate the number of children due to attend primary school.

Our estimation procedure is as follows: assuming that the appropriate age for primary school is between ages six and twelve, we can estimate the percentage of individuals who fall within this age cohort in 2005. We then multiply the percentage number by 100 to obtain the rough number of children who are between six and twelve. By logic, we can then estimate the number of children who fall into the cohort of ages seven to thirteen in 2004 and the number of children who fall into the cohort of ages five to eleven in 2006. By this procedure, we obtain the number of children due for primary school annually from 2000 to 2010.

2. Key Independent Variables

Inspired by Lindert's (2004, vol. I, 88–99; vol. II, 43–46) three indicators that measure the overall redistributive effect of a country's education policy and three "fingerprints" that capture the elitist bias in a country's education policy, we first develop five indicators for measuring a county's nominal level of public investment in basic education.

1. IV1: Public expenditure for basic education per capita = total funding for basic education of a county divided by the total population of a county.
2. IV2: Public expenditure for basic education per student = total funding for basic education of a county divided by the number of students in basic education within a county.
3. IV3: Total public expenditure for basic education as a portion of the total budget of the county.
4. IV4: Ratio between the growth rate of public expenditure for basic education and the growth rate of government revenue within a county.
5. IV5: Ratio between the growth rate of public expenditure for basic education and the growth rate of GDP per capita within a county.

All these values are calculated from data compiled from SYPCL from 2000 to 2009. The first two indicators (IV1 and IV2) directly measure the absolute amount of public spending on basic education, whereas the remaining three indicators (IV3, IV4, and IV5) measure the relative contributions of public spending and private budgets to basic education, albeit indirectly.

For each of these indicators, we then create a Z value for all the counties within a province to capture the relative standing of a county in terms of its education policies within the province. This is again directly inspired by Lindert's (2004, vol. II, 43–50) logic. These Z values more closely tap into the relative contribution of public spending and private budgets to basic education than the original indicators (i.e., IV1 to IV5), but still do so indirectly.

Notably, Lindert deployed a country's relative standing in these indicators within a group of countries with similar per capita income to capture the degree of elitist bias within a country's education system: a below-average level indicates an elitist bias. We believe that Lindert's logic is sound, but reason that the Z value is a more precise measurement than Lindert's dichotomous variable (i.e., above or below the means).

TABLE 4.1. Descriptions of Variables

Dependent variable	Explanation
ERPS	Enrollment rate for primary school
TREATMENT VARIABLES	
IV1 (in RMB ¥)	Public expenditure for basic education per capita = (total funding for basic education of a county) divided by (the total population of a county)
IV2 (in RMB ¥)	Public expenditure for basic education per student = (total funding for basic education of a county) divided by (the number of students in basic education within a county)
IV3 (in %)	Total public expenditure for basic education as a portion of the total budget of the county
IV4	Ratio between the growth rate of public expenditure for basic education and the growth rate of government revenue within a county
IV5	Ratio between the growth rate of public expenditure for basic education and the growth rate of GDP per capita within a county
Z-IV1	Z value of IV1
Z-IV2	Z value of IV2
Z-IV3	Z value of IV3
Z-IV4	Z value of IV4
Z-IV5	Z value of IV5
CONTROL VARIABLES	
GDP per capita	GDP per capita within a county
Budgetary income per capita	Budgetary income per capita within a county

Together, we have 10 indicators that measure a county's nominal and relative public support for basic education.[9] Definitions of variables are in table 4.1, and summary statistics of variables are in table 4.2.

C. STATISTICAL PROCEDURES AND RESULTS: OLS ESTIMATIONS

From the model in section II, our empirical predictions are straightforward: the higher the nominal value or ratio of these indicators, and the higher the Z value (as a relative measure), the higher a county's public support for basic education, the better for poor families investing in human capital, and the

TABLE 4.2. Summary Descriptive Statistics of Dependent Variable (DV) and Key Independent Variables (IVs)

Variable	No. of Observations	Mean	Standard Deviation
DV: ERPS (in %)	22,134	95.06	2.97
IV1 (in RMB ¥)	18,105	210.24	229.54
IV2 (in RMB ¥)	18,063	1452.91	1481.96
IV3 (in %)	18,110	24.23	6.98
IV4	15,193	0.81	9.66
IV5	15,004	1.53	6.06
Z-IV1	18,103	0.00	0.99
Z-IV2	18,061	0.01	1.02
Z-IV3	18,129	0.01	1.06
Z-IV4	15,047	0.00	1.01
Z-IV5	15,227	0.02	1.09

Sources: Statistical Yearbook of Prefecture and County Level (2000–2009) and China's 2005 national census (1% population scale).

Note: All actual numbers of income or spending are adjusted to the 2000 price level. The sample covers data from 2,794 countries in China from 2000 to 2009.

higher the growth rate of human capital accumulation within the county. We first employ two-way, fixed-effect OLS models to test our hypotheses.

The equation for estimation is as follows:

$$y_{it} = \alpha + \beta ED_{it} + X\delta + \text{county}_i + \text{year}_t + \varepsilon_{it}$$

y_{it} is ERPS within county i in year t. ED_{it} is the key explanatory variable that captures the level of public support for basic education within a county i in year t. ε_{it} is the error term, assumed to be randomly distributed across the sample.

Vector X denotes two key control variables that may impact the relationship between the explanatory variable and the dependent variables: (1) budgetary expenditure per capita and (2) GDP per capita within a county. We also control for two additional sets of fixed effects. The first set of fixed effects is the time-invariant fixed effects that may impact public investment in basic education within a county (county$_i$ in estimation equations). These fixed effects include: whether the county is a designated a "poor county," whether the county is a designated "minority ethnic group autonomous county," the distance between the county's capital and the provincial capital, and the quality of local governance within the county. The second set of fixed effects is year-specific macro-level factors that impact all counties such as economic cycle and macroeconomic policies (year$_t$ in estimation equations).

We first test the effect of public education expenditure per capita (IV1) on ERPS. As shown in table 4.3, public education expenditure per capita has a significant positive effect on ERPS within a county: a 1% increase in public education expenditure per capita leads to a 0.2% increase in the enrollment rate. Other control variables show consistent signs. For instance, budgetary revenue per capita has a significantly positive effect on the dependent variable. Interestingly, per capita GDP does not have a significant effect on the dependent variable, although it has a negative sign. This finding implies that ERPS is determined more by how much revenue a local government controls and how much money the local government decides to invest in basic public education (as an instrument of redistribution), consistent with our theory.

We further reason that public education expenditure per actually enrolled student (IV2) should have a more direct impact on ERPS than public education expenditure per capita. We set out to test this hypothesis, and the results are shown in table 4.4. Again, results are consistent with our hypothesis. Similar to the results reported in table 4.3, public education expenditure per actually enrolled student has a significantly positive impact on ERPS. Other control variables have similar levels of statistical significance and correct signs. Again, GDP per capita has no significant effect on the dependent variable and has a negative sign.

The two sets of regressions reported in tables 4.3 and 4.4 indicate that the absolute level of public education spending has a significant positive effect on ERPS. We then test whether the willingness of local government to invest in basic public education has a significant impact on ERPS. As shown in table 4.5, the ratio of public expenditure in basic education versus the budget of a county (IV3) has a significant positive effect on ERPS within a county. A 1% increase in the ratio of public expenditure in basic education to the budget of a county corresponds to a 0.02% increase in ERPS within the county.

In tables 4.6 and 4.7, we estimate the impact on ERPS of the ratio between the growth rate of public education expenditure and the growth rate of government revenue (IV4; table 4.6) and the ratio between the growth rate of public education expenditure and the growth rate of GDP (IV5; table 4.7). Both indicators have a positive impact on ERPS. Although the ratio between the growth rate of public education expenditure and the growth rate of government revenue is only significant at $p < 0.1$, the ratio between the growth rate of public education expenditure and the growth rate of GDP is significant at $p < 0.001$. More precisely, if public education expenditure grows 1% faster

TABLE 4.3. Public Expenditure for Basic Education per Capita (IV1) and ERPS

	(1)	(2)	(3)	(4)
IV1 (ln)	0.206**	0.179**	0.209**	0.183*
	(0.105)	(0.105)	(0.105)	(0.106)
Budgetary income per capita (ln)		0.157**		0.165**
		(0.076)		(0.0779)
GDP per capita (ln)			−0.031	−0.0448
			(0.042)	(0.0429)
Time trend	−0.0117	−0.083	0.006	−0.0209
	(0.0241)	(0.085)	(0.247)	(0.0256)
Constant	116.6**	146.661***	106.001***	134.3***
	(47.53)	(493487)	(48.795)	(50.42)
Observations	17,869	17,864	17,722	17,717
County fixed effect	Yes	Yes	Yes	Yes
Year fixed effect	Yes	Yes	Yes	Yes
R-squared	0.001	0.001	0.001	0.001
No. of countries	2,793	2,792	2.758	2,757

Note: Huber robust standard error is in parentheses. Error terms allow for within-province correlation.
*** $p < 0.01$, ** $p < 0.05$, * $p < 0.1$.

TABLE 4.4. Public Expenditure for Basic Education per Student (IV2) and ERPS

	(1)	(2)	(3)	(4)
IV2 (ln)	0.343***	0.334***	0.347***	0.340***
	(0.0764)	(0.076)	(0.077)	(0.077)
Budgetary income per capita (ln)		0.150**		0.157**
		(0.076)		(0.077)
GDP per capita (ln)			−0.030	−0.044
			(0.042)	(0.043)
Time trend	0.502*	−0.062***	−0.039**	−0.057**
	(0.258)	(0.022)	(0.021)	(0.023)
Constant	−908.8*	219.503***	174.992***	208.1***
	(515.9)	(43.99)	(42.019)	(44.91)
Observations	17,824	17,816	17,680	17,675
County fixed effect	Yes	Yes	Yes	Yes
Year fixed effect	Yes	Yes	Yes	Yes
R-squared	0.002	0.002	0.002	0.002
No. of counties	2,774	2,772	2,744	2,743

Note: Huber robust standard error is in parentheses. Error terms allow for within-province correlation.
*** $p < 0.01$, ** $p < 0.05$, * $p < 0.1$.

TABLE 4.5. Total Public Expenditure for Basic Education as a Portion of the Total Budget of the County (IV3) and ERPS

	(1)	(2)	(3)	(4)
IV3 (%)	0.017***	0.019***	0.016***	0.018***
	(0.006)	(0.006)	(0.006)	(0.006)
Budgetary income per capita (ln)		0.212***		0.216***
		(0.077)		(0.078)
GDP per capita (ln)			−0.026	−0.044
			(0.042)	(0.043)
Time trend	0.032***	0.005	0.037***	0.0121
	(0.012)	(0.015)	(0.013)	(0.0159)
Constant	29.62	82.607	19.577	68.860**
	(23.58)	0.015	(26.063)	(31.451)
Observations	17,848	17,842	17,701	17,696
County fixed effect	Yes	Yes	Yes	Yes
Year fixed effect	Yes	Yes	Yes	Yes
R-squared	0.001	0.002	0.001	0.002
No. of counties	2,794	2,792	2,758	2,757

Note: Huber robust standard error is in parentheses. Error terms allow for within-province correlation.
*** $p < 0.01$, ** $p < 0.05$, * $p < 0.1$.

TABLE 4.6. Ratio between the Growth Rate of Public Expenditure for Basic Education and the Growth Rate of Government Revenue within a County (IV4) and ERPS

	(1)	(2)	(3)	(4)
IV4	0.006*	0.006*	0.005*	0.005*
	(0.003)	(0.003)	(0.003)	(0.003)
Budgetary income per capita (ln)		0.164*		0.181**
		(0.086)		(0.088)
GDP per capita (ln)			−0.060	−0.077
			(0.499)	(0.050)
Time trend	0.375***	0.349***	0.402***	0.376***
	(0.098)	(0.099)	(0.100)	(0.101)
Constant	−658.3***	−606.867***	−711.515***	−660.6***
	(197.5)	(199.297)	(201.691)	(203.2)
Observations	14,953	14,947	14,861	14,860
County fixed effect	Yes	Yes	Yes	Yes
Year fixed effect	Yes	Yes	Yes	Yes
R-squared	0.002	0.003	0.003	0.003
No. of counties	2,667	2,661	2,637	2,636

Note: Huber robust standard error is in parentheses. Error terms allow for within-province correlation.
*** $p < 0.01$, ** $p < 0.05$, * $p < 0.1$.

TABLE 4.7. Ratio between the Growth Rate of Public Expenditure for Basic Education and the Growth Rate of GDP per Capita within a County (IV5) and ERPS

	(1)	(2)	(3)	(4)
IV5	0.011***	0.011***	0.011***	0.011***
	(0.004)	(0.004)	(0.004)	(0.004)
Budgetary income per capita (ln)		0.161*		0.182**
		(0.087)		(0.088)
GDP per capita (ln)			−0.057	−0.074
			(0.050)	(0.051)
Time trend	0.020	−0.003	0.027*	0.004
	(0.014)	(0.018)	(0.015)	(0.019)
Constant	55.700**	99.138***	40.760	85.280**
	(28.091)	(36.460)	(30.969)	(37.640)
Observations	14,763	14,759	14,761	14,757
County fixed effect	Yes	Yes	Yes	Yes
Year fixed effect	Yes	Yes	Yes	Yes
R-squared	0.001	0.001	0.001	0.001
No. of counties	2,609	2,608	2,608	2,607

Note: Huber robust standard error is in parentheses. Error terms allow for within-province correlation.
*** $p < 0.01$, ** $p < 0.05$, * $p < 0.1$.

than government revenue, ERPS will increase 0.6%. If public expenditure in basic education grows 1% faster than the rate of GDP per capita within a county, ERPS will increase 0.1%.

Finally, we test the impact of a county's relative standing within a province when it comes to investing in basic education (as captured by the Z values of the five IVs) on ERPS. As shown in table 4.8, of the five Z values, four have a positive and statistically significant relationship with ERPS. Only the Z value of IV1 does not have a statistically significant relationship with ERPS, and it has a negative sign.

These results strongly support the key insight from our model, indicating that the more critical constraint in shaping a household's decision about investing in their children's basic education is the relative burden rather than the absolute cost imposed by basic education. In other words, even if the absolute cost of basic education is high, households are more likely to invest in their children's education when the state shoulders a sufficient share of the overall burden, ceteris paribus. In contrast, even if the absolute cost for basic education is low, households are less likely to invest in their

TABLE 4.8. A County's Relative Positioning within a Province in Public Support for Primary Education (as Captured by Z Values) and ERPS

	(1)	(2)	(3)	(4)	(5)
Z-IV1	−0.058				
	(0.044)				
Z-IV2		0.119***			
		(0.0329)			
Z-IV3			0.0735*		
			(0.0388)		
Z-IV4				0.0423*	
				(0.0239)	
Z-IV5					0.0512**
					(0.0227)
Budgetary income	0.146**	0.207***	0.157**	0.174**	0.174**
per capita (ln)	(0.078)	(0.0776)	(0.0779)	(0.0883)	(0.0879)
GDP per capita (ln)	−0.023	−0.0436	−0.0420	−0.0723	−0.0729
	(0.043)	(0.0428)	(0.0429)	(0.0507)	(0.0506)
Time trend	−0.001	0.0120	0.0150	0.00558	0.00715
	(0.016)	(0.0159)	(0.0159)	(0.0190)	(0.0189)
Constant	110.680***	69.51**	64.06**	82.97**	79.84**
	(31.360)	(31.42)	(31.45)	(37.57)	(37.32)
Observations	17,715	17,715	17,674	14,800	14,902
County fixed effect	Yes	Yes	Yes	Yes	Yes
Year fixed effect	Yes	Yes	Yes	Yes	Yes
R-squared	0.002	0.002	0.001	0.001	0.001
No. of counties	2,757	2,757	2,743	2,608	2,617

Note: Huber robust standard error is in parentheses. Error terms allow for within-province correlation.
*** $p < 0.01$, ** $p < 0.05$, * $p < 0.1$.

children's education when the state shoulders an inadequate share of the overall burden, ceteris paribus.

D. STATISTICAL PROCEDURES AND RESULTS: SYSTEM GMM ESTIMATIONS

Although we believe that endogeneity is not a serious issue in our dataset and OLS estimations, we still deploy system GMM estimation to address the possible endogeneity problem (Bond et al. 2001). Table 4.9 shows the system GMM results. Overall, GMM results are consistent with the OLS

TABLE 4.9. Public Support for Basic Education and ERPS: System GMM Estimations

	(1) ERPS	(5) ERPS	(7) ERPS	(8) ERPS
IV2 (ln)	0.390***			
	(0.133)			
IV5		0.0116*		
		(0.00691)		
Z-IV2			0.114***	
			(0.045)	
Z-IV3				0.112**
				(0.0515)
ERPS lagged one year	0.292	0.0837	0.084	0.183
	(0.187)	(0.195)	(0.180)	(0.169)
Control variables	Yes	Yes	Yes	Yes
Year fixed effect	Yes	Yes	Yes	Yes
Time trend	Yes	Yes	Yes	Yes
Observations	14,683	11,856	14,679	14,713
AR(1) test	−2.754	−2.358	−3.149	−2.615
AR(1) test p value	0.00588	0.0184	0.00164	0.00894
AR(2) test	−0.240	−0.440	0.0755	−0.337
AR(2) test p value	0.811	0.660	0.940	0.736
Hansen test	102.4	86.74	98.66	82.63
Hansen test p value	0.526	0.518	0.629	0.930

Note: Huber robust standard error is in parentheses. Error terms allow for within-province correlation. *** $p < 0.01$, ** $p < 0.05$, * $p < 0.1$.

results reported above: all 10 independent variables have the correct (i.e., positive) sign. However, only four of them (IV2, IV5, Z-IV2, and Z-IV3) are statistically significant at conventional thresholds. These results suggest that OLS estimation may have overestimated the effect of public investment in basic education on households' decisions to invest in education. This may be due to the fact that some omitted variables also impact households' decisions to invest in human capital, but they cannot be adequately controlled due to the lack of data.

E. SUMMARY

Overall, our empirical results strongly support the key empirical prediction of our theoretical model: a higher level of public support for basic education significantly contributes to the accumulation of human capital. By focusing on the stage of primary education that is least likely to be affected by household incomes and students' efforts and performance in schools, as well as demonstrating that low-income households face strong financial constraints on investing in the education of their children when public investment in primary education is inadequate, our empirical results are not subject to the ambiguities of interpretation associated with data at a higher level of education. By utilizing data from a single country (i.e., China), thus holding the macroinstitutional system constant, we avoid the noisiness of cross-country data and are able to identify or isolate the impact of different levels of public spending on primary education more explicitly. These results thus crystallize our key argument that for many of the least developed countries or regions, adequate public support for basic education is the most critical instrument of good redistribution because budgetary constraints for low-income households remain the most critical barrier to even basic education.

IV. Discussion and Conclusion

Public investment in education, especially basic education, has long been identified as one of the most beneficial redistributive measures, with its central mechanism being that public investment in education reduces the financial burden for low-income families of investing in the human capital of their children, ceteris paribus. Yet, establishing the underlying mechanism in empirical exercises has not been easy. This chapter thus seeks to establish the central mechanism and the two central determining factors with greater clarity.

The mechanisms singled out and the results in our study are consistent with some recent contributions. For example, Dhuey (2011) found that extending the number of hours children spend in kindergarten benefits children from low-income families more (see also Raudenbush and Eschmann 2015). Likewise, Heckman and his colleagues have demonstrated the importance of early life conditions in shaping multiple life skills (reviewed in Heckman and Mosso 2014). Our model and results also suggest that earlier intervention can neutralize some of the most negative impacts on children from low-income families. Put differently, if a state wants to reduce the inequality of the general population brought on by households' unequal socioeconomic status, it needs to intervene earlier because it simply becomes too late after a certain stage (say, high school). More recently, Betthäuser (2017, 633) showed that Germany's compulsory schooling reform has indeed contributed to "a substantial narrowing of the gap in educational attainment between different social origin groups, [which in turn] "translated into a reduction in the inequality in labor market chances between people from different social class backgrounds, thus increasing intergenerational social mobility."

Although we do not explore the outcome of attainment resulting from China's education policy reform, partly because nationwide data at an aggregate level is extremely hard to come by, our model and results are consistent with those from several studies that use smaller, survey-based datasets. For instance, Yi et al. (2012) studied the dropout rate in junior high schools in rural areas with survey data from 64 counties in four provinces. They showed that poverty within the household is the most critical cause of students dropping out of junior high school, although other factors (such as poor grades) also matter.[10] On the other hand, Yang et al. (2014) reported that with rising income, educational attainment by high school students in rural areas has been picking up. Again, their results are consistent with our model that resources are the most critical limiting factor in hindering educational achievement, especially in rural areas in China.

Our study also provides possible explanations for some results from other studies with survey data from rural areas that seem to contradict conventional wisdom. For instance, Chyi and Zhou (2014) found that an early policy that put an upward limit on tuition had little impact on enrollment in basic education. Such a result contradicts conventional wisdom and thus demands an explanation.

Our model points to the possibility that putting an upward limit on tuition has little impact on enrollment in basic education because such a policy does not reduce the total minimal cost of education (i.e., E_{min} in our model).

When this is the case, poor rural households still cannot afford to invest in their children's education, exactly as the first scenario of our model predicts (i.e., $T < E_{min} - E_{pu}$). Thus, the *liangmian yibu* policy, which concretely reduces the relative burden of private investment in basic education within the total cost of basic education, has been found to have a powerful, positive impact on the student enrollment rate in rural areas in almost all existing empirical studies.

In contrast, because China only began to implement a more robust support scheme for high school education in poor regions in the western part of the country in 2017, the enrollment rate for high school in those regions has been extremely disappointing. Indeed, Yang et al. (2014) found an alarmingly high rate of dropouts in high schools in rural areas and that poverty within the household was one of the most critical causes for this outcome. Again, their results are consistent with our model that financial constraints are the most critical limiting factor in hindering educational achievement, especially in rural areas in China. If this is the case, it can be expected that China's new and more robust support scheme for high school education in poor regions will lead to encouraging results in the near future.

Our study also has implications beyond China. Lindert (2004) and Ansell (2010) have documented the fact that most Latin American countries and India continue to have quite elitist educational systems (i.e., higher education gets more public support than basic education). Meanwhile, comparing increases in the level of education across different regions, Checchi (2005, 2–4) showed that North Africa and the Middle East had the highest increase in tertiary educational attainment (almost 10 times), while Latin America had the second highest (6.8 times) from 1960 to 1995. In contrast, Confucian East Asian economies (China, Singapore, South Korea, Taiwan, and Vietnam) have invested heavily in basic education (Lindert 2004; Ansell 2010). According Checchi (2005, 2–4), East Asia had the highest increase in primary educational attainment (45.4% increase from 1960 to 1995) and the third highest increase in secondary educational attainment (34%), even though East Asia started with a higher level of secondary educational attainment (25.8%). These facts suggest that East Asia, as a whole, has implemented a less elitist institutional education system. This key policy may have been critical in the making of the East Asian miracle (Lucas 1988; World Bank 1993; Ansell 2010).

Thus, echoing Lindert (2004) and many others, our exercises yield one clear-cut policy implication, especially for developing countries. Developing countries should adopt a nonelitist public funding regime for education, namely, generous public funding for primary and secondary education but less for tertiary education. If possible, for all developing countries, primary and secondary education should be made not only mandatory but also essentially free.

Finally, although we do not address the persistent gender gap in investing in education and the overall high dropout rate in secondary school (junior high and high school) in rural areas, our model does shed light on some of the results from studies on these two issues. For instance, Chyi and Zhou (2014, 104) find that the *liangmian yibu* policy has had "a significant impact upon school enrollment of rural girls but not rural boys and this gender differential effect results from the improvement in the enrollment of girls who live in poor households." Due to a heavy bias favoring male children, rural households generally are reluctant to invest in girls' education. As such, boys' education is weighted more heavily in household budgetary considerations. Consequently, when public support for basic education is inadequate, rural households facing budgetary constraints will most likely refuse to invest in girls' education (Hannum et al. 2009, 2011; Zeng et al. 2014).[11] Although our study does not address this possibility directly, our model can accommodate such an outcome.

As demonstrated by numerous studies, in secondary schools, students' academic performance becomes a more important factor in shaping households' decisions to invest in human capital (Zhao and Glewwe 2010; Yi et al. 2012, 2015; Shi et al. 2016). In particular, combining survey data with in-depth interviews, Shi et al. (2016) advanced two possible causes for students' decisions to drop out of junior high and high school: rational calculation (i.e., dropping out because the costs exceed the benefits) and impulsive choice dropout (i.e., short-term stresses vs. benefits).

Our model can readily accommodate the two factors that underpin the rational calculation of dropping out: financial cost and capability concerns (i.e., academic performance) as opportunity costs. Yet, students' academic performance is also partly underpinned by socioeconomic factors at the household level (e.g., children have been left behind by their parents because their parents have gone to the cities as migrant workers), the community level (e.g., that fact that a whole village has failed to produce few, if any, college students), and the school level (e.g., bullying among students, insults by teachers, competitive examination system). These factors may well impact students' "impulsive choice" to drop out. Our study does not consider this critical issue, and more inquiries are urgently needed.

5

Hierarchy, Liberty, and Innovation

A NEW INSTITUTIONAL THEORY
AND QUALITATIVE EVIDENCE

The democratic institutions . . . alone can guarantee the freedom of
critical thought, and the progress of science.
—KARL POPPER ([1945] 1966, VOL. 2, 223)

Nowhere is freedom more important than where our ignorance is
greatest—at the boundaries of knowledge.
—FRIEDRICH A. HAYEK (1960, 394)

The relationship between political regime and economic development has
been an enduring question.[1] However, there has been no firm consensus on
which type of regime—most prominently, democracy or autocracy—is more
conducive to development.

On the theoretical front, while many have eloquently argued that democracy is more conducive to growth than autocracy (e.g., Olson 1993; Bhagwati
2002; North et al. 2009; Acemoglu and Robinson 2012), equally many have
forcefully contended that autocracy may actually be good for growth (e.g.,
Huntington 1968; Bhagwati 1982; Olson 1982). On the empirical front, robust
relationships between regime and growth have long been elusive, although
some recent works seem to identify a democratic advantage in prompting
growth (see the literature review in appendix 5-A at the end of the book for

details). Overall, the jury is still out as to whether democracy holds some important, if any, advantage in prompting growth over autocracy.

We believe that a key reason behind our failure to uncover a robust empirical relationship between regime and growth is that our assault on this *problématique* so far has been too blunt. More concretely, we have failed to explicitly, not to mention adequately, address two more specific interrelated questions. First, is democracy's advantage in promoting growth over autocracy, if any, conditional or not? Second, is democracy's advantage in promoting growth over autocracy, if any, all-around or specific?

We further reason that, to tackle the two questions, a possible starting point is to search for channel(s) in which an autocracy simply cannot possibly match democracy, even if the autocracy wants growth dearly. If we can identify such channel(s), we can reveal that democracy's advantage in promoting growth is both channel specific and conditional, because being channel specific essentially means that democracy's overall advantage in promoting growth is contingent upon social, economic, and political contexts (i.e., it requires the operation of other channels).

Bringing together the classic defense of democracy, endogenous growth theory, institutional economics, and the political economy of hierarchy, we contend that *democracy does hold a unique advantage in promoting growth over autocracy, but this advantage is conditional and channel specific.* More concretely, democracy holds a *unique* advantage over autocracy in promoting growth, but only when an economy enters the stage of growth via innovation, because the channel of liberty to (institutional and technological) innovation is the most critical channel in which democracy's advantage shines.[2]

We begin by underscoring that the coming of hierarchy in human society poses two opposing dynamics for economic development. On the one hand, hierarchy facilitates development, most critically because it provides sociopolitical order and stability. On the other hand, however, hierarchy also inherently hinders innovation and thus development because it demands "obedience to authority" (OTA) and OTA hinders bottom-up innovation. Since bottom-up innovation is indispensable to economic development, this means that the state, as a hierarchical organization, must strike a delicate balance between maintaining order and stability and facilitating bottom-up innovation in order to achieve development.

Drawing from the classic defense of liberty and democracy, we then contend that *liberty is the most effective way to achieve the delicate balance between maintaining order and stability by demanding OTA and encouraging innovation under hierarchy.* Further, because economic development goes through the stages of growth via imitation and then innovation, liberty may not be crucial when growth mostly depends on imitation. When growth has to depend more on innovation, however, liberty becomes more critical because only liberty protects and prompts innovation. As such, democracy is more conducive to growth via innovation because it counters hierarchy's structural impediments against innovation better than autocracy while maintaining order and stability.

Our theory has two straightforward empirical predictions. First, democracy is a necessary, though insufficient, condition for protecting major scientific breakthroughs that may challenge orthodoxies. Second, there should be a visible turning point in democracy's effect on growth. More concretely, below a certain income level (measured in GDP per capita), democracy may or may not hold significant overall advantages over autocracy in promoting growth. After an economy reaches a certain income level and growth comes to depend to a greater degree on innovation, however, democracy's advantage over autocracy in promoting growth should become more significant.

In this chapter, I present qualitative evidence for the first prediction by examining three prominent historical cases, leaving systematic quantitative evidence for our second prediction to chapter 6. Evidence from these three historical cases demonstrates that although key scientific breakthroughs can indeed pop up under autocracies, our first prediction holds: democracy is a necessary, though insufficient, condition for protecting major scientific breakthroughs that may challenge orthodoxies.

Four caveats are in order. First, we are only interested in uncovering democracy's advantages that cannot be matched by autocracies. We thus do not deny that democracy may hold additional advantages over autocracies in other channels when it comes to growth (e.g., investing in education, redistribution), especially when other social, economic, and political conditions are favorable. What we do suggest is that those other advantages can be mimicked by autocracies, in principle if not often in the real world. Second, we are not concerned with what happens after a country (democratized or not) becomes a developed country. We are thus agnostic about the possibility that specific institutions under democracy may actually hinder growth after a country becomes a fully developed country because developed democratic countries may possess some growth-retarding dynamics, such as pork barrel politics and polarized partisan politics (e.g., Olson 1982). Third, by defending the economic value of democracy, we do not deny that democracy itself is a normative value to be desired and defended for its own sake. In fact, we strongly concur with Ober (2008, 5–6) that when defending democracy, "ought" and "is" should be more tightly conjoined (see also Mackie 2003). Fourth, because the literature on democracy and growth is too voluminous for a brief critique, we have delegated our critique of the existing literature on this topic to appendix 5-A at the end of the book.

The rest of this chapter is structured as follows. Section I introduces the four intellectual pillars of our theory. Section II advances our theory. Section III presents qualitative evidence, demonstrating that only autocracies have killed major scientific breakthroughs and autocracies have almost invariably thwarted the social sciences. Section IV draws theoretical and empirical implications and concludes.

I. The Intellectual Foundation of Our Theory: Four Pillars

Our more integrated institutional theory regarding regime and growth is built on four intellectual pillars. The first is the endogenous growth model centered on knowledge (or ideas). The second is the political economy of hierarchy. The third is the classic definition and defense of democracy. The fourth is the notion that economic development can be divided into two different stages.

Because the fourth pillar is straightforward, we shall merely state its conclusion here. Focusing on technological learning alone, this literature stipulates that for developing countries to become developed countries they have to go through two stages of growth: growth via imitation and growth via innovation (Kim 1997).[3] During the stage of growth via imitation, developing countries "merely" need to copy the good things from developed countries and adopt them to local conditions. In this stage, little innovation is needed (Lewis 1955, 80). As an economy moves up the ladder of technology, however, it needs to innovate more and more simply because there are increasingly fewer things that it can readily copy. Despite being intuitively appealing and empirically sound, however, this thesis of growth via stages is purely about technology. As such, key institutional factors, such as regime, have only a marginal role in this literature. Our theory remedies this.

A. IDEAS AND GROWTH: THE ENDOGENOUS GROWTH MODEL

After a long hiatus, economists have rediscovered Smith's fundamental insight that knowledge—or the "skill, dexterity, and judgment" of a population, in Smith's original words ([1776] 1981, 1)—is indispensable for production, and therefore, for growth. The key insight of the "endogenous growth model" is that because knowledge is a nonrivalrous good (i.e., others' use of it does not diminish, and may even increase, one's own utility), the aggregate production function must eventually be increasing returns to scale, rather than constant returns to scale. This nonrivalrous nature of knowledge has been a crucial force that has enabled human society to eventually escape the Malthusian trap (for an excellent review, see Jones 2005).

Existing endogenous growth models centered on knowledge, however, suffer from three critical and interrelated deficiencies. First, they mostly treat knowledge—explicitly or implicitly—as technological knowledge alone, although our knowledge consists of both technological knowledge and social knowledge and both types of knowledge are indispensable for production and thus development (Hayek 1945, 521–22; Lewis 1955, 164–66). Second, they have yet to take the *quality* dimension of knowledge into account, although all too apparently knowledge has both a quantity dimension and a quality dimension. Third, institution, long identified as a critical force in shaping development through time and space by the new institutional economics (NIE), has been ominously missing in this literature. As such, existing endogenous growth literature has been mostly silent on the relationship between regime and growth (Tang and Gao 2020).

B. THE POLITICAL ECONOMY OF HIERARCHY

The second pillar of our theory is the political economy of hierarchy, a topic that has been only sporadically addressed in political science, economics, business management, and anthropology and only marginally integrated with the literature on growth (e.g., Etzioni-Halevy 1983; Sah and Stiglitz 1987; Sah 1991).

Hierarchy poses two opposing dynamics for learning and growth. On the one hand, hierarchy facilitates growth, through at least four mechanisms: facilitating individualistic innovation and accumulation; reducing individuals' uncertainty and risk for taking socially productive initiatives and, hence, encouraging investment in skills and capital; enabling scale mobilization of human power and resources; and partially overriding the problem of free riding in collective action (see appendix 5-B at the end of the book for details). On the other hand, however, hierarchy also brings a new force that discourages innovation and hence growth, and that force is obedience to authority (OTA; for a more detailed discussion with references, see appendix 5-B).

For our purpose here, OTA fundamentally encourages individuals within an organization to respect authority more and care about truth less (again, see appendix 5-B for elaboration). Because individuals' material and positional advances in a hierarchy critically depend on whether that they obey authority, individuals tend to obey more often than not. At the most extreme, everybody pretends to agree with the authority on everything and dares not question it, even if the authority is evidently wrong, for fear of being identified as disobedient. (Remember the "emperor with no clothes"?) Conformity and compliance thus become the culture of the whole organization. Unfortunately, while conformity and compliance are conducive to stability and order, they inevitably hinder innovation. As such, in order to achieve growth, a society needs to tread a fine balance between maintaining order and stability and facilitating innovation.

C. INSTITUTIONAL CHANGE AND THE GROWTH OF KNOWLEDGE: CLASSIC DEFENSES OF LIBERTY

For our purpose here, democracy can be understood on two fronts. First, democracy is the "form of political constitution which makes possible the adaptation of the government to the wishes of the governed without violent struggle" (Mises [1962] 1996, 42). Placed in the context of institutional change, this argument implies that democracy holds a unique advantage over autocracy in allowing and thus promoting peaceful institutional innovation or changes, especially bottom-up ones. Second, democracy is a metapolitical arrangement that best protects liberty, as Hayek ([1979] 1982, 5) put it: "Though democracy itself is not freedom . . . it is one of the most important safeguards of freedom." Most critically, many classic defenders of liberty have done so for the sake of accumulating new knowledge and thus solving new problems, based on two fundamental insights.

First, critical thinking is indispensable to scientific progress, and only liberty adequately protects critical thinking. "*The democratic institutions . . . alone can guarantee the freedom of critical thought, and the progress of science*" (Popper [1945] 1966, vol. 2, 223, emphasis added). Likewise, Polanyi (1941) defended the scientists' rights to resist governmental coordination precisely on the grounds that liberty is the prerequisite for science's pursuing of innovation: "The Liberal conception is that freedom is the only method by which we can continue to discover the regions of yet undisclosed truth in which we are advancing" (448; see also Polanyi 1962, 67–68; 1966; Sah 1991, 70). As such, "*nowhere is freedom more important than where our ignorance is greatest—at the boundaries of knowledge*" (Hayek 1960, 394, emphasis added).

Second, no omnipotent leader or coordination is possible. As Lewis (1955, 80) put it: "The case for the superiority of individual freedom in economic matters rests on the belief that the chief has no superior source of knowledge, and that individuals seeking in many directions are more likely to discover open doors than a chief with a monopoly of manoeuver." (See also Lewis 1955, 44, 166, and 178.) Similarly, Hayek (1960, 29–30) asserted that "the case for individual freedom rests chiefly on the recognition of the inevitable ignorance of all of us concerning a great many of the factors on which the achievement of our ends and welfare depend." (See also Hayek 1944, 12; 1945; 1960, ch. 2.)

In sum, classic defenders of democracy and liberty have argued that for a society to solve its practical problems with necessary innovations, individuals' liberty to pursue and try out new ideas must be protected. Unfortunately, these classic defenses of liberty have yet to be firmly linked with the endogenous growth literature, the NIE on growth, and the political economy of hierarchy.

II. Democracy's Unique Advantage in Promoting Growth Restated

We now advance a more integrated institutional theory that identifies democracy's unique advantage in prompting growth.[4] *We contend that the liberty-to-innovation channel is the primary, if not the only, channel in which democracy holds an exclusive advantage over autocracy when it comes to promoting growth because democracy better counters hierarchy's detrimental effects on innovation than autocracy, all else being equal.* Fundamentally, democracy achieves a better balance between maintaining order and stability and encouraging innovation by protecting liberty better than autocracy. In contrast, autocracy depresses growth because it suppresses liberty and thus innovation for the sake of order and stability by demanding excessive OTA from its subjects.

The liberty-to-innovation channel is thus a channel in which autocracy cannot possibly match democracy. Unlike efforts in other channels (e.g., property rights) that can generate growth without directly jeopardizing autocratic rule and may actually prolong it, the liberty-to-innovation channel vitally threatens autocratic rule: an autocrat's survival fundamentally depends on limiting bottom-up institutional innovations; thus, autocratic rulers can ill afford to protect the liberty-to-innovation channel even if they want growth dearly.

Although autocrats can easily impose institutional changes, they have inherently limited information of the whole social system, as all central planners do. As such, autocrats cannot possibly design a sound institutional system all by themselves (Lewis 1955, 80; Hayek 1960, 29–30). Democracy solves the problem of ignorance in decision making by allowing (if not encouraging) bottom-up innovations, both institutional and technological. As such, when it comes to the possibility of installing a more sound institutional system for the whole society, democracy should outduel autocracy, all else being equal.

Moreover, the virtue of liberty becomes more critical when an economy reaches the stage of having to grow via innovation, because innovation fundamentally requires liberty, as Adams, Hayek, Lewis, Polanyi, and Popper recognized long ago. Because democracy is a near necessary condition for system-wide, bottom-up innovations, technological but especially institutional democracy is a near necessary condition for growth via innovation.

Of course, a more sound institutional system increases citizens' confidence in their ability to change the system for the better via peaceful means (including the state as a protector of individuals' overall welfare, protection of property rights, etc.), and thus increases a society's stability. As such, individuals in democracies are more willing to invest in education, research, innovation, and enterprises than individuals in autocracies, all else being equal. These advantages in turn bestow democracies with a unique advantage over autocracy in promoting growth via innovation.

Finally, precisely because democracy allows for system-wide, bottom-up institutional change, a democracy maintains order and stability with less actual violence and threat of violence, thus incurring a smaller cost on its economy. In contrast, because autocracy does not allow system-wide, bottom-up institutional innovations, it must rely on the threat and actual use of violent force to maintain political stability. Inevitably, an autocracy's maintaining of order and stability entails a much larger cost for its economy.

The chain of logic behind our argument can be straightforwardly summarized. (1) System-wide, bottom-up innovation is necessary for growth via innovation. (2) Innovation requires the freedom to challenge existing ideas and institutions. (3) Because democracy protects liberty better than autocracy, democracy promotes bottom-up innovation and thus growth via innovation better than autocracy (figure 5.1).

So how does democracy promote innovation by limiting OTA and protecting liberty, especially at the micro level? As noted briefly in section I and

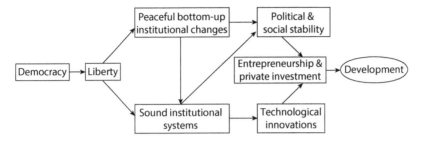

FIGURE 5.1. Democracy's Unique Advantage in Promoting Development.

in more detail in appendix 5-B at the end of the book, due to the impera-tives of OTA, there is an intrinsic tension between maintaining order and stability and facilitating innovation under hierarchy (Etzioni-Halevy 1983, 38). Because the growth of knowledge via innovation is the most critical engine of growth, in order to achieve growth, a state therefore has to charter a delicate balance between maintaining stability by demanding OTA from its citizens and facilitating innovation and thus growth by minimizing OTA's negative impact on learning. It is on this delicate balance that democracy and autocracy differ from each other fundamentally, because they employ diametrically opposite approaches to achieving it. Whereas democracy achieves this balance by protecting liberty, autocracy sacrifices innovation and growth for the sake of stability by suppressing liberty. The impact on innovation and growth of these opposite approaches is profound.

First, by protecting liberty, democracy limits the likelihood that individu-als will suffer negative repercussions if they challenge authority. Democracy thus facilitates diversity in individuals' innovation, encourages individuals to freely communicate their personal (tacit) knowledge, and allows indi-viduals to compete freely in the marketplace of ideas. Because diversity in innovation, free communication of ideas, and free competition are vital to the production of new knowledge, democracy facilitates the production of new knowledge. And because the growth of new knowledge is a criti-cal engine of growth, democracy facilitates growth, especially growth via innovation.

To begin with, diversity in individual innovation and free communication of ideas limit the possibility of monopolies of ideas in a society. Also, the rate of innovation reflects the intensity of competition (Hayek 1978; North 1994, 362). By protecting free communication of ideas and stimulating the competition of ideas, democracy facilitates the production of new knowl-edge and prevents monopolies of ideas better than autocracy.

Moreover, by allowing individuals to freely communicate their knowledge without fear of punishment, liberty limits OTA's negative effects on growth and thus contributes to the growth of new knowledge. With liberty protected, individuals are more willing to communicate their tacit knowledge in the public domain, thus increasing the portion of nonrivalrous knowledge and strengthening the cumulative effect in the production of new knowledge. Consequently, increasing returns to scale in knowledge production and growth tend to be more robust under democracy than under autocracy (Jones 2005). With free communication of ideas protected, the chances that new ideas will be tested are also enhanced. As a result, bad ideas are more easily—and more likely to be—weeded out. Consequently, less resources are wasted in pursuing scientifically unjustified goals, and the rate of return in the production of new knowledge again increases.

Second, democracy self-consciously limits its own authority in the realm of seeking knowledge, thus again limiting OTA's potential negative impact on innovation: democracy usually lets (natural and social) scientists run their own business (Polanyi 1941, 1956).

Third, by allowing, if not encouraging, bottom-up institutional changes by giving voice to individuals, democracy tends to depend on force and threat of force for maintaining political and social stability less than autocracy does. This in turn frees up more human and other resources for investing in innovation. All these dynamics suggest that the production of new knowledge is more likely to enter a virtuous cycle under democracy.

In contrast, under autocracy, where freedom is severely limited, people produce and communicate few new ideas, and having fewer ideas produced and communicated further strengthens the monopolies of ideas. Indeed, under autocracy, monopolies of ideas often run rampant, in addition to the more apparent manifestations of official ideologies, dogmas, and taboos (see also appendix 5-B). Moreover, under autocracy, most of the organizations that foster innovation (especially those organizations for higher learning, such as universities, R&D facilities, and think tanks) are run by state bureaucrats for the sake of internal control (Polanyi 1941, 454–56). Because these bureaucrats in turn demand OTA inside their own organizations, the barriers against innovation must necessarily permeate the whole society far more pervasively under autocracy than under democracy. Finally, autocracy almost always has to spend a disproportional part of its manpower and wealth on the apparatus of repression to maintain order and stability. As such, autocracy almost always invests fewer resources in innovation than it could. Under autocracy, therefore, the production of new knowledge is more likely to enter a vicious cycle.

Overall, whereas democracy is more likely to be "a society of explorers" that sets few limits on human inquiry (Polanyi 1966; Knight 1967, 785), autocracy is more likely to be "a society of conformists (and dissidents)" that sets few limits on the authority.

Yet, economic development inevitably generates new issues and challenges that have no readily available solutions and thus can only be tackled by innovation, both institutional and technological. Innovation thus gradually becomes more critical, especially when an economy reaches the stage of growth via innovation. Because liberty facilitates bottom-up innovation whereas OTA hinders it, democracy should hold a unique advantage over autocracy when it comes to growth, especially growth via innovation.

III. Autocracies against Natural and Social Sciences

Among scientists, historians, and philosophers of natural science, there is a remarkable consensus on a critical reason why modern science, as a key engine of modern economic development, first came to and flourished in the West. The consensus is that "the West successfully organized its scientists with very little use of hierarchical management" (Rosenberg and Birdzell 1986, 255). Polanyi (1962, 67–68) put it forcefully: "Throughout the formative centuries of modern science, the rejection of authority was its battle-cry. . . . When we rejected today the interference of political or religious authorities with the pursuit of science, we must do this in the name of the established scientific authority which safeguards the pursuit of science." (See also Polanyi 1941, 1966; Jacob 1997, ch. 8.)

We believe this insight that liberty from the interference of authority is indispensable for the flourishing of science holds crucial implications for understanding the relationship between regime and growth, not least because growth is partly but fundamentally powered by scientific and technological innovation, and innovation requires the freedom to try out new things and new ideas.

As predicted by our theory (see also section I and appendix 5-B), too much OTA under hierarchy inevitably stifles innovation. This section presents evidence from three prominent historical cases, demonstrating that autocracies have indeed killed major scientific breakthroughs or critically delayed scientific progress by limiting liberty and demanding OTA. By so doing, we demonstrate that although key scientific breakthroughs can indeed pop up under autocracies, democracy is a necessary, though insufficient, condition for protecting major scientific breakthroughs that may challenge orthodoxies.

The first two cases, the Inquisition against Galileo and the reign of Lysenko's (pseudo)genetics in the Soviet Union, show not only how autocracies indeed killed major scientific breakthroughs or critically delayed possible scientific progress by limiting liberty and demanding OTA but also that autocracies had done so primarily in order to sustain monopolies of bad ideas, just as our theory predicts.

In the third case, we present a massive but much neglected set of evidence that should constitute the most powerful indictment against autocracy: autocracies have invariably stifled social sciences because all social sciences are inherently "critical theories" (Bhaskar [1979] 1998, 1986). In so doing, however, autocracies drain one of the key springs of knowledge for bottom-up institutional innovations, because social sciences are a key provider of the ideas for possible institutional innovations or changes (Campbell [1971] 1988; Ruttan 1984; Tang 2011b).

A. THE INQUISITION, PROTESTANTISM, AND THE SHIFT OF THE SCIENTIFIC REVOLUTION FROM CONTINENTAL EUROPE TO BRITAIN, 1540–1680

With hindsight, one must wonder why the Industrial Revolution started in Protestant Britain but not Catholic (continental) Europe. After all, Copernicus, Tycho Brahe, Kepler, and Galileo, leading figures who started the Scientific Revolution, were all living in Catholic Europe,[5] and the Scientific Revolution had undoubtedly been a key propeller behind the Industrial Revolution. In light of our theory, there may be a straightforward explanation for this outcome: the Catholic Church's theocratic monopoly of ideas—most starkly symbolized by the Inquisition and the condemnation of Galileo in 1633–1634—had prevented the sparks of the Scientific Revolution from igniting and spreading across the European continent and thus killed continental Europe's chances of starting the Industrial Revolution.

The timeline behind the Inquisition is well known and a brief recount is sufficient here. In 1632, Galileo published *Dialogue on the Two Chief World Systems*, in which he pitted the two theories about the celestial systems, namely, (Aristotelian-) Ptolemaic and Copernican, against each other and ended up defending the Copernican system that the earth revolves around the sun. This book triggered the Inquisition and the eventual condemnation of Galileo in 1633.[6]

To be sure, none of the giants who started the Scientific Revolution had intended to dethrone God entirely. Indeed, Copernicus dedicated his treatise on heliocentrism to the Pope; Brahe patched geo-heliocentrism to retain harmony between heliocentrism and geocentrism. Likewise, Kepler tried to combine his astronomy with God to achieve mystical "harmony," and Galileo attempted to insulate the church from the implications of further scientific progress (Hall 1989; Cohen 1994, 120).[7] The crux of the problem was that scientists had ended up discovering things that increasingly rendered the theological teachings of the Catholic Church untenable.

Historians and sociologists have offered several explanations for the flourishing of the Scientific Revolution in England. Most prominently, taking a line from Weber (1958), Merton ([1938] 1970) argued that Protestantism (or more precisely, Puritanism) was a key cultural trait behind the flourishing of science in England in the seventeenth century (for critical discussions, see Hall 1961; Cohen 1994, 314–21, 333–36). Specifically, Merton advanced that Puritanism allowed scientists (and their families) to legitimate their scientific activities. Others have singled out the combination of the Greek worldview and the biblical view, especially the Protestant ethic, which adores earthly work (e.g., Hooykaas 1987; see also Cohen 1994, esp. chs. 4 and 5).

These explanations are mostly cultural or ideational. Missing from them is a political or institutional dimension: even with a scientific ethic—which might have a Protestant influence (in addition to others, such as Baconian empiricism)—in place, only under a political regime that could have shielded scientific inquiry from the Inquisition and the long reach of the Roman Catholic Church could science have flourished. And one finds such a situation only in England (and to a lesser extent in the Netherlands) back then.

The trial and eventual condemnation of Galileo essentially meant that communication, not to mention the pursuit of scientific knowledge, along the path of Copernicus and Galileo became dangerous on continental Europe. As Jacob (1997, 27–29) put it: "Anyone attracted by the ideas of Copernicus, if living in Catholic, as opposed to Protestant, Europe, now has to think very carefully about how to announce that support." By contrast, England and the Netherlands, being Protestant, were able to pick up the historical opportunities offered by those giants' revolutionary ideas and bring the revolution started by Copernicus into full force, because the Roman theocracy had limited power over monopolizing the marketplace of ideas there. It was no accident that Galileo's last major work, *Discorsi*

(*Discourses and Mathematical Demonstrations Relating to Two New Sciences*), was published in the Netherlands in 1638, not in his native Italy or Catholic Europe. "Many historical consequences can be traced back, in some ultimate sense, to the 'victory' over Galileo of a few Aristotelian professors, some Florentine and Jesuit clergymen, and the bureaucracy of the Roman Inquisition" (Jacob 1997, 29).

Here, it is critical to point out that while finding out the exact culprits behind the Inquisition and Galileo's eventual condemnation is of historical interest (for detailed references, see appendix 5-B), it is of only marginal interest for defending the liberty of pursuing knowledge. Whether or not the Inquisition had been pursued by professors of (natural) philosophy or even friends of Galileo who wanted to prevent him from being accused and convicted of even harsher crimes, or even that Galileo intended to protect the church and the Bible from any possible scientific progress, the Catholic Church simply had no business in deciding whether Copernicus's and Galileo's scientific theory was wrong or right.

Moreover, without the backing of the church, there should be little doubt that Galileo (and Copernicus) would have won the battle against Aristotle-Ptolemy sooner on continental Europe. At the very least, without the Catholic Church (and the Bible), Galileo's enemies would have had to go to some other source of authority to challenge him. The fate of Galileo and heliocentrism thus is a typical case in which bad ideas, by relying on political power, are able to monopolize the marketplace of ideas and slow down a scientific revolution, just as our theory predicts.

B. THE REIGN OF LYSENKO'S PSEUDOGENETICS IN THE FORMER SOVIET UNION

The second case we present is the disastrous reign of Lysenkoist (pseudo) genetics in the Soviet Union from 1936 to 1965. In the 1910s to 1920s, the study of genetics in the Soviet Union was not too far behind that in the United States. Yet, the reign of Lysenko set back genetics and biological research in the Soviet Union for almost three decades, if not more (Soyfer 1994; 2001).[8] Indeed, the reign of Lysenko had a devastating impact on biological sciences in all other communist countries, with the exception of East Germany due to strong resistance by prominent East German biologists who had achieved worldwide stature before WWII (Hagemann 2002).

The saga of Lysenko is now infamous, and again only a brief recounting is necessary here (for detailed treatments, see Soyfer 1994; see also Joravsky 1970; Roll-Hansen 2005).[9] Trofim Denisovich Lysenko (1896–1976) began to experiment with vernalization (i.e., exposing plants to a period of low temperature to influence the timing of flowering) in the second half of the 1920s, and shortly afterward (as early as 1927) he began to make wild claims of producing crops with high yield under Russia's demanding climate without actually backing his claims with data. He simply could not, because he violated all of the most fundamental principles of Mendel-Weismann-Morgan genetics. Instead, at the very beginning, Lysenko regularly and blatantly forged data. Yet, because Lysenko's wild claims gave the Soviet Union a false hope of ending the devastating famine caused by the Soviet's forced collectivization in 1928–1931, the Soviet Union provided Lysenko with some initial support.

In 1929, the Soviet Union established the Lenin Academy of Agricultural Science under the leadership of Nikolai Vavilov (1887–1943). In order to speed up the completion of his "Seedbank (of crops)" under heavy Soviet pressure, Vavilov decided to support Lysenko's vernalization scheme even though Lysenko did not have any proper training in genetics.[10] Beginning in 1929, Lysenko also began to blend his ideas of vernalization with the pseudogenetic theories of Michurin (1855–1935) as a version of Lamarckian inheritance—a possibility that was nullified by the presence of "Weismann's barrier" but unfortunately remained popular back then. Essentially, Lysenko claimed that even if a plant had been manipulated nongenetically, its offspring would be able to inherit those acquired characteristics. By 1934–1936, Lysenko had achieved the status of a "model Soviet scientist": he was "elected" not only to the Ukraine Academy of Science and the Lenin All-Union Academy of Agricultural Sciences but also to the USSR Supreme Soviet Council (as deputy chairman) in 1935.

In 1934, Lysenko, facing mounting criticism and doubt because his repeated claims of increasing crop output had never materialized, began to charge that Mendel-Weismann-Morgan genetics was "bourgeois science" that was incompatible with the Marx-Engels doctrine that nature can be easily "dominated" by human knowledge, whereas his combination of Michurinist genetics and vernalization was thoroughly consistent with Marxism-Leninism (Soyfer 2001, 724–26).[11] As a result, Lysenko's pseudoscience gained favor with the Soviet top leadership, and the Soviet Union gradually began to enshrine Lysenkoist genetics as orthodoxy. Stalin gave Lysenko key initial support in 1936, which eventually culminated in the Great Purge in Soviet biological sciences. During the purge from 1936 to 1938, many prominent Soviet biologists who were against Lysenko were removed from top official science positions, and many of them were arrested and tried on forged crimes and sentenced to death; the purge was only interrupted by

Hitler's invasion of the Soviet Union in 1940 (Joravsky 1970; Soyfer 1994, 91–158). By the time Lysenko became the president of the Lenin Academy in 1938 (replacing Vavilov), any criticism of Lysenko and his pseudoscience had become extremely difficult, if not entirely impossible.

Shortly after WWII, Lysenko worked to prolong his reign. He wrote to Stalin in 1947 and asked for the dictator's support. In his reply, Stalin gave his blessing to Lysenko, writing as follows: *"The Michurinist view is the only scientific view. The Weismannists and their followers who are rejecting heredity of acquired characters do not deserve the right to speak a long time about them. The future belongs to Michurin"* (as quoted in Soyfer 2001, 725, emphasis added). This political intervention eventually culminated in a Soviet polit-buro decree in 1948 that completely outlawed Mendel-Weismann-Morgan genetics as "reactionary and bourgeois pseudoscience," surely with Stalin's backing (Soyfer 2001). With the decree in hand, Lysenko and his followers went on to finish their business of purging all opponents.

There is no doubt that Lysenko's rise to power and subsequent reign was partially due to the fact that his pseudoscience promised a potential windfall for Soviet agriculture and fitted into Marxist-Leninist ideology (Roll-Hansen 2005). Yet, without the backing of brutal Soviet political power, Lysenko could not possibly have achieved and maintained the monopoly of his bad ideas in genetics in the Soviet Union (Joravsky 1970; Soyfer 1994, 2001). This is simply because his results would be subjected to replication and his claims would be quickly falsified and thus rejected (Popper [1937] 1959). In other words, in an "open society" or a republic of science protected by liberty via democracy, there is little possibility that Lysenko could have achieved and maintained his monopoly of bad ideas.

Overall, the reign of Lysenko's pseudogenetics and the Inquisition and eventual condemnation of Galileo are strikingly similar: monopolies by bad ideas were erected and enforced by inferences from authority, religious (and political) in one case and political in another. Put bluntly, Lysenko's disastrous long reign over genetics in the former Soviet Union could only have been possible under autocracy, just as the infamous prosecutions against Galileo and Bruno could only have been possible under theocracy.

C. THE FATE OF SOCIAL SCIENCES UNDER AUTOCRACY

Technological knowledge alone does not guarantee growth because growth also critically depends on social knowledge (Lewis 1955, 166; Hayek 1960, 25–26). Because social knowledge is inherently tied to politics and ideology, all social science knowledge is potentially subversive and thus dangerous and undesirable in autocracies (Polanyi 1966, 84; Ruttan 1984, 551). Moreover, social sciences are innately critical and provide knowledge for possible institutional changes (Campbell [1971] 1988; Bhaskar [1979] 1998, 1986; Ruttan 1984; Tang 2011b). Unsurprisingly, autocracies from all over the world have severely limited the social sciences. Indeed, autocracies have strenuously tried to make social sciences a docile servant to the state. As a result, a critical chunk of knowledge that is absolutely necessary for growth cannot be freely pursued and this cannot but be bad for growth.

Take China as an example. Although the Republic of China (1927–1949) under Chiang Kai-shek was also an autocracy and Chiang was certainly no friend of social scientists, China before 1949 had a decently thriving social sciences community. The communist takeover in 1949, however, ushered in a total assault against all social sciences. Beginning in 1952, under the tutelage of the Soviet Union, the People's Republic of China (PRC) began to abolish all major branches of (bourgeois) social sciences. Instead, universities in the PRC would teach only Marxism, Leninism, and Maoism, in addition to science, technology, production management, and economic planning. The result was nothing short of devastating.[12]

Most starkly, all departments of law (which included political sciences back then) were singled out as "targets that must be annihilated" because they were reactionary. By 1953, only six universities retained departments of law, and faculties in law and politics were reduced by more than half (or 0.8% of the total faculty in universities) and students in law and politics were reduced from 24% of the total student body to a meager 0.46%. Worse, only Marxist-Leninist-Maoist ideology was to be taught as political science: political science thus became synonymous with ideology and political indoctrination.

Sociology suffered a similar fate. In 1949, there were 22 universities with a department of sociology. By 1952, there were only two, and by 1953, they were all eliminated with the rationale that historical materialism could replace sociology.

Along the way, all faculty members in the social sciences were to be "reeducated" as servants of the proletarian dictatorship or to be banished to teaching English or other foreign languages. From 1957 to 1976, with two waves of political purges (the Anti-Rightist Campaign and the Great Proletarian Cultural Revolution), tens of thousands of social scientists were purged, banished to labor camps, sentenced to death, or beaten to death. Many committed suicide due to insufferable humiliation or languished without shelter and basic food supplies until they died.

After China's opening and reform in 1978, the Communist government reinstalled social sciences. Yet, social sciences have remained under the ideological grip of the Communist Party. Periodically, the Communist Party, through its Department of Propaganda, has initiated "recorrection campaigns" to reinforce its ideological grip on social sciences and the discussions on social issues in the wider society. Indeed, just recently, the government issued a decree forbidding the discussion of constitutional government, civil society, freedom of the press, and judicial independence, among other topics.

By stifling if not totally annihilating social sciences, autocracies drain one of the key springs of knowledge for institutional innovation because social sciences are a key provider of ideas for possible institutional innovation and change, especially from the bottom up. Under autocracies, therefore, almost all institutional changes are dictated from the top down. Unfortunately, due to the lack of liberty, autocrats cannot even learn about, much less correct, their misguided institutional changes imposed from the top because almost all dissenting voices are forbidden. In fact, lacking vibrant social sciences due to a lack of liberty has been a key cause of the numerous policy fiascoes under autocracies, with collective farms under the Soviet Union and China's "Great Leap Forward" being just some of the most devastating examples.

D. SUMMARY

All three historical cases presented above strongly support our theory. The first case attests to the fact that autocracies have indeed killed major scientific breakthroughs primarily because the breakthroughs challenged the orthodoxies underpinning the autocratic order. The second case shows that bad ideas, when backed by autocratic power, can suffocate scientific progress. Finally, the third case proves that social sciences inevitably suffer under autocracies. Together, the three cases demonstrate that although key scientific breakthroughs can indeed pop up under autocracies, democracy is a necessary, though insufficient, condition for protecting major scientific breakthroughs that may challenge orthodoxies, as classic defenses of liberty have long contended (e.g., Popper [1945] 1966; Hayek 1960).

After the Scientific Revolution and the Industrial Revolution, economic progress came to depend critically on scientific and technological progress, underpinned by a sound institutional foundation. In light of our new theory and evidence, it perhaps has not been mere coincidence that after the Scientific Revolution and the Industrial Revolution, without exception, the most technologically advanced state has always been the more liberal society of its age (Great Britain in 1700–1900 and the United States since 1900), and no leading autocratic power has ever won a race of long-run growth over the leading democracy. For a brief period, Nazi Germany and the Soviet Union did lead in some aspects of nuclear and space technology; but the democratic advantage eventually manifested itself fully even in these two cases. Nazi Germany's program of building a nuclear bomb was undermined by its heinous (and illiberal) policy against the Jews, and the Soviet Union could not fully explore the spillover potential provided by its lead in space exploration because it greatly limited the diffusion of knowledge (Gomulka 1995, 214–19).

IV. Implications and Concluding Remarks

We have put forward a more integrated defense that democracy does hold some advantage over autocracy when it comes to prompting growth. Unlike other possible channels identified in the literature, the channel of liberty to (institutional and technological) innovation, which derives directly from the classic defense of liberty and democracy, does not require additional and often ad hoc assumptions about the personality, (political and economic) preferences, and skills of rulers to operate. Because every state is a hierarchy, and there is innate tension between OTA and innovation, and innovation is critical to growth, all states have to tread a balance between maintaining stability and facilitating innovation when it comes to growth. On this front, democracy and autocracy adopt diametrically different approaches: democracy achieves a rough balance between maintaining stability and encouraging innovation by protecting liberty, while autocracy suppresses liberty and thus innovation for the sake of maintaining stability. Democracy thus better counters hierarchy's detrimental effects on innovation than does autocracy. As a result, democracy holds a unique advantage over autocracy when it comes to promoting growth, especially when an economy reaches the stage of growing via innovation.

Our theory holds important theoretical and empirical implications for understanding the relationship between democracy and growth, and, more broadly, the relationship between institutions and growth. Theoretically, our theory reinforces the notion that democracy's impact on growth is deeply contextual and historical, rather than linear, monotonic, context-free, and transhistorical (e.g., Lindert 2003; Gerring et al. 2005). This insight points to new possibilities for reconciling seemingly contradictory evidence and theories and shedding light on some empirical evidence that does not have a good theoretical explanation.

Practically and morally, our discussion underscores that democracy holds an inherent advantage when it comes to growth via innovation. Fundamentally, by protecting liberty, democracy protects our right to innovate and change and thus our hope for continuous progress. In contrast, by taking away our liberty, autocracy takes away our right of innovation, thus our hope for continuous progress (Popper [1945] 1966, vol. 2, 223; Polanyi 1956; Knight 1967, 785). Although autocracies may achieve robust growth for a period of time during growth via catching up by investing heavily in physical infrastructure, heavy equipment, and science and technology, autocracies cannot compete with democracies in the long run because autocracies are inherently inimical to innovation, technological and institutional. Lack of liberty therefore is a natural road to not only serfdom but also economic stagnation, when growth via imitation inevitably runs out of steam. By revealing democracy's unique advantage in promoting growth, we take away autocrats' ultimate justification for their survival, and state loudly and clearly that democracy is not only morally right but also economically productive. Our discussion also suggests that while democracy is inherently virtuous, the timing of democratization may be critical for how a developing country fares on its road toward prosperity.

In this chapter, we present qualitative evidence showing that autocracies have indeed killed key scientific breakthroughs that challenge the orthodoxies underpinning an autocratic order and have consistently stymied the growth of the social sciences because social sciences are inherently critical and thus considered subversive. Democracy is thus a necessary, though insufficient, condition for protecting major scientific breakthroughs that may challenge orthodoxies. In the next chapter, we present quantitative evidence to further substantiate our theory. Together, these two chapters complete a redefense of democracy's unique but conditional and channel-specific advantage in promoting growth over autocracy.

6

Democracy's Unique Advantage in Promoting Development

QUANTITATIVE EVIDENCE

Chapter 5 advances a new institutional theory regarding democracy's unique advantage in promoting growth, especially growth via innovation, by bringing together the classic defense of liberty and democracy, the political economy of hierarchy, endogenous growth theory, and the new institutional economics on growth. The new theory echoes the emerging consensus that political regime impacts growth through specific channels and is thus indirect, but it goes further on two fronts. First, we identify the channel of liberty to (institutional and technological) innovation as the channel in which democracy holds a unique advantage over autocracy when it comes to promoting growth.[1] Second, we further hold that democracy's unique positive effect on the channel of liberty-to-innovation is conditioned by the level of economic development. Moreover, unlike other possible channels identified in the literature, the channel of liberty-to-innovation does not require additional and often ad hoc assumptions about the personality, preferences, and skills of rulers to operate.

Our theory, centered on the channel of liberty-to-innovation, is thus more parsimonious than other theories on regime and growth that are explicitly or implicitly centered on other channels. The theory has two straightforward empirical predictions. The first prediction is that, historically, only autocracies have killed key scientific innovations. Chapter 5 presents qualitative evidence for the theory's first prediction by examining three prominent his-torical cases: the Roman Catholic Church's Inquisition against Galileo, the reign of Lysenko's pseudoscience over genetics in the former Soviet Union, and the suffocating of social sciences in communist countries.

The second prediction is that there should be a visible turning point in democracy's indirect effect on growth via the channel of liberty-to-innovation, conditioned by the level of economic development (see section I below). In this chapter, we present quantitative evidence for this prediction. Based on data of 1970–2010 from 79 (or 112) developing countries, we obtain strong empirical support for my theory.[2] To the best of our knowledge, we are the first to propose such an indirect and conditional effect of democracy on economic growth and to provide systematic, quantitative evidence.

Two caveats are in order here. First, because the empirical literature on democracy and growth is too voluminous for a brief critique, we have delegated our critique of the existing literature on this topic to appendix 5-A at the end of the book. Suffice it to note three key points. (1) There may be more than a single channel through which democracy impacts growth, and these channels interact with each other. (2) The channels through which democracy holds advantages versus autocracy when it comes to promot-ing growth may have been historically contingent: democracies might have held different advantages over autocracies in different historical times and contexts (e.g., Lindert 2003; Wu 2012). This suggests a nonlinear, if not a nonmonotonic, relationship between democracy and growth. (3) To the best of our knowledge, none of the existing works have theorized about and uncovered a channel in which democracy holds a unique advantage over autocracy.

Second, although at first glance our theory bears some similarities to Knutsen's (2015) thesis that democracy outgrows autocracy in the long run because democracy promotes faster growth of total factor productiv-ity (TFP), our exercise differs from Knutsen's work on three key fronts. (1) Our theory is a far more integrated effort than Knutsen's theorization. (2) Our theory singles out the channel of liberty-to-innovation as the chan-nel in which democracy holds a unique advantage over autocracy, whereas Knutsen treats TFP growth as just another channel in which democracy may hold an advantage over autocracy (see also Acemoglu et al. 2019). (3). Our theory emphasizes that democracy's impact on growth via the channel of liberty-to-innovation is conditioned by the level of economic development (i.e., only after GDP per capita reaches a certain level does democracy's advantage kick in), whereas Knutsen (2015) argues that democracy's effect on TFP growth is unconditional.[3]

The rest of the chapter is structured as follows. Section I presents quantitative evidence for our new theory. Section II draws key theoretical and empirical implications. Section III follows with a brief conclusion.

I. Quantitative Evidence for the New Theory

Recall that our theory has two straightforward empirical predictions. First, democracy is a necessary, though insufficient, condition for protecting major scientific breakthroughs that may challenge orthodoxies. Second, there should be a visible turning point in democracy's effect on growth. More concretely, below a certain income level (measured in GDP per capita), democracy may or may not hold significant overall advantages over autocracy in promoting growth. However, after an economy reaches a certain income level and growth comes to depend more extensively on innovation, democracy's advantage over autocracy in promoting growth should become more significant. Moreover, the channel of liberty-to-innovation is unique: democracy has no similar indirect and conditional effect on other channels through which democracy may impact economic development. In this section, we provide systematic, quantitative evidence for the second empirical prediction of our theory.

A. SAMPLE AND DATA

As noted above, our theory predicts that below a certain level of economic development when growth mostly depends on imitation or catching up, democracy holds no statistically significant impact over the channel of liberty-to-innovation. After the economy reaches a certain level of development, and growth comes to depend more on innovation, however, democracy's positive effect on the channel of liberty-to-innovation becomes more critical. We further argue that specific institutions under democracy may actually hinder growth after a country becomes a fully developed country because developed democratic countries may possess growth-retarding dynamics (e.g., pork barrel politics, polarized partisan politics; Olson 1982). Accordingly, we should test our theory both with countries that have achieved developed country status relatively recently and with countries that have yet to achieve developed country status.[4]

For the sake of availability of sound macroeconomic data and other data, we choose countries that had not yet become developed economies in 1970. Following standard practices in cross-country growth regressions (CCGRs), we also exclude "oil economies" (e.g., Kuwait, Saudi Arabia) and economies with a population of less than a half million. Other countries excluded include newly independent countries (republics of the former Soviet Union) and former Eastern European socialist countries due to a lack of quality historical data before 1992. This leaves us with a sample of 79 countries or economies (table 6-A.1 in appendix 6-B at the end of the book). The time span of our sample is 1970 to 2010. In this chapter, we report the main results from this dataset. Descriptive statistics of our main dataset are shown in table 6.1. Extensive robustness tests are available from the author upon request.

As a set of robustness checks, we have also run the same set of regressions, including all the robustness tests, with data from 112 countries that include former Eastern and Central European socialist countries, even though these countries lack reliable data before 1992.[5] We obtain essentially identical results with this larger group of countries. Again, these additiomal robustness results are available from the author upon request.

B. STRATEGIES FOR EMPIRICAL TESTING

Our theory predicts two interacting pathways that connect democracy and growth via the channel of liberty-to-innovation (see figure 5.1). More specifically:

(1) Liberty (protected by democracy) to institutional innovation, to political stability, to private investment (which may reflect both political stability and technological innovation), and finally to economic growth

(2) Liberty (protected by democracy) to institutional innovation, to technological innovation, to private investment, and finally to economic growth

In reality, however, it is difficult to disentangle these two pathways. Moreover, the linkage between institutional innovation and technological innovation cannot be easily established with quantitative data, due to the lack of data on either bottom-up institutional innovation or technological innovation, even in developed countries. Indeed, most developing countries did not have a sound patent system until fairly recently, and patents capture only a very small fraction of technological innovations. Also, to the best

TABLE 6.1. Descriptive Statistics of Variables

Variables	Explanation	Observations	Mean	Median	Standard deviation	Max	Min
GDPpc	GDP per capita (constant 2005 price, taken log 10)	3,091	3.218	3.195	0.572	4.724	2.136
Growth	Growth rate of GDP per capita (%)	3,117	1.794	2.112	5.156	37.128	−47.723
GDP deflator	GDP deflator (%)	3,117	49.945	8.417	628.649	26,765.9	−29.173
GCF	Gross capital formation (%)	3,065	22.062	21.636	8.111	73.495	−5.740
Pop. growth	Population growth rate (%)	3,239	2.134	2.233	1.100	11.181	−6.343
Polity2	Polity2 score	3,235	0.647	0	7.113	10	−10
Lexical	Lexical index	3,237	3.432	3	2.413	6	0
Stability	Stability	3,153	25,086	26,062	2,058	26,187	0
Openness	Openness (%)	3,161	68.792	57.35	48.023	453.44	4.83
ELF6	Ethnolinguistic fractionalization	3,239	0.386	0.376	0.293	0.910	0.000
Schooling	Average school years	3,075	5.464	5.36	2.574	11.85	0.29
EA	East Asia	3,239	0.089	0	0.284	1	0
SSA	Sub-Saharan Africa	3,239	0.342	0	0.474	1	0
LAC	Latin America and the Caribbean	3,239	0.278	0	0.448	1	0
Landlocked	Landlocked or not	3,239	0.203	0	0.402	1	0
Tropical	Tropical (proportion)	3,239	0.635	1	0.456	1	0
Mortality	Child mortality (ln)	3,211	4.116	4.270	1.028	5.991	1.030
Life exp.	Life expectancy (ln)	3,239	4.107	4.149	0.184	4.402	3.287
CTFP	Current TFP level	2,288	0.620	0.600	0.299	2.388	0.0732
CTFP growth	Growth rate of current TFP level	2,267	0.0130	−0.00418	0.426	18.853	−0.543
RTFP	Real TFP level	2,288	1.032	1	0.232	2.238	0.359
RTFP growth	Growth rate of real TFP level	2,267	0.000709	0.00264	0.0624	0.797	−0.564

of our knowledge, there is no existing dataset that measures institutional innovations.

We therefore resort to a partial and indirect empirical strategy that tests these two pathways together. We seek to establish two key links within the causal pathway from liberty to stability and from stability to economic growth. We first show that stability directly contributes to economic growth. Next, we show that democracy has an indirect effect on stability, conditioned by the level of economic development. We reason that more bottom-up institutional innovation reduces social conflict and hence enhances stability. As such, democracy should enhance stability, and this effect is conditioned by the level of economic development.[6] With liberty and bottom-up institutional innovation, political instability tends to be low and individuals tend to invest more in the economy. And when individuals invest more in the economy, it can be expected that more technological innovations will be produced. Both dynamics thus imply more growth. Hence, by identifying democracy's positive effect on political stability that is conditioned by the level of economic development, we indirectly identify the effect of the liberty-to-innovation channel on economic development, conditioned by the level of economic development.

As noted above, our theory does not exclude the possibility that democracy (via liberty) can and perhaps does impact growth via other channels, either positively or negatively. These channels may range from human capital to openness of the economy and gross capital formation (see appendix 6-A for details). What we contend is that the channel of liberty-to-innovation is the only channel in which democracy holds a distinct advantage: nondemocracy cannot imitate democracy on this front, fundamentally. As such, our theory predicts that democracy's conditional effect on the channel of liberty-to-innovation via political stability to private investment and finally to growth should be unique. In other words, democracy's effect on political stability conditioned by the level of economic development should be robust, whereas democracy should not have the same robust conditional effect on other channels even if these channels may contribute to economic growth.

C. MODELS, PROCEDURES, AND RESULTS

We estimate the following model for specific channels that may link democracy with economic development.[7]

$$Y_{i,t} = \alpha_i + \beta_1 \text{Demo}_{i,t} + \beta_2 \text{GDPpc}_{i,t} + \beta_3 (\text{Demo}_{i,t} * \text{GDPpc}_{i,t}) + \gamma Z_{i,t} + \varepsilon_{i,t}$$

where $Y_{i,t}$ is the dependent variable of interest (e.g., growth rate of GDP per capita, political stability, gross capital formation, etc.) of country i at time t. Demo$_{i,t}$ is the democracy score of country i at time t. GDPpc$_{i,t}$ is the level of GDP per capita (as the indicator of the level of economic development) of country i at time t. To make the interpretation of results with interaction terms easier, we take log 10 for GDP per capita. $Z_{i,t}$ is the set of control variables for country i at time t. Finally, $\varepsilon_{i,t}$ is the error term. All standard errors are clustered to countries.

For all the models, we are mostly interested in β_3, that is, the beta-coefficient in front of the interaction term of democracy score and level of economic development. We expect β_3 to be positive and significant only when the dependent variable is political stability but not with indicators for other channels. And these results should be quite robust with different indicators of democracy and model specifications.

For all the results reported here, we performed extensive robustness tests. These tests include (1) lagging all independent variables one to three years; (2) using the very recent lexical index, which is supposedly a more rigorous conceptualization for measuring electoral democracy than the Polity2 score (Skanning et al. 2015); (3) converting all data to three-year or five-year averages to minimize the possible impact of shocks; and (4) employing data from 112 countries. Suffice it to say that our results hold throughout all these extensive robustness tests. Again, these robustness tests are available from the author upon request.

We admit that endogeneity may pose a problem for our results. Unfortunately, we do not see any viable instrumental variable because we are exploring interaction models. Although system GMM may be a useful technique, results from system GMM tend to be quite fragile (e.g., Bazzi and Clemens 2013; Murtin and Wacziarg 2014). Most critically, because our theory predicts a unique channel in which democracy holds a conditional positive effect, if we can show that this channel is indeed unique and robust to a variety of robustness checks, we shall have dispelled any doubt about our results.

1. Democracy's Uncertain Direct Effect on Growth

Table 6.2 presents the results that test democracy's direct effect on economic growth, with the Polity2 score as the indicator for democracy. The dependent variable here is the growth rate of GDP per capita. Consistent with several recent studies (e.g., Murtin and Wacziarg 2014; Truex 2017; cf. Acemoglu et al. 2019), we also find that the direct relationship from democracy to economic growth is uncertain. Model 1 is the baseline growth model.

TABLE 6.2. Baseline Growth Models with Polity2 Score

(Dependent variable: Growth rate of GDP per capita)

	(1) FE	(2) FE	(3) FE	(4) FE	(5) FE	(6) RE	(7) RE	(8) FE
Polity2		0.0192 (0.0258)	0.0129 (0.0259)	0.0217 (0.0260)	0.0272 (0.0328)	0.0355 (0.0222)	0.0419* (0.0244)	0.583*** (0.145)
GDPpc	−0.211 (1.223)		1.278 (1.439)	−0.344 (1.194)	−0.178 (1.292)	−0.431 (0.307)	−0.401 (0.299)	2.129 (1.337)
GCF	0.225*** (0.0252)			0.224*** (0.0253)	0.223*** (0.0249)	0.211*** (0.0224)	0.211*** (0.0222)	
Population growth	−0.251 (0.247)			−0.240 (0.249)	−0.253 (0.261)	−0.253 (0.211)	−0.270 (0.219)	
Time trend					−0.0465 (0.139)		−0.0722 (0.120)	
Polity2 * GDPpc								−0.183*** (0.0476)
EA						1.431*** (0.547)	1.430*** (0.550)	

	(1)	(2)	(3)	(4)	(5)	(6)	(7)	(8)
SSA						-0.290	-0.249	
						(0.393)	(0.411)	
LAC						-0.0739	-0.0911	
						(0.394)	(0.391)	
Landlocked						0.240	0.254	
						(0.375)	(0.378)	
Tropical						-0.457	-0.450	
						(0.378)	(0.377)	
ELF6						0.428	0.469	
						(0.585)	(0.589)	
Constant	-1.933	1.781***	-2.308	-1.536	-1.911	-0.910	-0.808	-4.757
	(4.052)	(0.0210)	(4.630)	(3.953)	(4.110)	(1.196)	(1.219)	(4.299)
Observations	3,002	3,115	3,079	3,000	3,000	3,000	3,000	3,079
R-squared	0.072	0.000	0.001	0.072	0.072	0.545	0.550	0.010
No. of countries	78	79	78	78	78	78	78	78

Note: All models are OLS models. Robust standard errors are clustered to country. Robust standard errors in parentheses; *** p < 0.01, ** p < 0.05, * p < 0.1. All tables in this chapter are reported in this format, unless indicated otherwise.

Consistent with the well-known thesis of "conditional convergence" in economic development, GDP per capita (in constant 2005 prices) has a negative sign but just misses the cutoff level of significance.[8] Meanwhile, gross capital formation has a positive sign and is highly significant. Model 2 regresses the Polity2 score alone while model 3 controls for GDP per capita; the Polity2 score is insignificant in both models. Model 4 inserts the Polity2 score in the full baseline growth model, and it remains insignificant. The effect of the Polity2 score remains insignificant after controlling for time trends (model 5). The Polity2 score becomes marginally significant after inserting more control variables and with random effects models (6 and 7). Overall, whether Polity2 is significant critically depends on model specification, suggesting that whether democracy has an overall and direct effect on economic growth is at least uncertain. We obtain essentially identical results whether we lag all explanatory variables one year, two years, or three years.[9] We obtain essentially the same results when using the lexical index as the indicator for democracy. Again, these robustness tests are available from the author upon request.

The key result of interest from table 6.2, however, is that democracy has no positive conditional effect on economic growth, regardless of whether the Polity2 score (or lexical index) is the indicator for democracy (model 8). This result holds whether we lag all explanatory variables one year, two years, or three years. These results suggest that there is a distinction between democracy's direct effect on growth and its indirect effect on growth via specific channels (see the results reported immediately below).

2. Establishing That Political Stability Contributes to Economic Growth

Next, we establish a key link in the causal pathway proposed by our theory, that is, political stability contributes to economic growth. As shown in table 6.3, stability is positively associated with economic growth, and its impact is highly significant and robust across models and samples.

3. Establishing the Positive Effect on Political Stability of Democracy * GDPpc

In table 6.4, we provide evidence for our central empirical hypothesis, that is, democracy positively contributes to political stability, and this effect is conditioned by the level of economic development. This is indeed what we found: the interaction term of the Polity2 score (or lexical index) and GDP

TABLE 6.3. Political Stability Contributes to Economic Growth

(Dependent variable: GDP per capita growth rate)

	(1) FE	(2) FE	(3) FE	(4) FE	(5) RE	(6) RE
Stability	0.000302***	0.000291***	0.000234***	0.000233***	0.000208***	0.000208***
	(6.90e-05)	(6.81e-05)	(5.96e-05)	(6.01e-05)	(5.79e-05)	(5.84e-05)
GDPpc		0.751	−0.672	−0.778	−0.380	−0.368
		(1.510)	(1.284)	(1.313)	(0.342)	(0.323)
GCF			0.218***	0.219***	0.202***	0.202***
			(0.0262)	(0.0258)	(0.0230)	(0.0227)
Population growth			−0.241	−0.233	−0.270	−0.275
			(0.238)	(0.255)	(0.206)	(0.222)
Time trend				0.0231		−0.0144
				(0.117)		(0.115)
EA					1.524***	1.522***
					(0.526)	(0.525)
SSA					−0.432	−0.425
					(0.383)	(0.392)
LAC					0.0969	0.0963
					(0.392)	(0.391)
Landlocked					0.337	0.342
					(0.386)	(0.391)
Tropical					−0.476	−0.472
					(0.370)	(0.366)
ELF6					0.557	0.566
					(0.616)	(0.615)
Constant	−5.722***	−7.840	−6.145	−5.871	−6.051***	−6.062***
	(1.732)	(5.094)	(4.484)	(4.549)	(1.992)	(1.978)
Observations	3,033	2,997	2,918	2,918	2,918	2,918
R-squared	0.012	0.012	0.078	0.078	0.516	0.517
No. of countries	79	78	78	78	78	78

Note: Robust standard errors in parentheses; *** $p < 0.01$, ** $p < 0.05$, * $p < 0.1$.

per capita is positive and highly significant, and this result is highly robust across different models. This result holds in our extensive robustness checks.

Democracy's effect on stability conditioned by the level of GDP per capita is graphically depicted in figure 6.1 with the Polity2 score (based on model 2 of table 6.4). As shown in figure 6.1, the Polity2 score has no significant

TABLE 6.4. Conditional Effect of Polity2 Score on Political Stability at Different Levels of GDP per Capita

(Dependent variable: Political stability)

	(1) FE	(2) FE	(3) FE	(4) FE	(5) RE	(6) RE
Polity2	23.72*	−155.4**	−191.4***	−198.9***	−173.4***	−197.7***
	(13.58)	(65.91)	(68.57)	(72.80)	(63.08)	(67.73)
GDPpc	1,698***	1,433***	1,245***	1,089*	735.3**	547.1*
	(531.0)	(491.2)	(465.5)	(563.3)	(305.5)	(303.9)
Polity2 * GDPpc		57.59**	71.20***	72.18***	62.25***	65.74***
		(22.57)	(23.21)	(23.67)	(20.70)	(21.46)
GCF			27.53***	28.16***	30.52***	31.83***
			(7.277)	(7.398)	(7.152)	(6.984)
Population growth			51.78	62.08	44.23	80.82*
			(64.40)	(54.55)	(58.01)	(45.97)
Time trend				39.19		123.0*
				(80.56)		(67.62)
EA					−544.7	−545.4
					(537.5)	(518.6)
SSA					890.5**	756.3*
					(452.3)	(438.1)
LAC					−342.9	−299.4
					(396.0)	(375.3)
Landlocked					221.8	147.1
					(247.0)	(240.6)
Tropical					331.7	280.9
					(364.1)	(332.4)
ELF6					−117.2	−221.5
					(413.4)	(412.5)
Constant	19,583***	20,344***	20,173***	20,540***	21,458***	21,756***
	(1,711)	(1,571)	(1,512)	(1,708)	(1,148)	(1,110)
Observations	3,007	3,007	2,926	2,926	2,926	2,926
R-squared	0.022	0.029	0.040	0.040	0.138	0.179
No. of countries	79	79	79	79	79	79

Note: Robust standard errors in parentheses; *** $p < 0.01$, ** $p < 0.05$, * $p < 0.1$.

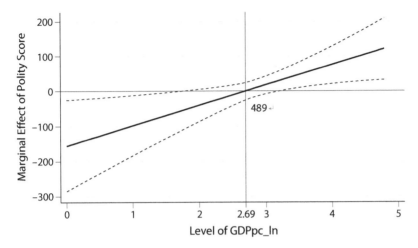

FIGURE 6.1. Marginal Effect of Polity2 Score on Stability at All Levels of GDPpc_log 10. Graph is based on model 2 of table 6.4. The number 489 (US$, constant 2005 price) is the level of GDP per capita where the Polity2 score begins to have a significant positive effect on stability. Dashed lines represent the 95% confidence interval.

conditional effect on stability below the GDP per capita level of of 489 (in constant 2005 US$), but it begins to have a positive conditional effect on stability above that level. This positive conditional effect becomes stronger as the level of GDP per capita goes higher. The same pattern holds for the lexical index, although the threshold is lower for it than for the Polity2 score.[10]

With the results from tables 6.3 and 6.4, we can now calculate the growth rate of GDP per capita under different combinations of GDPpc and Polity2 scores. These results are presented in table 6.5.

With the Polity2 score as the indicator of democracy, at the level of GDP per capita of $500 USD (constant 2005 prices), the growth rate of GDP in a fully autocratic country (i.e., Polity2 score is −10) is identical to that in a fully democratic country (i.e., Polity2 score is 10). At the level of GDP per capita of $1000 USD, a fully democratic country will only grow about 5.5% faster than a fully autocratic country (annual growth rate for democracy is 1.93% vs. 1.83% for autocracy). At the level of GDP per capita of $2000 USD, however, a fully democratic country will now grow about 12.5% faster than a fully autocratic country (annual growth rate for democracy is 1.87% vs. 1.66% for autocracy).

Moreover, this "democratic advantage" widens as the GDP per capita of an economy increases. At the level of GDP per capita of $4000 USD, a fully democratic country will grow about 20% faster than a fully autocratic country (annual growth rate for democracy is 1.8% vs. 1.5% for autocracy). At the

TABLE 6.5. Growth Rate of GDPpc with Different Combinations of Polity2 Scores and GDPpc

(GDP per capita in constant 2005 US$)

GDPpc	Polity = −10		Polity = −5		Polity = 0		Polity = 5		Polity = 10	
	Stability	Growth (100%)	Stability	Growth (100%)	Stability	Growth (100%)	Stability	Growth (100%)	Stability	Growth (100%)
100	23,867.97	2.37	23,622.97	2.32	23,377.97	2.26	23,132.97	2.20	22,887.97	2.14
500	24,241.07	1.99	24,245.27	1.99	24,249.47	1.99	24,253.67	1.99	24,257.87	1.99
1,000	24,400.97	1.83	24,511.97	1.85	24,622.97	1.88	24,733.97	1.90	24,844.97	1.93
2,000	24,560.87	1.66	24,778.67	1.71	24,996.47	1.76	25,214.27	1.81	25,432.07	1.87
4,000	24,720.77	1.50	25,045.37	1.57	25,369.97	1.65	25,694.57	1.73	26,019.17	1.8
8,000	24,880.67	1.33	25,312.07	1.43	25,743.47	1.54	26,174.87	1.64	26,606.27	1.74
10,000	24,933.97	1.28	25,400.97	1.39	25,867.97	1.5	26,334.97	1.61	26,801.97	1.72

Note: Growth rate of GDPpc calculated according to model 3 of table 6.3 and model 3 of table 6.4, with control variables taking the mean value.

level of GDP per capita of $8000 USD, the democratic advantage widens to 30% faster (1.74% vs. 1.33%). At the level of GDP per capita of $10,000 USD, the democratic advantage further widens to 35% faster (1.72% vs. 1.28%).

Indeed, as the GDP per capita of an economy increases, even a half-democratic country (i.e., Polity2 score is 5) will enjoy some significant democratic advantages over a half-autocratic country (i.e., Polity2 score is −5). At the level of GDP per capita of $4000 USD, even a half-democratic country will grow about 10% faster than a half-autocratic country (1.73% for the former vs. 1.57% for the latter). At the level of GDP per capita of $8000 USD, this advantage widens to 14% (1.64% vs. 1.43%).

Here, it is interesting to note that consistent with the conditional convergence thesis in economic development (as captured in the baseline growth model), the growth rate of GDP per capita decreases as the GDP per capita of an economy increases. Yet, consistent with our core theoretical prediction, after crossing the threshold level of GDP per capita (i.e., the turning point), democracy's (relative) advantage over autocracy becomes stronger as the GDP per capita of an economy increases and as a country becomes more democratic. A similar pattern emerges with the lexical index as the indicator of democracy.

4. Democracy * GDPpc Has No Similar Effect on Other Channels

Next, we show that democracy has no such conditional effect on other channels. We have tested all the channels for which we have reliable data. The only channel that we have not tested is "state capacity," because there is much conceptual and measurement uncertainty with indicators of state capacity and the relationship between indicators of state capacity with economic growth may be quite complex and nonmonotonic (Hendrix 2010; Hanson and Sigman 2013; see also the 2014 special issue of *Democratization*, vol. 21, no. 7).[11]

The channels we have tested include human capital (measured in average school years), economic openness, total factor productivity (TFP, measured in either current or constant dollars; data from Penn World Table 7.0), growth rate of TFP, and gross capital formation. Suffice it to say that we have found no conditional effect of democracy * GDPpc other than the channel of gross capital formation. Interestingly, democracy * GDPpc has a negative conditional effect on gross capital formation, and this effect is also highly robust. Together, these results strongly suggest that the channel of liberty-to-innovation via political stability is indeed a unique channel in which democracy holds a distinct advantage over autocracy.

D. SUMMARY

Overall, our extensive quantitative results strongly support our theory. Democracy has a strong, indirect, and positive effect on political stability, conditioned by the level of economic development, and this effect is highly robust. Also consistent with our theory, democracy's indirect and positive effect on political stability becomes stronger as the level of economic development gets higher. Because political stability contributes to economic growth directly, these results suggest that democracy also has a strong, indirect, and positive effect on economic growth, conditioned by the level of economic development. Equally important, the channel of stability-to-growth is unique in the sense that democracy has no similar conditional effect on other possible channels through which democracy may impact economic growth.

II. Implications

We have advanced a new institutional theory that singles out the channel of liberty-to-innovation as the channel in which democracy holds a unique advantage over autocracy when it comes to prompting growth. In chapter 5, we presented qualitative evidence showing that only autocracies have killed key scientific breakthroughs and consistently stymied the growth of the social sciences. In this chapter, we present systematic, quantitative evidence for our theory. Together, these two chapters complete our defense of democracy's indirect and conditional advantage for promoting economic growth, especially growth via innovation.

Our theory holds important theoretical and empirical implications for understanding the relationship between democracy and growth and the relationship between institutions and growth in general. Theoretically, a key conclusion shared by our theory and a few others is that democracy's impact on growth is deeply contextual and historical rather than linear, monotonic, context-free, and transhistorical (e.g., Lindert 2003; Wu 2012). This insight gives us a possible direction for reconciling many seemingly contradictory pieces of evidence and theories and illuminating some of the empirical evidence that currently does not have a good theoretical explanation.

Empirically, our results provide a possible explanation for the many conflicting results from CCGR studies that show that democracy seems to hold a positive, negative, or no discernible advantage over autocracy when it comes to prompting growth (see the literature review in appendix 5-A).[12] Other than the more commonly acknowledged problems, such as quality of data (conceptualization, measurement, and selection bias), model specification, differences in estimation techniques, and several underappreciated methodological problems in growth regressions with cross-sectional and panel data (for earlier discussions, see Temple 2000; de Haan 2007; Truex 2017), there may be two additional causes behind the inconclusiveness: the systemic nature of growth and the different demands on a society's institutions in different phases of economic development (see chapter 8).

First and foremost, rather than impacting growth directly, political regimes influence growth indirectly through the institutional foundations they lay down and the economic policies they make and implement (Easterly 2005; Rodrik 2005; Persson and Tabellini 2006). Moreover, achieving and sustaining growth is a systemic effort: a state has to play with the combinations of channels, and both democracies and autocracies can get some channels right but some channels wrong. When this is the case, a regime's positive effects and negative effects in different channels may cancel each other out. *This possibility makes it difficult to reveal a clear-cut direct overall advantage for democracy in CCGRs.* As such, a better strategy may be to pit democracy against autocracy in specific channels that may link regimes with growth and then assess the performance of democracy versus autocracy in these channels.

Second, different phases of economic development may require overlapping but nonidentical institutional systems. As such, regressions with all the countries in the world may not reveal any clear-cut relationship between regime and growth, and a more sensible strategy is to divide countries into samples according to their different stages of development and then compare regression results across the different samples of countries.

Take the liberty-to-innovation channel, for example. When countries are in the phase of growth via catching up, their growth largely depends on imitation, and they can grow "simply by modeling themselves on the more dynamic features of the more advanced" (Lewis 1955, 80). In contrast, when a country approaches the technological frontier (i.e., it has already caught up significantly), innovation becomes crucial for its growth. Hence, while autocracies may indeed catch up (or imitate) well when they are governed by a "wise" autocrat (e.g., Chiang Ching-kuo, Deng Xiaoping, Lee Kuan Yew, Park Chung-hee, and Pinochet), they simply cannot innovate well enough when their economies demand more innovation. Consequently, as an autocracy catches up, it may have to democratize in order to sustain further growth at the technological frontier, and autocracies that do not democratize will be less likely to sustain their growth momentum. Because the liberty-to-innovation channel is only one of many channels that underpin growth, however, democracy cannot hope to achieve growth automatically just by getting the liberty-to-innovation channel right. Moreover, because all modern states, democratic or autocratic, are heavily bureaucratic societies and they all require OTA to function, the difference in OTA between democracies and autocracies is only a matter of degree, and OTA may still prevail more often than it should even in democracies. Such a possibility inevitably makes revealing a clear-cut direct overall advantage for democracy in growth regressions more difficult.

Theoretically, if the notion holds that the impact of regime on growth is both contextual and historical, it may allow us to synthesize many divergent theoretical insights.

To begin with, as Rose-Ackerman (2003) perceptively noted, Mancur Olson (1982, 1993) had expounded two evidently conflicting theories on the relationship between regimes and growth. Whereas Olson (1982) had argued that vested interest groups are inimical to growth and periodical shattering of a society's power structure may be necessary for restarting the economy (e.g., Japan and Germany after WWII), Olson (1993) contended that although a "stationary bandit" (i.e., autocracy) is definitely better than "roving (petty) bandits" (i.e., anarchy) in promoting growth in the beginning of organized economic life, only democracy can protect property rights credibly and thus sustain growth in the long run. The tension between "framework [i.e., institutional] stability" and "coalitional stability" within Olson's two stances is all too apparent. Unfortunately, although Rose-Ackerman (2003, esp. 164–68) correctly grasped this tension within Olson's oeuvre and pointed out that Olson's two stances started with two different background assumptions, neither she nor Olson (2000) could resolve the tension satisfactorily.

Our theory points to a possible dynamic solution to Olson's self-contradiction. The solution is that the institutional system for starting and sustaining growth in most developing countries, which contain more autocracies than democracies until very recently, may be different, if not very different, from the institutional system for sustaining growth in developed countries that are mostly democracies. For most late developing countries, basic political order, essential state capacity most prominently embodied in political power that monopolizes violence and infrastructural power (such as a Weberian and effective bureaucracy), and secure property rights are the most critical requirements (Mann 1986, 1993; Evans and Rauch 1999; Kohli 2004; Slater 2010; Vu 2010a).

In contrast, for developed countries that are also mature democracies, preventing the capture of the state by vested interest groups (hence limiting unproductive redistribution, which may include unsustainable welfare spending) and sustaining a work ethic despite the increasing welfare state become more critical. Also, good governance is crucial for sustained growth regardless of regime type (Easterly 2005; Rodrik 2005).

Indeed, Olson was grappling with the possible different institutional foundations for growth in different developmental stages, even though both Olson and Rose-Ackerman (2003) have failed to grasp it. Whereas Olson (1982) dealt with growth in democratic developed countries, Olson (1993) dealt with economic development in the very beginning of organized economic activities in human history and the (re)establishment of order in late developers. When economic development varies greatly across time and space, we need a social evolutionary approach for understanding it (for a more detailed discussion, see chapter 7 and Tang 2020).

Second, Lindert (2003) links voice (which can only be adequate under full democracy, via franchising) to human capital and argues that democracy increasingly contributes to growth via human capital as history moves from the seventeenth through nineteenth centuries to the twentieth century. Our theory and evidence suggest the impact of voice on growth may not be due to the accumulation of human capital alone, but also to the fuller realization of the potential of human capital under democracy. Because democracy protects liberty and thus facilitates bottom-up innovation better than autocracy, human capital reaps greater returns under democracy, especially at the stage of growth via innovation.

Third, the notion that the impact of regime on growth is both contextual and historical suggests a new twist to the empirically well-supported Lipset thesis that countries with a higher development (or income) level are more likely to have democratic governments (Lipset 1959; Barro 1997, ch. 2; Przeworski et al. 2000). Because democracy is critical to sustaining growth via bottom-up innovation, democratic regimes are more likely to deliver better economic performances in middle-income countries or above. As a result, democracies are more likely to acquire performance-based legitimacy in these countries and thus are more likely to survive. This suggests that a robust correlation between high income and democracy is observed precisely because democracy becomes more critical at a relatively high level of economic development.

Fourth, in light of the notion that the impact of regime type on growth is both context dependent and historical, the almost exclusive focus on property rights (as "credible constraints on the extractive/predatory executive or Leviathan") in much of the NIE literature on growth has been unwarranted, if not misguided (e.g., North and Thomas 1973; North 1981; North and Weingast 1989; Olson 1993, 2000; Acemoglu et al. 2005; Acemoglu and Robinson 2012). Although the channel of property rights is certainly a key dimension in the overall institutional foundation of growth, it is not the only dimension (Bardhan 2005a). After all, long before NIE became dominant, Milton Friedman (1962, 10) had pointed out that while all liberal democracies have secure property rights, it is not the case that every state with secure property rights is a liberal democracy.

Therefore, NIE must (re)connect with the literature on comparative economic development, most prominently represented by the literature on the developmental state (e.g., Gerschenkron 1962; Johnson 1982, 1995; Deyo 1987; Amsden 1989; Haggard 1990; Wade 1990; Evans 1995; Kohli 2004; Slater 2010; Vu 2010a; for a similar call, see Bardhan 2016). In short, we need "a more nuanced theory of the state" (Bardhan 1989; see also Lewis 1984). At the very least, NIE must grasp that the state can do far more than just protecting or not protecting property rights. The key question for any useful economic theory of development is thus as much about the positives of making the state a helping hand as it is about the negatives of preventing states from being a grabbing hand.

Finally, our discussion also holds all too apparent implications for understanding the different challenges faced by two key developing countries: China and India. According to my theory and results, China will be increasingly hard-pressed to sustain its phenomenal growth without (smooth) democratization, now that it has reached the level of $8000 USD in per capita GDP (2015 prices, World Bank). Whether and when China will democratize relatively smoothly therefore has huge political and economic implications. Meanwhile, India faces a different set of problems. Due to a lack of strong state capacity from its colonial and democratic legacies, India has been slow in adopting necessary policy changes and building adequate infrastructure (including human capital). Hence, these two countries face two very different sets of problems, and it is not always enlightening to compare them on equal grounds (see also chapter 8).

III. Concluding Remarks

We have developed a more integrated and parsimonious theory regarding democracy's unique advantage in promoting economic development. Our discussion underscores that democracy holds an inherent advantage when it comes to growth via innovation. By protecting liberty, democracy protects our rights to innovate bottom-up and change thus also our hope for continuous progress. In contrast, by taking away our liberty, autocracy takes away our rights of continuous innovation, thus our hope for continuous progress (Popper [1945] 1966, vol. 2, 223; Polanyi 1956).

When defending the virtues of liberty and democracy, many have argued either that liberty is the best solution to the problem of knowledge (Polanyi 1941; Hayek 1945, 1960, ch. 2, 394; Lewis 1955, 80) or that liberal democracy is the best solution to social stability by allowing peaceful transfer of power (Mises [1962] 1996, 42). In light of our theory, these two arguments become two sides of the same coin: liberty presents the best solution for achieving the delicate balance between maintaining order and social stability and promoting the accumulation of knowledge (thus growth) under hierarchy, because liberty limits the negative impacts of hierarchy and OTA on learning without jeopardizing order and stability. Hence, the central challenge of liberalism is not merely reconciling freedom with authority but rather achieving a balance between freedom and authority for the most desirable social outcome (Preston 1983; see also Bhagwati 2002; Rose-Ackerman 2003).

7
Development as a Social Evolutionary Process

Why is economics not an evolutionary science?
—THORSTEIN VEBLEN (1898)

The Mecca of the economists lies in economic biology rather than in economic dynamics.
—ALFRED MARSHALL ([1920] 1982, XII)

The essential point to grasp is that in dealing with capitalism we are dealing with an evolutionary process.
—JOSEPH SCHUMPETER ([1943] 2003, 82)

This chapter underscores the simple yet underappreciated fact that development is a social evolutionary process, in a double sense, and then explores its implications for understanding development. IFED is a system by definition: it consists of several dimensions, with each dimension having many specific institutional arrangements interacting with each other. As such, it has to be understood with a systemic approach (Jervis 1997). Because every system populated by human beings is also a social evolutionary system, however, IFED also has to be understood through a social evolutionary approach (Tang 2020), in addition to a systemic approach. My discussion proceeds in two parts.

In the first part (sections I and II), I explore the (evolutionary) systemic nature of IFED and its theoretical and empirical implications for understanding the role of institutions in development. In the second part (sections III and IV), I outline some initial ideas regarding the fact that development is a social evolutionary process, along with the theoretical and empirical implications of those ideas for understanding development (Tang 2020).[1] Section V offers some concluding thoughts.

All together, this chapter lays some of the groundwork for addressing a far more complex and challenging puzzle (i.e., the "new development triangle") in chapter 8.

I. IFED as an Evolutionary System and Its Theoretical Implications

The fact that IFED is an evolutionary system dictates three immediate implications. First and foremost, because institutions interact with each other (and institutions often require other institutions to function), "the efficiency of a particular institutional arrangement cannot be assessed without referring to the other related institutional arrangements in that society. An institutional arrangement that is efficient in one society may not be efficient in other societies" (Lin 1989, 3–7; see also Ogilvie and Carus 2014, 461–69).

By logical extension, even if two economies are performing comparably, they may contain different individual institutional arrangements: "very different institutional structures have often been found to be reasonable substitutes for each other, both in dissimilar as well as similar contexts" (Engerman and Sokoloff 2005, 641; see also 647–48). In other words, growth and stagnation can happen in a variety of institutional settings.

Second, the six dimensions and specific arrangements within those dimensions in different societies have evolved in different historical settings. Two quick observations regarding the evolutionary history of the six dimensions can be made: (1) each dimension of IFED has evolved gradually, perhaps taking centuries, sometimes millennia; and (2) there may have been a rough historical sequence through which different institutions came to exist (Diamond 1997). Social and political stability provided by band or tribe came first. Once hierarchy came to exist, the positional market began to take shape. The channel of social mobility also came to exist, but only in a very limited sense because high social status in most traditional societies could only be achieved by inheritance or social revolt. Once some sort of specialization existed within a tribe, there could be an exchange of goods, and a market (not in the modern sense of a regulated market) came to exist. Yet, large markets evolved from intratribal exchange to intertribal exchange, long-distance exchange, a national market, and finally the extensively regulated and protected international trade system today. Private property rights came first, and property rights exempt from state expropriation came to exist much later. Liberty definitely came after social mobility in history. And for most of our history, redistribution has been one-way: from the subjects (or the poor) to the ruling class (or the rich). Institutionalized income redistribution for the poor is a very modern phenomenon.

Third, and immediately following from the second implication, just because good and bad things tend to cluster today (i.e., they are correlated with each other) does not mean that they came as "clusters" or had common roots historically (cf. Besley and Persson 2011). Even for developed countries, good things came in a mostly haphazard and messy way rather than in one tidy package. Certainly, state capacity, internal peace, and high income could not have come together in historical time in one stroke in the real world, even in Western Europe (Elias [1939] 1994; Hintze 1975; Tilly 1975, 1990). Indeed, internal peace within a core territory, not to mention essential state capacities, comes very slowly (see also Slater 2010; Vu 2010a). In short, for most of our history, few states have ever had all the good or bad things in place at one time, and it is misleading to believe that clustering is key to development in most developing countries.

The key point here is that different societies have come to possess their different institutions through various routes and means. As a result, equifinality is the key to understanding their evolution. Unfortunately, many have failed to grasp this key point and its implications. Consequently, their interpretations of economic history, some of which have become conventional wisdom, are wanting (Ogilvie and Carus 2014).

For instance, many have argued that Europe's fortune was its disunity, while imperial China's misfortune was its unity (Jones 2003; Chaudhry and Garner 2007; Diamond 1997, 414–16; Epstein 2000, 25–28; Landes 1998, 35–39). From a systemic perspective, however, this argument is half right at best (see also Mokyr 2002, 278–82; cf. Olson 1982).

By itself, unity under hierarchy is undoubtedly a boon for development (see chapter 2). Unity means a larger population and a larger market, and a larger population means more talent for innovation while a larger market means greater potential returns for innovations and entrepreneurship (Jones 2005; Simon 1981; Sokoloff 1988). Unity also usually means a common language, a common measurement system, a common currency, and a common legal code, and each of these measures reduces transaction costs greatly.

Immediately after unifying China in 221 BC, Emperor Qin Shi-huang did exactly those four things: unify the Chinese written language, unify the measurement system, introduce a common currency, and of course, impose a common legal order. While the Qin dynasty did not last long (a mere 15 years), these four institutional measures laid down a key part of the foundation for the first Chinese "efflorescence" in the Han dynasty that followed (202 BC to AD 220). In fact, all of China's episodes of efflorescence occurred in periods where unity was at its core—in the Han, Tang, Song, Ming, and Qing dynasties (Goldstone 2002; see also Epstein 2000; Wang 2004).[2] Indeed, these institutional foundations have continued to play critical roles in sustaining China's development in the past four decades or so.

Today, by introducing the euro and establishing the European Parliament, the European Union is doing two to three of the four things that Emperor Qin did. Just imagine how much transaction costs could be reduced if European states had a common language; it would surely reduce the cost of translation in Brussels![3] (See Shiue and Keller 2007; Ko et al. 2017.)

In contrast, without political unity and thus social and political stability, investment faces much uncertainty (Epstein 2000, 7–9). Because nation-states not only reduce coordination costs and transaction costs but also increase potential returns, unity by itself is a boon for development. It was perhaps no accident that modern development first emerged in European countries that had achieved political unification and centralization earlier (i.e., Britain, France; see Elias [1939] 1994; Epstein 2000; Pagano 2003; Huang and Tang 2018).

Yet, hierarchy that underpins political and economic unity is only one dimension of IFED, and it does not operate independently from other dimensions of IFED: when paired with an oppressive regime, hierarchy may well become a disadvantage rather than an advantage. Without sufficient internal competition of ideas or liberty protected by democracy, hierarchy may well kill creativity and lead to stagnation and decay (see chapters 5 and 6). Hence, political disunity resulted in good fortune for Europe while political unity was a misfortune for China—not because of disunity or unity per se, but because there was no liberal society on both continents at that time. Today, with the free competition of ideas guaranteed by democracy, political unity in Europe is a virtue (see chapters 5 and 6; see also Mokyr 2017, ch. 16).

A somewhat related consequence of failing to grasp the three key implications has been an overemphasis of any one dimension (e.g., property rights) within IFED, while neglecting the interaction between different institutions (Williamson 2000; Engerman and Sokoloff 2005; Glaeser et al. 2004). Thus, several important works on institutions and growth have essentially argued that autocracy cannot work (Acemoglu and Robinson 2012; Besley and Persson 2011; see also Engerman and Sokoloff 2012), implicitly or explicitly. Yet, because liberty protected by democracy is only one dimension of IFED and is not necessary for development, it should not be a surprise that development can happen without full democracy (see chapters 5 and 6; see also Besley and Kudamatsu 2008).

Overall, without the social evolutionary component, NIE theorists have often found their theorization to be unable to accommodate economic history and hence have tended to squeeze facts into their ill-fitting framework (for a similar take, see Mokyr 2017).

II. IFED as an Evolutionary System and Its Empirical Implications

Since Barro (1991), Levine and Renelt (1992), and Mankiw et al. (1992), cross-country growth regressions (CCGRs) have taught us many valuable things. Yet, the existing CCGR literature has yet to take seriously the notion that IFED is a system in which many institutional arrangements interact with each other. By comparison, more recent comparative case studies of economic development have done a better job than CCGRs, but even these studies have failed to explicitly acknowledge this key point. This section outlines the key implications for our empirical effort to understand the role of institutions in development held by the systemic (and evolutionary) nature of IFED,[4] for both CCGR and comparative case studies, although my discussion here focuses on the former.

As Aron (2000, 100) pointed out, due to the lack of a systemic understanding of just what constitutes IFED, the CCGR literature that tries to link institutions with economic performance suffers from "a range of serious problems with data, methodology, and identification." (See also Temple 1999.) Among other things, seven key deficiencies stand out.

Foremost, many studies treat different dimensions of IFED as a single entity and test their effects on growth. This problem is especially severe in studies trying to correlate political regimes with development. Political regimes, as meta-institutions, impact development not directly but only indirectly through specific institutions. Hence, to understand a political regime's impact on development, we need to understand how the regime shapes specific institutions, which in turn shape development. When this is not done, regime type has been found to have no consistent direct and unconditional effect on development in most CCGRs (see chapters 5 and 6; see also Knutsen 2012; Truex 2017).

Second, blunt typologies, either dichotomous or even trichotomous, may be useful theoretical heuristics as starting points (e.g., Olson 2000; Kohli 2004; North et al. 2009; Acemoglu and Robinson 2012), but they are simply too static and hence of little theoretical value. Also, the same notion may denote very different practical meanings in different times and spaces. For instance, whereas the liberal concept of freedom today underpins the ideology of shared citizenship within modern states, premodern freedoms challenged the state's claim to undivided and final sovereignty (Epstein 2000, 15). Indeed, the concept of freedom as privilege is central to modern understandings of freedom (Epstein 2000, ch. 2).

Third, some indicators that supposedly measure institutional qualities do not actually measure the quality of specific institutional arrangements, but rather "bundled institutions." As Glaeser et al. (2004) have pointed out, this might have been a major problem with some of Acemoglu et al.'s (2001, 2002, 2005) empirical work emphasizing the role of secure property rights and constraints on the executive. When all the good things are bundled under or taken as measuring protection of property rights, surely one can find that secure property rights are conducive to development (see also Besley and Persson 2011).

Fourth, some indicators that supposedly measure institutional qualities actually measure the (combined) effect of several institutional arrangements or even development itself. This problem is far more debilitating for our empirical effort than the problem of endogeneity.

The quality of governance (QoG) is one prominent example. QoG is an outcome rather than a cause of development (see chapter 8 for details; see also Kurtz and Schrank 2007).[5] A similar case can be made regarding the role of social trust in development. The level of general social trust, as an important indicator of social capital, has been argued to have a positive correlation with development (e.g., Putnam 1993; Knack and Keefer 1997; Zak and Knack 2001). Yet, as Knack and Keefer (1997, 1277–84) themselves have admitted, the level of general social trust most likely reflects historical outcomes shaped not only by institutional arrangements, such as the restraining of executives and enforcement of contracts, but also by socioeconomic development itself (Algan and Cahuc 2014). As such, the positive correlation between social trust and development does not mean that much, even if it is robust. Certainly, trust is not very "cultural" in the conventional sense because it can change rather rapidly. According to Williamson (2000), culture belongs to the first level of institutions, and its time frame for change is usually in the range of 100 to 1,000 years. Yet, the level of general social trust in the 29 countries within Knack and Keefer's sample decreased from about 60% in the 1950s to about 30% in the 1990s (1997, 1267).[6]

Fifth, there has been much redundancy among the indicators: many indicators that supposedly measure different dimensions of IFED may actually be measuring the same thing. When several indicators that measure overlapping things are put onto the right side of regression models, causal inference becomes deeply problematic.

Sixth, different dimensions of IFED can shape each other via intermediating outcomes, including development itself. Hence, most (if not all) institutional factors that are on the right side of CCGRs are subject to dynamic interactions among themselves and other variables. As a result, few robust linear correlations between institutions and development can be obtained in CCGRs, especially with panel data that covers a long period of time (i.e., more than one decade or more). This problem does not go away even if we design a set of indicators that independently measure different dimensions of IFED. Most CCGRs have so far had, and will continue to have, a hard time capturing this interaction among different institutional factors (Pack 1994, 68–69; Manski 2000, 117). Indeed, CCGRs have mostly ignored this interaction and its potential impact on growth (Ghosh and Wolf 1998).

Seventh, many have stressed interactions between informal constraints (e.g., culture, ideology, social capital) and formal institutions as a fundamental force behind institutional and economic changes (Denzau and North 1994; Fedderke et al.1999; Greif 1994, 1998; North 1981, 1990; Ruttan and Hayami 1984). Without specifying dimensions of IFED and measuring them, however, it is difficult to understand this interaction and assess its impact on formal institutions and development.

To address these shortcomings, four improvements are urgently needed. First, we need to reject simplistic CCGRs without theorization. Second, we need to implement better econometric practices when running CCGRs, now guided by better theorization. Third, we need to combine CCGRs with in-depth case studies with process tracing in order to better understand development. We simply cannot rely on CCGRs to truly prove that a particular dimension of an institution is fundamental for growth. We need to examine different actual development paths with process tracing. The institutional approach toward development has been, and perhaps will continue to be, a mainly historical approach. Fourth, and most critically, we need a set of indicators that better measure the quality of institutional arrangements. By providing a systemic understanding of IFED, our framework may just provide the basis for designing such a set of indicators.

Aron (2000) posited two principles for constructing the indicators: (1) measurements of *quality of institutions* rather than *attributes* of institutions should be preferred for correlating institutions with economic performance, and (2) objective indexes should be preferred because subjective indexes can be easily colored by dramatic events and cognitive biases. Besides Aron's principles, two more should be added: measuring institutions as defined and measurement with parsimony. The first, measuring institutions as defined, means that indicators must truly measure institutions rather than intermediating outcomes or economic development itself. For instance, among the five "striking points" identified by the World Bank (2008) for high-growth countries in its *Growth Report*, only one (credible commitment) can be reasonably understood as capturing the quality of some institutions.[7] Similarly, Rodrik (2007) listed six institutions, but only two can reasonably be understood as institutions (as rules), whereas the other four are organizations or bureaucracies. The second principle, measurement with parsimony, means that more parsimony is needed to reduce redundancy among indicators. By parsimony, we mean that different indicators must actually measure "independent" dimensions of IFED. Otherwise, as redundant indicators multiply, parsimony gets lost, and "it becomes harder and harder to believe in an underlying structural, reversible relation [that might have been uncovered in CCGRs]" (Solow 1994, 51).

With a better constructed set of indicators, we may finally be able to compare countries' institutional qualities and correlate them with economic performance, through both CCGR and comparative case studies with process tracing. We can also begin to explore the dynamic interactions between institutions and other factors (including development itself) with more precision in the coming years. If so, we may finally be able to offer some realistic and welfare-enhancing policy advice for LDCs (cf. Easterly 2001, 2005).

III. Development as an Evolutionary System and Its Implications

This section explores the theoretical and empirical implications of an evolutionary approach toward development, thus also preparing part of the groundwork for addressing a far more challenging puzzle, the new development triangle, in chapter 8. If development is an evolutionary system (Schumpeter [1943] 2003; Nelson and Winter 1982; Hodgson and Knudsen 2010; Tang 2017), what should we do when trying to understand development?

First of all, we need to reject the notion that the economic system has ever been a "natural" or "self-organized" system; this is the "invisible hand" myth populated by Smith ([1776] 1981) and Hayek (1979). Because politics and economy have never been separated other than in the minds of modern economics and economists, no economy has ever been a natural outcome. Rather, all economic systems have been a product of social evolution, deeply and extensively shaped by social-political power (Elias [1939] 1994; Polanyi [1944] 2001; Mann 1984; Tang 2020). Modern property rights and credible commitments have been outcomes of political struggles (Narizny 2019). Publicly funded education has been even more so the outcome of political processes and struggles, with Britain as the first industrialized country being a laggard in mass education for a very long time (Lindert 2003). Without exception, equality of opportunity for women and minority groups and democracy everywhere have always been outcomes of political struggles.

Second, searching for uni-causal linkages between production factors (labor, capital, and technology), institutions, and natural endowment (e.g., land) on the one hand and development on the other is missing the point because these factors are components of the same evolutionary system (Ang 2016).

The recent quarrel on the relative importance of natural endowment (land, original population, and colonial settlement), institutions, and human capital is illustrative. On one side, Engerman and Sokoloff (2005) argued that noninstitutional factors, especially colonies' different initial settings, had a long-lasting impact on their prosperity. Presenting a slightly different interpretation about the natural experiment of European colonies, Acemoglu et al. (2001) contended that institutions are the fundamental cause of long-term growth. In contrast, Glaeser et al. (2004) argued that human capital may be more decisive than institutions.

In light of the framework developed here, their differences can be easily bridged. In fact, when espousing the critical role of institutions, Acemoglu et al. (2001) explicitly admitted that initial settings of the colonies, along with settlers' mortality rate and initial prosperity, were critical factors for determining what institutions were introduced historically, thus echoing Engerman and Sokoloff's point that institutions are endogenous. Meanwhile, Glaeser et al. (2004) were right to point out that both Acemoglu et al. and

Engerman and Sokoloff neglected the potential impact of European settlers' human capital on development. Yet, Glaeser et al. (2004) might have failed to note that human capital, meaning the knowledge embedded in individuals, is also actually critical for constructing institutions. One can easily imagine that in colonies with few European settlers, introducing growth-facilitating institutions is not only more costly but also more difficult because of the shortage of tactical knowledge or human capital to run the institutions. The rational choice for European settlers, therefore, was to introduce exploitative institutions that required less human capital to operate. Hence, the three different positions can be readily synthesized, and together they provide us with a more holistic and more convincing picture, proving again that understanding the interactions among different factors as components of an evolutionary system called development is a more productive exercise than debating which factor is the most pivotal.

The shifting role of war, revolution, and external pressure or threat in shaping development also illustrates the evolutionary nature of development as a system. There is no doubt that war, revolution, and external pressure, as political competition, can lower the barriers to innovation and reform (e.g., Jones 2003; Olson 1982; Tilly 1990). Yet, war also destroys. And if liberalism encourages a "war of ideas", real wars become redundant. Certainly, much of the discussion about war's independent stimulating effect on development collapses with a counterfactual: What would happen if there was no war? (See Kuznets 1968, 57.)

Third, a theory of development cannot be anything else but *endogenous*. Inside the system, other than land at the very beginning, all other factors are dynamically linked and cannot be given exogenously. Each dimension of the institutional foundations evolves interactively with not only other institutional dimensions but also other production factors. Both institutions and culture are endogenous rather than exogenous, and institutions or culture alone cannot cause growth (Engerman and Sokoloff 2002, 2005; Sokoloff and Engerman 2000; Glaeser et al. 2004; Acemoglu et al. 2005; cf. Inglehart et al. 2000; Mokyr 2017).

Fourth, there may be some rough requirements on institutions and state capacity in different phases of economic development, as shown in table 7.1. Put somewhat simplistically, different phases of economic development may well require different institutions and state capacities.

Finally, some seemingly opposite forces should be taken as two faces of the same dynamic, and overemphasizing one while neglecting the other is counterproductive. In other words, a proper approach toward development

TABLE 7.1. Changing Demands on IFED in Different Stages of Economic Development

Ingredients\phases	Catching up I: Starting/initiating (very low income level)	Catching up II: Taking off (low income level)	Innovation I (in pockets): Sustaining (middle income level)	Innovation II (frontier): Maturing (high income level)
"Must have" institutions (regardless of regime type)	Order and stability National market Property rights: Rules and contracts Basic education and health care Some higher education	Besides those in phase I: More middle to higher education	Besides those in phases I and II: Universal basic education plus health care Extensive higher education Democratization and democracy	Besides those in phase III: Fully democratic
State capacity required	Some state autonomy Some leadership at the highest level Delivering basic infrastructure (electricity, roads, clean water, etc.)	High state autonomy (i.e., a good bureaucracy) Some decision-making capacity at lower levels Delivering more basic infrastructure	High state autonomy (i.e., a good bureaucracy) High policy-making capacities across all levels Learning capacity (imitation and innovation) More basic infrastructure	High state autonomy (i.e., a good bureaucracy) High policymaking capacities across all levels Learning capacity (imitation and innovation) More basic infrastructure
Is democracy absolutely necessary?	No	No	Yes, at least some democratization	Yes, almost necessary condition
Democracy's Achilles' heel?	Too much populist redistribution politics, low capital formation	Too much populist redistribution politics, low capital formation	Vested interest groups, entrenched welfare state	Vested interest groups, entrenched welfare state

must accommodate some seemingly opposing forces and factors. Thus, we have to bring together individualistic initiatives and collective actions, gradual changes and revolutionary changes, external incentives and intrinsic motivations, material and nonmaterial calculations, factors driven by demand and factors driven by supply, positive and negative feedback, changes and stability, the inevitable and the accidental, and the reduction of transaction costs and the reaping of profits in our new approach to institutional change. These seemingly opposing forces are what have made the economic system integrative, dynamic, and evolutionary. If we continue with the old approach that pits one force against the other, we can easily fall into logical inconsistency.

Olson's two self-contradicting positions perfectly illustrate the point above. Olson (1982) emphasized that interest groups are bad for development, therefore, a state needs to break up its vested interest groups periodically, with revolution, purge, and even war if necessary. In contrast, Olson (1993, 1996, 2000) called for constraints on the executives (as in democracies), thus explicitly suggesting that the state cannot be allowed to become too powerful. Obviously, Olson's earlier logic of breaking up interest groups and later logic of constraining executives cannot be easily reconciled (Ackerman 2003; McLean 2000).

Among the incomplete list of seemingly diametrically opposed forces or dynamics, I single out three dyads: material versus nonmaterial, external incentives versus intrinsic motivations, and individual initiatives versus collective action.

While Becker (1976) insisted that the economic approach should be applicable to the nonmaterial side of human motivation, the economic approach toward human interactions has usually been about utility maximization. As a result, it has paid little attention to behavior for nonmaterial gains from social status and achievement satisfaction.

Yet, with the accumulation of knowledge at the heart of economic progress, we must acknowledge that a major driving force behind the accumulation of knowledge has always been nonmaterial incentives (Marshall 1920, 3–5; Rosenberg and Birdzell 1986, 243; Merton 1973; Stephan 1996; Mokyr 2017). Material gain is certainly a major channel through which learning is encouraged, and nonmaterial gain (mostly through social status) is definitely another. Both channels influence individuals' incentives for achieving upward social mobility, for social mobility is not only about wealth but also about prestige and a place in history. This is especially true when it comes to explaining scientists' motivations. Scientists like Galileo, Newton, and

Einstein were perhaps more motivated by the drive to have a place in history than by potential material gain.

For too long, mainstream economics has tended to dismiss intrinsic motivations and take external incentives to be behind all human actions. Yet, it would be extremely difficult to imagine what kind of external incentives we can employ to explain the actions of revolutionaries like Gandhi, Mandela, Lenin, Park Chun-hee, Mao Tse-tung, Ho Chi-min, and Deng Xiaoping. In science, what external (material) incentives can we employ to explain Bruno, Galileo, and Darwin's stand against the Church and Stephen Hawking's heroic effort when facing so much pain? If economics indeed claims to study all human activities, then we must develop some understanding of how intrinsic motivations drive behaviors that ultimately drive economic changes.

Finally, economics tends to focus on individual initiatives and dismisses collective actions as irrational unless they make individual sense (Olson 1965). Yet, time and again, we have seen that leaders take actions to mobilize the public into collective action. Since institutional changes do not occur spontaneously, it requires collective action to design, modify, and even revolutionize them. By taking the position that collectivism is not part of the economic approach, economics has been missing the forest for the trees.

IV. A Niche Construction–Based Approach to Development

Schumpeter (1947, 4) noted that "development influences . . . all the factors 'on which it depends,'" as well as that *the essential point to grasp is that in dealing with capitalism we are dealing with an evolutionary process"* ([1943] 2003, 82, emphasis added). What he was conveying in these two statements is that development is not only an evolutionary system but also an evolutionary process that drives changes beyond the economic system (see also Hayek 1960, ch. 3; Boulding 1966; Loasby 1999; Evans 2004).

This section develops Schumpeter's insight more fully and draws broad implications for understanding how development itself can impact the state, institutions, culture, and economic agents (i.e., individuals, families, and organizations). The key message here is that development can be understood as a process of human niche construction, and therefore we need to adopt a niche construction approach toward development itself.

In biological evolution, there have been several exciting advances that extend the Modern Synthesis, and one of them has been niche construction, first introduced by Lewontin (1983). Since then, niche construction has received significant theoretical extension and strong empirical support (e.g., Odling-Smee 1988, 2010; Laland et al. 2000; Odling-Smit et al. 2003; Danchin et al. 2011; Odling-Smee and Laland 2011; Kendal et al. 2011).

Briefly, niche construction theory (NCT) starts with the self-evident observation that organisms not only adapt to the environment in which they operate but also actively modify their environment (Lewontin 1983). In other words, an organism's environment is not externally independent from an organism's life cycle. Rather, there is feedback from an organism's life cycle to the environment, which thus entails possible "stable and directional changes in environmental conditions" in the long run, and constructed niches very often pass from one generation to the next, resulting in "ecological inheritance" (Odling-Smee 2010; Odling-Smee and Laland 2011). These modified niches therefore come back to shape the fitness of the organisms' offspring and other organisms. In short, organisms and their environment coevolve. Thus, NCT has four key components: niche, niche construction, ecological inheritance, and coevolution of organisms and niches (as the environment).

Initially, niche construction was defined too broadly as any modification or change of an organism's environment that resulted from that organism's metabolism and activities (e.g., Lewontin 1983; Odling-Smee et al. 2003; Odling-Smee 2010; Odling-Smee and Laland 2011). Defined as such, there is no doubt that in the very long run all organisms perform some kind of niche construction. When this is the case, niche construction is simply too broad for any analytical purpose (Sterelny 2005).

Accordingly, evolutionary biologists have now settled on a narrower definition for both niche and niche construction (Laland and Sterelny 2006, 1760). A niche is a subdomain of the larger environment of an organism or a group of organisms, such as a pond, a riverbank, or a piece of terrain. Niche construction, then, is a process through which an organism or a group of organisms "engineers" its niche (i.e., a subdomain of its environment) via its metabolism and activities over a significant period of time. Moreover, although niche construction is purely biological and unintentional for most nonhuman species (i.e., group animals, such as ants), it can be "intentional" or "purposeful" for some mammals (e.g., beavers constructing a dam). Defined as such, niche construction is a process, and hence a potential mechanism, just like variation-selection-inheritance (VSI) in biological evolution, even though the former is less central than the latter (Laland and Sterelny 2006).

By any measure, human beings are the most powerful niche constructor as we know it (Laland et al. 2000; Kendal et al. 2011; O'Brien and Laland 2012). Humans impact their environment via their metabolism and activities either unintentionally or intentionally, just as other organisms do. Human beings, however, engineer both their physical and social environment pervasively and profoundly. Take, for example, the coming of settled agriculture (Diamond 1997; O'Brien and Laland 2012). When initiating settled agriculture, our ancestors had to clear underbrush to make fields, construct settled living spaces (e.g., hamlets), and domesticate animals by keeping them alive and fostering reproduction rather than killing them for instant consumption. Besides settled agriculture, the Industrial Revolution, megacities, the internet revolution, and global warming are just a few examples of the grand cultural and physical niche constructions by our species. Equally critical, along the way, human beings have created economic and political organizations and institutions—two critical niches for our daily social lives. In short, economic development is a niche construction process on the grandest scale.

For social niche construction (SNC), we also adopt a narrow requirement: niche construction by human beings (as human or social niche construction) must be *intentional* (cf. Laland et al. 2000; Kendal et al. 2011). This does not mean that intentional construction always leads to desired outcomes because all outcomes are subject to selection, both natural and artificial, but merely that human agents seek to achieve goals with calculated strategies. This allows us to differentiate intentional niche construction from intentional adaptation to the natural and social environment (e.g., conformism).

Concurring with some other social scientists, especially anthropologists (Laland et al. 2000, 2010; O'Brien and Laland 2012), we believe that NCT is a potentially powerful theorization tool for understanding human society, especially for understanding how development shapes human society, including the physical and social dimensions. We therefore import NCT to evolutionary economics. More concretely and ontologically:

(1) Via their actions and interactions, human beings construct their niches as aspects or pockets of the social system all the time. A newly constructed environment impacts the agent itself but also other agents. Whether the new environment benefits the organism itself or other organisms depends on artificial selection within the new constructed system. Hence, SNC is not parallel,

but secondary, to the central mechanism of social evolution (i.e., artificial VSI/SVI).

(2) Development, as an emergent process of agents' action and interaction through time and space, is one of the most powerful processes of human niche construction. As becomes clear in chapter 8, development shapes state capacity, institutional foundations, and economic policies, which together come back to shape developmental outcomes.

(3) Agents, especially more powerful ones, do not merely adapt to the social system but also actively seek to shape or modify it to suit them better. All else being equal, the more powerful the agent is, the larger the impact of its niche construction. Development is not a process in which individuals participate and benefit equally: inequality in terms of capability/power, resources, and benefits is the norm in development.

(4) Agents deploy strategic behaviors to achieve niche construction, but the exact outcomes include both intended and unintended ones. All the resources, whether material (e.g., wealth, number of allies and opponents) or ideational (e.g., religious, ideological, and cultural) can enter agents' calculations of picking niches and yield specific strategies for construction (Elias [1939] 1994; Bourdieu 2005).

(5) There are always multiple agents who can construct the niche, and they almost inevitably have different preferences for outcomes, resulting in conflicts of interest. Moreover, their attempts at niche construction interact with each other. Hence, SNC demands a conflictual and interactive approach rather than a cooperative and atomistic approach toward how agents shape their environment and each other.

(6) Agents learn from their own and others' experiences to draw lessons for constructing their environment. This learning process itself is a process of artificial selection.

(7) Agents pick a domain or a niche within a social system to modify. Most of the time, however, agents can only construct a niche that has been handed down to them from the last round of construction, perhaps by other agents. In other words, an agent can only construct a niche within the existing constraints (O'Brien and Laland 2012, 436). Thus, more often than not, the scope for niche construction is limited, piecemeal, and gradual, even though the impact of the new niche can be quite significant, especially in the long run.

Epistemologically, how can we understand development as a niche construction process?

(1) SNC is only one aspect or dimension of the social evolution paradigm (SEP). Specifically, SNC is useful for understanding how development and agents (individuals and collectives) interact and how their interactions change both of them. This calls for a social evolutionary approach toward development (Tang 2020), and such an approach subsumes the social system paradigm (Bunge 1999; Jervis 1997).

(2) To understand the economic system as part of the social system (i.e., the dynamics of an economic system and how these dynamics sustain and eventually transform an economic system), the right starting questions include asking how agents interact with each other within the economic system while being constrained and enabled by the system, how agents and the system interact with each other, and how agents and the system mutually constitute and transform each other. After identifying or describing these patterns, we then go on to ask the "why" questions: why agents have interacted with each other within the economic system as they have, why agents and the system have interacted with each other as they have, and why the economy (as part of a society) has persisted and then changed or why the economy has survived or collapsed or broken down.

(3) As an extension of point 2, an SNC approach should look into how different social institutions, organizations, and other parts of a society have come to exist and operate in a mix of both compatibility and incompatibility. These parts and their interactions produce intended and unintended outcomes, driven not only by agents' actions/interactions with each other but also by their interactions with existing social institutions, organizations, and other parts during the development process.

(4) Empirically, an SNC approach calls for a figuration and relational construction perspective pioneered by Elias ([1939] 1994) and restated by Emirbayer (1997), rather than the mechanistic approach in mainstream neoclassical economics. SNC may also provide a way for bridging the gap between microeconomics and macroeconomics. The key is to bring our scattered understanding about agent/agency, interaction, and emergent properties (e.g., institutions, development, and state capacity) together.

V. Concluding Remarks

More than a century ago, Veblen (1898) asked rhetorically, "Why is economics not an evolutionary science?" To Veblen's question, Marshall's ([1920] 1982, xii) response was unequivocal: "The Mecca of the economists lies in economic biology rather than in economic dynamics." (See also Veblen [1899] 1967; Nelson and Winter 1982; Hodgson and Knudsen 2010). Unfortunately, many have failed to heed the advice from Veblen, Marshall, and Schumpeter. Hence, more than a century after Veblen and Marshall, evolutionism has remained in the margins of economics (Mokyr 2017).

   This chapter attempts to reinvigorate the evolutionary approach toward development by insisting that both IFED and development are not only evolutionary systems but that development itself is an evolutionary process. Consequently, our approach toward development must also be evolutionary (Tang 2017, 2020). This chapter also suggests key directions for adopting a social evolutionary approach toward not only IFED but also development itself. By so doing, this chapter lays part of the foundation for understanding development beyond IFED, which is the task of the next chapter.

8

The New Development Triangle

STATE CAPACITY, INSTITUTIONAL FOUNDATION, AND SOCIOECONOMIC POLICY

[The wealth of nations] must be regulated by two different circumstances: first, the skill, dexterity, and judgment with which its labor is generally applied; and secondly, the proportion between the number of those who are employed in useful labor, and that of those who are not so employed.
—ADAM SMITH ([1776] 1981, 10)

On the very first page of *The Wealth of Nations*, Adam Smith made it clear that the most critical factor shaping economic performance across time and space is the (mis)allocation of production factors by economic, political, and social decisions: *who—under what institutions, policies, and power relationships—decides to deploy what knowledge and other production factors to make what outputs.* If this is true, we can easily conclude that the state is the most powerful, hence the most critical, player in shaping economic performance across time and space (Lewis 1955, 408–15; North 1981, 20).

Unfortunately, the role of the state has been mostly marginalized in the voluminous literature on institutions and development, dominated by NCE-inspired NIE and NCE itself, contrary to the old institutional economics (e.g., Veblen [1899] 1967; Commons 1934). In fact, the implicit message before 2000 was that a minimal state is almost always the best solution, as pronounced by the neoliberal Washington Consensus. Somewhat crudely, whereas classic political economy had deemed that the proper limits of government function was a "disputed question" and predicted the discussion would increase rather than diminish (Mill [1871] 2006, 205), NCE and NIE have often called for a minimal or even an ultra-minimal state "that is limited to the narrow functions of protection against force, theft, fraud, enforcement of contracts, and so on" (Nozick 1974, ix). Indeed, Coase's (1959, 1960) seminal contribution on transaction costs implicitly points to a minimal state merely laying down property rights and enforcing contracts.[1]

Fortunately, there was a fundamental rethinking of the role of the state in development in the early 1980s in some corners of political science and historical sociology.[2] Although the notion of a "developmental state" can be traced back to Alexander Hamilton (1791), Friedrich List ([1841] 1885), and Alexander Gerschenkron (1962), it was Chalmers Johnson's (1982) *MITI and the Japanese Miracle* that really opened up the debate. (For reviews on this literature on the developmental state, see Öniş 1991; Woo-Cumings 1999; Routley 2012; Haggard 2015, 2018; for Johnson's own reflection, see Johnson 1999.) By examining a handful of East Asian countries or economies with an interdisciplinary, historical-comparative, and (deeply) institutional approach (HCIA),[3] this literature has forcefully demonstrated that the state can indeed be a constructive, if not absolutely indispensable, player in facilitating development (Amsden 1989; Wade 1990; Haggard 1990; Evans 1995). Their conclusion thus breaks radically from the NCE/NIE orthodoxy.

By the early 1990s, the notion that the state can do (and some states have indeed done) a lot to facilitate development began to surface in some very unlikely places, where neoclassical economics had long reigned (e.g., the IMF, the World Bank). Initially, in *The East Asian Miracle*, authors from the World Bank (1993) admitted some role for the state only grudgingly and still insisted on the righteousness of the neoliberal Washington Consensus. In *The State in a Changing World*, different authors from the World Bank (1997, 1) asserted unequivocally that "*the determining factor behind the contrasting development is the effectiveness of the state*" (emphasis added). The intellectual tide had indeed turned (see also World Bank 2002, 2005, 2017).[4]

Today, the thesis that development—especially late development by developing countries—needs a strong state is indisputable (for reviews, see Evans 1995; Chang 1999; Woo-Cumings 1999; Kohli 2002; Vu 2010a; Hoffman 2015; Bardhan 2016, 866–71; Haggard 2004, 2018; Johnson and Koyama 2017; Foa 2017). In fact, the new consensus is that becoming a

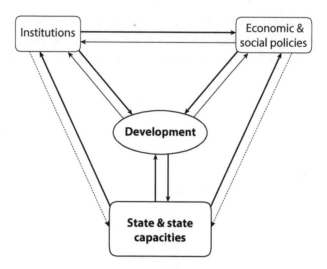

FIGURE 8.1. The New Development Triangle. Solid arrows denote direct effects; dashed arrows show indirect effects. The thickness of the solid arrows denotes the size of the possible impact.

developmental state is a near necessary condition for jump-starting and sustaining development.

Via this new institutionalist literature on the developmental state, "state capacity" has become a buzzword, even among newly converted NIE theorists (e.g., North et al. 2009; Besley and Persson 2011; Acemoglu and Robinson 2012). Yet, the existing discussions have often been mostly inductive and fragmentary. This chapter seeks to provide a more integrative framework for understanding how a state can facilitate economic development, by drawing, extending, and integrating existing discussions.

I start with a simple premise: state power or capacity by itself does not produce development, and a state has to deploy its power (if it possesses power) as an instrument to shape development (Johnson 1982; Amsden 1989; Wade 1990; Haggard 1990; Evans 1995; Kohli 2004; Vu 2010a). Straightforwardly, the state can deploy two primary instruments for shaping development in both the long and short runs: institutions and policies (World Bank 1997, 2008). Yet, effectively exercising these two instruments requires a state with some key capacities. As such, I argue that *state capacity, the institutional system, and economic policy constitute the "(new) development triangle"* (NDT; figure 8.1).

Understanding NDT is immensely challenging. Because all the key dimensions are interconnected, and feedback is rampant within the triangle, understanding the causal effects with conventional econometric methods becomes extremely difficult, if not entirely impossible. Even with more in-depth comparative case studies, untangling the causal linkages within the triangle will be extremely demanding. Thus, this chapter sets itself a mod-est task: to outline some tentative steps toward understanding the complex triangle and to explore its implications for understanding and shaping eco-nomic development, especially for developing countries.

Before I can elaborate on NDT's three key pillars, however, we need to get some important concepts right and provide initial yardsticks for mea-suring these concepts.

I. State Capacity and Governance: Conceptualization and Measurement

Since Mann ([1984] 1988, 1986, 1993; see also Tilly 1975; Skocpol 1979; Migdal 1988), there has been a resurging interest in state capacity and other related notions, such as state effectiveness and state autonomy (Soifer 2008). More recently, there has also been a growing interest in quality of gover-nance or government (QoG) and other governance-related notions, such as accountability, transparency, and rule of law (Kaufmann and Kraay 2008; Rothstein 2011). Along the way, many empirical studies have also attempted to link either state capacity or QoG with economic, political, and social outcomes, including economic development (e.g., Enriquez and Centeno 2012; Bardhan 2016; Centeno et al. 2017).

So far, however, consistent and robust results that link either state capac-ity or QoG with economic, political, and social outcomes have been lacking. A critical cause, I argue, has been conceptual confusion, theoretical inad-equacy, and operational (i.e., measurement) deficiency when handling these difficult concepts. (For earlier discussions, see Kurtz and Schrank 2007; Thomas 2010; Enriquez and Centeno 2012; Soifer 2015; Centeno et al. 2017; and the special issue of *Studies in Comparative International Development*, 2008.)

This section draws from a more detailed conceptual analysis advanced elsewhere (Tang 2022). Table 8.1 summarizes some key conceptual clari-fications. Very importantly, although my discussion of state capacity also starts with Mann's ([1984] 1988, 1986, 1993) framework (e.g., despotic power and infrastructural power), I depart from his discussion and many of his followers significantly (e.g., Saylor 2013; Soifer 2008; Soifer and vom Hau 2008; Hanson and Sigman 2013; Hanson 2017). Indeed, I argue that Mann's

TABLE 8.1. Conceptual Clarifications

Notions or terms	Comments
State capacity	The combinatorial outcome of *material and ideological resources* plus *coercive, extractive,* and *administrative capacities* commanded by a state; these resources and capabilities in turn allow the state to achieve certain goals *if it so chooses.*

State effectiveness	A complex outcome underpinned by state capacity, quality of bureaucracy, the cooperation of the population, and the will of the state. Unsuitable as an explanatory variable.
State autonomy	A complex outcome, most critically underpinned by state capacity and state-society relations (Mann [1984] 1988, 1993; Evans 1995; Migdal 1988, 2001).
Quality of bureaucracy (i.e., Weberian or not): a subdimension within state capacity	A complex outcome, most critically underpinned by institutions governing social mobility (i.e., meritocracy in promoting), equality of opportunity (i.e., meritocracy in recruiting), and redistribution (i.e., education). See Evans and Rauch (1999).

Quality of governance (QoG)	A complex outcome that is somewhat parallel to development. QoG is also underpinned by state capacity, institutions, and policies. Unsuitable as an explanatory variable for development.
(Degree of) the rule of law; transparency	Subdimensions within QoG. They are still complex outcomes underpinned by state capacity, institutions, and policies. Not well suited as an explanatory variable for development.
Accountability (of officials and state apparatuses)	A complex outcome, most critically underpinned by regime type and institutions (Soifer 2008). Can be part of QoG.
Corruption	A complex outcome, most critically underpinned by state capacity, institutions (e.g., rules for deterring, preventing, and punishing corruption), and accountability, which are in turn shaped by regime type and institutions.

Road density, clean water, educational achievement, and other social outcomes	Historical outcomes underpinned by state capacity, institutions (including regime type), policies, and states' intentions and will for achieving objectives. They should not be treated as linear proxies for state capacity.

framework is partly flawed because it conflates the constitutive components of state capacity with its regulatory factors.[5]

A. STATE CAPACITY DEFINED

I define *state capacity* as the outcome of *material and ideological resources* plus *coercive, extractive,* and *administrative capacities* commanded by a state (Skocpol 1985, 16–17; see also Mann [1984] 1988; 1993, ch. 3). These resources and capacities in turn allow the state to achieve certain goals *if it so chooses*. My definition thus explicitly states that state capacity contains two kinds of things: resources and capabilities, which together constitute a state's capacity. By resources, I mean "anything that can serve as a source of power in social interactions" (Sewell 1992, 9–10).

Material resources have to be part of any definition of state capacity. Ideological resources capture Mann's (1986) emphasis on ideological power, especially for modern states. However, resources and capacities are not the same. From AD 1500 on, Spain had commanded vast resources from its early conquest of Latin America but remained a weak state (Elliott 1989; Lynch 1992; Grafe 2012). Likewise, France before 1789 was a relatively weak state even though it too had commanded serious resources (Rosenthal 1992; Collins 1995).

By defining state capacity purely in terms of resources and capabilities, my definition is also normatively neutral (Centeno et al. 2017), thus avoiding the danger of conflating state capacity with other factors that may regulate state capacities and state performance (e.g., regime type, democratic procedures, or ideologies), as these regulators themselves are not state capacities.

By defining state capacity purely in terms of resources and capabilities, my definition avoids the danger of conflating state capacity with outcome or performance—an error committed by many, including Mann himself ([1984] 1988, 1986, 1993; see more on this below). Hence, although we may have to measure certain dimensions of state capacity indirectly by measuring outcomes that are partly underpinned by state capacities, we must bear in mind that these results are underpinned by state capacity and the state's will to achieve the results. As such, we cannot simply assume that lacking a certain set of results necessarily means a state is lacking state capacity; the other possibility is that the state lacks the will to achieve such a result (Bardhan 2016, 863). Drawing useful elements from a voluminous literature, I contend that state capacity comprises four key subdimensions (see also Tilly 1992; Fritz 2007; Soifer 2008; Slater 2010).

Coercive capacities. This dimension is mostly a function of a state's level of monopoly of violence (Elias [1939] 1994; Tilly 1990). This is the most foundational dimension of state capacities: unless a state can command a threshold degree of monopoly of violence, it cannot do anything else (including extractive). In fact, unless a roving bandit can command a minimal degree of monopoly of violence within a territory, it cannot even claim to be a state (Mann 1993; Olson 1993).

Extractive capacities (taxation). This dimension is the one that most directly contributes to states' material resources (Elias [1939] 1994; Tilly 1990). Without some capacity to extract resources from the society, a state is essentially a sham that cannot really function. However, extractive capacities must be based on a state's coercive capacities: extraction has to be backed by the threat of violence and actual violence if necessary.

Administrative capacities I. This subdimension includes administrative capacities that actually run a state or rule the subjects within the state. Most critically, it includes capacities for enforcing rules and delivering service, from bureaucrats at the top of the power echelon to desk clerks at the bottom. We can call this subdimension "delivering capacity." At the core of this subdimension is the quality of the bureaucracy, which is in turn underpinned by institutions and policies that regulate the quality of bureaucracy. Of course, in order to deliver any service, a state needs resources, which in turn depends on extraction.

Administrative capacities II. The second subdimension of administrative capacities includes the capacity for gathering information and making quality decisions. This dimension is underpinned by both the quality of the bureaucracy and the quality of leadership.

The first three dimensions are widely accepted by students of state capacity. For instance, Besley and Persson (2011) identified three dimensions of state capacity: fiscal, legal, and military (coercive). Their military and fiscal capacity corresponds to coercive and extractive capacity as described in this chapter, and their legal capacity is part of administrative capacities I, also as defined above (see also Fukuyama 2013; Kurtz 2013; Saylor 2013; Soifer 2008, 2015; Hanson and Sigman 2013).[6]

I, however, insist that a definition of state capacity with only the first three dimensions is incomplete: the fourth dimension—information and leadership—is also critical. Only with the fourth dimension will leadership count. Without this dimension, leadership has no role in state capacity.[7] Yet, leaders are a special kind of agent and wield enormous power.

This is especially important for economic development: unless the upper echelon within the central bureaucracy can make mostly correct policies and change the institution, little can be done by the bottom. As such, the quality of leadership must be part of the state capacity, especially for many developing countries that are not mature democracies. Consider what would have happened to Botswana, China, Mauritius, Singapore, South Korea, and Taiwan without Seretse Khama, Deng Xiaoping, Seewoosagur Ramgoolam, Lee Kuan Yew, Park Chung-hee, and Jiang Jing Guo (e.g., Amsden 1989; Wade 1990; Haggard 1990; Evans 1995; Kohli 2004; see also Fritz 2007; Lin 2009; Centeno et al. 2017, 11–12). Indeed, even in mature democracies, leadership counts when it comes to economic performance in critical times, as the tenures of David Cameron, Theresa May, Boris Johnson, Angela Merkel, and of course Donald Trump attest.[8]

Meanwhile, even wise leaders must base their decisions on quality information, which can only be obtained by a decently capable state bureaucracy (Lee and Zhang 2016). Indeed, a key task of state bureaucracy is actually information gathering, and for a state to function properly, local and low-level officials must be able to gather information (and make local decisions).

Within the modern state bureaucracy, the apparatuses for information gathering are both functionally and structurally different from those for implementing rules or delivering services (Zuo and Tang 2013). Hence, although both the third and the fourth dimensions are mostly underpinned by the quality of bureaucracy, they are different. Consequently, it is more desirable to separate the two subdimensions of administrative capacities than to conflate them all under bureaucratic capacity or infrastructural power (e.g., Mann ([1984] 1988, 1993; Fukuyama 2013).

Obviously, all four subdimensions of state capacity are underpinned by institutions and policies within the state. From coercive and extractive capacities to quality of bureaucracy and constraints on executives, only proper institutions and policies can underpin them. Pulling all these together, therefore, state capacity is inherently multidimensional, multilayered, multicausal, cumulative/historical, and hence dynamic and evolutionary (figure 8.2).

Moreover, each dimension within state capacity is connected and impacted by other dimensions. Hence, in figure 8.2, unidirectional arrows capture the key conceptual points: when we think about state capacity, we have to differentiate factors into layers before we can understand the possible relationships between factors and layers. In contrast, bidirectional arrows

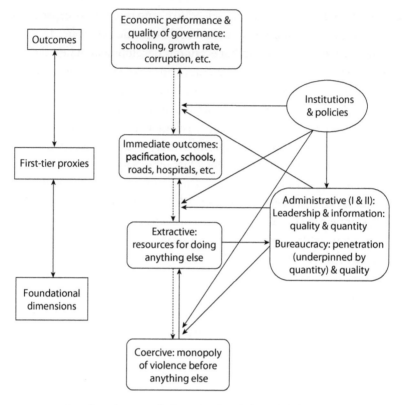

FIGURE 8.2. State Capacity as a Multidimensional, Multilayered, and Multicausal Concept. As noted in the text, I hold that coercive and extractive capacities are the most foundational dimensions of state capacity. Other proxies that indirectly and only partly measure state capacity include pacification, schools, roads, and so on. Both institutions and policies indirectly affect state capacity. Solid arrows denote directions with a more robust effect; dashed arrows indicate directions with a less robust effect.

denote the self-evident fact that in the real world factors and outcomes at different levels impact each other. The oval with institutions and policies recaptures the idea that, underpinned partly by state capacity, institutions and policies come back to impact state capacity as well.

B. STATE CAPACITY VERSUS STATE AUTONOMY, STATE EFFECTIVENESS, AND QOG

With state capacity defined as above, we can now differentiate it from several related concepts—most critically, state effectiveness (as performance) and state autonomy. Since a detailed conceptual analysis of these concepts is provided elsewhere (Tang 2022), I shall be brief here.

State capacity is obviously different from *state autonomy*, commonly defined as the degree of freedom that a state enjoys when making its policies (Skocpol 1979, 29–31; 1985, 9–20; Mann [1984] 1988; 1993, ch. 3; Migdal 1988, ch. 1; Evans 1995; Slater 2010, 256–57; Fukuyama 2013, 2016). State autonomy is therefore an institutional outcome underpinned by societal forces.

State autonomy may also partly underpin QoG (see below). Hence, although state autonomy may be useful as an instrument for explaining economic performance and QoG, it is most useful as a regulatory factor that captures the quality of policymaking and implementation. State autonomy is unsuitable as an intervening variable for explaining either economic performance or QoG (cf. Fukuyama 2016). Moreover, as a supposedly specific concept, measuring state autonomy in specific issue domains is difficult, if not almost impossible (cf. Evans 1995), and yet measuring it holistically is invalid. Overall, therefore, state autonomy may not be of much practical value for understanding state effectiveness.

State effectiveness is an outcome that is a function of a state's capacity, intention, and will, with intention and will being regulated by additional institutional and social factors (Tang 2013; Centeno et al. 2017). Evidently, capacity is different from either (political) intention and will (or resolve) to act or the eventual outcome. Thus, even if a state has the necessary capacities for getting a task done, it is not certain the task will get done if it does not have the will to do the task.

Meanwhile, the state's will is certainly not only a function of leadership but also a function of accountability that is underpinned by institutions. This is true not only in democracies but also in electoral autocracies or even autocracies without elections (Miller 2015; Weeks 2014). Obviously, accountability is a subcomponent of QoG. Hence, state effectiveness is a function of state capacity and will, which in turn are a function of leadership and accountability. Furthermore, the eventual effectiveness of a policy or an action is a function of at least the resources devoted to it, the capabilities of agents devoted to it, and the degree of cooperation among agents for it.

Moreover, *state effectiveness is inherently subdomain or subissue specific.* We mostly talk about state effectiveness in funding education, controlling crime, and delivering specific services rather than in abstract or aggregate terms. In contrast, within a specific domain (e.g., coercive, extractive), state capacity in principle is adaptable and fungible across different subdomains and subissues, even though the state may have different capacities in different domains. Hence, state capacity is different from state effectiveness.

Finally, QoG is the effectiveness of government policies and actions in terms of advancing the collective interest of the general public (or the subjects within a state).[9] Hence, QoG is about the quality of the exercising of state capacities by the state. In light of this, QoG is also an outcome that is partly underpinned by state capacities, just as economic development is; and just as economic development is a historical and cumulative outcome, so is QoG. Thus, one should expect to find a strong correlation between the level of economic development and QoG.

This is indeed what we have found: QoG has a high correlation with GDP per capita (as cumulative outcome), but not with the growth rate of GDP per capita (Baland et al. 2010, 4615–20; World Bank 2017, fig. 5.2, fig. 5.3, 99, 139–40). Indeed, existing measurements of QoG are really measuring GDP per capita, as revealed by a latent variable exercise (Halleröd et al. 2014). As such, QoG, as an outcome itself, is unsuitable for being an explanatory variable for economic development and social outcomes (cf. Kaufman et al. 2010; Baland et al. 2010).

Unfortunately, many have conflated state capacity and QoG. For instance, Soifer and Hau (2008, 225) identified accountability as part of state capacity. Clearly, accountability is a key dimension of QoG (Agnafors 2013). Similarly, the World Bank (2017, 7–11) talks about power asymmetries in three forms: exclusion, capture, and clientelism (patrimony). Evidently, whereas capture is part of state autonomy, exclusion and clientelism are more about QoG.

More prominently, Fukuyama (2013, 2016) has essentially equated QoG with state capacity by defining governance as "a government's ability to make and enforce rules, and to deliver services, regardless of whether that government is democratic or not." Fukuyama then went on to admit that he was more interested in Mann's notion of "infrastructural power." Even for understanding state capacity, however, Fukuyama was confused. Although he usefully talked about procedural (i.e., Weberian) capacity (as resource), output, and autonomy, he essentially settled on capacity and autonomy as measurements of state capacity. Yet, as noted above, state autonomy does not constitute but only regulates state capacity. Fukuyama's whole discussion thus has been a conceptual muddle (see also Baland et al. 2010).

C. MEASURING STATE CAPACITY

Measuring state capacity properly is no easy task. Again, because I devote a separate paper to the conceptual analysis of state capacity (Tang 2022), I shall be brief here.

To begin with, without a decent conceptual analysis, measuring the different dimensions of state capacity separately or aggregately is not only infeasible but also misleading, even if they are done with latent variables or simple factor analysis. For instance, Hendrix (2010), using latent variables, identified three dimensions for state capacity, including rational legality, rentier-autocraticness (fiscal dependence on commodity exports), and neopatrimoniality. His whole exercise, however, has no conceptual foundation and is hence invalid. Obviously, in light of the conceptual analysis above, what Hendrix measured was not state capacity alone but a mix of state capacity with political regime and state-society relations (Saylor 2013, 375). The same criticism applies to Hanson and Sigman (2013), who employ similar techniques. Remarkably, although Hanson and Sigman (2013, 2) claim to have defined state capacity narrowly as "the ability of state institutions to effectively implement official goals," their final indicators draw from a host of datasets. Both Hendrix (2010) and Hanson and Sigman (2013) have replaced conceptualization with a latent variable exercise as a miracle worker.

The only viable way to measure state capacity is to unpack it and then measure its individual dimensions based on sound conceptualization. Briefly, two indicators are useful for measuring a state's coercive capacity: the size of its police force and the size of its military relative to its population and the size of its territory. In contrast, sociopolitical stability or instability is not a sound indicator of a state's coercive capacity because it is the combined outcome of state capacity and other socioeconomic conditions.

Taxation rate (i.e., tax revenue relative to total GDP) is a valid proxy of extractive capacity, but it may not be ideal. Two possible alternative and more-fined grained indicators are the share of income tax, property tax, and consumption tax within a state's total tax income (Lieberman 2002; Slater 2010; see also Hanson and Sigman 2013).

It is extremely difficult to measure administrative capacity I directly. Two possible proxies can be considered: outcomes in terms of investment in key infrastructure (e.g., roads, railways, airports, schools) and education (e.g., Besley and Persson 2014). These indicators, however, should be treated cautiously not only because they are already very close to economic performance (i.e., growth rate), but also because they are only partly underpinned by state capacity. Besides state capacity, both proxies are underpinned by a state's intention and will, and we cannot directly measure a state's intention or will to deliver.

Information capacity can be measured by the frequency and accuracy of census and other statewide information data (Lee and Zhang 2017).

A somewhat useful indicator in the early stages of development is the number of post offices across a country.

The quality of leadership is much tougher to measure ex post: we tend to attribute effective leadership to successful states after the state has succeeded. For measuring leadership ex ante, one may want to use a leader's quality of education, diversity of experience, and achievements prior to taking office. The same principle applies to cabinet members and key advisers. All else being equal, a leader with a better and higher level of education, more diverse experience, and more achievements is more likely to function more effectively.

II. NDT: A Preliminary Analytical Framework

The theoretical and empirical challenge for understanding the relationship between NDT and development is immense simply because development is an extremely complex social outcome, and NDT itself is a system. This section thus sets a modest aim: it seeks to outline some initial theoretical hunches toward a better understanding by pulling things together and advancing a tentative evolutionary framework. Hence, what I present below is not a theory but a preliminary analytical framework for constructing more specific theories. The next section addresses the empirical challenges for understanding NDT.

A caveat is in order. Because the preceding chapters have dealt with institutions and development extensively, this section does not repeat what has been said above. I merely stress one key point: there is no such thing as weak or strong institutions—only good, bad, or mixed. Weak or strong institutions mostly reflect underlying weak or strong state capacity (Migdal 1988). My discussion on policy and development is also brief because it too has been extensively addressed. I thus focus on (1) state capacity and development and (2) bringing the three components (i.e., state capacity, institutions, and policies) together.

A. CRITIQUE OF THE EXISTING LITERATURE

Much has been written on the various aspects of the complex relationship between state capacity, institutions, and policies on the one hand (especially state capacity and institutions and state capacity and policies) and developmental outcomes on the other hand. For the purpose of understanding NDT and development, however, the existing discussions suffer from seven key shortcomings, besides the theoretical and logical deficiencies identified in chapter 1 (i.e., tautology, blunt concepts, induction over deduction, etc.).

First, as noted above, much of the existing literature suffers from conceptual confusion and myriad measurement problems. In particular, many scholars have deployed invalid conceptual frameworks and variables for understanding the relationship between NDT and development. For instance, Waldner (1999) identified four aspects of institutionalized arrangements that shape development: state-society relations, the quality of bureaucracy, fiscal practice, and pattern of state economic intervention. Apparently, fiscal practice falls under economic policies (as instruments), whereas a pattern of state intervention is an outcome underpinned by both institutions and policies. In contrast, bureaucracy reflects key aspects of state capacity, whereas state-society relations are more related to state autonomy (Migdal 1988; Evans 1995). Hence, three of the four aspects that Waldner (1999) had in mind were not merely institution or policy but rather outcomes underpinned by institution, policy, and social-state interactions.

Second, some discussions lack at least one or even two of the three components within NDT. For a long time, much of the development literature has focused on the effect of economic policies on development (e.g., the "big push"; Easterly 2001, 2005). Others have addressed bilateral relationships, such as state capacity and institution, state capacity and policy, or institution and policy. For instance, the Northian NIE approach has mostly focused on institutions and development (e.g., North and Weingast 1989; North 1990; North et al. 2009; Acemoglu et al. 2000, 2001, 2005; Acemoglu and Robinson 2012), whereas Lin (2012b, 2012c) has focused almost exclusively on industrial policy and development. The former literature implicitly assumes that LDCs can make sound institutions and enforce them, while the latter implicitly assumes that LDCs can make sound industrial policies and implement them adequately. Yet, apparently, making and enforcing institutions as rules requires a minimal threshold of state capacity (Bardhan 2016; Johnson and Koyama 2017), whereas making and implementing sound industrial policies requires not only a minimal threshold of state capacity but also some sound institutions in place (Mao et al. 2021; Chen et al. 2022). Both bodies of literature thus have missed the critical role of state capacity.

Third, even if some of the existing discussions have all three components within the triangle, they lack an integrated and coherent framework as captured in NDT. For instance, an article by the World Bank (2017) touched on governance, state capacity, institutions, and policies. It not only addressed the politics of development, especially power asymmetries (i.e., exclusion/

domination, capture, and clientelism) but also acknowledged the need to focus on function rather than form. Yet, it failed to present a framework for understanding these issues as components within the NDT. Similarly, in a very thoughtful review essay, despite having clearly identified the interaction between state capacity, institutional foundation, and economic policies and providing a trenchant critique of the dominant NIE approach (e.g., North and Weingast 1989; North et al. 2009, 2013; Besley and Persson 2011; Acemoglu and Robinson 2012), Bardhan (2016) did not advance an integrated framework for understanding the whole NDT. The same criticism can be applied to Chang (1999, 2000, 2002), Rodrik (2007), Besley and Persson (2011, 2014), Hoffman (2015), and Johnson and Koyama (2017).

Fourth, even when a discussion contains at least two or even all three components within the NDT, the theorization has been sloppy. Most prominently, Besley and Persson (2011, 2014) talked about the clustering of high income, strong state capacity, and peacefulness. Yet, apparently, peacefulness must be a function of the control of violence as a key dimension of state capacity. The same criticism applies to North et al. (2009, 2013).

Fifth, the dominant methodological approach in mainstream economics (and partly so in economic history and political science) has been quantitative or econometric. While econometric exercises are good at identifying and establishing robust correlations between certain factors and economic outcomes, they are not good at integrating the various factors into a coherent framework. Somewhat ironically, each econometric exercise that links one factor within NDT with some economic outcomes treats the factor as if it is a sufficient cause of the outcomes. In reality, the factor identified is one of numerous factors that have shaped economic outcomes through time and space (Goertz and Mahoney 2012). To synthesize the numerous factors, we need a more integrated and coherent framework.

Sixth, much of the existing discussion has a heavy, normative tone. Implicitly and often explicitly, it has been argued that development is underpinned by high QoG and democracy, or at least rule of law (as part of QoG) and constraints on executives (as a proxy for democracy). Yet, as noted above, development and QoG are both underpinned by NDT. More critically, whether rule of law (or QoG) or constraints on executives (or democracy) has a direct or indirect positive effect on development should be an empirical rather than a normative question.

Finally, the existing discussion is far from an evolutionary framework that is necessary for understanding NDT and development, despite some implicit evolutionary elements (e.g., Chang 2003; for an exception, see Ang 2016).

More often than not, a linear and hence nonsystemic and nonevolutionary approach has reigned (e.g., North and Weingast 1989; North et al. 2009, 2013; Besley and Persson 2011; Acemoglu and Robinson 2012; for critiques, see Chang 2011; Bardhan 2016; see also chapter 1).

B. POLICIES AND DEVELOPMENT: BEYOND ECONOMIC POLICIES

By policies, I do not mean economic policies (e.g., fiscal and industrial policies) alone but also social and political policies that directly or indirectly impact economic performance in the short to medium run. Economic policies certainly include the usual suspects, such as monetary, fiscal, taxation, investment, and industrial policies; but social and political policies can range from educational policies to land reform, welfare policies (e.g., unemployment benefits), and short-term policies for dealing with social and political crises (Kohli 2002).

Unlike institutions, which are more difficult and slow to change, policies have to be constantly adjusted to changing situations. Thus, policies are instruments for absorbing, softening, or exacerbating short-term shocks or tools. Primary examples include different policies implemented by countries hit by a financial crisis (e.g., Pepinsky 2009).

Just like institutions, however, policies can also be understood as instruments for shifting the economy from one condition to another, often by reallocating resources from some sectors to other sectors (Smith [1776] 1981, 10; Tang and Gao 2020). Thus, the literature on the developmental state argues that for technological catch-up to occur, it may be necessary for states to implement coordinated industrial policies to induce firms to shift from producing low-tech goods to producing high-tech goods (e.g., Lin 2009; Lee 2013b; Bardhan 2016; Haggard 2018).

Although many policies are for short-term to medium-term objectives, they often have both short-term and long-term impacts. Moreover, because policies operate within a social system, their effects cannot always be assumed ex ante but only assessed ex post (Jervis 1997). Thus, when Indonesia and Malaysia implemented different policies in the wake of the 1997 Asian financial crisis, these two countries ended up on very different paths politically and economically, and the outcomes in Indonesia were not what was anticipated by its leaders at all (Pepinsky 2009). Likewise, the various stimulus packages implemented by major economies during the 2008 Great Recession also produced long-lasting impacts. In both crises, states implemented many policies in order to tackle a short-term crisis, but these policies have produced unintended impacts far beyond the immediate time frame.

Land reform illustrates these dynamics most powerfully. In many post-revolution states, land reform was implemented primarily as a political instrument for solidifying popular support for the new regime. Yet, properly implemented land reform has a critical and profound impact on long-term development: by providing poor, rural residents with secure property rights, land reform, as a key form of redistribution, significantly increases agricultural output and therefore frees up labor for industrialization in the long run. Hence, land reform can be understood as a policy shock for jump-starting near-term agricultural growth and laying a foundation for industrialization in the years to come.

Historically, different land policies in the New World by colonialists serve as another powerful illustration. In its early stage of colonization and expansion into Native American territories, the United States offered free land to new immigrants. Yet, no such policy was introduced in most Latin American countries. In fact, most Latin American states did just the opposite: land management and distribution policy was consistently tilted toward landlords with large holdings. These differences in land policies have continued to shape development of these countries up to this day: whereas North American countries have prospered, many Latin American countries have been stuck with high inequality and economic stagnation (Temin 1997; Sokoloff and Engerman 2000; Acemoglu et al. 2003; Nugent and Robinson 2010; Engerman and Skoloff 2011, 2012).

The comparison is reflective of the situation with India and the Philippines (which did not implement land reform or whose reform did not really go deep enough) on the one side and most East Asian countries on the other side, after WWII. At the same time, however, one must admit the possibility that land reform may actually have a negative impact on agricultural production in the short term because it may disrupt existing production (e.g., South Africa, Zimbabwe).

Similarly, although education policies (or investment in schooling) have long-term positive effects on development overall, if the provision of education is restricted to the upper class, it may have considerable and lasting negative effects on development. As Lindert (2003) has shown, in many Latin American countries and India, although states have invested quite significantly in education, their highly elitist biases mean that much has been spent on higher education (which tends to benefit the wealthier) and little on basic education (which tends to benefit the middle and lower classes). Such a policy has had significant detrimental effects on the development of these countries in the long run.

Note that all these policies require both state capacity to make and implement them and institutions to enforce them (Slater 2010; Vu 2010a). Simply preaching about institutions, industrial policy (e.g., Lin 2012b, 2012c; Stiglitz and Lin 2013), governance, and law is not enough (e.g., World Bank 2017). Focusing on policies alone is misguided; eventually, one has to admit that without a threshold level of state capacity and some institutions in place, policies most likely will not work (e.g., Kohli 2004, esp. 381–408; cf. World Bank 2005, 270–74). We therefore need to bring them into an integrated framework: the new development triangle.

C. NDT AND DEVELOPMENT: BRINGING THINGS TOGETHER

As the deepest determinant for modern development, state capacity is the foundation for economic development (Kohli 2002; Levi 2002, esp. 42–49). Yet, beyond this critical but mundane statement, understanding how state capacity impacts development is immensely challenging. Moreover, due to conceptual, theoretical, and operational problems, existing discussions tend to misfire.

Most prominently, the Northian NIE literature has mostly argued that state impacts on development are based almost exclusively on whether the state can protect property rights (Bardhan 2016, 862). More recent NIE literature has gone much further. For instance, Johnson and Koyama (2017, 8–14) identified six pathways or channels through which state capacity or the state in general impacts development: protection from external predation; state unification of the market, such as by reducing transaction costs and providing wider coverage of the law (Spaulding 2011; Acemolgu et al. 2011); more effective bureaucracy; general rule of law (i.e., legal capacity); nation building and reducing ethnic cleavages; and fiscal capacity. Apparently, Johnson and Koyama's scheme has mixed dimensions of state capacities, institutions, and immediate outcomes of development.

Among the recent discussions, Bardhan (2016, 862–64) has advanced a most thoughtful rethinking of the role of the state in development. He enlisted a host of issues for a state to intervene, including "resolution of coordination failures and collective-action problems, the conflicting issues of commitment and accountability, and the need for balancing the trade-offs they generate." He then identified several key missing pieces in the dominant

NIE literature, including "the possible importance of rent sharing in a political equilibrium, the advantage and problems of political centralization and decentralization." Unfortunately, Bardhan did not explicate what constitutes state capacity and IFED. Thus, although he called for a joining of "the stream of the literature on industrial policy with the mainstream on state capacity for market-supporting institutions," he did not advance an integrative analytical framework, such as NDT.

Building on the work of Bardhan and those previously mentioned, I believe we need to consider several principles for understanding how state capacity shapes development. First, each major dimension within state capacity may have a different and nonlinear relationship with development, indirectly via policies and institutions. For instance, before a certain threshold, extraction capacity must be positively correlated with state capacity. After reaching a certain threshold, however, more extraction has a negative effect on development because too much extraction means too little being put back into development. Similarly, a monopoly of violence (order and stability) is essential, partly underpinned by a state's oppression apparatus (e.g., army, police). Yet, if oppression becomes too severe or the oppression apparatus becomes too large, it must also mean that order and stability are fragile or that the cost for maintaining order and stability has become too great.

Second, different dimensions within state capacity inevitably interact with each other. Most evidently, a monopoly of violence and extraction, the bread and butter of state building, are mutually reinforcing (Hintze 1975; Elias [1939] 1994; Tilly 1975, 1992; Epstein 2000). Similarly, administrative capacities I and administrative capacities II also reinforce each other.

Third, by building up its extraction capacity, a state must have also installed other institutions and organizations for extracting. Such state-building efforts cannot help but have an impact on development. In fact, this is why a long state history, which usually implies stronger state capacity, is strongly and positively associated with long-term development.

III. Understanding the Triangle: Empirical Challenges

The interaction among the various dimensions and components within NDT is extremely complex. More critically, economic development itself is a powerful niche construction process that shapes other social and political developments, which in turn come back to shape almost every component within the triangle (Schumpeter [1943] 2000, 82; Myrdal 1974, 729–30; see also Besley and Persson 2014). State capacity is underpinned by GDP per capita, taxation rate, and QoG—outcomes that are partly underpinned by state capacity. Moreover, resources and capacities in the current period are outcomes of resources and capacities in previous periods and causes of resources and capacities in future periods. Certainly, the educational level and professionalization of government officials partly underpins state capacity, but these factors are also outcomes from earlier state capacity, institutions, and policies. There are so many potential interacting, moderating, and confounding arrows that simple unidirectional causality essentially does not exist. All these issues pose immense challenges for our effort to empirically understand NDT. This section outlines some initial steps toward understanding the triangle.

A. PRINCIPLES AND OPERATIONAL CONSIDERATIONS

I begin with some core principles and then lay out some operational considerations. First, state capacity is foundational, but the overall outcome depends on institutions and policies more immediately. Hence, NIE's singular focus on institutions (including type of regime or order) or even the combination of institutions and policies while neglecting state building cannot possibly be adequate for understanding economic development across time and space (e.g., Helpman 2008; Shirley 2008; North et al. 2009; North et al. 2013; Besley and Persson 2011; Acemoglu and Robinson 2011; Engerman and Sokoloff 2011; Costa and Lamoreaux 2011). Instead, we need more studies on how some states have managed to become strong developmental states while others have failed contribute to our understanding of state building (e.g., Waldner 1999; Slater 2010; Vu 2010a; Kurtz 2013; Saylor 2013; Soifer 2015; Johnson and Koyama 2017).

Second, state capacity both underpins institutions and policies and regulates the effect of institutions and policies at any given time. For example, although China has had strong state capacity since 1954, it has also had episodes of growth disasters, such as the Great Leap Forward and the Cultural Revolution. After China's open and reform policy, however, China's strong capacities have been able to deliver positive results quite effectively. In other words, when state capacity is strong, bad policies hurt people more while good policies deliver more good to the people. In contrast, when state capacity is weak, bad policies may have a greatly reduced effect because they are not enforced or implemented. Likewise, without a decent (threshold) level of state capacity, institutions cannot function well and policies cannot be

Institutions & Policies	State capacities	
	Strong	Weak
Good	Outcomes: best scenario	Outcomes: second best
Bad	Outcomes: worst scenario	Outcomes: second worst

FIGURE 8.3. Relationship between State Capacities and Institutions and Policies.

properly implemented. Hence, again, when state capacity is strong, bad institutions hurt people more while good institutions deliver more good to the people. All these possibilities mean that when considering the impact of institutions and policies state capacity should be a moderating factor. Figure 8.3 summarizes these dynamics.

Third, as also noted in chapter 7, development is a powerful niche construction process: it impacts everything, including state capacity, institutions, and policies. Hence, it is wrong to argue that institutions alone determine development (Acemoglu and Robinson 2012); but it is also wrong to argue that development requires state capacity in a static sense without a time frame (e.g., Wen 2016). Development is more causal in the short run, but state capacity is more causal in the long run.

Fourth, economics needs to draw from both political science (especially comparative politics) and sociology. The practice that economists mostly cite only other economists is detrimental to economics as a field. After all, state capacity has mostly been built by political agents and processes (Elias [1939] 1994; Foucault 2000; Tilly 1992; Ertman 1997), and so have institutions (Tang 2011; for empirical evidence, see Sangmpam 2007; Grassi and Memoli 2015).

For operational issues, key challenges include the following. First and foremost, even if we have all the datasets for the key components within NDT, there is no possibility of having exogenous variables for all the possible linkages, loops, or causal relations because almost every major component within NDT interacts with and impacts other components within NDT. We must accept the infeasibility of having robust econometric evidence for every node or link within the triangle (Linder 2011, esp. 366–69).

Second, existing discussions about China versus India or East Asia versus Latin America usually focus on one or two dimensions of institutions or policies and ignore the interactions among different dimensions of state capacity, different institutions, and various policies. Thus, they have often concluded with a simplistic picture: Russia was ruined because of monopoly, while China prospered for lack of it (e.g., Parente and Prescott 1999; Parente and Ríos-Rull 2005). On this front, even the much admired literature on EADS has missed a few key components within NDT.

In light of NDT, whenever feasible, it will be desirable to test how different interactions, rather than each individual dimension or component alone, have shaped development outcomes. In fact, one would conjecture that testing the effect of individual dimensions or components is not only relatively uninteresting but also potentially misleading.

Third, more often than not, interactions among different dimensions of state capacity, different institutions, and various policies are nonlinear. Even assessing the effect of institutions and policies and their interactions by holding state capacity as a given or slow-moving condition will be extremely challenging. Different institutions often contradict each other, and so do different policies. Moreover, institutions and policies often collide with each other. As a result, the effect of institutions and policies cannot be assessed without considering other policies and the overall institutional environment. Furthermore, policies can have both short-term and long-term impacts.

Of course, because state capacity and institutions cannot be changed overnight, to some degree, state capacity and institutions in period $t-1$ can be taken as exogenous for understanding the performance of an economy in period t. In contrast, because policies tend to be more situation oriented, policies in period $t-1$ cannot be taken as exogenous for understanding the performance of an economy in period t: policies are mostly endogenous to growth and development in the short to medium term. Also, at least in the long run, institutions and policies impact state capacity, which in turn impacts development.

Altogether, therefore, finding ideal exogenous instruments for all the arrows within the NDT is going to be extremely difficult, if not impossible (e.g., Lindert 2011, esp. 364–69). Also, information gathering and, especially, leadership are hard to quantify. Hence, focusing on leadership almost exclusively requires in-depth case studies of crisis situations when leadership matters the most (e.g., Samuels 2003; Lewis 2007).

Facing these obstacles, how can we make steady progress toward understanding NDT and development and with what kind of empirical tools? The first thing is to acknowledge that the prevailing dogma of causal inference is bad for economics, especially for understanding complex and challenging social facts, such as development (Bardhan 2016; Akerlof 2020). What we need instead is a combination of adequate quantitative and in-depth case study (i.e., mostly qualitative) evidence, plus logical deduction. Here, I conjecture that a promising way forward is to examine countries with similar growth experiences for one period and then very different experiences for the period after, with crises as key signposts. Consistent with our focus on LDCs, we can first identify LDCs that have managed to grow for a decade or more (10, 20, 30, 40, and 50 years) since 1960 and then explore what they have done right or wrong with in-depth comparative case studies (see table I.1 in the book's introduction for the list of countries).[10]

We start arbitrarily with an average annual growth rate of 4% of GDP per capita (GDPpc). Such a growth rate will double GDPpc in 20 years, triple it in 30 years, increase it close to five times (4.8) in 40 years, and increase it slightly more than 7.1 times in 50 years. Apparently, sustaining a 4% annual growth rate of GDPpc for even 20 years is no easy task.[11] In fact, not many LDCs have managed that, as evidenced by the following descriptive statistics:

- Only 6 economies have achieved 50 years of over 4% growth.
- Only 11 have achieved 40 years of over 4% growth (including the 6 above).
- Only 21 have achieved 30 years of over 4% growth (including the 11 above).
- Only 43 have achieved 20 years of over 4% growth (including the 21 above).
- Only 81 have achieved 10 years of over 4% growth (including the 43 above).

In other words, of the 81 economies with 10 years of 4% growth, only 43 of them have managed to grow for another 10 years, while 38 of them sank. Of the 43 economies that have managed to grow for 20 years, only 21 have managed to grow for another 10 years. Of the 21, only 11 have managed to growth for another 10 years (30 years in total). Undoubtedly, this is a depressing picture. Now the question becomes, What lessons can we draw from it?

More concretely, what cases (i.e., countries, economies) should we look into for discovering important theoretical and practical lessons for LDCs? How should we conduct the case studies? Drawing from existing discussions (e.g., Waldner 1999; Woo-Cumings 1999; Kohli 2004; Slater 2010; Vu 2010a), I believe that the following three points will serve as useful guidelines.

First, extremely weak states (e.g., Somalia) or states with adequate state capacity but where development is not seen as a central task do not meet the necessary starting conditions for obtaining development. Such states may seek predation (e.g., Democratic Republic of Congo) or simply do not have the state infrastructural power to play any role or generate development. These states are not very illuminating cases for uncovering useful lessons for development. Rather, their key tasks are for building states and gaining a mind-set for pursuing development.

Second, comparative case studies will be more useful than many single case studies scattered in the literature (e.g., some of the studies in Rodrik 2003; Chang 2007). Moreover, comparison of halfway cases (or half-negative cases) and successful cases promises to be more illuminating than the standard comparison of positive and negative cases. In other words, we should compare states that have pursued development and achieved some results but then became stagnant against successful states. Such comparisons should reveal important data about the necessary conditions (and even perhaps quasi-sufficient conditions) for success. Slightly less useful comparisons would be those between successful states and unsuccessful states despite their similar state capacities (e.g., Thailand and the Philippines during the 1997 Asian financial crisis).

Third, both inductions from a set of successful states that are somewhat similar and inductions from a set of unsuccessful states that are somewhat similar will still be useful for drawing lessons. Obviously, for these comparisons, important lessons for causal inferences when doing process tracing should be imported to arrive at more reliable causal explanations or theories.

For econometric exercises, state capacity and institutions in period $t-1$ can be taken as exogenous for understanding the performance of an economy in period t because state capacities are difficult to build and accumulate, whereas institutions tend to be quite durable. With sound datasets, we may be able to test the following hypotheses (summarized in table 8.2).

(1) Both extractive capacity and coercive capacity should have an inverted-U-shape relationship with economic growth: both are necessary for development, but a state cannot hope to extract too much from its economy or rely too much on coercion and still have robust growth. More concretely, overall tax rate and spending on security (coercion) apparatuses should have an inverted-U-shape relationship with economic growth.

(2) Inadequate investment in basic health care and basic education is always a bad policy.

(3) When policies are correct, the stronger the delivery capacity, the better for growth. When policies are wrong, the stronger the delivery capacity, the worse for growth.

TABLE 8.2. Possible Patterns and Hypotheses for Empirical Testing

Items\outcomes	Immediate outcomes: Road density, clean water, education, etc. (high or low)	"Final" outcomes: Development and QoG
Coercive capacity (high or low)	Overall effect is nonlinear; linear up to a point but then declines (i.e., spending too much on coercion is inimical to investment and development).	Nonlinear; linear up to a point but then declines. Relationship will be hard to establish, however, due to distance from state capacity to these outcomes.
Extractive capacity (high or low)	Overall effect is nonlinear; linear up to a point but then declines (i.e., too much extraction is inimical to investment and development)	Nonlinear; linear up to a point but then declines. Relationship will be hard to establish, however, due to distance from state capacity to these outcomes.
Delivery/ implementation (high or low)	Linear	Not sure. Relationship will be hard to establish, due to distance from state capacity to these outcomes, which are also affected by states' intention and will.
Information/decision (good or bad)	Linear	Not sure. Relationship will be hard to establish, due to distance from state capacity to these outcomes, which are also affected by states' intention and will.

(4) Too much unproductive redistribution (or redistributive policies/ politics) is always counterproductive and will be extremely harmful for early stages of development.

(5) Weak states are more likely to fall into and then remain trapped by poverty and other social ills.

B. AN EMPIRICAL ILLUSTRATION: CHINA VERSUS INDIA

Much has been said regarding the contrasting performance of economic development by China and India. For believers in democracy's economic advantages (e.g., North et al. 2009, 2013; Acemoglu and Robinson 2012), India should have grown much faster since independence in 1947 than China since the founding of the People's Republic during its civil war in 1949. Yet, before their respective reforms, India from 1947 to 1990 lagged behind China from 1949 to 1978 in almost every respect, despite the fact that China had inflicted two colossal disasters upon itself (i.e., the "Great Leap Forward" famine and the Cultural Revolution). Since their respective reform periods, China (1978–2020) has so far continued to maintain its growth edge over India (1990–2020). So how are we going to explain this fact (e.g., Bardhan 2010)?[12] NDT sheds some interesting new light on this puzzle.

Overall, China has stronger state capacity, partly due to its longer state history than that of India and partly due to its revolutionary roots (Vu 2010a; Wen 2016, esp. ch. 5).[13] In contrast, India has a much lower state capacity, especially in terms of coercion, extraction (the two foundational dimensions), and delivery: perhaps the only dimension within state capacity in which India enjoys an advantage is information because autocracy tends to obstruct the free flow of information (Sen 2000).

In terms of regulatory factors of state capacity, China also enjoys certain advantages. Certainly, penetration by the Chinese state is much deeper than penetration by the Indian state because China went through a top-to-bottom social revolution led by a revolutionary party. Also, the Chinese state enjoys more autonomy than the Indian state despite the fact that both have a high level of corruption. Together within China's competition for development, these features have provided local Chinese officials with more incentives and resources for development. Also, when it comes to industrial policies specifically, China has made many correct bets (Mao et al. 2021; Chen et al. 2022).[14] Thus, the only key component within the NDT for which India possesses key advantages over China is within institutions. Yet, even here, India does not enjoy overall advantages over China.

To begin with, democracy does not guarantee development because democracy has only an indirect, channel-specific, and conditional effect (see chapters 5 and 6). Very critically, because democracy becomes necessary (and more useful) only when a country reaches the world technology frontier, it does not bestow India with an inherent growth advantage because both India and China are still quite far away from the technological frontier.

Second, India's property rights protection is much more robust than China's, but this has proved to be a double-edged sword. The key is land property rights. In China, land is publicly owned and hence the state can easily seize land for developmental purposes (e.g., for Special Economic Zones, industrial parks, etc.). Yet, due to its property rights, India cannot do this.

Third, due to its persistent caste system, India has been a laggard in terms of redistribution as a form of empowering the people. Combined with its

TABLE 8.3. An Empirical Illustration of NDT: China versus India

Dimensions	China	India
STATE CAPACITY		
Coercion	+++	++
Extraction	+++	++
Administrative I (i.e., delivering)	+++	+ (partly constrained by its institution on property rights)
Administrative II, information	+ (autocracy tends to obstruct the free flow of information)	++
Administrative II, leadership	+ (leadership is uneven)	+ (leadership is uneven)
DIMENSIONS OF IFED		
IFED-1: Order and stability	+++ (e.g., unrest)	++ (e.g., insurgency)
IFED-2: Material market	++	++
IFED-3: Positional market	++	+ (i.e., caste system)
IFED-4: Redistribution	++	+
IFED-5: Equality of opportunity	++ (?)	+ (quota system)
IFED-6: Liberty for innovation	+	++
POLICIES		
Macroeconomic	++	++
Social	++	+
Industrial	++	+
QUALITY OF GOVERNANCE		
Procedural/due process	+	++
Gathering and aggregating subjects' opinions	+	++
Goals toward public interests	++	++
Transparency/corruption	+	+

Note: More plus signs indicate stronger performance.

weak delivery capacity, India has thus lagged far behind China in terms of supporting its population with basic education and health care.

Hence, overall, India does not possess better institutions than China; each country has its own counterproductive institutions, and both countries' quality of governance needs great improvement. China, however, has managed to compensate for its institutional deficiencies with stronger state capacity and sounder policies. Indeed, one can actually argue that China since 1978 has also come to possess better institutions for development (summarized in table 8.3). Since this is the case, although China remains a robust autocracy whereas India is a robust democracy, the former can develop itself better than the latter, at least in principle.

Finally, our new framework also resolves Fukuyama's amazement over why China has been ranked so low in governance (Fukuyama 2013, 2016; Kaufmann et al. 2010). Because the Worldwide Governance Indicators seek to measure governance, not state capacity (although they do capture some aspects of state capacity), it is no wonder China has low scores. Here, India enjoys some advantages over China.

IV. Concluding Remarks

This chapter has outlined a new framework that promises to integrate and even transcend several unfruitful debates regarding the role of different factors in economic development—most prominently, state capacity, institutions, policies, and governance. More concretely, I contend that state capacity, institutions, and policies constitute the new development triangle (NDT). In contrast, the quality of governance (QoG) should not be taken as a contributing factor in shaping economic development. Rather, QoG itself is an outcome underpinned by state capacity, institutions, and policies, just like development itself. Furthermore, I have outlined some useful directions for understanding the NDT. Yet, understanding how NDT impacts development will remain an extremely challenging task for which I can only call for more effort.

Conclusion

LAYING THE FOUNDATION
FOR DEVELOPMENT

Generating and then sustaining economic development will remain the perennial challenge for most LDCs for many decades to come. In this concluding chapter, I summarize some practical implications for tackling this tall task, especially when thinking about states' roles in shaping development. Obviously, I cannot possibly prescribe any comprehensive policy package for specific issues or domains. Rather, my purpose is to lay out a few principles for LDCs to craft institutions and policies in order to facilitate development. Sound institutions and policies, underpinned by state capacities, fulfill the critical functions of providing possibility, incentive, capability, and opportunity and thus lay a solid foundation for jump-starting and sustaining development (see table 2.1).

I. Becoming a Developmental State in the Midst of Globalization

As underscored repeatedly above, once we admit that institutions and policies matter for development, it must follow that the state is a key player in jump-starting and sustaining development. The ultimate question for LDCs can thus be put, How can an LDC become and remain a "developmental state" in the broader sense?

A growing body of literature has certainly provided much insight on how later-developing countries can catch up by becoming developmental states (e.g., Gerschenkron 1962; Johnson 1982, 1995; Deyo 1987; Amsden 1989; Haggard 1990; Wade 1990; Chaudhry 1993; Evans 1995; Epstein 2000; Kohli 2004; Slater 2010; Vu 2010a; for reviews, see Bardhan 2016; Haggard 2018). Moreover, the developmental state has not been an exclusively East Asian phenomenon: Mauritius and Ethiopia can be credibly claimed as African developmental states (Subramanian and Roy 2003; see also Evans 1998; Routley 2014). Hence, the EADS literature is not the end of the story. What we need is a more integrated theory of the developmental state that goes beyond East Asia (Bardhan 2000, 2016; Haggard 2018; see also Lewis 1984).

We begin by first admitting that the state can do far more than just protect property rights. The central question of development is thus as much about the positive aspects of making the state a helping hand as it is about the negative aspects of preventing states from being a grabbing hand. The notion that a free market ever existed and prospered all by itself is a myth. On the contrary, "the road to the free market was opened and kept open by an enormous increase in continuous, centrally planned organized and controlled interventionism" (Polanyi [1944] 2001, 140).[1]

The fate of post–Soviet Union economic reform in Russia is illustrative here. In the aftermath of the collapse of the Soviet Union, Russia initiated economic reform under a largely collapsed state, and the outcome was an economy mostly controlled by oligarchies. In this sense, the Russian state retreated too fast: it did not lay down enough proper rules, and it could not enforce the rules it did enact (Olson 2000). Before a state can retreat (and let the "free" market work), it first has to march forward.

Second, we must acknowledge that "natural endowment" is more than land and natural resources: state history, culture, and historical institutions are also part of a state's "natural endowment." Many sub-Saharan African states had never fully finished the process toward a coherent state structure and were instead abruptly ushered into the era of the modern state by decolonization. Consequently, these African states have had a hard time controlling violence and extracting taxes, and laying down IFED has been mostly beyond their state capacities: all these tasks require a threshold of state capacity to begin with, and many (if not most) sub-Saharan African states simply do not possess it (Easterly and Levine 1997; Van Arkadie 1999; Herbst 2000; Bates 2008). The recent African growth miracle has been partly underpinned by about half a century of state building by African states, first and foremost by controlling violence (Straus 2012; Rodrik 2018).

Third, because state building ultimately underpins state capacity, adequate state capacity cannot be built in a short time frame (for a review, see

Vu 2010b). Hence, the best option for a weak state is to have some growth in the short term, build on the momentum, and then put more effort and resources back into building its state capacities gradually, with the key being to generate positive feedback between growth of the economy in the near term and growth in state capacities via state building over time (Rodrik 2007; Lin 2012c).

Here, two aspects are perhaps crucial. The first is a universal consensus: a capable bureaucracy, which can only be built by meritocratic recruitment (Johnson 1982; Amsden 1989; Wade 1990; Haggard 1990; Evans 1995; Cheng et al. 1998; cf. Evans and Rauch 1999; Cornell et al. 2021). The second factor, perhaps a bit controversial, is nationalism as a sense of solidarity or collective identity within a community that extends beyond tribes and ethnic groups. Nationalism has been one of the most powerful ideologies in modern history, and a certain degree of nationalism is necessary for sustaining a modern nation-state (Gellner 1983; Mann 1993). Part of the value of nationalism to the state and development is similar to loyalty to an organization: without loyalty from its members, an organization's collective will and competence will suffer (Hirschman 1970; see also Lewis 1955, 28–29). Nationalism may be especially critical when a state faces an economic crisis (Doner et al. 2005). Fractionalization along ethnic, linguistic, and religious fissures is bad for growth, partly because it weakens nationalism (Alesina et al. 2003).[2]

Indeed, all of the major East Asian miracle economies had strong nationalist sentiments (Johnson 1962; Amsden 1989; Vu 2010a). In contrast, because many African countries have never fully experienced the long historical process of melding into a cohesive cultural entity as part of the foundation of a modern nation-state, fractionalization in these countries runs deep.

Finally, and no less importantly, in today's world LDCs have to develop under a globalized economy. The immense power of globalized capital and rules puts any country that wants to experiment with institutions and policies in a very difficult situation: no state can experiment with institutions and policies without heeding the ever-changing international environment, as Kiren Aziz Chaudhry (1993) perceptively noted long ago. In the post–Cold War era, the terrorist attacks of September 11 in 2001, the 2008 Great Recession, and now the COVID-19 pandemic have all drastically reshaped the international environment with profound and lasting consequences, and it is such a challenging environment under which LDCs must now operate.

II. Engineering IFED with Institutional Changes

For many LDCs, the primary challenge is to engineer institutional change; enforcing specific institutional arrangements comes only second. Therefore, without an adequate understanding of institutional change, it will be difficult, if not impossible, to understand the role of the state in laying the institutional foundation for development.

Here, a general theory of institutional change is crucial for understanding the role of the state in laying down the institutional foundations for social welfare (Tang 2011b). Our framework, however, has a cautionary note for the state when engineering IFED because a state faces four key challenges to installing institutions: our inherently limited knowledge, the distributional effect of institutions, IFED as a system, and natural endowments.

The inherent incompleteness of our knowledge. Other than realizing that "institutions matter," we have yet to adequately understand the many specific arrangements in the various dimensions of IFED and the interactions among the different institutional arrangements within the system of IFED. Equally important, we have inadequate knowledge about how people will respond to the various arrangements, not to mention to the whole institutional system (Przeworski 2004), partly because people may respond to incentives and constraints underscored by institutions in ways that designers of the institutions cannot anticipate.[3] With a vast gap in our knowledge, a state's ability to install a growth-facilitating IFED through "systemic" institutional transformation must necessarily be limited.

The distributional effect of institutions. The effect of institutions is rarely neutral: institutions almost always have distributional effects. In other words, most of the time, institutions only benefit some but not all agents. As a result, different agents will fight for institutions (Tang 2011b). Consequently, institutions that are eventually made are not necessarily public goods for all but rather private goods that serve the interests of some.

IFED as a system. Specific institutions within IFED interact with each other. Moreover, institutions also interact with culture and other components within the development triangle. From these interactions, friction and incompatibilities inevitably arise. An institution that seems to improve welfare independently may actually jeopardize welfare via its interaction with other institutions, and prescriptions based on identifying traps via some statistical associations cannot possibly be valid and mostly likely cannot work (e.g., Collier 2007). Similarly, some institutional arrangements that are economically optimal in one country may not perform well in other countries due to differences in their overall historical endowments; the critical role of context and localized knowledge in building growth-sustaining institutions cannot be overemphasized (Lin 1989, 3; Rodrik 2003, 17–18). Most of the time, sticking a theoretically optimal institutional framework into a random country without heeding local contexts and knowledge will not work (Przeworski 2004).

Natural endowments. Institutions are embedded within a state's "natural endowments" and are inherently conservative (North 1990; Williamson 2000; Greif and Laitin 2004). Moreover, any institution, once in place, has a life of its own; institutions themselves are "carriers of history" (David 1994; see also Greif 1998, 82). Hence, installing IFED via institutional changes faces many obstacles and cannot be achieved in a short period of time.

For LDCs, these challenges are both good news and bad news. The good news is that they do not have to heed all the smart advice from textbooks offered by outside experts. Instead, they can tailor institutions to their local conditions. The bad news is that installing IFED is a slow, long, and frequently difficult process. Moreover, experimenting with different institutional arrangements may or may not work because of existing institutions and a country's historical evolutionary path. Further, because development is a systemic and dynamic outcome, sustained development cannot be achieved by getting one or two things right in one or two periods. The fundamental challenge for LDCs is to find a fine balance between working toward a sound IFED and making transitional institutional arrangements work as efficiently as possible as development proceeds.

Our framework therefore calls for a cautious or piecemeal approach overall in installing IFED, with occasional bold changes when necessary. Attempts to transform the whole IFED overnight or impose a simple institutional solution usually produce more disasters than miracles. A new institutional system cannot be installed overnight. Consequently, the old institutional system should not be flushed away. When moving toward a better IFED, it is necessary to achieve a balance between changing some institutional arrangements and making other parts of the existing institutional system work as efficiently as possible.

As a result, an experimental approach toward institutional changes is perhaps essential, as conveyed pithily by Deng Xiaoping's dictum: "Cross the river by feeling the stones" (World Bank 2008, 3–5). In contrast, post–Soviet Russia's "big bang" rush to privatize, guided by the new institutional economics' overemphasis of property rights, proved to be another soured attempt at grand social engineering due to our ignorance of our ignorance (Williamson, 2000 609–10), as Hayek warned us a long time ago (Hayek 1945; 1960, ch. 3; see also Polanyi 1941; Popper [1945] 1966; Scott 1995).

As a principle, a state should initiate reform in areas that can jump-start growth to generate momentum and sustain the momentum with more reforms. If things do not work out, try something else. Of course, gradualism in engineering institutional change has its own drawbacks, such as entrenching too many vested interest groups, pork barrel politics, and institutional rigidity (Olson 1982; Rodrik 2000, 16–17). Hence, gradualism does not reject decisive actions that are necessary for overhauling some key aspects of IFED or overcoming critical obstacles, from time to time.[4] Here, a crisis mentality (when facing a real crisis) may indeed be needed for decisive policy turn-arounds and institutional changes.[5]

III. Making Policies: Balancing Short-Term and Long-Term Objectives

Whereas institutions are usually made for addressing medium-term to long-term issues, policies are usually made for addressing some short-term and medium-term challenges. The proper relationship between policies and institutions when it comes to economic development can thus be understood as follows:

> Igniting development and sustaining it are somewhat different enterprises. The former generally requires a limited range of (often unconventional [policy]) reforms that need not overly tap the institutional capacity of the economy. The latter challenge is in many ways harder, as it requires constructing a sound institutional underpinning to maintain productive dynamics and endow the economy with resilience to shocks over the longer term. The good news is that this institutional infrastructure does not have to be constructed overnight. (Rodrik 2007, 16)

In other words, there is no need for "big bang" reform in jump-starting development. Some policy changes first (and some institutional changes second) may be enough for jump-starting growth in the near term, although sustaining growth in the medium to long run and turning it into development will require deeper institutional changes.

Making policies for economic development also presents four key challenges: our inherently limited knowledge, the distributional effect of policies, policies operating within existing institutions and policies, and the trade-offs between the short term and medium to long term. Because the first three challenges are essentially similar to their counterparts in making institutions, I shall not repeat what has been said above. Instead, I focus on the fourth challenge here.

Within a system, any policy or action generally produces more than its designer had intended (Jervis 1997). Hence, policies made for addressing short- to medium-term challenges will have medium- to long-term effects, both intended and unintended. Some seemingly wonderful short-term policies may have unintended and undesired long-term consequences. Conversely, while a policy may be beneficial in the long run, it may be painful in the short run. When this is the case, a state often faces serious trade-offs when crafting policies. Economic policies that are necessary for addressing a pressing challenge in the short term may have a long-term growth-hindering effect on performance.

Of course, some policies are inherently growth hindering. Financialization of an economy is almost always bad (even without hindsight) because financial transactions do not produce added value by themselves (Haldane et al. 2010). What is more, financialization of an economy (as a policy) generates long-term impacts on institutions, partly through political contributions in either democracy or nondemocracy.

More often than not, however, a policy's short- to medium-term effects may be different from its medium- to long-term ones. For instance, policies designed to combat inflation (such as austerity) in the present may hinder growth in the medium term. Most prominently, financial crises—a very different beast—often require drastic actions to avoid an impending implosion. Yet, almost inevitably, policies made for the purpose of containing a financial crisis have medium- to long-run effects, and some of their effects do not necessarily facilitate growth. Moreover, different policies for containing a crisis may have different causal pathways and uneven (i.e., nonlinear and nonmonotonic) effects.

Furthermore, while explaining a policy's success is relatively simple (i.e., all has gone right), explaining a policy's failure is far more challenging. Besides the obvious possibility that the policy is bad, there are four additional possibilities that can contribute to its failure: a misleading assessment of the (changing) situation, inadequate resources devoted to the policy, bad implementation (e.g., corruption, ineptness), and contradictions with other policies. This key but often neglected point poses another challenge for us in drawing lessons from our past experiences (Zuo and Tang 2013).

Facing these difficulties, policymakers must be aware of potential trade-offs and then adopt a cautious approach toward making policies, even when facing a crisis, unless the crisis is a systemic one as in 2008. More often than not, it is more advisable to have some policies in place, allow them a bit of time to have an effect, and then assess what more needs to be done before more policies are poured into a situation.

IV. Basic Principles and Concluding Remarks

Other than countries that are undergoing systemic violence (e.g., civil war), states do have ample room for jump-starting growth with some basic policy changes (World Bank 1997; Rodrik 2007; Lin 2012c). The more challenging task is to sustain growth momentum with institutional changes and growing state capacities. Integrating and building on existing discussions, this section suggests some basic principles and concludes.

The first principle is a cautionary but central one: every state has to know and operate within its limits, and it has to match its tasks and roles with its capacities (World Bank 1997, esp. ch. 3). No state can do everything. In fact, one of the primary causes behind the numerous fiascoes in many episodes of "structural adjustments" dictated by the IMF and World Bank and led by the Washington Consensus is that structural adjustments almost always have demanded that LDCs get many things right within a short period of time.

Second, a state's central task in economic development is to expand not only the size but also the scope of the market with state power, as states accumulate more and more power. Scope also matters: the key is to let the market operate in places it should rather than to limit the market with political patronage and barriers (Olson 2000). Size also matters: without a state that is powerful enough, a state cannot integrate the market(s) within its borders, and the size of the market will remain small. Indeed, this was the real story behind the rise of the West. Epstein put it forcefully:

> The main institutional bottleneck in pre-modern [European] states did not arise from a lack of concern with contractual rules, despotic insouciance or parliamentary weakness, but from the coordination failures caused by the absence of undivided sovereignty over the political and

economic spheres. Multiple sovereignty was a source of both economic and political inefficiency. Because the state did not have a monopoly of power with its borders, feudal lords, cities, corporations, and other "public" or chartered bodies derived income from jurisdictional rights that constrained Smithian growth. (Epstein 2000, 36)

Third, because sound policies can substitute for institutional arrangements (at least for the short term), states have to prioritize sound policies when sound institutions require more time to build (Glaeser et al. 2004; Rodrik 2007). Also, policies can eventually evolve into formal institutions; for example, from a household responsibility system in the countryside to a constitutional protection of property rights in China. The key here is to maintain sound policies while engineering institutional changes for the better (World Bank 1997, 2008; Rodrik 2007; Lin 2012c; cf. North et al. 2009, 2013; Besley and Persson 2011; Acemoglu and Robinson 2012).

Fourth, the evolutionary and systemic nature of development dictates that states have to constantly adjust to the changing situation because economic development transforms human society (Lin 2012c). In other words, a state must retain some flexibility in its institutions and policies. With all the more recent good performers, such as China, India, and Vietnam, this has been the case (Qian 2003; Xu 2011; Yao 2014; Ang 2016).

Fifth, barring some exceptions (e.g., Singapore after independence), state capacity often takes a long period of time to build and accumulate.[6] Moreover, state capacities can be easily degraded by bad institutions and bad policies, as exemplified by China on the verge of collapse after Mao's purge of intellectuals in the Anti-Rightist Campaign (1956–1958) and the even more disastrous Great Leap Forward (1958–1961) and Cultural Revolution (1966–1976). Hence, the last and key principle is that every state should try to build and accumulate its capacities or at least not weaken its capacities with political and social revolution or upheaval unless the state is already on the verge of collapse.

Historically, there seem to have been only a few roads toward strong state capacity, including war and conquest (Elias [1939] 1994; Tilly 1990), a revolutionary single party (Johnson 1962; Vu 2010a), an antirevolutionary protection pact (Slater 2009), and perhaps in some cases colonialism (Mahoney 2010; Kurtz 2013; Soifer 2015; see also the special issue of *Studies in Comparative International Development*, 2008). Yet, as Jervis (2002) noted two decades ago—now supported with extensive data (Cederman et al. 2017)—both interstate and intrastate (especially ethnic) wars have decreased significantly. When this is the case, how can a weak state justify state-building measures that often require at least some sacrifices from its citizens? This may be a new challenge faced by weak states.

Finally, different institutions or policies and the different effects of a single institution or policy may pull in different directions. As a result, the effects of institutions and policies must be context specific and issue specific (Lin 1989, 3–7; Engerman and Skoloff 2005; World Bank 2005, 10–12; Rodrik 2007, esp. ch. 5). Consequently, human societies will never secure the perfect institutional foundations of development; there is no policy or institutional panacea for development, although there are some basic things that states can do if they want to achieve long-term development. All these facts pose imposing challenges for LDCs in finding their own paths toward sustained development, and they have to face these challenges with knowledge, wisdom, and sometimes, courage.

APPENDIX TO CHAPTER 4:
PROOFS OF THE SOLUTIONS

Let E_{min} denote the minimum total investment required for obtaining a certain level of education. Then $E_{min} - E_{pu}$ denotes the minimum private investment required for obtaining a certain level of education by a household.

From equation (1) in the text, we have $K_0 + E_{pr} = W_0 - C_0 - S_0$. Let $T(\geq 0)$ denote $K_0 + E_{pr} = W_0 - C_0 - S_0$ as the budgetary constraint after excluding other factors.

We have two basic scenarios. The first scenario is $T < E_{min} - E_{pu}$. In this scenario, a household cannot afford to provide any schooling. The second scenario is $T \geq E_{min} - E_{pu}$. In this scenario, a household's minimal budgetary support is larger than the minimum investment required for education minus the public investment in education. Under this scenario, a household has to optimize its investment in education (and hence in production). Let E_{pr}^* denote the optimal level of private investment in education. This scenario has two subscenarios.

The first subscenario is $E_{pr}^* + E_{pu} > E_{min}$. Under this subscenario, the minimum investment for education is low enough that every household can afford schooling. Yet, a household may voluntarily withhold its members from school if the household deems the return from schooling is actually lower than the return from investing the capital in production without schooling (e.g., knowledge taught in schools is of little practical value, when schools merely teach superstition and religious doctrines without any practical value).

The second subscenario is $E_{pr}^* + E_{pu} \leq E_{min}$. Under this subscenario, a household deems that the return from schooling is higher than the return from investing the capital in production without schooling because education is of real practical value (e.g., knowledge taught is mathematics, physics, chemistry, and biology, rather than superstitions and religious doctrines). Yet, due to budgetary constraints, under this subscenario, a household will only provide its members with some schooling up to a certain level, depending on the share of public investment out of the total cost of education. Under such a setup, it is straightforward to obtain the solutions for the two subscenarios of the second basic scenario.

I. Solutions for Subscenario $T \geq E_{min} - E_{pu}$ and $E_{pr}^* + E_{pu} > E_{min}$

Again, let E_{pr}^* denote the optimal level of private investment in education. When there is E_{pr}^* available, $Y_{max} > Y(E_{pr} = 0) > Y(E_{pr} = E_{pu} = 0)$. The solution is $E_{pr}^* + E_{pu} > E_{min}$. Put in lay terms, few households will withhold investment in education for budgetary reasons; however, households may still withhold investment in education under other circumstances.

Recall

$$T - (K_0 + E_{pr}) \geq 0$$

and

$$Y_1 = A \cdot H_1^\alpha \cdot K_1^{1-\alpha} = A \cdot [\gamma(E_{pr} + E_{pu}) + \beta \cdot H_0]^\alpha \cdot K_1^{1-\alpha}$$

Take the Lagrangian

$$L(K_1, E_{pr}) = A \cdot [\gamma(E_{pr} + E_{pu}) + \beta \cdot H_0]^\alpha \cdot K_1^{1-\alpha} + \lambda(T - K_1 - E_{pr}) \quad (1)$$

In turn, we obtain the conditions for maximizing Y_1.

$$\frac{\partial L}{\partial K_1} = A \cdot (1-\alpha) \cdot [\gamma(E_{pr} + E_{pu}) + \beta \cdot H_0]^\alpha \cdot K_1^{-\alpha} - \lambda = 0 \quad (2)$$

$$\frac{\partial L}{\partial E_{pr}} = A \cdot \gamma \cdot \alpha \cdot [\gamma(E_{pr} + E_{pu}) + \beta \cdot H_0]^{\alpha-1} \cdot K_1^{1-\alpha} - \lambda = 0 \quad (3)$$

$$\frac{\partial L}{\partial \lambda} = T - K_1 - E_{pr} = 0 \quad (4)$$

From equations (2) and (3), we obtain

$$\frac{A \cdot (1-\alpha) \cdot [\gamma(E_{pr} + E_{pu}) + \beta \cdot H_0]^\alpha \cdot K_1^{-\alpha}}{A \cdot \gamma \cdot \alpha \cdot [\gamma(E_{pr} + E_{pu}) + \beta \cdot H_0]^{\alpha-1} \cdot K_1^{1-\alpha}} = 1$$

or

$$\frac{(1-\alpha) \cdot [\gamma(E_{pr} + E_{pu}) + \beta \cdot H_0]}{\gamma \cdot \alpha \cdot K_1} = 1 \quad (5)$$

Inserting equation (4) into equation (5), we can eliminate K_1 and obtain

$$E_{pr}^* = \alpha \cdot T - (1-\alpha) \cdot E_{pu} - \frac{1-\alpha}{\gamma} \cdot \beta \cdot H_0 \quad (6)$$

From $E^*_{pr} + E_{pu} > E_{min}$, we obtain

$$\frac{E_{pu} + E^*_{pr}}{E_{min}} > 1 \tag{7}$$

Inserting equation (7) into equation (6), we obtain

$$\frac{\alpha \cdot T + \alpha \cdot E_{pu} - \dfrac{1-\alpha}{\gamma} \cdot \beta \cdot H_0}{E_{min}} > 1$$

or

$$\alpha \left(\frac{T}{E_{min}} + \frac{E_{pu}}{E_{min}} \right) - \frac{1-\alpha}{\gamma E_{min}} \cdot \beta \cdot H_0 > 1 \tag{8}$$

Apparently, the greater the budget a household has (i.e., T is large), the higher the raw intelligence possessed by a household (i.e., γ is large), the higher the rate of knowledge depreciation or rate of technological change (i.e., β is low), the more critical human capital is in production (i.e., α is large), and the larger the public support for education (i.e., E_{pu} is large), the more willing a household will be to invest in its children's education. In contrast, the higher the minimum amount of investment for education is (i.e., E_{min} is large) and the more initial human capital a household possesses (i.e., H_0 is large), the less willing a household is to invest in its children's further education. *Most critically, taken together, the greater the portion of the total cost for basic education that public support shoulders* $\left(\text{i.e., } \dfrac{E_{pu}}{E_{min}} \text{ is larger} \right)$, *the more willing a household will be to invest in its children's further education.*

II. Solutions for Subscenario $T \geq E_{min} - E_{pu}$ and $E^*_{pr} + E_{pu} \leq E_{min}$

Under such a setting, a household has the capacity for investing in education up to a certain level, yet the cost of education is so significant that a household must devote more resources to education than to production in order to invest in education up to a certain level. Under such constraints, a household cannot maximize Y by investing E^*_{pr}. Rather, the optimal solution is to maximize the level of education (i.e., investing up to that level) up to the point from which the return from investment in education becomes smaller than the return from investing in education. Formally, $Y(E_{pr} = E_{min} - E_{pu}) > Y(E_{pr} = E_{pu} = 0)$.

Under this setup, $E_{pr} + E_{pu} = E_{min}$, whereas with investment in production $K_1 = T - (E_{min} - E_{pu})$, we have

$$A \cdot [\gamma \cdot E_{min} + \beta \cdot H_0]^\alpha \cdot (T - E_{min} + E_{pu})^{1-\alpha} > A \cdot (\beta \cdot H_0)^\alpha \cdot T^{1-\alpha} \tag{9}$$

Simplifying the equation and letting M denote the simplified equation, we obtain

$$M = \left(\frac{\gamma \cdot E_{min}}{\beta \cdot H_0} + 1 \right)^{\alpha} \cdot \left(\frac{E_{pu} - E_{min}}{T} + 1 \right)^{1-\alpha} > 1$$

or

$$M = \left(\frac{\gamma \cdot E_{min}}{\beta \cdot H_0} + 1 \right)^{\alpha} \cdot \left(\frac{E_{min}\left(\frac{E_{pu}}{E_{min}} - 1 \right)}{T} + 1 \right)^{1-\alpha} > 1 \qquad (10)$$

with $E_{pu} - E_{min} < 0$.

Equation (10) yields similar implications as equation (8). In other words, the greater the budget a household has (i.e., T is large), the higher the raw intelligence possessed by a household (i.e., γ is large), the higher the rate of knowledge depreciation or rate of technological change (i.e., β is small), the more critical human capital is in production (i.e., α is large), the less initial human capital a household possesses (i.e., H_0 is small), and the larger the public support for education (i.e., E_{pu} is large), the more willing a household will be to invest in its children's education. Again, and more critically, *the higher the portion of the total cost for basic education that public support shoulders* $\left(\text{i.e., } \dfrac{E_{pu}}{E_{min}} \text{ is larger} \right)$, *the more willing a household will be to invest in its children's further education.*

Finally, we can establish the relationship between E_{min} and M. According to the chain rule,

$$\frac{\partial \ln M}{\partial E_{min}} = \frac{\partial M}{\partial E_{min}} \cdot \frac{\partial \ln M}{\partial M} = \frac{\partial M}{\partial E_{min}} \cdot \frac{1}{M}$$

we obtain

$$\frac{\partial M}{\partial E_{min}} = M \cdot \frac{\partial \ln M}{\partial E_{min}}$$

Taking the partial derivative of M with respect to E_{min}, we obtain

$$\frac{\partial M}{\partial E_{min}} = M \cdot \frac{\gamma \cdot \alpha \cdot T + \gamma \cdot \alpha \cdot E_{pu} - (1-\alpha) \cdot \beta \cdot H_0 - \gamma \cdot E_{min}}{(\gamma \cdot E_{min} + \beta \cdot H_0) \cdot (T - E_{min} + E_{pu})} \qquad (11)$$

Inserting equation (6) into equation (11), we obtain

$$\frac{\partial M}{\partial E_{min}} = M \cdot \frac{\gamma \cdot (E_{pr}^{*} + E_{pu} - E_{min})}{(\gamma \cdot E_{min} + \beta \cdot H_0) \cdot (T - E_{min} + E_{pu})} \qquad (12)$$

Recall the two conditions for the second subscenario of the second basic scenario,

$$T - E_{min} + E_{pu} > 0 \quad \text{and} \quad E_{pr}^* + E_{pu} - E_{min} < 0$$

We easily obtain

$$\frac{\partial M}{\partial E_{min}} < 0 \tag{13}$$

Equation (13) explicitly dictates that the larger E_{min} is, the lower the household's willingness to invest in the education of its members will be. Q.E.D.

5-A. Regimes and Growth: A Critical Literature Review

There are three broad bodies of literature on the relationship between regimes and growth. The first primarily addresses a regime's impact on growth on normative and theoretical grounds without systematic empirical evidence (e.g., Huntington 1968; Olson 1993; Bhagwati 2002). The second tries to establish some statistical correlation between regimes and growth. The third and more recent one seeks to reveal the specific channels through which regimes impact growth in addition to establishing statistical correlations between regimes and growth, often with panel data.[1] Because our theory partly builds on the first body of literature, we address it in the next section. The second trend is now dated and subsumed under the third body of literature; as such, we focus on the third here.

5-A.1. CROSS-COUNTRY GROWTH REGRESSION LITERATURE AND ITS INADEQUACIES

After the foundational works of Kormendi and Meguire (1985), Barro (1991), and Mankiw et al. (1992), the literature on regimes and growth, based primarily on cross-country growth regressions (CCGR) but sometimes in-depth case studies too, has been ever growing. Although a clear and robust empirical relationship between regimes and growth has yet to emerge (for recent reviews, see Knutsen 2012; Pozuelo et al. 2016; Truex 2017), a key consensus is that regimes impact growth only indirectly or via specific channels. Several channels have been singled out as the ones through which democracy can facilitate growth, including property rights, human capital, public health, redistribution, total factor productivity (TFP), state capacity, and political and economic stability (e.g., Sirowy and Inkeles 1990; Przeworski and Limongi 1993; Tavares and Wacziarg 2001; Lindert 2003; Gerring et al. 2005; Doucoulabos and Ulubaşoğlu 2008; Knutsen 2015; Acemoglu et al. 2019; Wang and Xu 2018). Table 5-A.1 summarizes these channels.

TABLE 5-A.1. Channels through Which Democracy May Impact Growth

Channels	Supporting	Dissenting
CHANNELS IN WHICH DEMOCRACY IS PURPORTED TO HOLD AN ADVANTAGE		
Property rights	North and Thomas 1973; North and Weingast 1989; Olson 1993; Barro 1996; Leblang 1996; Clague et al. 1996; Acemoglu et al. 2001, 2005; Lindert 2003; Doucoulabos and Ulubaşoğlu 2008	This link is a historical one (Lindert 2003).
Human capital, including education and health care	Engerman et al. 1998; Lake and Baum 2001; Tavares and Wacziarg 2001; Baum and Lake 2003; Feng 2003; Doucoulabos and Ulubaşoğlu 2008; Papaioannoun and Siourounis 2008; Wigley and Akkoyunlu-Wigley 2011; Gerring et al. 2012; Acemoglu et al. 2019	World Bank 1993; Lindert 2003; Ross 2006; Ansell 2010; Miller 2015; Treux 2017
Inflation/economic stability/volatility	Quinn and Wooley 2001; Feng 2003; Mobarak 2005; Doucoulabos and Ulubaşoğlu 2008; Klomp and de Haan 2009	None
Political stability	Acemoglu and Robinson 2000; Kurzman et al. 2002; Feng 2003; Rodrik 1999, 2000; Rodrik et al. 2004; Doucoulabos and Ulubaşoğlu 2008; Jong-A-Pin 2009; Goldstone et al. 2010	Perotti 1996; Tavares and Wacziarg 2001
Reduction of inequality	Muller 1988; Acemoglu and Robinson 2000; Besley and Burgess 2000; Sokoloff and Engerman 2000; Tavares and Wacziarg 2001	Aghion et al. 1999; Forbes 2000; Ansell 2010
Total factor productivity	Knutsen 2015	None
State capacity	Wang and Xu 2018. Knutsen (2013) reported an interactive effect on growth between regime type and state capacity. His results suggest that democracy facilitates economic growth only when state capacity is relatively low.	Tilly 1990; Slater 2010; Vu 2010; Hanson 2015
CHANNELS IN WHICH DEMOCRACY IS PURPORTED TO BE A DISADVANTAGE		
Accumulation of physical capital (democracy encourages wasteful consumption)	Tavares and Wacziarg 2001	

TABLE 5-A.1. (*continued*)

Channels	Supporting	Dissenting
Governmental spending (democracy encourages wasteful governmental spending)	Tavares and Wacziarg 2001; Kurzman et al. 2002	Sen 2000; Lake and Baum 2001; Baum and Lake 2003; Lindert 2003
Redistribution (democracy encourages non-productive if not counterproductive redistribution)	Olson 1982; Alesina and Rodrik 1994	Besley and Burgess 2000; Sokoloff and Engerman 2000; Feng 2003; Lindert 2003

Existing literature on regimes and growth, however, suffers from several shortcomings. First and foremost, the literature has become almost purely empirical to the point that it is only superficially theoretical, if not atheoretical. More often than not, this literature merely establishes some statistical correlation between regimes and growth without much prior theorizing. Most prominently, the literature has been largely disconnected from the classic defense and definition of democracy. As a result, we are often at a loss when trying to make sense of contradictory statistical correlations, and knowledge accumulation has often been limited, if not difficult (Aron 2000; de Haan 2007).

Second, and related to the first, most of the channels in which democracy holds (dis)advantage over autocracy that have been singled out by the literature are not necessarily unique to democracy, because many of the channels uncovered require additional ad hoc or implicit assumptions about the personality, political and economic preferences, and skills of rulers to operate. For instance, the thesis that protection of property rights requires democracy (e.g., North and Weingast 1989) can only be true when one assumes that all autocrats are predatory and thus unwilling to protect their subjects' property rights because they are "purely self-interested and having limited time-horizons" (Clark 1996, 566; see also Epstein 2000, 6). In principle, however, autocrats can commit to secure property rights as firmly as democracies when they have dynastic ambitions (Clark 1996, 566–67; see also Olson 1993), are fierce patriots (nationalists) or expansionists (Lewis 1955, 28, 79; Friedman 1962, 10; Przeworski and Limong 1993, 56), and/or face external threats (Epstein 2000, 25–27).

Indeed, many autocracies have matched democracy when it comes to protecting property rights (Przeworski and Limongi 1993, 52–4). South Korea and Taiwan before their respective democratization and Singapore and post-1978 China readily come to mind. More likely, the seemingly tight link between (illiberal) democracy and property rights has been a historical coincidence, as Lindert (2003) rightly noted: it just happened that (illiberal) democracies in historical times (e.g., Britain from the seventeenth to the early twentieth century) protected property rights better than most of their autocratic counterparts back then (see also Barro 1997, 22–23).

Similarly, the human capital channel, which includes both education and health care, is also based on an implicit assumption: (fully franchised) democracy provides mass education, thus facilitating the accumulation of human capital better than autocracy. Again, in principle, autocrats who strongly believe in the value of education can easily match democracy when it comes to investing in human capital. Indeed, all former socialist countries have invested heavily in education, especially education in natural sciences and technology. Moreover, although the amount of total investment in education certainly matters, the kind of investment also matters: elitist investment in mass education may actually heighten inequality and hinder growth. Yet, nonelitist mass education was achieved in Imperial Germany and most former communist countries. South Korea and Taiwan invested heavily in basic mass education long before they became democracies, and Singapore and Malaysia continue to do so. In contrast, education in illiberal, democratic Britain had a strong elitist bias before 1890, and India and many Latin American democracies continue to have a strong elitist bias in their educational policies (Lindert 2003; see also Dreze and Sen 2002, 143–186; Ansell 2010, ch. 3). Thus, while democracies may indeed have a positive effect on investment in education, they do not necessarily do a better job of investing in human capital than autocracies (Ross 2006). Certainly, some electoral autocracies do invest in human capital (McGuire 2015; Miller 2015). Similar criticisms can be applied to other channels, such as inequality, redistribution (which may also impact human capital), and state capacity.

In sum, partly due to the lack of prior theorizing, the channels singled out by the existing literature on regimes and growth are not really about regimes per se, but require implicit assumptions about the personality, preferences, and skills of autocratic rulers versus democratic rulers. In other words, in all these channels, nondemocracy can match democracy in principle and often in practice. As a result, we are often at a loss when trying to make sense of contradictory statistical correlations.

5-A.2. ECONOMIC AND SOCIOPOLITICAL STABILITY

Because the story behind the channel of economic and sociopolitical stability is a bit more complicated and our theory critically centers upon it, we address it in more detail. For many authors, there exists a fairly robust negative relationship between democracy and economic volatility or instability (e.g., Rodrik 1999; 2000; Quinn and Woolley 2001; Klomp and de Haan 2009). Existing literature has further suggested two possible pathways linking democracy with economic stability and in turn growth. The first pathway is that democracy reduces economic volatility because democracy favors risk-averse economic policy (Quinn and Woolley 2001). A second pathway is that democracy alleviates social conflict and thus copes with external economic shocks better than autocracy (Rodrik 1999; 2000). These works, however, suffer from critical methodological defects, such as measurement problems, invalid model specifications, and inadequate robustness testing (Yang 2008; cf. Klomp and de Hann 2009).[2] More critically, other than Quinn and Woolley (2001), all the works on economic volatility are also thoroughly atheoretical, and none of these works have presented a convincing case for why autocracy cannot also achieve economic stability.

Three possible pathways have been proposed to link democracy with growth via political stability. The first is reduction of inequality. According to this thesis, democracy tends to be more stable and thus more conducive to growth because democracy tends to do a better job in redistribution, thus reducing inequality (Muller 1988), and inequality is bad for growth (Aghion et al. 1999).

This pathway, however, faces major theoretical and empirical difficulties. Theoretically, as Bollen and Jackman (1985, 1995) perceptively pointed out, (factual) inequality does not necessarily lead to social instability because inequality is neither *inequity* nor *injustice*. Unless a large portion of the population perceives inequality as unjust, inequality does not necessarily lead to social instability. Unfortunately, as Gimpelson and Treisman (2018) have demonstrated, the public often misperceives (factual) inequality.

Empirically, CCGR evidence supporting the thesis that inequality is bad for growth has not been robust (Forbes 2000). Moreover, we have plenty of evidence that autocracies can actually be more egalitarian and pro-redistribution (and grow faster) than democracies, partly because land reform often requires "concentration of power" (Alertus 2015). South Korea, Singapore, and Taiwan all grew robustly while limiting inequality under autocracy (World Bank 1993; Ansell 2010). In contrast, inequality persists in India and many Latin America democracies: the level of inequality in these countries remains largely unchanged despite democracies and democratization (Bollen and Jackman 1995, 984).[3]

The second pathway through which democracy facilitates growth via political stability is social cleavage. Because social cleavages (e.g., ethnolinguistic fractionalization, political polarization) increase the probability of social conflict, they tend to reduce growth (Alesina et al. 2003; Desmet et al. 2012). Since democracy copes with social cleavages better than autocracy by encouraging social cooperation, democracy is more conducive to growth than autocracy (Rodrik 1999; 2000; Yang 2008).

The third pathway links democracy with political stability and private investment. Because private investment reflects individuals' confidence in returns from entrepreneurship and investment in human capital (Feng 2003, chs. 7 and 8), private investment is a key engine of growth. Implicitly, the second and third pathways link democracy with political stability via the classic defense of democracy: democracy, by definition, allows peaceful change of government through voice rather than force, thus leading to stability, which in turn encourages private investment and then economic growth.

The logic behind the liberty-stability channel through private investment is sound, but existing discussions still retain some key empirical and theoretical weaknesses. Empirically, as Rodrik (1999, 387–89) noted, while investment rates in developing countries tend to be persistent over time despite major regime changes and external shocks, growth rates in these countries have differed greatly since the 1970s. Growth collapsed in most developing countries in the mid-1970s, and most of the countries that avoided growth collapse were East Asian countries, none of them democracies at that time.

Meanwhile, Feng's (2003) study that supposedly linked democracy with growth via political stability must be treated with some caution. In addition to not using panel data, Feng has largely conflated investment in human capital and private investment as entrepreneurship, and he found that democracy impacts growth positively *only* through education. Also, Feng studied the linkage between democracy and growth and the linkage between political stability and growth separately as two competing causal pathways rather than two links along a single pathway from democracy to growth via stability. Moreover, his measurement of political instability is suspicious because it is an estimated probability of unconstitutional change within a country rather than an actual measurement of political instability. Finally, Feng (2003, 296–99) found that democracy has no statistically significant impact on growth overall.

More recently, Aisen and Veiga (2013) attempted to identify the specific channels through which political instability can impact growth. While they showed that "political instability adversely affects growth by lowering the rates of productivity growth and, to a smaller degree, physical and human capital accumulation," they also noted that "democracy may have a small negative effect" on growth. Perotti (1996) and Tavares and Wacziarg (2001) too found that democracy does not affect political stability.

Finally, all these studies are atheoretical. For our purpose here, they have failed to differentiate stability entailed by hierarchy from stability entailed by democracy. Because hierarchy alone brings order and stability, any observed political stability under democracy must be the combined effect of hierarchy and democracy. As such, we need to isolate democracy's effect on stability from hierarchy's effect on stability. Moreover, because both popular mandate and performance are sources of citizens' support for a regime, when an authoritarian regime delivers strong growth, it can become highly stable. Hence, it may be that poor growth causes political instability rather than the other way around. Without adequate prior theorizing, existing studies have great difficulty in differentiating these different causal relationships in different directions.

5-A.3. SUMMARY

To summarize, then, while democracy may indeed do a better job in the aforementioned three channels than autocracy, some autocracies may have managed to match, if not better, democracies' efforts in these channels. In fact, because an autocrat's legitimacy is more critically (or even solely) based on performance with respect to furthering the citizens' welfare, an autocrat may actually have greater incentive in pursuing economic development than a democratic leader (Krause 1995, 315) and thus have every reason to match the best practices that democracy can offer in those three channels. The channel in which democracy holds an exclusive advantage must be a channel that autocracy has yet to match so far and cannot possibly match in the future, even if an autocrat is pro-growth from the bottom of his heart. Without a rigorous prior theorization regarding the channel in which democracy holds an exclusive advantage over autocracy when it comes to prompting development, we remain unsure about the relationship between regimes and development.

Nonetheless, we have learned a lot regarding democracy and growth from this literature. First, all these works recognize that there may be more than a single channel through which democracy (or a regime) impacts growth. Moreover, these channels interact with each other. Second, the channels through which democracy holds advantages over autocracy when it comes to promoting development may have been historically contingent: *democracies might have held different advantages over autocracies in different historical times* (Lindert 2003). This suggests a nonlinear, if not nonmonotonic, relationship between democracy and development, as Barro (1996; 1997), Durham (1999), and Kurzman et al. (2002) noted very early on. The key task now becomes identifying the channel(s) in which democracy holds exclusive advantages over autocracy while simultaneously integrating the insights that democracy's impact over development is both historically contingent and nonlinear.

5-B. How Hierarchy/Obedience to Authority Both Facilitates and Hinders Innovation and Growth

The rise of political hierarchy in human societies in the form of chiefdoms and states around 4000 BC in ancient Mesopotamia was a watershed event in the history of humanity (Service 1971; Fried 1967). Since then, almost all human activities, including learning and growth, have operated under a hierarchy. Yet, hierarchy poses two opposing dynamics for learning and growth; as Etzioni-Halevy (1983, 38) put it, "Lack of hierarchy spells lack of coordination, too stiff a hierarchy spells lack of creativeness."

On the one hand, hierarchy facilitates growth through at least four mechanisms.[4] First, hierarchy facilitates individualistic innovation and accumulation and thus encourages growth. In contrast, in egalitarian societies, socially productive and accumulative initiatives (thus sustained economic growth) tend to be extremely difficult because egalitarian society discourages them: indeed, egalitarian societies intentionally level against individualistic accumulation and innovation (Boehm 1999; Miller and Cook 1998, 81–82).

Second, by gradually bringing order and stability via monopolizing and limiting violence within a community, hierarchy fundamentally reduces the uncertainty and risk of taking socially productive initiatives and encourages investment in skills and capital, thus making sustained growth possible (Olson 1993, 567).[5] A key prerequisite for sustained growth is to prevent individuals from engaging in socially destructive behaviors (e.g., theft) through "order and stability" so that they will be more willing to consider socially productive initiatives. Without order and stability, even if the human society is not a "brutish and nasty" place with everyone being a "roving bandit" (Olson 1993), it certainly would not be a very accumulative and productive one.

Third, hierarchy enables scale mobilization of human power and resources so that people as a group can take on more ambitious initiatives where an individual's effort is no longer adequate. Because hierarchy is fundamentally a mechanism for coordinating individual efforts under the division of labor (Rader 1992, 1383–92), hierarchy is foremost a means of extending human capability (Arrow 1974, 16; see also Loasby 1999, 87–93; Marshall [1920] 1982, 138–39).

Fourth, hierarchy is also a means to override the problem of free riding in collective action because every hierarchical organization is managed by a bureaucratic apparatus to limit shirking, stealing, and cheating. Moreover, with division of labor and social coordination under hierarchy, individuals do not have to face the challenges of life alone. Instead, they can rely on others' knowledge and skills and thus devote more time and energy to pursue the knowledge and skills they are most interested in and good at, thus further increasing their personal knowledge and capabilities as well as those of the wider populace. Of course, greater division of labor and better social coordination further encourages growth. The growing complexity of organizations thus has been a major driving force behind human progress. Without hierarchical organizations, there would be no pyramids, no Great Wall, no Panama Canal, and little human progress. Arrow (1964, 398) did not overstate when he remarked, "Truly among man's innovations, the use of [hierarchical] organization to accomplish his ends is among both his greatest and his earliest."

On the other hand, hierarchy also brings a new force that discourages innovation and hence growth; that force is obedience to authority (OTA). A hierarchy explicitly demands its members' OTA. In fact, a hierarchy can only be viable if there is enough OTA among its members because "it is extremely difficult and costly to maintain order once the will to obey breaks down" (Lewis 1955, 103; see also Weber 1978, 53–53, 212). Not surprisingly, since the beginning of hierarchy and through thousands of years, OTA has permeated every human organization. Indeed, the degree of OTA in modern societies has reached a frightening level, as the famous Milgram (1974) experiments on OTA vividly demonstrated. Milgram showed that individuals are extremely obedient even to fake authority—human beings seem to have an almost innate instinct of OTA.

Following Milgram's groundbreaking experiments, many have explored OTA's social and political implications (for a brief review, see Miller et al.

1995); yet, few have addressed its implications for understanding learning, innovation, and growth. For our purpose here, OTA fundamentally encourages individuals within an organization to respect authority more and care about truth less.

Within a hierarchy, the authority has a "legitimate" means to reward and punish. More often than not, the authority rewards those who obey or agree and punishes those who do not: this practice is the only means of maintaining authority for the ruler. The legitimate power to reward and punish essentially means that there exists a unidirectional deterrence relationship between authority figures and their subordinates. Under most circumstances, the ruler can credibly threaten the subordinate with certain consequences if the latter does not obey, but the latter cannot credibly threaten the former.[6] Under this relationship, most individuals choose to "gain promotion by pleasing [the] superior" (Polanyi 1941, 444).[7]

This unidirectional deterrence relationship between authorities and their subordinates has profound implications for a hierarchical organization's innovation. On the one hand, while a subject may not want to challenge the authority before considering potential consequences, the subject's acquiring of new knowledge may unintentionally challenge the authority—and sometimes the whole social order, either explicitly or implicitly—as new ideas are potentially subversive. On the other hand, the subject needs to obey the authority in order to obtain rewards from the authority. As such, there is an inherent tension between innovation and OTA. When individuals conform to OTA, they inevitably limit their innovation.

More concretely, hierarchy and OTA can hinder innovation, and growth resulting from innovation, on three interrelated fronts. First, an authority almost always favors certain ideas but disfavors others. As such, OTA induces individuals to pursue ideas that are more acceptable to the authority (Foucault 1980; see also Becker 1976, 11; North 1990, 78; Hodgson 2003). This self-censorship inevitably limits the diversity of individuals' innovation under hierarchy, and limiting the diversity of individual innovation has negative consequences for innovation throughout the whole organization.

Moreover, because the authority is in a position to allocate resources, it can allocate resources to groups or individuals who obey and take them away from those who do not. This means that under hierarchy individuals who are expected to produce ideas consistent with the authority's ideas are supported, while others who are expected to produce ideas inconsistent with the authority's ideas are undersupported, if supported at all. By the same token, the authority can allocate resources to those research areas that are expected to produce results consistent with the authority's ideas and away from those areas that are expected to produce results that are not consistent.[8] Since pursuing new knowledge always requires some investment of resources, by selectively supporting inquiries according to whether their expected outcomes will please the authority,[9] OTA again limits the diversity of new ideas.

Second, and related to the concept of an authority favoring certain ideas, OTA adversely impacts growth by reducing the production of new knowledge because OTA makes a monopoly of ideas more likely and long-lasting. Indeed, OTA can be taken as a "legitimate" tool for the authority to engineer and sustain monopolies of ideas.[10]

OTA necessarily means that individuals devote less effort and time to developing new ideas because new ideas may challenge the authority's ideas. As such, fewer new ideas join the competition of ideas as a whole. Both dynamics strengthen the possibility of monopolies of ideas favored by the authority. Because an organization's rate of innovation is a function of the intensity of competition (Hayek 1978; North 1994, 362), the more prevalent and profound the monopoly of ideas within an organization, the less productive the organization's innovation becomes. Because production is essentially a process of utilizing and generating knowledge (Smith 1776 [1981], ch. 1; Hayek 1945; Arrow 1962; Boulding 1966, 6; Rosenberg 1982; Becker and Murphy 1992; Loasby 1999, 130–136), the impact on growth of a monopoly of ideas must be similar to the impact on growth of a monopoly of goods or production processes (Parente and Prescott 1999)—it is detrimental to development.

Indeed, OTA's adverse impact on innovation cannot be completely eliminated, even if the authority is open-minded and actually encourages diversity of innovation. For instance, even if the authority merely serves as a gatekeeper, screening information flow and selecting potential projects, the organization's innovation still suffers. This is the case simply because a gatekeeper cannot possibly have complete knowledge (Polanyi 1941, 1956; Hayek 1945). Indeed, even if the gatekeepers have complete knowledge, they cannot possibly have all the time and brainpower to process all the knowledge. As such, facing information overload, the gatekeepers may become overly conservative. Eventually, few innovative projects may be supported and pursued (Sah 1991, 78–81; Nevis et al. 1995, 81; Jacob 1997, ch. 8).[11]

Third, OTA hinders communication of new ideas. When OTA dominates individuals' calculations of behavior, they refrain from communicating their new ideas to each other for fear of offending the authority. As a result, fewer new ideas are communicated under OTA. This reduction in the communication of new ideas produces two adverse effects on growth that have been extensively modeled by endogenous growth models.

Endogenous growth models have shown that the nonrivalrous nature of knowledge and the "standing-on-shoulders" effect are absolutely critical to increasing returns to scale in sustaining growth (Jones 2005; see also Hayek 1960, 43, 47; Romer 1989; 1990). Because OTA limits the communication of new ideas, the portion of knowledge that remains "tacit" increases (Polanyi 1966), while the portion of nonrivalrous knowledge decreases. Before any idea becomes nonrivalrous, it has to be shared or communicated first. Consequently, under OTA, the cumulative effect in the production of knowledge (or the standing-on-shoulders effect) inevitably weakens, and the whole society gets less than it potentially could from its investment in innovation. As such, reduced communication of new ideas under OTA necessarily entails less growth.

Moreover, within any organization, hampered communication of new ideas inevitably means that fewer new ideas are tried since the trial and error of ideas almost always first requires communication of ideas within the organization. Essentially, then, hampered communication of new ideas becomes a barrier to adoption of new ideas. Yet, the trial and error of ideas is indispensable for getting close to true(r) knowledge, as Popper (1937 [1959]) and Campbell (1960, 1974a, 1974b) persuasively contended. Without extensive trial and error, incorrect and false ideas are less likely to be weeded out, especially when those ideas happen to be favored by the authority. This inevitably reduces the speed of getting rid of the "bad apples," which in turn means that more resources are wasted in pursuing scientifically unjustified and unsound ideas, and the rate of return in the production of new knowledge is lowered. Again, Lysenko's disastrous long reign in Soviet genetics is a tragically perfect illustration of a naked emperor who just kept going (see chapter 5).

In sum, hierarchy and OTA not only hinder the production of knowledge by reducing the diversity of innovation and erecting monopolies of ideas; they also limit the contribution of innovation to growth by limiting the communication of knowledge, reducing the standing-on-shoulders effect and decreasing the speed of getting rid of the bad apples.

5-C. Additional Notes on the Cases

The historiography of the Scientific Revolution (1500–1700) is voluminous. For a detailed survey of the historiography up to the 1990s, including major explanations of the Scientific Revolution, see Cohen (1994). For a standard history of the Scientific Revolution, see Hall (1989). For some prominent explanations of the making of the Scientific Revolution, in addition to Merton (1938 [1970]), see Rabb (1965), Zilsel (1942), Hall (1961), and Hooykaas (1987).

Merton (1938 [1970], xvi–xvii) noted that even in Protestant England in the seventeenth to nineteenth centuries, many scientists did not openly challenge God. According to Merton, Puritan scientists "took it almost as self-evident that science made not for the dethronement of God but rather provided a means of celebrating His wisdom and the tidiness of the universe He had created." Another reason Merton cited was largely instrumental: "Before science had acquired a substantial autonomy as an institution, it needed those extraneous sources of legitimacy."

Many historians of the Scientific Revolution have noted the Netherlands' unique role in relaying the torch of the Scientific Revolution to England after the Inquisition. For instance, Cohen (1994, 362) noted, "The Netherlands, in particular, became a free haven for the publication of texts that Catholic authors could not have seen through the press at home. Thus, the Inquisition, in discouraging local printers, in forbidding publications, and consequently in stifling much daring thought, contributed its share to the preponderance of Protestantism throughout a large portion of the Scientific Revolution." In addition to Cohen (1994), Eisenstein (1979) presents an in-depth study on Protestant printing houses and their roles in the Scientific Revolution.

For a brief introduction to Galileo, see Drake (1980 [2001]). For key historical documents on the Inquisition of Galileo, see Finocchiaro (1989). For in-depth studies on some of the issues within the Inquisition of Galileo, see De Dantillana (1955), Langford (1961 [1992]), Redondi ([1983] 1987), Feldhay (1995), and Speller (2008).

In light of our new institutional explanation, Weber (1958) might have missed the most critical implication of the Protestant ethic because he barely touched on the relationship between the Protestant ethic and the rise of modern science. Weber's thesis cannot account for the timing and shifting of location from the Scientific Revolution to the Industrial Revolution:

whereas the Protestant Reformation and the Scientific Revolution started on the European continent in the sixteenth to seventeenth centuries, the Industrial Revolution began in the eighteenth century and started in Protestant Europe (Temin 1997, 268–69). In contrast, our explanation accounts for the timing and shifting of location from the Scientific Revolution to the Industrial Revolution.

"Bourgeois science" was Bukharin's label for sciences in the West. Bukharin was of course a theorist of the Soviet Union, and his speech in 1931 on the unity of science and politics was warmly received by many scientists in the West. See Polanyi (1941) for a rebuttal and further references (see also Polanyi 1956). Michurin, of course, had never been a friend of Mendelian genetics. As early as 1923, he declared, "Mendel's law is not applicable in fruit breeding" (quoted in Joravsky 1970, 48; see also 40–53). For an incomplete list of prominent Soviet scientists who were purged, see Joravsky (1970, appendix II).

5-D. Firm-Level Evidence: Japanese Firms versus Fordism in the 1980s–1990s

Our theory can also assimilate some firm-level evidence. During the 1980s and 1990s, many contrasted the performance of leading Japanese firms against the performance of leading American firms and attributed the better performance of the former to their less hierarchical style of management. Specifically, these authors argued that under the Ford-Taylorism management within American firms, decision making is usually concentrated in a highly bureaucratized management team, and most employees are expected to obey management's decisions and perform the assigned tasks without question (Temin 1997, 275). Essentially, this arrangement lets the management monopolize the production and competition of ideas. In contrast, many leading Japanese firms, while also maintaining a highly bureaucratized management team, nonetheless actively encourage employees to voice their suggestions freely to the management team by rewarding them. Thus, while hierarchies in Japanese firms are not necessarily flatter than those in American firms, Japanese firms do leave more space for employees to participate in decision making (Aoki 1986; 1995). In light of our theory, management in Japanese firms tries to limit hierarchy's structural impediments against the production and communication of new ideas and thus enables firms to innovate better. Because a firm's competitiveness critically depends on its innovation capability, Japanese firms come to enjoy some important advantages in their competition against companies managed under the more Ford-Taylorism style of management.

This firm-level evidence thus provides additional support for our theory that liberty under hierarchy facilitates innovation, productivity, and competitiveness.[12] In fact, two of the seven innovation orientations and four of the ten facilitating factors of organizational innovation as given by Nevis and his colleagues (1995, 71) are related to liberty under hierarchy. In addition, Sah and Stiglitz (1987) developed a similar argument when examining innovation in organizations with theoretical models: "polyarchy" (i.e., a hierarchy with multiple decision points) is more conducive to innovation than hierarchy with a single decision point (see also Sah 1991; for a review, see Rader 1992).

6-A. Further Notes on Data

For most social and economic indicators, we rely on the World Bank's World Economic Indicators. To measure economic growth, we rely on GDP per capita (GDPpc) in current prices, using a GDP deflator. As Pinkovskiy and Sala-i-Martin (2016) have shown recently, measuring growth rate with GDPpc in current prices calculated with a GDP deflator may be a better indicator for real economic activity than purchase-power parity measures. For total factor productivity (TFP), we rely on the Penn World Table 7.0.

For measuring democracies or political regimes, we rely on the widely used Polity2 scores. We also deploy a very recent measurement of democracy, the lexical index by Skaaning et al. (2015), which seems to be conceptually sound. We avoid Przeworski et al.'s (2000) or Boix et al.'s (2012) dichotomous measurements of democracy because they take political regimes to be a quality measurement and are thus too blunt. We also avoid indicators from the Vanhanen and Freedom House indexes due to their coding schemes (Munck 2009). Finally, by focusing on the period from 1970 to 2010, we also avoid the problem of retrospective coding with the same rules of measurement (Munck 2009).[1]

We transform Barro-Lee's human capital (schooling) five-year average data into annual data by linearly extrapolating the rate of increase of five years into a yearly increase, holding that that the level of schooling cannot increase very drastically.

For political instability, we use data from Databanks International (DBI; 2011). Compared to other existing indicators of political instability, not only does DBI data have longer temporal and wider spatial coverage, it is also more conceptually valid (Jong-A-Pin 2010). Most critically, it does not conflate political instability caused by irregular political protest or unrest with political instability caused by regular and constitutional governmental changes. According to our theory, which is explicitly rooted in the classic definition of democracy, one of democracy's great strengths is that government can change peacefully and policies can change from a peaceful bottom-up process in addition to imposition from the top down. Hence, regular governmental changes in democracies, despite leading to short-term policy uncertainties, are not political instability in a more fundamental sense. Indeed, Jong-A-Pin (2009, 20–22, table 4a–d) found that "countries that have high factor scores on the 'within' dimension [within regime instability, or changes in government without regime change] are typically countries that also have high scores on democracy indices, while countries that have low scores are typically autocracies. Indeed, the correlation between the 'within' variable and . . . the democracy variable [as measured by the polity index] . . . is 0.79." As such, political instability must be strictly defined as unconstitutional and hence nondemocratic governmental change, genocide, and politicide (e.g., Goldstone et al. 2010) so as to differentiate from constitutional governmental change that may incur short-term political and social uncertainties (cf. Alesina et al. 1996; Gurgal and Lach 2013). In contrast, the International Country Risk Guide takes governmental changes in democracies as equivalent to governmental instability in autocracies. Finally, although the Armed Conflict dataset by Gleditsch et al. (2002) covers a longer temporal period, the DBI dataset contains most of the data points of the Armed Conflict dataset. By relying on the DBI dataset, we retain more consistent coding and scoring.

For ethnolinguistic fractionalization (ELF), we use the more recent and better developed dataset of Desmet et al. (2012) rather than earlier datasets by Alesina et al. (2003) and Fearon (2003). The new dataset by Desmet and colleagues offers several key improvements over previous datasets, one of them being a kind of internal control: it offers several different levels of aggregation in measuring fractionalization, and these different levels of measurement have different impacts when it comes to political instability and economic growth. Specifically, they show that ELF6 is more powerful for predicting economic performance, whereas ELF1 is more useful for predicting political tension and instability. We have been able to duplicate their results.

Instead of the economic freedom composite index (either by the Fraser Institute or Freedom House), we use openness, measured as a percentage of trade in terms of total GNP as a control variable. As a composite index, the economic freedom index is on dubious conceptual ground, and it is heavily subjective because it is based on expert opinion. In contrast, the openness measure is mostly objective.[2]

The countries comprising the dataset are shown in table 6-A.1, and sources of data are given in table 6-A.2. Descriptive statistics for the variables appear in the chapter text (table 6.1).

Due to space limitations, additional appendixes to chapter 6 are available upon request from the author (twukong@fudan.edu.cn).

6-B. Other Technical Issues

6-B.1. BASELINE MODEL AND CONFOUNDING VARIABLES

Within the cross-country growth regressions (CCGR) literature, methodological issues—especially those related to growth theories, econometric measurement, data sources, and econometric estimation techniques—have attracted increased scrutiny (e.g., Levine and Renelt 1992; Sala-i-Martin 1997; Brunetti 1997; Temple 1999; Aron 2000; Wacziarg 2002; Durlauf et al. 2005; de Haan 2007; Kurtz and Schrank 2007). We do not repeat the essentials emphasized by others here, other than noting two underappreciated aspects.

First, many growth regressions violate key premises and conclusions of growth models (from the Solow growth model to an endogenous growth model) and have based their estimations on invalid baseline growth models. This is so not only among political scientists and sociologists but also among economists themselves (for earlier critiques, see Temple 1999; Wacziarg 2002, 909–911; Durlauf et al. 2005).

We believe that a baseline growth model is essential for assessing the credibility of the statistical relationship between an explanatory variable and growth. From the growth modeling literature and the empirical growth literature, we believe that the baseline model, in which annual growth rate of GDPpc is the dependent variable, should have the following control variables: (1) initial GDPpc (should have a negative sign, consistent with the conditional convergence thesis); (2) rate of population growth (should have a negative sign); (3) gross investment ratio, with human capital investment being part of it (should have a positive sign); and (4) inflation (should have a negative sign, consistent with basic macroeconomics). All growth regressions should first establish the validity of this baseline model and then deploy it to assess specific hypotheses by inserting other explanatory variables of interest (Temple 1999; Wacziarg 2002). Needless to say, making sure all the essential control variables have the expected signs in the baseline model serves as a useful check on the overall quality of the dataset.

We therefore first establish a baseline growth model. The full baseline model contains the following control variables: GDPpc, rate of population

TABLE 6-A.1. List of the 79 Countries Comprising the Dataset

1	Algeria	41	Kenya
2	Argentina	42	Korea, South
3	Bahrain	43	Madagascar
4	Bangladesh	44	Malawi
5	Benin	45	Malaysia
6	Bolivia	46	Mali
7	Botswana	47	Mauritius
8	Brazil	48	Mexico
9	Burundi	49	Morocco
10	Cameroon	50	Nepal
11	Central African Republic	51	Nicaragua
12	Chad	52	Niger
13	Chile	53	Nigeria
14	China	54	Oman
15	Colombia	55	Pakistan
16	Congo, Democratic Republic of	56	Panama
17	Congo, Republic of	57	Paraguay
18	Costa Rica	58	Peru
19	Cyprus	59	Philippines
20	Dominican Republic	60	Portugal
21	Ecuador	61	Rwanda
22	Egypt	62	Senegal
23	El Salvador	63	Sierra Leone
24	Fiji	64	Singapore
25	Gabon	65	South Africa
26	Ghana	66	Spain
27	Greece	67	Sri Lanka
28	Guatemala	68	Syria
29	Guyana	69	Tanzania
30	Haiti	70	Thailand
31	Honduras	71	Togo
32	Hungary	72	Trinidad
33	India	73	Tunisia
34	Indonesia	74	Turkey
35	Iran	75	Uganda
36	Ireland	76	Uruguay
37	Israel	77	Venezuela
38	Ivory Coast	78	Zambia
39	Jamaica	79	Zimbabwe
40	Jordan		

TABLE 6-A.2. Explanatory and Control Variables: Included versus Excluded

Dependent variable: Annual growth rate of GDP per capita*

KEY EXPLANATORY VARIABLE

Polity2 score and lexical index	Skanning et al. 2015

CONTROL VARIABLES INCLUDED

Variable	*Sources*
Polity score (Pv2)	Polity IV project
Human capital (average of education years among adults 25 years old and above), in %	Barro and Lee 2013
GDP per capita, inflation, growth rate of GDP per capita (%), population growth rate (%)	World Bank
Total investment rate (%)	World Bank/Penn World Table 2010
Percentage of private investment in total fixed asset investment	World Bank
Government consumption rate (%)	World Bank
Openness (openness at current prices, %)	Penn World Table 2010
Ethnolinguistic fractionalization	Desmet et al. 2012
Land area (in thousands of square meters)	Frankel and Romer 1999
Latitude (distance of capital city from the equator measured as absolute latitude)	Rodrik et al. 2004
Landlocked (landlocked or not)	Sachs 2003
Tropics (percentage of tropical land area)	Gallup et al. 1999
Political instability (domestic 9)	Databanks International 2011

POSSIBLE CONTROL VARIABLES EXCLUDED

Variables	*Reason for exclusion*
Quality of democracy	Potential confounding variables
Quality of governance, state capacity (extraction/taxation rate/public goods provision), corruption, rule of law/country risk indicator, protection of property rights	Potential confounding variables
Public investment (as a percentage of GDP)	Contains both growth-promoting (e.g., education) and growth-hindering dimensions (e.g., pork barrel and wasteful projects)
Inequality/redistribution	Potential confounding variables
Economic freedom composite index	Measurement problems
Colonial experiences/colonial legacies	Potential confounding variables
Religion (e.g., Christian vs. non-Christian, percentage of Muslim population) and legal origin	Potential confounding and intervening variables

* We also test our models with annual growth rate of GNP as the dependent variables. The results are almost identical. Additional results are available upon request (twukong@fudan.edu.cn).

growth, and gross capital formation (model 1 in Table 6.2). All variables in the partial or full baseline model have the correct signs (i.e., GDPpc and population growth are negative but insignificant, whereas gross capital formation is positive and highly significant).

Second, lacking rigorous prior theorizing, many growth regressions are "kitchen sink" or "garbage can" regressions: they simply put whatever variables that have data into the right side of the equation, often due to a misplaced concern for omitted control variables (Temple 1999; Wacziarg 2002). This practice, however, makes obtaining consistent results and interpretation of results extremely difficult, if not essentially impossible (Achen 2002; 2005; Ray 2003). Moreover, the payoff of putting more control variables into the right side of regression equations can be both positive and negative (Clark 2005; see also Freedman 2010). We thus should heed the advice of Achen (2002, 2005) and Ray (2003): rather than putting all possible control variables into the regression equation, we should insert key explanatory variables one at a time into the baseline model to test their statistical significance while making sure the baseline model remains valid. Doing so facilitates the interpretation of results.

Third, following the basic logic of regression, certain confounding variables should be excluded when testing specific hypotheses (Ray 2003). The following possible control variables are thus excluded because they may be confounding and intervening variables between regime and growth (i.e., they are partly underpinned by growth, or worse, by both growth and regime), and they may have quite complex relationships with growth, regime type, regime stability, and transition (i.e., stability of regime, de-/democratization). These variables include

(1) Inequality (whether measured by the Gini coefficient or other measures). Inequality is a product of political regimes (e.g., democracy vs. nondemocracy), government policies (e.g., health care, education), factor endowment, and economic development itself (e.g., Engerman and Sokoloff 2002; Lindert 2003; Ansell 2010; Boix 2010). In addition, inequality may be bad for democracy but good for democratization (Acemoglu and Robinson 2000; Boix 2003; Houle 2009; Haggard and Kaufman 2012).

(2) Protection of property rights. Many measurements of property rights are subjective and, more critically, easily conflated with features of democracy (e.g., measured as constraints on executives, political constraints, judicial constraints).

(3) Colonial experiences. Colonial experiences (or lack of them) have been shown to impact both regimes and economic development (e.g., Acemoglu et al. 2001; 2002; Olsson 2009; Hariri 2012; for a more sophisticated study, see Lee and Paine 2019).

(4) Religion. Religious factors may influence both democracy and economic development (e.g., Weber 1958; Tawney 1936; Barro and McCleary 2003; McCleary and Barro 2006).

(5) State capacity, political extraction capacity (e.g., Abertman and Kugler 1997; Bäck and Hadenius 2008; Kugler and Tammen 2012; Charron and Lapuente 2010), corruption (Transparency International), quality of governance (e.g., Worldwide Governance Indicators), and country risk indicators (International Country Risk Guide). These indicators are at least partly determined by both regimes and economic performance. More critically, some of these datasets are suspect in terms of validity and reliability due to their deeply subjective means of construction (for a systematic critique, see Kurtz and Schrank 2007).

Excluded variables are listed in table 6-A.2.

6-B.2. WORKING WITH INTERACTION TERMS

We explicitly posit an interactive relationship: the effect of democracy on political stability is contingent on the level of economic development (measured in GDP per capita). We thus heed the advice of these works on interaction terms (e.g., Braumoeller 2004; Brambor et al. 2005; Berry et al. 2012). Recently, Hainmueller et al. (2019) also found that many studies with interaction terms fail to check whether their results are mostly driven by extreme, uneven distribution of data. We also run these tests, and we show that our data is quite evenly distributed and our results are thus not driven by uneven distribution of data. All these additional robustness tests are available from the author upon request (twukong@fudan.edu.cn).

NOTES

Introduction

1. Of course, the notion that institutions matter for economic development is not new. For a succinct historical survey, see Reinert (2007). For a more thorough survey on institutional economics, see Hodgson (2004).

2. Chapter 1 provides a more detailed critique of these major works.

3. For why we need to combine both individualism and collectivism, see Tang 2011b.

4. For instance, overfinancialization of an economy is certainly driven by greater incentives for bankers, but these incentives were the most direct cause of the 2008–2009 crash (Turner et al. 2010).

5. In other words, I focus on the functions performed by institutions rather than the exact forms of institutions: after all, the same function can be performed by different forms of institutions. On this key understanding, see Chang 2007b, 17–21. Also see the discussion in chapter 1.

6. Keynes's ([1936] 2013) *General Theory* is mostly a theory about the short to medium run. In contrast, Lewis's (1955) *Theory of Economic Growth*, Myrdal's *Asian Drama* (1968), and North and Thomas's (1973) *The Rise of the Western World* are clearly about development in the long run, whereas Diamond's (1997) *Guns, Germs, and Steel* is about economic and political development in the very long run. Of course, many have transgressed both the long run and the short run (e.g., Hirschman 1958, 1970; Schumpeter [1934] 1968; Rodrik 2007).

7. Many have failed to maintain this distinction. For instance, after explicitly adopting Lin and Nugent's (1995, 2306–7) definition of institutions as rules, Rodrik (2007, ch. 5) singled out five different sets of institutions: property rights, regulatory institutions, institutions for macro-economic stabilization, institutions for social insurance, and institutions of conflict management. Apparently, he has conflated organization and institution.

8. In fact, North (1990, 16) came close to such a position when he wrote, "Institutions are not necessarily or even usually created to be socially efficient; rather they, or at least the formal rules, are created to serve the interests of those with the bargaining power to devise new rules." Unfortunately, North did not stay with this key insight and eventually fell into the functionalism fallacy. Not all NIE theorists embrace North's focus on incentive and transaction costs (e.g., Olson 1982, 2000; Ostrom 1986), and different theorists may differ on specific aspects of transaction costs (e.g., Williamson 1975, 1985). Nonetheless, NIE remains a mostly functionalist approach.

9. For an earlier discussion on the relationship between institutional and noninstitutional explanations of development, see Engerman and Sokoloff (2005, esp. 641–45).

10. Jones's (1995) time-series tests of growth theory showed that while real investment in R&D grew by more than 20%, there had been little change in the growth rate of developed economies. This can be explained by two possible causes other than that the models may be inappropriate. First, innovation has become more difficult as easy ones have been accomplished (i.e., the

"standing-on-shoulders" effect has become less robust). Second, utilization of innovation has been hindered by institutions. Of course, without increasing R&D investment, even the 2% rate might not have been maintained.

11. For a witty takedown of the various theses on growth, see McCloskey (2010). For two earlier but equally entertaining and strongly opinionated surveys of these searches for "primary movers," see Meier (2001) and Adelman (2001) and the comments following them.

12. Here, I adopt Haggard's (1990, 23) definitions of strategies and policies: strategies consist of packages of policies. Moreover, a long-term strategy must be underpinned by institutions and policies.

13. By putting more weight on institutions than on culture, I am not suggesting that culture has no role in shaping economic development. I am merely contending that culture is less central than institutions.

14. Lin sometimes equates policies with ideas. This is not precise: only some ideas are made into policies (or institutions). Here, I refrain from engaging the debate on the specifics of NSE. On this front, see Lin (2012b).

15. For our own work on development strategies and industrial policies, see Mao et al. (2021).

16. Indeed, Lin was a firm institutionalist very early on! (See, e.g., Lin 1989, 1995; Lin and Nugent 1995.)

17. As noted by Aron (2000) back in 2000, more than two dozen institutional factors have been found to be associated with development!

18. In contrast, as John Hicks (1965) noted, "Growth theory (as we [i.e., economists] shall understand it) [or growth models] has no particular bearing on underdevelopment economics, nor has the underdevelopment interest played any essential part in its development."

19. Compared to these foundational problems, the problem of scaling up from micro experiments to macro- or meso-level outcomes is rather minor (e.g., Ravallion 2012; Besley and Persson 2014, 929–30).

Chapter 1: Laying the Groundwork

1. Bardhan (2016, 866, fn. 7) was kind enough to note that Acemoglu and Robinson's definition is "somewhat vague."

2. It should be noted that Fukuyama (2013, 2016) mostly addresses dimensions of state capacity, especially the dimension of infrastructural power that underpins governance quality—such as the quality of bureaucracy and the autonomy of the bureaucracy (Mann 1986)—rather than governance per se.

3. For a recent study that does suggest that "absolute deprivation" (which can be understood as capturing factual inequality) leads to civil war, see Baten and Mumme (2013).

4. In other words, ideological components have been present in the ancient, in the old, and in the new institutional economics of development (Hodgson 1989, 1993; Reinert 2007).

5. Asia has no entry in the index of Acemoglu and Robinson (2012) or the index of Besley and Persson (2011), even though Africa, the Americas, and (of course) Europe are there! Political correctness might have been another cause (Smith 2013).

6. Even France's installing a system of selling public offices can be taken as the right measure for raising revenue within a short period of time when other measures simply could not meet the immediate demand.

7. For general treatments on institutional change with an NIE paradigm, see Greif and Laitin (2004); Knight (1992); Lin (1989); and Ruttan and Hayami (1984). For an earlier review of this larger literature, see Lin and Nugent (1995). Criticizing the existing literature, Tang (2011b) advanced a general theory of institutional change.

Chapter 2: A Systematic Statement of IFED

1. As a concept, order has often been talked about but rarely defined. For a conceptual analysis of order and a framework for measuring order, see Tang (2016b).

2. Constrained by his NIE straightjacket, Olson (1993) had conflated order (under hierarchy) and property rights. Order is not property rights although the former underpins the latter. Moselle and Polak (2001) developed a model suggesting that predatory stationary bandits may be worse than anarchy.

3. In this sense, politics is no tragedy after all (cf. Buchanan 2003).

4. Regarding the positional market as a means for allocating resources (in this case, human talent), the functionalist school of sociology actually shares a perspective similar to classical economists' laissez-faire view on the material market (Davis and Moore 1945), although it has faced far more criticism from sociologists and political scientists (e.g., Buckley 1958; Tumin 1953). For details, see the discussion in chapter 3.

5. Olson (1982, 161–65) briefly mentioned South Africa under apartheid as a case of enforcing extreme inequality of opportunity and suggested that discrimination against blacks was detrimental to development.

Excursion: Three Inequalities

1. Ever since Rawls, most theorists on equality have rightly rejected utilitarianist "equality of welfare" mostly because welfare is very subjective (e.g., Dworkin 2000; Sen 1992).

Chapter 3: The Positional Market and Development

1. Here, we are primarily interested in the vertical dimension of social mobility. Functionalism argued that social stratification serves a social purpose of "placing and motivating individuals in the social structure," thus implying that it may play a role in economic growth. See Davis and Moore (1945), 242.

2. Service (1971, 1975) reviewed and interpreted the available evidence back then. He reached the same two conclusions without stating them as explicitly as I do here.

3. We should differentiate two types of positional inequality (or hierarchy): domestic versus political (Service 1975, 49–50). Domestic hierarchy operates within a family or a clan. In contrast, political hierarchy extends beyond a family or a clan. We are interested in political hierarchy here.

4. Of course, this does not mean that occupation of any leadership position in human society thereafter is always materially rewarding, at least not in the short run.

5. I retain the label of "positional goods" because it has gained currency.

6. As perceptively pointed out by Trigg (2001) and Tilman (2006), some critics of Veblen's theory of conspicuous consumption (and by implication, Bourdieu's work too) have been using a very restricted reading into the phenomenon of conspicuous consumption, thus missing a great deal of social reality.

7. A luxury tax is one measure to strike such a balance, and income tax to a lesser extent. In fact, Frank (1989, 1997) advocated for a progressive consumption tax explicitly on the grounds of curbing conspicuous consumption and increasing happiness. Ng (1997) endorsed Frank's position.

8. Most economists have treated knowledge as if it has only a quantity dimension. The fact that knowledge has a quality dimension has profound implications for understanding economic growth. We develop a growth model that takes the quality dimension of knowledge into account elsewhere (Tang and Gao 2020).

9. *Discrimination* means to make a distinction between people on the basis of class or category, without regard to their merit. Defined as such, discrimination captures a very broad phenomenon, including an individual's dislike of another individual (i.e., prejudice, as a form of individual discrimination). *Institutionalized discrimination* usually denotes formally legalized discrimination (e.g., slavery in the antebellum American South, apartheid in South Africa). *Institutional discrimination* here covers both informal and formal discrimination that is backed by explicit or implicit power or domination, in Weberian terms (Weber 1978, 53–54, 61–62, 341–43, 926–27, 941–46). Thus, institutional discrimination is broader than institutionalized discrimination but narrower than discrimination. Institutional discrimination is related to other concepts, such as social closure/exclusion/barrier, power/domination, stratification, class, status, and inequality, all of which cannot be elaborated here.

10. The most extreme form of social immobility is ethnic cleansing, under which one group seeks to completely eliminate another group's chances of social mobility by physically annihilating them.

11. For earlier discussions on the interaction between the two markets and its impact on growth, often without explicitly differentiating the two markets, see Baumol (1990); Fershtman and Weiss (1993); Fershtman et al. (1996); Hirsch (1977); Knell (1999); and Pagano (2003, 640–42).

12. Apparently, what level of incentives is adequate is both an objective and a subjective question.

13. Hence, positional competition became a universal trait of human beings *only* after human society evolved into a hierarchical society, as Rousseau ([1755] 1993) recognized long ago. Rousseau thus provided the first (though rough) explanation for the origin of our quest for status, recognition, honor, and the like. (Shaver 1989). Interestingly enough, Karl Popper ([1945] 1966, 174) labeled tribal society as "closed society" and posttribal society as "open society," and stated explicitly that in open societies "many members strive to rise socially, and to take the places of others."

14. Vietnam, being similar to China, is also a type III society. Indeed, most sociologists studying transitional economies put Vietnam and China in the same category (Walder 2003). India may also belong to the type III category, although in a different way. In India, the caste system still stigmatizes upward social mobility for individuals from lower castes. For much of the twentieth century, most Latin American countries have been also been type III societies. See the discussion in section VIII.

15. Brown was sloppy here: most economic historians probably would not identify the economic growth of Britain between 1540 and 1640 as "industrial capitalism." For a critique, see Beier 1975.

16. There is seemingly a contradiction here: If Imperial China's channel of social mobility was strongly against those who pursued science and technology, why did Imperial China lead technologically for such a long time? The short answer is twofold. First, Imperial China had a large population, thus a large talent pool to draw from. Hence, even when its institutional arrangements were strongly against those who pursued science and technology, there were some innovations. Second, for much of the time, Imperial China was a unified state with a unified language, currency, and legal code. This unity greatly reduces transaction costs (Epstein 2000; Olson 1993). I address the Needham puzzle in greater detail elsewhere.

17. Evidently, Lewis's "lack of vertical mobility" is equivalent to social immobility according to our definition.

18. For the thesis that (American Negro) slavery was actually good for economic growth in the South (at least for that period), see Fogel and Engerman (1974, 4–6, 191–232).

19. I thank a reviewer for alerting me to this literature on compensatory consumption.

20. Evidently, a partial theory of revolt and revolution can be developed from Gellner's and Hirschman's thesis on individuals' demands for redistribution. One can certainly take institutional

discrimination as a source of injustice (or a form of fundamental injustice), and injustice can induce revolt (Moore 1978).

21. Because (in principle) it may be possible to achieve mass education without public funding, I specify publicly funded mass education to avoid confusion.

22. These countries include China (including the Chinese mainland, Hong Kong, Macau, and Taiwan), Japan, North Korea, Singapore, South Korea, and Vietnam.

23. The doctrine of the "three represents" proclaims that the CCP always represents "the demand by advanced production force, the direction of advanced culture, and the interest of most Chinese people."

24. As Walder (1995) noted, the institutional arrangement that nonparty loyalists can only become another type of elite means that the Chinese political system has an inherent vulnerability. The "three represents" can be understood as a measure designed to partially reduce this vulnerability.

25. Although one can argue that neoclassical economics is compatible with ideationalism by stating, for instance, "I did this because I got high by doing this," doing so renders neoclassical economics tautological and any testing of neoclassical economics explanations impossible (Bunge 1996, esp. 366–70). Raymond Boudon's "cognitive rationalism" was moving toward adopting the nonmaterialist approach, but even he admitted the problem of being tautological (Boudon 1998, 826).

Chapter 4: Redistribution and Development

1. Because we focus on developing countries, "basic education" here denotes primary school and junior high school. Recently, Cohodes et al. (2014) showed that "expanding health insurance coverage for low-income children has large effects on high school completion, college attendance and college completion." Their results thus corroborate the argument that basic health care for the disadvantaged contributes to their human capital formation (thus reduces inequality 2), which in turn contributes to development and reduces inequality 1.

2. We now have a greater appreciation for Theodore Schultz's early focus on institutions and the profound insight that education is foremost about investing in educating the poor in a sound institutional environment, when he pioneered the research on human capital (e.g., Schultz 1960, 1961, 1981, 1993). In one place, Schultz lamented, "Economists who specialize in growth models seldom mention institutions. There is no hiding the fact that our new analytical cupboards are bare on thinking by economists about institutions" (1993, 231). At the same time, Singer (1995, 890) rightly criticized Schultz for not paying much attention to the issue of redistribution, although Schultz was strongly against any institutional and personal discrimination against the less fortunate.

3. Chen et al. (2011) and Mo et al. (2012) examine the impact of other policy changes on educational inequality in rural areas. Yuan and Zhang (2015) focus on urban areas and model how urban families can allocate their resources when public investment increases. Because these studies are not directly relevant for our discussion here, we refrain from engaging with them further.

4. As Lindert (2004) noted, this was the norm for much of human history. The state did not shoulder any burden of a household's investment in education: public spending on education did not exist until the nineteenth century.

5. This is consistent with insights obtained by Galor and Moav (2000, 2004), with different models.

6. In such a situation, the ultimate result, of course, is more growth for the overall economy. This is why adequate public support for primary education is a form of growth-promoting

redistribution. For nonelitist and elitist education systems, see Lindert (2004) and the discussion in section III.

7. For a comprehensive review of these policies, see Hannum et al. 2008.

8. This policy has been variously translated as "two waivers, one subsidy" (Yi et al. 2012), "two exempts and one compensation" (Chyi and Zhou 2014), and "two exemptions, one subsidy" (Yang et al. 2014; Shi 2016). To avoid confusion, we use the policy's name in Chinese pinyin, that is, *liangmian yibu.*

9. It would be ideal to have the ratio between private education spending per student and public education spending per student as a key independent variable. Data on households' private spending on education per student (or even per household), however, cannot be obtained. Nonetheless, we trust that our 10 indicators are more than adequate for gauging the redistributive effect of a county's policies on basic education. Also, empirical results from survey data at the household level strongly suggest that budget constraints remain a powerful determining factor in shaping a household's decision to spend money on their children's education (see the studies cited above).

10. It is important to note that poor grades may be due to the fact that the student is from a household with low socioeconomic status and hence has developed cognitive skills more slowly during early childhood.

11. Yi et al. (2012) also find that parents' attitudes toward female children is a significant determining factor for female students, whereas poor academic performance is a significant determining factor for both genders.

Chapter 5: Hierarchy, Liberty, and Innovation

1. Throughout this chapter, *regime* refers to political regime. By *liberty*, we mean political liberty or freedom. We use *economic freedom* (rather than economic liberty) to describe aspects of economic governance (e.g., property rights).

2. Hereafter, unless stated otherwise, innovation denotes both institutional and technological innovation.

3. Rostow's (in)famous "five stages of economic growth" (e.g., takeoff) is an induction of the whole history of economic development rather than a theory of growth per se.

4. Some earlier works have touched on some of the key components of our theory. For instance, Ober (2008) defended the virtue of democracy on the distribution and use of knowledge within a democracy (i.e., Athens). In contrast, we focus on the creation of knowledge under hierarchy. Ober's work and our work thus complement each other. Ober (2008, esp. 102–6), however, might have erred in pitting democracy against hierarchy, following Williamson's (1975, 1985) earlier mistakes. Properly understood, democracy is a form of governance for hierarchy. In other words, the proper antonym for democracy is nondemocracy such as autocracy rather than hierarchy per se. See also Mokyr (1990, 2002, esp. chs. 6 and 7); Acemoglu and Robinson (2012). None of them, however, have developed an integrative theory as we have done here.

5. It is important to stress that our question is not the beginning of the Scientific Revolution per se, but rather why the revolution did not flourish on the European continent.

6. The historiography of the whole Galileo affair is voluminous. For a more detailed bibliography and additional notes on this and the second case, see appendix 5-C.

7. Indeed, even in Protestant England in the seventeenth to nineteenth centuries, many scientists did not openly challenge God, as Merton ([1938] 1970, xvi–xvii) rightly noted.

8. As Soyfer (2001) noted, Soviet biologists, such as Nikolai Koltsov and Gregory Filippov, before 1934 made many key scientific breakthroughs, some of them of Nobel Prize caliber.

9. The narratives here draw heavily from these three authors. For a brief account, see Soyfer 2001.

10. Ironically and tragically, Vavilov later was purged for his criticism against Soviet policies for agricultural sciences and Lysenko genetics in 1938. Vavilov was arrested and tried as a spy for Britain. He was sentenced to death and died in prison in 1943.

11. Michurin had never been an admirer of Mendelian genetics. As early as 1923, he declared, "Mendel's law is not applicable in fruit breeding" (quoted in Joravsky 1970, 48; for additional details, see 40–53).

12. "The Death and Revival of the Chinese University, 1952" (in Chinese), available online at http://www.21ccom.net/articles/lsjd/lsjj/article_2012061261768.html (accessed May 20, 2013).

Chapter 6: Democracy's Unique Advantage in Promoting Development

1. Hereafter, unless stated otherwise, innovation denotes both institutional and technological innovation.

2. Aghion et al. (2008) found that the closer a country is to the technological frontier, the more critical democracy becomes for growth. Their results thus similarly imply that more advanced economies benefit more from democratic institutions. They, however, do not directly test this implication but rather infer it from results based on sector-specific data. Also, they hold that it is the freedom of entry that explains democracy's advantage in promoting growth in more advanced sectors. List of 112 countries and additional empirical results wih 112 countries are available from the author upon request.

3. Our empirical results also show that democracy's effect on TFP growth is unconditionally insignificant when using TFP data from the more widely used Penn World Table dataset. Knutsen (2013) reported that democracy prompts growth by interacting with low state capacity. Again, he does not theorize this interaction effect as a unique channel through which democracy impacts growth (see also Hanson 2015). Democracy may also contribute to state capacity, at least in the long run (e.g., Wang and Xu 2015).

4. Doing so also reduces the weight of the highly unrealistic implicit assumption of sample homogeneity (i.e., all countries are similar or even the same through time and space) in our empirical inquiries. The practice of having all the countries in the same sample heavily depends on this unrealistic assumption (de Haan 2007).

5. For a study that focuses on these "transitional economies," see Peev and Mueller (2012). This study does explore a political regime's indirect effect on growth but not with the interaction terms as we do here.

6. In other words, sociopolitical stability is a manifestation of particular social conditions plus institutional arrangements, and it critically depends on the liberty to (institutional) innovation channel: with liberty, people can demand and achieve more institutional changes than without liberty. Without liberty, political unrest is almost inevitable or superficial stability comes with a heavy price to growth: autocracies can only deploy more and more repressive forces to prevent outbreaks of unrest. For empirical evidence, see Goldstone et al. (2010). For an interesting study that examines how stability in entrenched autocracy and new democracy impacts business at the firm level, see Nur-tegin (2014).

7. Due to space limitations, we address other technical issues in detail in appendix 6-A.

8. Because we use GDP per capita in constant dollars, we do not include inflation rate in our regressions. When we use GDP per capita in current prices, we do include inflation rate in our regressions. The results are almost identical, with only numerical differences in terms of beta coefficients and standard errors.

9. We perform these tests because Acemoglu et al. (2019) suggest that lagging three to five years is necessary for revealing the positive effect of democracy on economic growth.

10. Again, these additional results are available from the author upon request.

11. Indeed, both Knutsen (2012) and Hanson (2015) have found that democracy seems to be a replacement for state capacity when it comes to contributing to economic growth—that is, the interaction term of democracy and state capacity has a negative effect on economic development, suggesting that the relationship between indicators of state capacity and economic growth may indeed be complex and nonmonotonic.

12. More recently, Pozuelo et al. (2016) challenged that the positive associative results between democratization/democracy and economic growth obtained by Papaioannou and Siourounis (2008) and Acemoglu et al. (2019) are mostly driven by endogeneity.

Chapter 7: Development as a Social Evolutionary Process

1. For earlier reviews of evolutionary economics, which suffer from various shortcomings, see Nelson (2006, 2007) and Hodgson and Knudsen (2010). For instance, inspired by cultural evolutionism (e.g., Boyd and Richerson 1985; Richerson and Boyd 2005), Mokyr (2017) adopted an explicitly evolutionary approach, but his approach was only culturally evolutionary, not socially evolutionary. The mostly genetic or biological approach (e.g., Galor and Moav 2002; Ashraf and Galor 2013; Clark 2007) is a dead end because it smacks of genetic or biological determinism. For a more detailed critique, see Tang (2020). See also Mokyr (2017, 22–34).

2. The term *efflorescence* is Goldstone's (2002) phraseology.

3. See BBC, "Translating Is EU's New Boom Industry," April, 8, 2004.

4. I do not discuss the problem of endogeneity (e.g., the impact of development on institutional changes) here. For a good discussion, see Aron (2000) and Przeworski (2004).

5. Kurtz and Schrank (2007) were criticizing the Worldwide Governance Indicators compiled by Kaufmann et al. (2010).

6. The contrast between the former Yugoslavia before and after the Bosnian War and the contrast between China before and after 1957 (when it experienced the Anti-Rightist Campaign, the Great Leap Forward, and the Cultural Revolution) should readily prove that general trust can be shattered by traumatic events in a relatively short period of time.

7. The other four are openness to the global economy, macroeconomic stability, high saving and investment rates, and leadership and governance.

Chapter 8: The New Development Triangle

1. Here, theory fits with ideology perfectly (Evans 1995, 23). Chang (2000, 5–6) argued that there was a tacit "unholy alliance" of NCE (and hence NIE) and neoliberalism.

2. Although Albert Hirschman, Arthur Lewis, and Gunnar Myrdal all advocated for a key role for the state, their work was mostly in the form of advocacy rather than empirical evidence.

3. Thelen and Steinmo (1992) called it "historical institutionalism in comparative politics," while Evans (1995) called it a "comparative institutional approach (CIA)." Some NIE theorists have referred to it as "historical and comparative institutional analysis," but their understanding remains stuck in NIE orthodoxy (e.g., Aoki 2001; Greif 1998).

4. The World Bank's (1993) *East Asian Miracle* did not really embrace the East Asian developmental state (EADS) model. In fact, the lead author of *The East Asian Miracle* insisted that East Asia was mostly a successful neoclassical story. For an emphatic critique, see Amsden (1994). See also Woo-Cumings (1999, 29).

5. I also leave operational issues to other venues. For state, I adopt Mann's (1993, 54–56) modified Weberian definition: the state is a differentiated set of institutions (i.e., organizations) and personnel embodying centrality, in the sense that political relations radiate to and from a center, to

cover a territorially demarcated area over which it exercises some degree of authoritative, binding rule making, backed up by some organized physical force. Hence, the state is an organization—a very special and highly complex one. The state is not an institution (as rules) even though it must use or deploy institutions (e.g., laws) and other suborganizations (e.g., bureaucracies) to govern.

6. Besley and Persson (2014), however, had three different dimensions: fiscal, legal, and collective. Apparently, their legal and collective capacity correspond to administrative capacities I here. They did not provide any rationale for why coercive or military capacity was dropped. Thus, Besley and Persson have been inconsistent.

7. Here, it is important to differentiate decision-making capacity from leadership (cf. Fritz 2007), even though leadership is not a term that can be easily defined and measured. By leadership, I mean the (individual and collective) capacity of a country's top leaders (or rulers) in making tough decisions and taking decisive actions.

8. In mainstream economic literature on development, only a handful studies have explicitly identified leadership as a key factor for successful development (e.g., Jones and Olken 2005; World Bank 2008, 26–28; Lin 2009, 2012c).

9. Again, I can only provide a more detailed conceptual analysis of QoG elsewhere. Suffice it to say that QoG is also multidimensional, multilayered, multicausal, cumulative/historical, and hence dynamic and evolutionary.

10. Two earlier attempts, without much in-depth research and follow-up, were Rodrik (1999) and Pritchett (2000). Both relied on econometric exercises exclusively. See also Easterly et al. (1993) and Bruno and Easterly (1998). The World Bank (2008) identified only 13 cases of successful stories that had experienced 30 years of over 7% annual growth of GDP after WWII: Botswana, Brazil, China, Hong Kong (China), Indonesia, Japan, South Korea, Malaysia, Malta, Oman, Singapore, Taiwan (China), and Thailand. I believe a 7% growth rate is too high a bar for us to draw more applicable lessons from a larger sample. Also, within the 13 cases, Japan should be counted as an industrialized state rather than a standard LDC.

11. Crafts and O'Rourke (2014, 314–18) noted that Western Europe had also managed to achieve a 4% average growth rate in GDP per capita from 1950 to 1973 (before the first oil shock came). Because Western European countries had already developed before WWII, however, I do not consider them together with LDCs.

12. A similar comparison of the Philippines and Vietnam can be performed (e.g., Pritchett 2003). Strikingly, in North et al. (2013), there were two chapters focusing on the Philippines and India, respectively, but no comparative chapters.

13. Thus, it is also wrong to pit state capacity against institutions: you need both. On this front, Wen Yi (2016) made the opposite mistake of Acemoglu and Robinson (2012).

14. Hence, China's experiences should be closely studied but cannot be easily copied. China is unique in the sense that it has several features that, when combined, make it incomparable to other LDCs. Other advantages include a vast market and huge population, investment in human capital before the open and reform policy, and overseas Chinese citizens' willingness to invest in China in the beginning.

Conclusion: Laying the Foundation for Development

1. Thus, contrary to Amsden (1989), even the first industrialization was not built on laissez-faire principles (Epstein 2000; see also Olson 2000). The second industrial revolution (US, Germany, and Japan before WWI) was surely built with powerful state interventions (i.e., infant industry protection), and this has been true of the most recent industrialization in East Asia to an even greater extent (Chang 2000; see also Amsden 1989, 143–44; Wade 1990).

2. Of course, narrow-minded nationalism or xenophobia that results in a refusal to learn anything from a foreign country is harmful for growth, as the Qing Empire of China demonstrated

amply. Notably, nationalism does not equate to protectionism or economic nationalism as Olson (1987) understood it.

3. It is here that field experiments, with institutional elements being explicitly taken into account, can help. Unfortunately, much of the RCT literature within the Banerjee and Duflo (2011) tradition has consciously avoided testing institutions.

4. A prime case might have been the Chinese state that mobilized all its power of propaganda to forcefully overcome the initial resistance against market reform among its mid- to low-level cadres (Nee 2001), even though China has mostly worked with a gradualist model (see also Lin 2012c, ch. 8).

5. Indeed, only with this realization can we understand Andy Grove's famous quote, "Only the paranoid survive," and the Chinese adage "Thinking about danger when feeling comfortable" (*ju-an-si-wei*). This argument is echoed by organizational learning literature. For example, Kim (1997) argued that South Korea's Hyundai has been resorting to engineering crises, thus creating a crisis mentality among its employees to stimulate learning. In the South Korean case, strong nationalism might have been one of the major motivations that propelled South Koreans to learn faster and compete with the world's best companies.

6. Hence, state antiquity is strongly and positively associated with long-term development (Diamond 1997; Bockstette, Chanda, and Putterman 2002; Chanda and Putterman 2007; Borcan, Olsson, and Putterman 2018).

Appendixes to Chapter 5

1. Panel data offers significant advantages over cross-sectional or time-series data, especially in growth regressions. For a more technical discussion, see Temple (1999, 125–33).

2. For instance, although Rodrik (1999) deployed a long list of indicators that measure the quality of institutions, many of these indicators (such as QoG) suffered from conceptual sloppiness, selection biases, and heavily subjective ratings (Kurtz and Schrank 2007). See also Yang (2008).

3. Indeed, it is tenuous to argue that India and many Latin American states (when they were democratic) have been more stable than authoritarian states like South Korea, Singapore, Taiwan, or even Indonesia before the 1997 Asian financial crisis.

4. When discussing obedience to rules in organizations, Clague (1993, 412) pointed out that a certain level of obedience to rules is necessary, though not sufficient, for growth.

5. Of course, this does not mean social order is impossible within an egalitarian society.

6. Although a subordinate can threaten the authority with revolt, the individual chooses to submit to the authority most of the time because revolt is often extremely risky and difficult.

7. In this sense, individuals in power may deem at least some innovations potentially threatening or destabilizing because innovation may bring a shift of power from the incumbent to the powerless (Acemoglu and Robinson 2006; see also Lewis 1955, 178–79; Olson 1963; North 1981, 29; Mokyr 1992). Some of these authors have conflated innovation and growth and thus deemed both to be destabilizing. In contrast, we maintain that only innovation and growth that cannot be controlled by the powerful are destabilizing to the authority.

8. The case of Lysenko's reign over genetics in the Soviet Union is illustrative here (see chapter 5).

9. In modern science, this practice is a form of a "bad funding regime." For a brief discussion, see Stephan (1996, 1219–26). Again, the case of Lysenko is tragically illustrative here.

10. Limiting the diversity of individuals' innovation is different from the actual establishment of a monopoly of ideas. Again, the Lysenko case is illustrative here.

11. An illustration of too much hierarchical control leading to retardation of innovation is France's rather unsuccessful attempt to catch up with Britain in the eighteenth century by putting

overwhelming oversight power on innovations into the hands of a centralized bureaucracy, the Parisian Academy of Sciences. Under this arrangement, potential innovations had to be approved by the academy before being explored. Unsurprisingly, the result was that few projects were approved and France did not catch up with England (Jacob 1997, ch. 8).

12. Of course, this does not explain why many leading Japanese firms have since fallen behind.

Appendixes to Chapter 6

1. For instance, Lindert (2003) identifies England after 1800 as a democracy, yet England was an illiberal democracy in which a large portion of its population did not have voting rights.

2. We do note that economic freedom (e.g., economic liberalization from state control and planned economy) is positively correlated with economic growth (e.g., Jong-A-Pin and de Haan 2011).

BIBLIOGRAPHY

Abramovitz, Moses. 1956. "Resource and Output Trends in the United States since 1870." *American Economic Review* 46 (2): 5–23.

Abramovitz, Moses. 1986. "Catching Up, Forging Ahead, and Falling Behind." *Journal of Economic History* 46 (2): 385–406.

Acemoglu, Daron, Mario A. Bautista, Pablo Querubin, and James A. Robinson. 2008. "Economic and Political Inequality in Development: The Case of Cundinamarca, Colombia." In *Institutions and Economic Performance*, edited by Elhanan Helpman, 181–245. Cambridge, MA: Harvard University Press.

Acemoglu, Daron, Davide Cantoni, Simon Johnson, and James A. Robinson. 2011. "The Consequences of Radical Reform: The French Revolution." *American Economic Review* 101 (7): 3286–307.

Acemoglu, Daron, Simon Johnson, and James A. Robinson. 2001. "The Colonial Origins of Comparative Development: An Empirical Investigation." *American Economic Review* 91 (5): 1369–401.

Acemoglu, Daron, Simon Johnson, and James A. Robinson. 2002. "Reversal of Fortune: Geography and Institutions in the Making of the Modern World Income Distribution." *Quarterly Journal of Economics* 117 (4): 1231–94.

Acemoglu, Daron, Simon Johnson, and James A. Robinson. 2003. "An African Success Story: Botswana." In *In Search of Prosperity: Analytic Narratives on Economic Growth*, edited by Dani Rodrik, 80–119. Princeton, NJ: Princeton University Press.

Acemoglu, Daron, Simon Johnson, and James A. Robinson. 2005a. "Institutions as the Fundamental Cause of Long-Run Growth." In *Handbook of Economic Growth*, vol. 1A, edited by Philippe Aghion and Steven Durlauf, 385–472. Amsterdam: Elsevier North-Holland.

Acemoglu, Daron, Simon Johnson, and James A. Robinson. 2005b. "The Rise of Europe: Atlantic Trade, Institutional Change, and Economic Growth." *American Economic Review* 95 (3): 546–79.

Acemoglu, Daron, Suresh Naidu, Pascual Restrepo, and James A. Robinson. 2019. "Democracy Does Cause Growth." *Journal of Political Economy* 127 (1): 47–100.

Acemoglu, Daron, and James A. Robinson. 2000. "Why Did the West Extend the Franchise? Democracy, Inequality, and Growth in Historical Perspective." *Quarterly Journal of Economics* 115 (4): 1167–99.

Acemoglu, Daron, and James A. Robinson. 2006. "Economic Backwardness in Political Perspective." *American Political Science Review* 100 (1): 115–31.

Acemoglu, Daron, and James A. Robinson. 2012. *Why Nations Fail: The Origins of Power, Prosperity, and Poverty*. New York: Crown Publishing Group.

Achen, Christopher H. 2002. "Toward a New Political Methodology: Microfoundations and ART." *Annual Review of Political Science* 5: 423–50.

Achen, Christopher H. 2005. "Let's Put Garbage-Can Regressions and Garbage-Can Probits Where They Belong." *Conflict Management and Peace Science* 22 (4): 327–39.

Adams, John. 1765. *A Dissertation on the Canon and Feudal Law*. http://teachingamericanhistory .org/library/document/a-dissertation-on-the-canon-and-feudal-law/ (accessed November 18, 2016).

Adelman, Irma. 2001. "Fallacies in Development Theory and Their Implications for Policy." In *Frontiers of Development Economics: The Future in Perspective*, edited by Gerald M. Meier and Joseph E. Stiglitz, 103–34. Oxford, UK: Oxford University Press.

Aghion, Philippe, Alberto Alesina, and Francesco Trebbi. 2008. "Democracy, Technology, and Growth." In *Institutions and Economic Performance*, edited by Elhanan Helpman, 511–44. Cambridge, MA: Harvard University Press.

Aghion, Philippe, Eve Caroli, and Cecilia Garcia-Penalosa. 1999. "Inequality and Economic Growth: The Perspective of the New Growth Theories." *Journal of Economic Literature* 37 (4): 1615–60.

Aghion, Philippe, and Alexandra M. Roulet. 2014. "Growth and the Smart State." *Annual Review of Economics* 6 (1): 913–26.

Agnafors, Marcus. 2013. "Quality of Government: Toward a More Complex Definition." *American Political Science Review* 107 (3): 433–45.

Aisen, Ari, and Francisco José Veiga. 2013. "How Does Political Instability Affect Economic Growth?" *European Journal of Political Economy* 29 (1): 151–67.

Aizer, Anna, and Janet Currie. 2014. "The Intergenerational Transmission of Inequality: Maternal Disadvantage and Health at Birth." *Science* 344 (6): 856–61.

Akerlof, George A. 1997. "Social Distance and Social Decisions." *Econometrica* 65 (3): 1005–27.

Akerlof, George A. 2002. "Behavioral Macroeconomics and Macroeconomic Behavior." *American Economic Review* 92 (3): 411–33.

Akerlof, George A. 2007. "The Missing Motivations in Macroeconomics." *American Economic Review* 97 (1): 5–36.

Akerlof, George A. 2020. "Sins of Omission and the Practice of Economics." *Journal of Economic Literature* 58 (2): 405–18.

Akerlof, George A., and Rachel E. Kranton. 2000. "Economics and Identity." *Quarterly Journal of Economics* 115 (3): 715–53.

Akerlof, George A., and Robert J. Shiller. 2008. *Animal Spirits: How Human Psychology Drives the Economy, and Why It Matters for Global Capitalism*. Princeton, NJ: Princeton University Press.

Albertus, Michael. 2015. *Autocracy and Redistribution: The Politics of Land Reform*. Cambridge, UK: Cambridge University Press.

Alesina, Alberto, Arnaud Devleeschauer, William Easterly, Sergio Kurlat, and Romain Wacziarg. 2003. "Fractionalization." *Journal of Economic Growth* 8 (2): 155–94.

Alesina, Alberto, and Paola Giuliano. 2015. "Culture and Institutions." *Journal of Economic Literature* 53 (4): 898–944.

Alesina, Alberto, and Eliana La Ferrara. 2005. "Preferences of Redistribution in the Land of Equal Opportunities." *Journal of Public Economics* 89 (5–6): 897–931.

Alesina, Alberto, Sule Ozler, Nouriel Roubini, and Phillip Swagel. 1996. "Political Instability and Economic Growth." *Journal of Economic Growth* 1 (2): 189–211.

Alesina, Alberto, and Dani Rodrik. 1994. "Distributive Politics and Economic Growth." *Quarterly Journal of Economics* 109 (2): 465–90.

Algan, Yann, and Pierre Cahuc. 2014. "Trust, Growth, and Well-Being: New Evidence and Policy Implications." In *Handbook of Economic Growth*, vol. 2, edited by Philippe Aghion and Steven Durlauf, 49–120. Amsterdam: Elsevier North-Holland.

Allen, Robert C. 2008. "A Review of Gregory Clark's *A Farewell to Alms: A Brief Economic History of the World.*" *Journal of Economic Literature* 46 (4): 946–73.

Allen, Robert C. 2009. *The British Industrial Revolution in Global Perspective.* Cambridge, UK: Cambridge University Press.

Amsden, Alice H. 1989. *Asia's Next Giant: South Korea and Late Industrialization.* New York: Oxford University Press.

Amsden, Alice. H. 1994. "Why Isn't the Whole World Experimenting with the East Asian Model to Develop? Review of *The East Asian Miracle.*" *World Development* 22 (4): 627–33.

Amsden, Alice. H. 2007. *Escape from Empire: The Developing World's Journey through Heaven and Hell.* Cambridge, MA: MIT Press.

Anderson, Lykke E. 2000. "Social Mobility in Latin America." Manuscript, Instituto de Investigaciones Socio-Económicas (IISEC), Universidad Católica Boliviana.

Anderson, Lykke E. 2001. "Low Social Mobility in Bolivia: Causes and Consequences for Development." Working paper 1046, Kiel Institute for the World Economy.

Andrews, Matt. 2013. *The Limits of Institutional Reform in Development.* Cambridge, UK: Cambridge University Press.

Ang, Yuen Yuen. 2016. *How China Escaped the Poverty Trap.* Ithaca, NY: Cornell University Press.

Ankarloo, Daniel. 2002. "New Institutional Economics and Economic History." *Capital and Class* 78: 9–36.

Ankarloo, Daniel, and Giulio Palermo. 2004. "Anti-Williamson: A Marxian Critique of New Institutional Economics." *Cambridge Journal of Economics* 28 (3): 413–29.

Ansell, Ben W. 2010. *From the Ballot to the Blackboard: The Redistributive Political Economy of Education.* New York: Cambridge University Press.

Aoki, Masahiko. 1986. "Horizontal vs. Vertical Information Structure of the Firm." *American Economic Review* 76 (5): 971–83.

Aoki, Masahiko. 1995. "Decentralizing Information Processing and Hierarchical Monitoring: The Case of Japan." In *Social Capability and Long-Term Economic Growth*, edited by Bon Ho Koo and Dwight H. Perkins, 159–80. London: Palgrave Macmillan.

Aoki, Masahiko. 2001. *Toward a Comparative Institutional Analysis.* Cambridge, MA: MIT Press.

Arbetman, Marina, and Jacek Kugler, eds. 1997. *Political Capacity and Economic Behavior.* Boulder, CO: Westview.

Arneson, Richard J. 1989. "Equality and Equal Opportunity for Welfare." *Philosophical Studies* 56: 77–93.

Arneson, Richard J. 1999. "Against Rawlsian Equality of Opportunity." *Philosophical Studies* 93 (1): 77–112.

Aron, Janie. 2000. "Growth and Institutions: A Review of the Evidence." *World Bank Research Observer* 15 (1): 99–135.

Arrow, Kenneth J. 1962. "The Economic Implication of Learning by Doing." *Review of Economic Studies* 29 (3): 155–73.

Arrow, Kenneth J. 1964. "Control in Large Organizations." *Management Science* 10 (3): 397–408.

Arrow, Kenneth J. 1974. *The Limits of Organization.* New York: W. W. Norton.

Ashraf, Quamrul, and Oded Galor. 2013. "The 'Out of Africa' Hypothesis, Human Genetic Diversity, and Comparative Economic Development." *American Economic Review* 103 (1): 1–46.

Atkinson, A. B., and F. Bourguignon, eds. 2000. *Handbook of Income Distribution*, vol. 1. Amsterdam: Elsevier North-Holland.

Autor, David H. 2014. "Skills, Education, and the Rise of Earning Inequality among the 'Other 99 Percent.'" *Science* 344 (6186): 843–51.

Bäck, Hanna, and Axel Hadenius. 2008. "Democracy and State Capacity: Exploring a J-Shaped Relationship." *Governance* 21 (1): 1–24.

Baland, Jean-Marie, Karl Ove Moene, and James A. Robinson. 2010. "Governance and Development." In *Handbook of Development Economics*, vol. 5, edited by Dani Rodrik and Mark Rosenzweig, 4597–656. Amsterdam: North-Holland.

Balazs, Etienne. 1964. *Chinese Civilization and Bureaucracy*. Translated by H. M. Wright. New Haven, CT: Yale University Press.

Banerjee, Abhijit V., and Esther Duflo. 2003. "Inequality and Growth: What Can the Data Say?" *Journal of Economic Growth* 8 (3): 267–99.

Banerjee, Abhijit, and Esther Duflo. 2011. *Poor Economics: A Radical Rethinking of the Way to Fight Global Poverty*. New York: Public Affairs.

Bardhan, Pranab. 1989. "The New Institutional Economics and Development Theory: A Brief Critical Assessment." *World Development* 17 (9): 1389–95.

Bardhan, Pranab. 2000. "Understanding Underdevelopment: Challenges for Institutional Economics from the Point of View of Poor Countries." *Journal of Institutional and Theoretical Economics* 156 (1): 216–35.

Bardhan, Pranab. 2005a. "Institutions Matter, but Which Ones?" *Economics of Transition* 13 (3): 499–532.

Bardhan, Pranab. 2005b. *Scarcity, Conflicts, and Cooperation: Essays in the Political and Institutional Economics of Development*. Princeton, NJ: Princeton University Press.

Bardhan, Pranab K. 2010. *Awakening Giants, Feet of Clay: Assessing the Economic Rise of China and India*. Princeton, NJ: Princeton University Press.

Bardhan, Pranab K. 2016. "State and Development: The Need for a Reappraisal of the Current Literature." *Journal of Economic Literature* 54 (3): 862–92.

Barro, Robert J. 1991. "Economic Growth in a Cross Section of Countries." *Quarterly Journal of Economics* 106 (2): 407–43.

Barro, Robert J. 1996. "Democracy and Growth." *Journal of Economic Growth* 1 (1): 1–27.

Barro, Robert J. 1997. *Determinants of Economic Growth*. Cambridge, MA: MIT Press.

Barro, Robert J. 2000. "Inequality and Growth in a Panel of Countries." *Journal of Economic Growth* 5 (1): 5–32.

Barro, Robert. J. 2008. "Inequality and Growth Revisited." Working paper 11, Regional Economic Integration, Asian Development Bank.

Barro, Robert J., and Jong-Wha Lee. 2013. "A New Data Set of Educational Attainment in the World, 1950–2010." *Journal of Development Economics* 104: 184–98.

Barro, Robert J., and Rachel M. McCleary. 2003. "Religion and Economic Growth across Countries." *American Sociological Review* 68 (5): 760–81.

Baten, Joerg, and Christina Mumme. 2013. "Does Inequality Lead to Civil Wars? A Global Long-Term Study Using Anthropometric Indicators (1816–1999)." *European Journal of Political Economy* 32: 56–79.

Bates, Robert H. 2008. *When Things Fell Apart: State Failure in Late-Century Africa*. Cambridge, UK: Cambridge University Press.

Baum, Matthew A., and David A. Lake. 2003. "The Political Economy of Growth: Democracy and Human Capital." *American Journal of Political Science* 47 (2): 333–47.

Baumol, William J. 1990. "Entrepreneurship: Productive, Unproductive, and Destructive." *Journal of Political Economy* 98 (5): 893–921.

Bazzi, Samuel, and Michael A. Clemens. 2013. "Blunt Instruments: Avoiding Common Pitfalls in Identifying the Causes of Economic Growth." *American Economic Journal: Macroeconomics* 5 (2): 152–86.

Becker, Gary S. [1957] 1971. *The Economics of Discrimination*. 2nd ed. Chicago: University of Chicago Press.

Becker, Gary S. [1964] 1993. *Human Capital: A Theoretical and Empirical Analysis, with Special Reference to Education*. Chicago: University of Chicago Press.

Becker, Gary S. 1976. *The Economic Approach to Human Behavior*. Chicago: University of Chicago Press.

Becker, Gary S., Edward L. Glaeser, and Kevin M. Murphy. 1999. "Population and Economic Growth." *American Economic Review* 89 (2): 145–49.

Becker, Gary S., and Kevin M. Murphy. 1992. "The Division of Labor, Coordination Costs, and Knowledge." *Quarterly Journal of Economics* 107 (4): 1136–60.

Beier, Augustus Leon. 1975. "Industrial Growth and Social Mobility in England, 1540–1640." *British Journal of Sociology* 26 (2): 242–44.

Bénabou, Roland. 1996. "Unequal Societies." Economic research report 9617, New York University C. V. Starr Center.

Bénabou, Roland. 2002. "Tax and Education Policy in a Heterogeneous-Agent Economy: What Levels of Redistribution Maximize Growth and Efficiency?" *Econometrica* 70 (2): 481–517.

Bénabou, Roland, and Efe A. Ok. 2001. "Social Mobility and the Demand for Redistribution: The Poum Hypothesis." *Quarterly Journal of Economics* 116 (2): 447–87.

Bénabou, Roland, and Jean Tirole. 2002. "Self-Confidence and Personal Motivation." *Quarterly Journal of Economics* 117 (3): 871–915.

Bénabou, Roland, and Jean Tirole. 2006. "Belief in a Just World and Redistributive Politics." *Quarterly Journal of Economics* 121 (2): 699–746.

Berry, William D., Matt Golder, and Daniel Milton. 2012. "Improving Tests of Theories Positing Interaction." *Journal of Politics* 74 (3): 653–71.

Bertrand, Marianne, and Sendhil Mullainathan. 2004. "Are Emily and Greg More Employable Than Lakisha and Jamal? A Field Experiment on Labor Market Discrimination." *American Economic Review* 94 (4): 991–1013.

Besley, Timothy, and Robin Burgess. 2000. "Land Reform, Poverty Reduction and Growth: Evidence from India." *Quarterly Journal of Economics* 115 (2): 389–430.

Besley, Timothy, and Masayuki Kudamatsu. 2008. "Making Autocracy Work." In *Institutions and Economic Performance*, edited by Elhanan Helpman, 452–510. Cambridge, MA: Harvard University Press.

Besley, Timothy, and Torsten Persson. 2011. *Pillars of Prosperity*. Princeton, NJ: Princeton University Press.

Besley, Timothy, and Torsten Persson. 2014. "The Causes and Consequences of Development Clusters: State Capacity, Peace, and Income." *Annual Review of Economics* 6 (1): 927–49.

Betthäuser, Bastian. 2017. "Fostering Equality of Opportunity? Compulsory Schooling Reform and Social Mobility in Germany." *European Sociological Review* 33 (5): 633–44.

Bhagwati, Jagdish N. 1982. "Directly Unproductive, Profit-Seeking (DUP) Activities." *Journal of Political Economy* 95 (5): 988–1002.

Bhagwati, Jagdish N. 2002. "Democracy and Development: Cruel Dilemma or Symbiotic Relationship?" *Review of Development Economics* 6 (2): 151–62.

Bhaskar, Roy. [1979] 1998. *The Possibility of Naturalism: A Philosophical Critique of the Contemporary Human Sciences*. 3rd ed. London: Routledge.

Bhaskar, Roy. 1986. *Scientific Realism and Human Emancipation*. London: Routledge.

Bian, Yanjie, Xiaoling Shu, and John L. Logan. 2001. "Communist Party Membership and Regime Dynamics in China." *Social Forces* 79 (3): 805–41.

Bockstette, Valerie, Areendam Chanda, and Louis Putterman. 2002. "States and Markets: The Advantage of an Early Start." *Journal of Economic Growth* 7 (4): 347–69.

Boehm, Christopher. 1999. *Hierarchy in the Forest: The Evolution of Egalitarian Behavior*. Cambridge, MA: Harvard University Press.

Boix, Carles. 2009. "The Conditional Relationship between Inequality and Development." *PS: Political Science & Politics* 42 (4): 645–49.

Boix, Carles. 2010. "Origins and Persistence of Economic Inequality." *Annual Review of Political Science* 13: 489–516.

Boix, Carles. 2015. *Political Order and Inequality: Their Foundations and Their Consequences for Human Welfare.* New York: Cambridge University Press.

Boix, Carles, Michael Miller, and Sebastian Rosato. 2012. "A Complete Data Set of Political Regimes, 1800–2007." *Comparative Political Studies* 46 (12): 1523–54.

Boldrin, Michele, David K. Levine, and Salvatore Modica. 2013. "A Review of Acemoglu and Robinson's *Why Nations Fail.*" http://www.dklevine.com/general/aandrreview.pdf (accessed March 24, 2016).

Bollen, Kenneth A., and Robert W. Jackman. 1985. "Political Democracy and the Size Distribution of Income." *American Sociological Review* 50 (4): 438–57.

Bollen, Kenneth A., and Robert W. Jackman. 1995. "Income Inequality and Democratization Revisited: Comment on Muller." *American Sociological Review* 60 (6): 983–89.

Bond, Stephen R., Anke Hoeffler, and Jonathan R. W. Temple. 2001. "GMM Estimation of Empirical Growth Models." Working paper, University of Oxford. http://www.nuff.ox.ac.uk/Economics/papers/2001/w21/bht10.pdf.

Borcan, Oana, Ola Olsson, and Louis Putterman. 2018. "State History and Economic Development: Evidence from Six Millennia." *Journal of Economic Growth* 23 (1): 1–40.

Boudon, Raymond. 1998. "Limitations of Rational Choice Theory." *American Journal of Sociology* 104 (3): 817–28.

Boulding, Kenneth E. 1966. "The Economics of Knowledge and the Knowledge of Economics." *American Economic Review* 56 (1/2): 1–13.

Bourdieu, Pierre. 1984. *Distinction: A Social Critique of the Judgment of Taste.* London, UK: Routledge.

Bourdieu, Pierre. 2005. *The Social Structures of the Economy.* London, UK: Polity Press.

Bourguignon, Francois, and Thierry Verdier. 2000. "Oligarchy, Democracy, Inequality and Growth." *Journal of Development Economics* 62 (1): 285–313.

Boyd, Robert, and Peter J. Richerson. 1985. *Culture and the Evolutionary Process.* Chicago: University of Chicago Press.

Brambor, Thomas, William Roberts Clark, and Matt Golder. 2005. "Understanding Interaction Models: Improving Empirical Analyses." *Political Analysis* 14 (1): 63–82.

Braumoeller, Bear F. 2004. "Hypothesis Testing and Multiplicative Interaction Terms." *International Organization* 58 (4): 807–20.

Breen, Richard. 1997. "Inequality, Economic Growth and Social Mobility." *British Journal of Sociology* 48 (3): 429–49.

Brown, Richard H. 1973. "Social Mobility and Economic Growth: A Renaissance Example." *British Journal of Sociology* 23 (1): 58–66.

Brown, Richard H. 1976. "Social Theory as Metaphor: On the Logic of Discovery for the Sciences of Conduct." *Theory and Society* 3 (2): 169–97.

Brunetti, Aymo. 1997. "Political Variables in Cross-Country Growth Analysis." *Journal of Economic Surveys* 11 (2): 163–90.

Bruno, Michael, and William Easterly. 1998. "Inflation Crises and Long-Run Growth." *Journal of Monetary Economics* 41 (1): 3–26.

Buchanan, James M. 2003. "Politics as Tragedy in Several Acts." *Economics & Politics* 15 (2): 181–91.

Buckley, Walter. 1958. "Social Stratification and the Functional Theory of Social Differentiation." *American Sociological Review* 23: 369–75.

Bunge, Mario. 1996. *Finding Philosophy in Social Science*. New Haven, CT: Yale University Press.

Bunge, Mario. 1999. *The Sociology-Philosophy Connection*. New Brunswick, NJ: Transaction Publishers.

Campbell, Donald T. 1960. "Blind Variation and Selective Retention in Creative Thought as in Other Knowledge Processes." *Psychological Review* 67 (6): 380–400.

Campbell, Donald T. [1971] 1988. "The Experimental Society." In *Methodology and Epistemology for Social Science: Selected Papers*, edited by E. Samuel Overman, 290–314. Chicago, IL: University of Chicago Press.

Campbell, Donald T. 1974a. "Evolutionary Epistemology." In *The Philosophy of Karl Popper*, edited by Paul Arthur Schilpp, 413–63. La Salle, PA: Open Court.

Campbell, Donald T. 1974b. "Unjustified Variation and Selective Retention in Scientific Discovery." In *Studies in the Philosophy of Biology: Reduction and Related Problems*, edited by Francisco J. Ayala and Theodosius Dobzhansky, 139–61. Berkeley: University of California Press.

Caplovitz, David. 1967. *The Poor Pay More: Consumer Practices of Low-Income Families*. London: Macmillan.

Cartwright, Nancy. 2010. "What Are Randomized Controlled Trials Good for?" *Philosophical Studies* 147 (1): 59–70.

Cederman, Lars-Erik, Kristian S. Gleditsch, and Halvard Buhaug. 2013. *Inequality, Grievances, and Civil War*. Cambridge, MA: Cambridge University Press.

Cederman, Lars-Erik, Kristian S. Gleditsch, and Julian Wucherpfennig. 2017. "Predicting the Decline of Ethnic Civil War: Was Gurr Right and for the Right Reasons?" *Journal of Peace Research* 54 (2): 262–74.

Centeno, Miguel Angel, Atul Kohli, and Deborah J. Yashar. 2017. "Unpacking States in the Developing World: Capacity, Performance, and Politics." In *State in the Developing World*, edited by Miguel Angel Centeno, Atul Kohli, and Deborah J. Yashar, 1–32. Cambridge, UK: Cambridge University Press.

Chanda, Areendam, and Louis Putterman. 2007. "Early Starts, Reversals and Catch-up in the Process of Economic Development." *Scandinavian Journal of Economics* 109 (2): 387–413.

Chang, Ha-Joon. 1999. "The Economic Theory of the Developmental State." In *The Developmental State*, edited by Meredith Woo-Cumings, 182–99. Ithaca, NY: Cornell University Press.

Chang, Ha-Joon. 2000. "An Institutionalist Perspective on the Role of the State: Toward an Institutionalist Political Economy." In *Institutions and the Role of the State*, edited by Leonardo Burlamaqui, Ana Celia Castro, and Ha-Joon Chang, 3–26. Northampton, UK: Edward Elgar.

Chang, Ha-Joon. 2002. "Breaking the Mould: An Institutionalist Political Economy Alternative to the Neo-liberal Theory of the Market and the State." *Cambridge Journal of Economics* 26 (5): 539–59.

Chang, Ha-Joon. 2003. *Kicking Away the Ladder: Development Strategy in Historical Perspective*. London: Anthem.

Chang, Ha-Joon. 2007a. *Institutional Change and Economic Development*. Tokyo: United Nations University Press.

Chang, Ha-Joon. 2007b. "Understanding the Relationship between Institutions and Economic Development: Some Key Theoretical Issues." In *Institutional Change and Economic Development*, edited by H.-J. Chang, 17–33. Tokyo: United Nations University Press.

Chang, Ha-Joon. 2011. "Institutions and Economic Development: Theory, Policy and History." *Journal of Institutional Economics* 7 (4): 473–98.

Chang, Ha-Joon, and Peter Evans. 2000. "The Role of Institutions in Economic Change." Paper prepared for the meeting of the "Other Canon" Group, Venice, Italy.

Charron, Nicholas, and Victor Lapuente. 2010. "Does Democracy Produce Quality of Government?" *European Journal of Political Research* 49 (4): 443–70.

Chaudhry, Azam, and Philip Garner. 2007. "Do Governments Suppress Growth? Institutions, Rent-Seeking, and Innovation Blocking in a Model of Schumpeterian Growth." *Economics and Politics* 19 (1): 35–52.

Chaudhry, Kiren Aziz. 1993. "The Myths of the Market and the Common History of Late Developers." *Politics and Society* 21 (3): 245–73.

Che, Jiahua, and Yingyi Qian. 1998. "Insecure Property Rights and Government Ownership of Firms." *Quarterly Journal of Economics* 113 (2): 467–96.

Checchi, Daniele. 2005. *The Economics of Education.* Cambridge, UK: Cambridge University Press.

Chen, Shiyi, Gary H. Jefferson, and Jun Zhang. 2011. "Structural Change, Productivity Growth and Industrial Transformation in China." *China Economic Review* 22 (1): 133–50.

Chen, Wei, Jie Mao, Shiping Tang, Zhiguo Xiao, and Qiang Zhi. 2022. "The Political Logic of Developmental State: Bureaucratic Coordination and Industrial Policy." Working paper, Fudan University.

Cheng, Tun-Jen, Stephan Haggard, and David Kang. 1998. "Institutions and Growth in Korea and Taiwan: The Bureaucracy." *Journal of Development Studies* 34 (6): 87–111.

Chetty, Raj, Nathaniel Hendren, Maggie R. Jones, and Sonya R. Porter. 2018. "Race and Economic Opportunity in the United States: An Intergenerational Perspective." Working paper 24441, NBER.

Chou, Chien-Fu, and Gabriel Talmain. 1996. "Redistribution and Growth: Pareto Improvements." *Journal of Economic Growth* 1 (4): 505–23.

Chyi, Hau, and Bo Zhou. 2014. "The Effects of Tuition Reforms on School Enrollment in Rural China." *Economics of Education Review* 38 (1): 103–23.

Ciccone, Antonio, and Marek Jarociński. 2010. "Determinants of Economic Growth: Will Data Tell?" *American Economic Journal: Macroeconomics* 2 (4): 222–46.

Clague, Christopher. 1993. "Rule of Obedience, Organizational Loyalty, and Economic Developing." *Journal of Institutional and Theoretical Economics* 149 (2): 393–414.

Clague, Christopher, Philip Keefer, Stephen Knack, and Mancur Olson. 1996. "Property and Contract Rights in Autocracies and Democracies." *Journal of Economic Growth* 1 (2): 243–76.

Clark, Gregory. 1996. "The Political Foundations of Modern Economic Growth: England, 1540–1800." *Journal of Interdisciplinary History* 26 (4): 563–88.

Clark, Gregory. 2007. *A Farewell to Alms: A Brief Economic History of the World.* Princeton, NJ: Princeton University Press.

Clark, Kevin A. 2005. "The Phantom Menace: Omitted Variable Bias in Econometric Research." *Conflict Management and Peace Science* 22 (2): 341–352.

Clarke, Harold D., Allan Kornberg, Chris McIntyre, Petra Bauer-Kaase, and Max Kaase. 1999. "The Effect of Economic Priorities on the Measurement of Value Change: New Experimental Evidence." *American Political Science Review* 93 (3): 637–47.

Coase, Ronald H. 1937. "The Nature of the Firm." *Economica* 4 (16): 386–405.

Coase, Ronald H. 1959. "The Federal Communications Commission." *Journal of Law and Economics* 2 (2): 1–40.

Coase, Ronald H. 1960. "The Problem of Social Cost." *Journal of Law and Economics* 3 (1): 1–44.

Coffman, D'Maris, Adrian Leonard, and Larry Neal. 2013. *Questioning Credible Commitment: Perspectives on the Rise of Financial Capitalism.* Cambridge, UK: Cambridge University Press.

Cohen, H. Floris. 1994. *The Scientific Revolution: A Historiographical Inquiry.* Chicago: University of Chicago Press.

Cohodes, Sarah, Daniel Grossman, Samuel Kleiner, and Michael F. Lovenheim. 2014. "The Effect of Child Health Insurance Access on Schooling: Evidence from Public Insurance Expansions." Working paper 20178, NBER .

Collier, David, and James E. Mahon. 1993. "Conceptual 'Stretching' Revisited: Adapting Categories in Comparative Analysis." *American Political Science Review* 87 (4): 845–55.

Collier, Paul. 2007. *The Bottom Billion: Why the Poorest Countries Are Failing and What Can Be Done about It*. Oxford, UK: Oxford University Press.

Collier, Paul, et al. 2003. *Break the Conflict Trap: Civil War and Development Policy*. Oxford, UK: Oxford University Press.

Collins, James B. 1995. *The State in Early Modern France*. Cambridge, UK: Cambridge University Press.

Collins, Randall. 1979. *Conflict Sociology: Toward an Explanatory Science*. New York: Academic Press.

Commons, John R. 1924. *Legal Foundations of Capitalism*. New York: Macmillan.

Commons, John R. 1934. *Institutional Economics: Its Place in Political Economy*. New York: Macmillan.

Cook, Lisa D. 2014. "Violence and Economic Activity: Evidence from African American Patents, 1870–1940." *Journal of Economic Growth* 19 (2): 221–57.

Cornell, Agnes, Carl Henrik Knutsen, and Jan Teorell. 2021. "Bureaucracy and Growth." *Comparative Political Studies* 53 (14): 2246–82.

Costa, Dora L., and Naomi R. Lamoreaux. 2011. *Understanding Long-Run Economic Growth: Geography, Institutions, and the Knowledge Economy*. Chicago: University of Chicago Press.

Costalli, Stefano, Lugi Moretti, and Constantino Pischedda. 2017. "The Economic Costs of Civil War: Synthetic Counterfactual Evidence and the Effects of Ethnic Fractionalization." *Journal of Peace Research* 54 (1): 80–98.

Crafts, Nicholas, and Kevin H. O'Rourke. 2014. "Twentieth Century Growth." In *Handbook of Economic Growth*, vol. 2, edited by Philippe Aghion and Steven Durlauf, 263–346. Amsterdam: Elsevier North-Holland.

Cramer, Christopher. 2003. "Does Inequality Cause Conflict?" *Journal of International Development* 15 (4): 397–412.

Dahrendorf, Ralf. 1968. *Essays in the Theory of Society*. Stanford, CA: Stanford University Press.

Danchin, Étienne, et al. 2011. "Beyond DNA: Integrating Inclusive Inheritance into an Extended Theory of Evolution." *Nature Reviews Genetics* 12: 475–86.

Databanks International. 2011. *Cross-National Time-Series Data*. Jerusalem: Databanks International.

David, Paul A. 1994. "Why Are Institutions the 'Carriers of History'? Path Dependence and the Evolution of Conventions, Organizations and Institutions." *Structural Change and Economic Dynamics* 5 (2): 205–20.

Davis, Kingsley, and Wilbert E. Moore. 1945. "Some Principles of Stratification." *American Sociological Review* 12 (2): 242–49.

Deaton, Angus, and Nancy Cartwright. 2018. "Understanding and Misunderstanding Randomized Controlled Trials." *Social Science & Medicine* 210: 2–21.

Deaton, Angus. 2010. "Instruments, Randomization, and Learning about Development." *Journal of Economic Literature* 48 (2): 424–55.

De Dantillana, Giorgio. 1955. *The Crime of Galileo*. Chicago: University of Chicago Press.

De Haan, Jakob. 2007. "Political Institutions and Economic Growth Reconsidered." *Public Choice* 131 (3): 281–92.

Denzau, Arthur T., and Douglass C. North. 1994. "Shared Mental Models: Ideologues and Institutions." *Kyklos* 47 (1): 3–31.

Desmet, Klaus, Ignacio Ortuño-Ortín, and Romain Wacziarg. 2012. "The Political Economy of Linguistic Cleavages." *Journal of Development Economics* 97 (2): 322–38.

Deyo, Frederic, ed. 1987. *The Political Economy of the New Asian Industrialism*. Ithaca, NY: Cornell University Press.

Dhuey, Elizabeth. 2011. "Who Benefits from Kindergarten? Evidence from the Introduction of State Subsidization." *Educational Evaluation and Policy Analysis* 33 (1): 3–22.

Diamond, Jared. 1997. *Guns, Germs, and Steel*. New York: W. W. Norton.

Dickson, Bruce J. 2008a. *Wealth into Power: The Communist Party's Embrace of China's Private Sector*. New York: Cambridge University Press.

Dickson, Bruce J. 2008b. "Who Consents to the 'Beijing Consensus': Crony Communism in China." Presented at the "'Washington Consensus' versus 'Beijing Consensus'" Conference, University of Denver, May 29–June 1, 2008.

Dincecco, Mark. 2010. "Fragmented Authority from Ancient Regime to Modernity: A Quantitative Analysis." *Journal of Institutional Economics* 6 (3): 48–103.

Dincecco, Mark. 2011. *Political Transformation and Public Finance, Europe, 1650–1913*. Cambridge, UK: Cambridge University Press.

Dixit, Avinash, and Mancur Olson. 2000. "Does Voluntary Participation Undermine the Coase Theorem?" *Journal of Public Economics* 76 (3): 309–35.

Doner, Richard F., Bryan K. Ritchie, and Dan Slater. 2005. "Systemic Vulnerability and the Origins of Developmental States: Northeast and Southeast Asia in Comparative Perspective." *International Organization* 59 (2): 327–61.

Doorenspleet, Renske. 2019. *Rethinking the Value of Democracy: A Comparative Perspective*. New York: Palgrave Macmillan.

Dorsch, Michael T., and Paul Maarek. 2019. "Democratization and the Conditional Dynamics of Income Distribution." *American Political Science Review* 113 (2): 385–404.

Doucoulabos, Hristos, and Mehmet Ali Ulubaşoğlu. 2008. "Democracy and Economic Growth: A Meta-Analysis." *American Journal of Political Science* 52 (1): 61–83.

Drake, Stillman. [1980] 2001. *Galileo: A Very Short Introduction*. Oxford, UK: Oxford University Press.

Dreze, Jean, and Amartya Sen. 2002. *India: Development and Participation*. New Delhi: Oxford University Press.

Duesenberry, James. 1949. *Income, Saving, and the Theory of Consumer Behavior*. Cambridge, MA: Harvard University Press.

Durham, J. Benson. 1999. "Economic Growth and Political Regimes." *Journal of Economic Growth* 4 (1): 81–111.

Durlauf, Steven, Paul Johnson, and Jonathan Temple. 2005. "Growth Econometrics." In *Handbook of Economic Growth*, vol. 1A, edited by Philippe Aghion and Steven Durlauf, 555–677. Amsterdam: Elsevier North-Holland.

Dworkin, Ronald. 2000. *Sovereign Virtue: The Theory and Practice of Equality*. Cambridge, MA: Harvard University Press.

Earle, Timothy H. 1997. *How Chiefs Come to Power: The Political Economy in Prehistory*. Stanford, CA: Stanford University Press.

Easterlin, Richard A. 1981. "Why Isn't the Whole World Developed?" *Journal of Economic History* 41 (1): 1–19.

Easterly, William. 2001. *The Elusive Quest for Growth: Economists' Adventures and Misadventures in the Tropics*. Cambridge, MA: MIT Press.

Easterly, William. 2005. "National Policies and Economic Growth: A Reappraisal." In *Handbook of Economic Growth*, vol. 1A, edited by Philippe Aghion and Steven Durlauf, 1015–59. Amsterdam: Elsevier North-Holland.

Easterly, William, Michael Kremer, Lant Pritchett, and Lawrence H. Summers. 1993. "Good Policy or Good Luck?" *Journal of Monetary Economics* 32 (2): 459–83.

Easterly, William, and Ross Levine. 1997. "Africa's Growth Tragedy: Policies and Ethnic Divisions." *Quarterly Journal of Economics* 112 (4): 1203–50.

Easterly, William, and Ross Levine. 2001. "It's Not Factor Accumulation: Stylized Facts and Growth Models." *World Bank Economic Review* 15 (2): 177–219.

Easterly, William, and Ross Levine. 2003. "Tropics, Germs, and Crops: How Endowments Influence Economic Development." *Journal of Monetary Economics* 50 (1): 3–39.

Eisenstein, Elizabeth L. 1979. *The Printing Press as an Agent of Change: Communication and Cultural Transformation of the Early-Modern Europe.* 2 vols. Cambridge, UK: Cambridge University Press.

Elias, Norbert. [1939] 1991. *The Society of Individuals.* Malden, MA: Blackwell.

Elias, Norbert. [1939] 1994. *The Civilizing Process.* Malden, MA: Blackwell.

Elliott, John Huxtable. [1963] 2002. *Imperial Spain, 1469–1716.* London: Penguin Press.

Elliott, John Huxtable. 1989. *Spain and Its World 1500–1700.* New Haven, CT: Yale University Press.

Emirbayer, Mustafa 1997. "Manifesto for a Relational Sociology." *American Journal of Sociology* 103 (2): 281–317.

Engerman, Stanley L., Elisa Mariscal, and Kenneth L. Sokoloff. 1998. "Schooling, Suffrage, and the Persistence of Inequality in the Americas, 1800–1945." Working paper, University of California, Los Angeles.

Engerman, Stanley L., and Kenneth L. Sokoloff. 1997. "Factor Endowments, Institutions, and Differential Paths of Growth among New World Economics." In *How Latin America Fell Behind*, edited by Stephen Haber, 260–304. Stanford, CA: Stanford University Press.

Engerman, Stanley L., and Kenneth L. Sokoloff. 2002. "Factor Endowments, Inequality, and Paths of Development among New World Economies." *Economica* 3: 41–88.

Engerman, Stanley L., and Kenneth L. Sokoloff. 2005. "Institutional and Non-institutional Explanations of Economic Differences." In *Handbook of New Institutional Economics*, edited by Claude Menard and Mary M. Shirley, 639–66. Berlin: Springer.

Engerman, Stanley L., and Kenneth L. Sokoloff. 2011. "Once upon a Time in the Americas: Land and Immigration Policies in the New World." In *Understanding Long-Run Economic Growth: Geography, Institutions, and the Knowledge Economy*, edited by Dora L. Costa and Naomi R. Lamoreaux, 13–48. Chicago: University of Chicago Press.

Engerman, Stanley L., and Kenneth L. Sokoloff. 2012. *Economic Development in the Americas since 1500: Endowments and Institutions.* Cambridge, UK: Cambridge University Press.

Enriquez, Elaine, and Miguel Angel Centeno. 2012. "State Capacity: Utilization, Durability, and the Role of Wealth vs. History." *International and Multidisciplinary Journal of Social Sciences* 1 (2): 130–62.

Epstein, Stephan R. 2000. *Freedom and Growth: The Rise of States and Markets in Europe, 1300–1750.* London: Routledge.

Ertman, Thomas. 1997. *Birth of the Leviathan: Building States and Regimes in Medieval and Early Modern Europe.* Cambridge, UK: Cambridge University Press.

Etzioni-Halevy, Eva. 1983. *Bureaucracy and Democracy: A Political Dilemma.* London: Routledge.

Evans, Peter B. 1995. *Embedded Autonomy: State and Industrial Transformation.* Princeton, NJ: Princeton University Press.

Evans, Peter B. 1998. "Transferable Lessons? Re-examining the Institutional Prerequisites of East Asian Economic Policies." *Journal of Development Studies* 34 (6): 66–86.

Evans, Peter B. 2004. "Development as Institutional Change: The Pitfalls of Monocropping and Potentials of Deliberation." *Studies in Comparative International Development* 38 (4): 30–53.

Evans, Peter B. 2007. "Extending the Institutional Turn: Property, Politics, and Development Trajectories." In *Institutional Change and Economic Development*, edited by Ha-Joon Chang, 35–52. Tokyo: United Nations University Press.

Evans, Peter B., and James E. Rauch. 1999. "Bureaucracy and Growth: A Cross-National Analysis of the Effects of 'Weberian' State Structures on Economic Growth." *American Sociological Review* 64 (5): 748–65.

Fearon, James D. 2003. "Ethnic and Cultural Diversity by Country." *Journal of Economic Growth* 8 (2): 195–222.

Fedderke, Johannes, Raphael de Kadt, and John Luiz. 1999. "Economic Growth and Social Capital: A Critical Reflection." *Theory and Society* 28: 709–45.

Feinstein, Leon. 2004. "Mobility in Pupil's Cognitive Attainment during School Life." *Oxford Review of Economic Policy* 20 (2): 213–29.

Feldhay, Rivka. 1995. *Galileo and the Church: Political Inquisition or Critical Dialogue?* Cambridge, UK: Cambridge University Press.

Feng, Yi. 2003. *Democracy, Governance, and Economic Performance.* Cambridge, MA: MIT Press.

Fershtman, Chaim, Kevin M. Murphy, and Yoram Weiss. 1996. "Social Status, Education, and Growth." *Journal of Political Economy* 104 (1): 108–32.

Fershtman, Chaim, and Yoram Weiss. 1993. "Social Status, Culture and Economic Performance." *Economic Journal* 103 (419): 946–59.

Fewsmith, Joseph. 2003. "Studying the Three Represents." *China Leadership Monitor* 8 (1): 1–11.

Finocchiaro, Maurice A., ed. 1989. *The Galileo Affair: A Documentary History.* Berkeley: University of California Press.

Fleischer, Belton M., Haizheng Li, and Min Qiang Zhao. 2010. "Human Capital, Economic Growth, and Regional Inequality in China." *Journal of Development Economics* 92 (2): 215–31.

Foa, Roberto S. 2017. "Persistence or Reverse of Fortune? Early State Inheritance and the Legacies of Colonial Rule." *Politics and Society* 45 (2): 301–24.

Fogel, Robert W. 2011. "The Impact of the Asian Miracle on the Theory of Economic Growth." In *Understanding Long-Run Economic Growth,* edited by Dora L. Costa and Naomi R. Lamoreaux, 311–54. Chicago: University of Chicago Press.

Fogel, Robert W., and Stanley L. Engerman. 1974. *Time on the Cross: The Economics of American Negro Slavery.* Boston: Little, Brown.

Forbes, Kristin J. 2000. "A Reassessment of the Relationship between Inequality and Growth." *American Economic Review* 90 (4): 869–87.

Foucault, Michel. 1980. *Power/Knowledge: Selected Interviews and Other Writings, 1972–1977,* edited by Colin Gordon. New York: Pantheon.

Foucault, Michel. 2000. *Power,* vol. 3 of *Essential Works of Foucault (1954–1984),* edited by James D. Faubion. New York: New Press.

Frank, Andre Gunder. 1967. *Capitalism and Underdevelopment in Latin America.* New York: Monthly Review Press.

Frank, Robert H. 1985. *Choosing the Right Pond: Human Behaviour and the Quest for Status.* New York: Oxford University Press.

Frank, Robert H. 1989. "Frames of Reference and the Quality of Life." *American Economic Review* 79 (2): 80–85.

Frank, Robert H. 1997. "The Frame of Reference as a Public Good." *Economic Journal* 107 (445): 1832–47.

Frank, Robert H. 2005. "Positional Externalities Cause Large and Preventable Welfare Losses." *American Economic Review* 95 (2): 137–41.

Frankel, Jeffrey A., and David H. Romer.1999. "Does Trade Cause Growth?" *American Economic Review* 89 (3): 379–99.

Freedman, David A. 2010. *Statistical Models and Causal Inference: A Dialogue with the Social Sciences.* Cambridge: Cambridge University Press.

Fried, Morton. 1967. *The Evolution of Political Society.* New York: Random House.

Friedman, Milton. 1962. *Capitalism and Freedom.* Chicago: University of Chicago Press.

Fritz, Verena. 2007. *State-Building: A Comparative Study of Ukraine, Lithuania, Belarus, and Russia.* Budapest, Hungary: Central European University Press.

Fukuyama, Francis. 2013. "What Is Governance?" *Governance* 26 (3): 347–68.

Fukuyama, Francis. 2016. "Governance: What Do We Know, and How Do We Know It?" *Annual Review of Political Science* 19: 89–105.

Furubotn, Erik G., and Rudolf Richter. 1991. "The New Institutional Economics: An Assessment." In *The New Institutional Economics*, 1–34. Tübingen, Germany: Mohr Siebeck.

Gallup, John Luke, Jeffrey D. Sachs, and Andrew D. Mellinger. 1999. "Geography and Economic Growth." *International Regional Science Review* 22 (2): 179–232.

Galor, Oded. 2011. "Inequality, Human Capital Formation, and the Process of Development." In *Handbook of the Economics of Education*, vol. 4, edited by Eric A. Hanushek, Stephen Machin, and Ludger Woessmann, 441–93. Amsterdam: Elsevier North-Holland.

Galor, Oded, and Omer Moav. 2000. "Ability-Biased Technological Transition, Wage Inequality, and Economic Growth." *Quarterly Journal of Economics* 115 (2): 469–97.

Galor, Oded, and Omer Moav. 2002. "Natural Selection and the Origin of Economic Growth." *Quarterly Journal of Economics* 117 (4): 1133–91.

Galor, Oded, and Omer Moav. 2004. "From Physical to Human Capital Accumulation: Inequality and the Process of Development." *Review of Economic Studies* 71 (4): 1001–26.

Galor, Oded, Omer Moav, and Dietrich Vollrath. 2009. "Inequality in Landownership, the Emergence of Human-Capital Promoting Institutions, and the Great Divergence." *Review of Economic Studies* 76 (1): 143–79.

Galor, Oded, and David N. Weil. 2000. "Population, Technology, and Growth: From Malthusian Stagnation to the Demographic Transition and Beyond." *American Economic Review* 90 (4): 806–28.

Garcia-Jimeno, Camilo, and James A. Robinson. 2011. "The Myth of the Frontier." In *Understanding Long-Run Economic Growth*, edited by Dora L. Costa and Naomi R. Lamoreaux, 49–88. Chicago: University of Chicago Press.

Gates, Scott, Håvard Hegre, Håvard Mokleiv Nygård, and Håvard Strand. 2012. "Development Consequences of Armed Conflict." *World Development* 40 (9): 1713–22.

Gellner, Ernest. 1983. *Nations and Nationalism*. Ithaca, NY: Cornell University Press.

Gerring, John, Philip Bond, William T. Barndt, and Carola Moreno. 2005. "Democracy and Economic Growth: A Historical Perspective." *World Politics* 57 (3): 323–64.

Gerring, John, Styrom C. Thacker, and Rodrigo Alfaro. 2012. "Democracy and Human Development." *Journal of Politics* 74 (1): 1–17.

Gerschenkron, Alexander. 1962. *Economic Backwardness in Historical Perspective*. Cambridge, MA: Harvard University Press.

Ghosh, Atish R., and Holger Wolf. 1998. "Thresholds and Context Dependence in Growth." Working paper 6480, NBER.

Giddens, Anthony. 1976. *New Rules of Sociological Method*. 2nd ed. London: Polity Press.

Giddens, Anthony. 1979. *Central Problems in Social Theory: Action, Structure, and Contradiction in Social Analysis*. Berkeley: University of California Press.

Giddens, Anthony. 1984. *The Constitution of Society: Outline of the Theory of Structuration*. London: Polity Press.

Gimpelson, Vladimir, and Daniel Treisman. 2018. "Misperceiving Inequality." *Economics and Politics* 30 (1): 27–54.

Glaeser, Edward L., Rafael La Porta, Florenico Lopez-de-Silanes, and Andrei Shleifer. 2004. "Do Institutions Cause Growth?" *Journal of Economic Growth* 9 (3): 272–303.

Gleditsch, Nils Petter, et al. 2002. "Armed Conflict 1946–2001: A New Dataset." *Journal of Peace Research* 39 (5): 615–37.

Glewwe, Paul. 2002. "Schools and Skills in Developing Countries: Education Policies and Socioeconomic Outcomes." *Journal of Economic Literature* 40 (2): 436–82.

Glewwe, Paul, Eric A. Hanushek, Sarah D. Humpage, and Renato Eavina. 2011. "School Resources and Educational Outcomes in Developing Countries: A Review of the Literature from 1990–2010." Working paper 17554, NBER.

Glewwe, Paul, and Michael Kremer. 2006. "Schools, Teachers and Education Outcomes in Developing Countries." In *Handbook of the Economics of Education*, vol. 2, edited by Eric Hanushek and Finis Welch, 945–1017. Amsterdam: Elsevier North-Holland.

Glewwe, Paul, and Karthik Muralidharan. 2015. "Improving School Education Outcomes in Developing Countries: Evidence, Knowledge Gaps, and Policy Implications." Working paper 15–001, RISE, Oxford University.

Glomm, Gerhard, and B. Ravikumar. 1992. "Public versus Private Investment in Human Capital: Endogenous Growth and Income Inequality." *Journal of Political Economy* 100 (4): 818–34.

Glomm, Gerhard, and B. Ravikumar. 1993. *Endogenous Expenditures on Public Schools and Persistent Growth*. No. 85. Minneapolis, MN: Federal Reserve Bank.

Glomm, Gerhard, B. Ravikumar, and Ioana C. Schiopu. 2011. "The Political Economy of Education Funding." In *Handbook of the Economics of Education*, vol. 4, edited by Eric A. Hanushek, Stephen Machin, and Ludger Woessmann, 615–80. Amsterdam: Elsevier North-Holland.

Goertz, Gary. 2005. *Social Science Concepts: A User's Guide*. Princeton, NJ: Princeton University Press.

Goertz, Gary, and James Mahoney. 2012. *A Tale of Two Cultures: Qualitative and Quantitative Research in the Social Sciences*. Princeton, NJ: Princeton University Press.

Goldstone, Jack A. 2000. "The Rise of the West—or Not? A Revision of Socio-Economic History." *Sociological Theory* 18 (2): 175–94.

Goldstone, Jack A. 2002. "Efflorescences and Economic Growth in World History: Rethinking the 'Rise of the West' and the Industrial Revolution." *Journal of World History* 13 (2): 323–89.

Goldstone, Jack A., et al. 2010. "A Global Model for Forecasting Political Instability." *American Journal of Political Science* 54 (1): 190–208.

Goldthorpe, John H. 1985. "On Economic Development and Social Mobility." *British Journal of Sociology* 36 (4): 549–73.

Gomulka, Stanislaw. 1995. "The Puzzles of Fairly Fast Growth and Rapid Collapse under Socialism." In *Social Capability and Long-Term Economic Growth*, edited by Bon Ho Koo and Dwight H. Perkins, 203–20. London: Palgrave Macmillan.

Gorodnichenko, Yuriy, and Gerard Roland. 2017. "Culture, Institutions and the Wealth of Nations." *Review of Economics and Statistics* 99 (3): 402–16.

Grafe, Regina. 2012. *Distant Tyranny: Markets, Power, and Backwardness in Spain, 1650–1800*. Princeton, NJ: Princeton University Press.

Graham, Carol. 2015. "A Review of William Easterly's *The Tyranny of Experts*." *Journal of Economic Literature* 53 (1): 92–101.

Granato, Jim, Ronald Inglehart, and David Leblang. 1996. "The Effect of Cultural Values on Economic Development: Theory, Hypotheses, and Some Empirical Tests." *American Journal of Political Sciences* 40 (3): 607–31.

Grassi, Davide, and Vincenzo Memoli. 2015. "Political Determinants of State Capacity in Latin America." *World Development* 88 (1): 94–106.

Greif, Avner. 1994. "Cultural Beliefs and the Organization of Society: A Historical and Theoretical Reflection on Collectivist and Individualist Societies." *Journal of Political Economy* 102 (5): 912–50.

Greif, Avner. 1998. "Historical and Comparative Institutional Analysis." *American Economic Review* 88 (2): 80–84.

Greif, Avner. 2006. *Institutions and the Path to the Modern Economy: Lessons from Medieval Trade*. Cambridge, UK: Cambridge University Press.

Greif, Avner, and David Laitin. 2004. "A Theory of Endogenous Institutional Change." *American Political Science Review* 98 (4): 633–52.

Grossman, Gene M., and Elhanan Helpman. 1991. *Innovation and Growth in the Global Economy*. Cambridge, MA: MIT Press.

Guiso, Luigi, Paola Sapienza, and Luigi Zingales. 2006. "Does Culture Affect Economic Outcomes?" *Journal of Economic Perspectives* 20 (1): 23–49.

Guiso, Luigi, Paola Sapienza, and Luigi Zingales. 2009. "Cultural Biases in Economic Exchange." *Quarterly Journal of Economics* 124 (3): 1095–131.

Guiso, Luigi, Paola Sapienza, and Luigi Zingales. 2016. "Long-Term Persistence." *Journal of the European Economic Association* 14 (6): 1401–36.

Gurgul, Henryk, and Lukasz Lach. 2013. "Political Instability and Economic Growth: Evidence from Two Decades of Transition in CEE." *Communist and Post-Communist Studies* 46 (2): 189–202.

Hagemann, Rodolf. 2002. "How Did East German Genetics Avoid Lysenkoism?" *Trend in Genetics* 18 (6): 320–24.

Haggard, Stephan. 1990. *Pathways from the Periphery: The Politics of Growth in the Newly Industrializing Countries.* Ithaca, NY: Cornell University Press.

Haggard, Stephan. 2004. "Institutions and Growth in East Asia." *Studies in Comparative International Development* 38 (4): 53–81.

Haggard, Stephan. 2015. "The Developmental State Is Dead: Long Live the Developmental State!" In *Advances in Comparative-Historical Analysis*, edited by James Mahoney and Kathleen Thelen, 39–66. Cambridge, UK: Cambridge University Press.

Haggard, Stephan. 2018. *Developmental States.* Cambridge, UK: Cambridge University Press.

Haggard, Stephan, and Robert R. Kaufman. 2012. "Inequality and Regime Change: Democratic Transitions and the Stability of Democratic Rule." *American Political Science Review* 106 (3): 495–516.

Hainmueller, Jens, Jonathan Mummolo, and Yiqing Xu. 2019. "How Much Should We Trust Estimates from Multiplicative Interaction Models? Simple Tools to Improve Empirical Practice." *Political Analysis* 27 (2): 163–92.

Haldane, Andrew, Simon Brennan, and Vasileios Madours. 2010. "What Is the Contribution of the Financial Sector: Miracle or Mirage?" In *The Future of Finance: The LSE Report*, edited by Adair Turner et al., 87–120. London: LSE Press.

Hall, Alfred Rupert. 1961. "Merton Revisited, or Science and Society in the Seventeenth Century." *History of Science* 2 (1): 1–16.

Hall, Alfred Rupert. 1989. *The Revolution in Science, 1500–1750.* 3rd ed. London: Longman.

Hall, Robert E., and Charles I. Jones. 1999. "Why Do Some Countries Produce So Much More Output per Worker Than Others?" *Quarterly Journal of Economics* 114 (1): 83–116.

Halleröd, B., H. Ekbrand, and D. Gordon. 2014. "Good Governance—What We Think It Is and What We Really Measure." Paper presented at the Quality of Government and the Performance of Democracies seminar, Gothenburg, Sweden, May 20–22, 2014.

Hamilton, Alexander. 1791. "Report on the Subject of Manufactures." https://founders.archives .gov/documents/Hamilton/01-10-02-0001-0007 (accessed January 21, 2020).

Hanley, Ryan Patrick. 2014. "The 'Wisdom of the State': Adam Smith on China and Tartary." *American Political Science Review* 108 (2): 371–82.

Hannum, Emily, Xuehui An, and Hua-Yu Sebastian Cherng. 2011. "Examinations and Educational Opportunity in China: Mobility and Bottlenecks for the Rural Poor." *Oxford Review of Education* 37 (2): 267–305.

Hannum, Emily, Jere Behrman, Meiyan Wang, and Jihong Liu. 2008. "Education in the Reform Era." In *China's Great Economic Transformation*, edited by Loren Brandt and Thomas G. Rawski, 215–49. New York: Cambridge University Press.

Hannum, Emily, Peggy Kong, and Yuping Zhang. 2009. "Family Sources of Educational Gender Inequality in Rural China: A Critical Assessment." *International Journal of Educational Development* 29 (5): 474–86.

Hanson, Jonathan K. 2015. "Democracy and State Capacity: Complements or Substitutes?" *Studies in Comparative International Development* 55 (3): 304–30.

Hanson, Jonathan K. 2017. "State Capacity and the Resilience of Electoral Authoritarianism: Conceptualizing and Measuring the Institutional Underpinnings of Autocratic Power." *International Political Science Review* 39 (1): 17–32.

Hanson, Jonathan K., and Rachel Sigman, 2013. "Leviathan's Latent Dimensions: Measuring State Capacity for Comparative Political Research." Working paper, University of Michigan.

Hariri, Jacob Gerner. 2012. "The Autocratic Legacy of Early Statehood." *American Political Science Review* 106 (3): 471–94.

Harrison, Lawrence E., and Samuel P. Huntington, eds. 2000. *Culture Matters: How Values Shape Human Progress*. New York: Basic Books.

Hayek, Friedrich A. 1944. *The Road to Serfdom*. Chicago: University of Chicago Press.

Hayek, Friedrich A. 1945. "The Use of Knowledge in Society." *American Economic Review* 35 (4): 519–30.

Hayek, Friedrich A. 1960. *The Constitution of Liberty*. Chicago: University of Chicago Press.

Hayek, Friedrich A. 1978. *New Studies in Philosophy, Politics, Economics and the History of Ideas*. London: Routledge.

Hayek, Friedrich A. 1979. *Law, Legislation, and Liberty*, vol. III of *The Political Order of a Free People*. London: Routledge.

Hayek, Friedrich A. [1979] 1982. *The Political Order of a Free People*. London: Routledge.

Heckman, James J., and Stefano Mosso. 2014. "The Economics of Human Development and Social Mobility." *Annual Review of Economics* 6 (1): 689–733.

Helpman, Elhanan, ed. 2008. *Institutions and Economic Performance*. Cambridge, MA: Harvard University Press.

Hendrix, Cullen S. 2010. "Measuring State Capacity: Theoretical and Empirical Implications for Studying Civil Conflict." *Journal of Peace Research* 47 (3): 273–85.

Herbst, Jeffrey. 2000. *States and Power in Africa: Comparative Lessons in Authority and Control*. Princeton, NJ: Princeton University Press.

Herlihy, David. 1973. "Three Patterns of Social Mobility in Medieval History." *Journal of Interdisciplinary History* 3 (4): 623–47.

Herrendorf, Berthold, Richard Rogerson, and Akos Valentinyi. 2014. "Growth and Structural Transformation." In *Handbook of Economic Growth*, vol. 2, edited by Philippe Aghion and Steven Durlauf, 855–941. Amsterdam: Elsevier North-Holland.

Herrmann-Pillath, C. 2010. "What Have We Learnt from 20 Years of Economic Research into Culture?" *International Journal of Cultural Studies* 13 (4): 317–35.

Hertel, Florian R., and Olaf Groh-Samberg. 2019. "The Relation between Inequality and Intergenerational Class Mobility in 39 Countries." *American Sociological Review* 84 (6): 1099–133.

Hicks, John. 1965. *Capital and Growth*. Oxford, UK: Oxford University Press.

Hintze, Otto. 1975. "The Formation of States and Constitutional Development: A Study in History and Politics." In *The Historical Essays of Otto Hintze*, edited by F. Gilbert, 157–77. New York: Oxford University Press.

Hirsch, Fred. 1977. *Social Limits to Growth*. London: Routledge.

Hirschman, Albert O. 1958. *The Strategy of Economic Development*. New Haven, CT: Yale University Press.

Hirschman, Albert O. 1970. *Exit, Voice, and Loyalty: Responses to Decline in Firms, Organizations, and States*. Cambridge, MA: Harvard University Press.

Hirschman, Albert O. 1973. "The Changing Tolerance for Income Inequality in the Course of Economic Development." *World Development* 1 (12): 29–36.

Hirschman, Albert O. 1977. *The Passions and the Interests: Political Arguments for Capitalism before Its Triumph*. Princeton, NJ: Princeton University Press.

Ho, Ping-Ti. 1962. *The Ladder of Success in Imperial China: Aspects of Social Mobility, 1368–1911*. New York: Columbia University Press.

Hobbes, Thomas. [1651] 1985. *Leviathan*, edited by C. B. Macpherson. New York: Penguin Press.

Hodgson, Geoffrey M. 1989. "Institutional Economic Theory: The Old versus the New." *Review of Political Economy* 1 (3): 249–69.

Hodgson, Geoffrey M. 1993. "Institutional Economics: Surveying the Old and the New." *Metroeconomica* 44 (1): 1–28.

Hodgson, Geoffrey M. 2003. "The Hidden Persuaders: Institutions and Individuals in Economic History." *Cambridge Journal of Economics* 27 (1): 159–75.

Hodgson, Geoffrey M. 2004. *The Evolution of Institutional Economics: Agency, Structure, and Darwinism in American Institutionalism*. London: Routledge.

Hodgson, Geoffrey M., and Thorbjørn Knudsen. 2010. *Darwin's Conjecture: The Search for General Principles of Social and Economic Evolution*. Chicago: University of Chicago Press.

Hoffman, Philip T. 2015. "What Do States Do? Politics and Economic History." *Journal of Economic History* 75 (2): 303–32.

Hooykaas, R. 1987. "The Rise of Modern Science: When and Why?" *British Journal of History of Science* 20 (4): 453–73.

Houle, Christian 2009. "Inequality and Democracy: Why Inequality Harms Consolidation but Does Not Affect Democratization." *World Politics* 61 (4): 589–622.

Houle, Christian. 2019. "Social Mobility and Political Instability." *Journal of Conflict Resolution* 63 (1): 85–111.

Huang, Zhenqian, and Shiping Tang. 2018. "Tickets to Modernization: A Qualitative Comparative Analysis of the Rise of Modern European States." *CASS Journal of Political Science* 6: 26–41 (in Chinese).

Huntington, Samuel P. 1968. *Political Order in Changing Societies*. New Haven, CT: Yale University Press.

Inglehart, Ronald, et al. 2000. *World Values Surveys and European Values Surveys, 1981–1984, 1990–1993, and 1995–1997*. ICPSR study 2790. Ann Arbor, MI: Inter-university Consortium for Political and Social Research.

Jackman, Robert W., and Ross A. Miller. 1996a. "The Poverty of Political Culture." *American Journal of Political Science* 40 (3): 697–716.

Jackman, Robert W., and Ross A. Miller. 1996b. "A Renaissance of Political Culture?" *American Journal of Political Science* 40 (3): 632–59.

Jacob, Margaret C. 1997. *Scientific Culture and the Making of the Industrial West*. New York: Oxford University Press.

Jefferson, Thomas. 1779. "A Bill for the More General Diffusion of Knowledge." http://founders .archives.gov/documents/Jefferson/01-02-02-0132-0004-0079 (accessed April 20, 2014).

Jennings, Colin. 2013. "Institutions and Prosperity." *European Journal of Political Economy* 29 (1): 252–58.

Jervis, Robert. 1997. *System Effects: Complexity in Political and Social Life*. Princeton, NJ: Princeton University Press.

Jervis, Robert. 2002. "Theories of War in an Era of Leading-Power Peace." *American Political Science Review* 96 (1): 1–14.

Johnson, Allen W., and Timothy Earle. 1987. *The Evolution of Human Societies: From Foraging Group to Agrarian State*. Stanford, CA: Stanford University Press.

Johnson, Chalmers. 1962. *Peasant Nationalism and Communism Power: The Emergence of Revolutionary China, 1937–1945*. Stanford, CA: Stanford University Press.

Johnson, Chalmers. 1982. *MITI and the Japanese Miracle: The Growth of Industrial Policy*. Stanford, CA: Stanford University Press.

Johnson, Chalmers. 1987. "Political Institutions and Economic Performance: The Government-Business Relationship in Japan, South Korea and Taiwan." In *The Political Economy of the New Asian Industrialism*, edited by Frederic Deyo, 136–64. Ithaca, NY: Cornell University Press.

Johnson, Chalmers. 1995. *Japan: Who Governs? The Rise of the Developmental State*. New York: Norton.

Johnson, Chalmers. 1999. "The Developmental State: Odyssey of a Concept." In *The Development State*, edited by Meredith Woo-Cumings, 32–60. Ithaca, NY: Cornell University Press.

Johnson, Noel D., and Mark Koyama. 2017. "States and Economic Growth: Capacity and Constraints." *Explorations in Economic History* 64 (1): 1–20.

Jones, B. F., and B. A. Olken. 2005. "Do Leaders Matter? National Leadership and Growth since World War II." *Quarterly Journal of Economics* 120 (3): 835–64.

Jones, Charles I. 1995. "Times Series Tests of Endogenous Growth Models." *Quarterly Journal of Economics* 110 (2): 495–525.

Jones, Charles I. 1997. "On the Evolution of the World Income Distribution." *Journal of Economic Perspectives* 11 (3): 19–36.

Jones, Charles I. 2001. "Was an Industrial Revolution Inevitable?" *Advances in Macroeconomics* 1 (2): Article 1. http://elsa.berkeley.edu/~chad/bc400.pdf (accessed November 2005).

Jones, Charles I. 2005. "Ideas and Growth." In *Handbook of Economic Growth*, edited by Phillippe Aghion and Steven Durlauf, vol. 1B: 1063–111. Amsterdam: Elsevier North-Holland.

Jones, Charles I., and Paul Romer. 2010. "The New Kaldor Facts: Ideas, Institutions, Population, and Human Capital." *American Economic Journal: Macroeconomics* 2 (1): 224–45.

Jones, Eric. 2003. *The European Miracle*. 3rd ed. Cambridge, UK: Cambridge University Press.

Jong-A-Pin, Richard. 2009. "On the Measurement of Political Instability and Its Impact on Economic Growth." *European Journal of Political Economy* 25 (1): 15–29.

Jong-A-Pin, Richard, and Jakob de Haan. 2008. "Growth Accelerations and Regime Changes: A Correction." *Economic Journal Watch* 5 (1): 51–58.

Jong-A-Pin, Richard, and Jakob de Haan. 2011. "Political Regime Change, Economic Liberalization and Growth Accelerations." *Public Choice* 146 (1): 93–115.

Joravsky, David. 1970. *The Lysenko Affair*. Cambridge, MA: Harvard University Press.

Kahhat, Jaime. 2011. "Markets and the Dynamics of Inequality: Theoretical Perspectives." Background paper prepared for "Markets, the State and the Dynamics of Inequality: How to Advance Inclusive Growth." United Nations Development Program, Bureau of Development Policy, Poverty Group.

Kaldor, Nicholas. 1961. "Capital Accumulation and Economic Growth." In *The Theory of Capital*, edited by F. A. Lutz and D. C. Hague, 177–222. New York: St. Martin's Press.

Kanbur, R. 2000. "Income Distribution and Development." In *Handbook of Income Distribution*, edited by A. B. Atkinson and F. Bourguignon, 791–842. Amsterdam: Elsevier Science.

Kang, Seonjou, and James Meernik. 2005. "Civil War Destruction and the Prospects for Economic Growth." *Journal of Politics* 67 (1): 88–109.

Karnani, Aneel. 2009. "Romanticizing the Poor Harms the Poor." *Journal of International Development* 21 (1): 76–86.

Kaufmann, Daniel, and Aart Kraay. 2008. "Governance Indicators: Where Are We, and Where Should We Be Going?" *World Bank Research Observer* 23 (1): 1–30.

Kaufmann, Daniel, Aart Kraay, and Massimo Mastruzzi. 2010. "The Worldwide Governance Indicators: Methodology and Analytical Issues." Working paper 5430, World Bank Policy Research.

Keefer, Philip. 2000. "Review of *Power and Prosperity*." *Journal of Economic History* 60 (3): 919–21.

Keefer, Philip, and Stephen Knack. 2005. "Social Capital, Social Norms and the New Institutional Economics." In *Handbook of New Institutional Economics*, edited by Claude Menard and Mary M. Shirley, 701–25. Berlin: Springer.

Keeley, Lawrence H. 1996. *War before Civilization: The Myth of the Peaceful Savage*. New York: Oxford University Press.

Kendal, Jeremy, Jamshid J. Tehrani, and John Odling-Smee. 2011. "Human Niche Construction in Interdisciplinary Focus." *Philosophical Transactions of the Royal Society B: Biological Sciences* 366 (1566): 783–934.

Keynes, John Maynard. [1936] 2013. *The General Theory of Employment, Interest and Money*. Cambridge, UK: Cambridge University Press.

Kiiza, Julius. 2007. "Developmental Nationalism and Economic Performance in Africa: The Case of Three 'Successful' African Economies." In *Institutional Change and Economic Development*, edited by Ha-Joon Chang, 281–300. Tokyo: United Nations University Press.

Kim, Lin-su. 1997. *From Imitation to Innovation: The Dynamics of Korean Technological Learning*. Cambridge, MA: Harvard Business School Press.

Klomp, Joeren, and Jakob de Haan. 2009. "Political Institutions and Economic Volatility." *European Journal of Political Economy* 25: 311–26.

Knack, Stephen, and Philip Keefer. 1997. "Does Social Capital Have an Economic Payoff? A Cross-Country Investigation." *Quarterly Journal of Economics* 112 (4): 1251–88.

Knell, Markus. 1999. "Social Comparisons, Inequality, and Growth." *Journal of Institutional and Theoretical Economics* 155 (4): 664–95.

Knight, Frank H. 1967. "Laissez Faire: Pro and Con." *Journal of Political Economy* 75 (6): 782–95.

Knight, Jack. 1992. *Institutions and Social Conflict*. Cambridge, UK: Cambridge University Press.

Knight, John, Terry Sicular, and Ximing Yue. 2013. "Educational Inequality in China: The Intergenerational Dimension." In *Rising Inequality in China: Challenges to a Harmonious Society*, edited by Li Shi, Hiroshi Sato, and Terry Sicular, 142–96. New York: Cambridge University Press.

Knutsen, Carl Henrik. 2012. "Democracy and Economic Growth: A Survey of Arguments and Results." *International Area Studies Review* 15 (4): 393–415.

Knutsen, Carl Henrik. 2013. "Democracy, State Capacity, and Economic Growth." *World Development* 43 (1): 1–18.

Knutsen, Carl Henrik. 2015. "Why Democracies Outgrow Autocracies in the Long Run: Civil Liberties, Information Flows and Technological Change." *Kyklos* 68 (3): 357–84.

Ko, Chiu Yu, Mark Koyama, and Tuan-Hwee Sng. 2017. "Unified China and Divided Europe." *International Economic Review* 59 (1): 285–327.

Kohli, Atul. 2002. "States and Societies." In *Political Science: The State of the Discipline*, edited by Ira Katznelson and Helen V. Milner, 84–117. New York: W. W. Norton.

Kohli, Atul. 2004. *State-Directed Development: Political Power and Industrialization in the Global Periphery*. Cambridge, UK: Cambridge University Press.

Kormendi, Roger C., and Philip G. Meguire. 1985. "Macroeconomic Determinants of Growth: Cross-Country Evidence." *Journal of Monetary Economics* 16 (2): 141–63.

Krause, Lawrence H. 1995. "Social Capability and Long-Term Economic Growth." In *Social Capability and Long-Term Economic Growth*, edited by Bon Ho Koo and Dwight H. Perkins, 310–27. London: Palgrave Macmillan.

Kremer, Michael. 1993. "Population Growth and Technological Change: One Million B. C. to 1990." *Quarterly Journal of Economics* 108 (3): 681–716.

Kugler, Jaeck, and Ronald L. Tammen, eds. 2012. *The Performance of Nations*. Lanham, MD: Rowman and Littlefield.

Kurtz, Marcus J. 2013. *Latin American State Building in Comparative Perspective*. Cambridge, UK: Cambridge University Press.

Kurtz, Marcus J., and Andrew Schrank. 2007. "Growth and Governance: Models, Measures, and Mechanisms." *Journal of Politics* 69 (2): 538–54.

Kurzman, Charles, Regina Werum, and Ross E. Burkhart. 2002. "Democracy's Effect on Economic Growth: A Pooled Time-Series Analysis, 1951–1980." *Studies in Comparative International Development* 37 (1): 3–33.

Kuznets, Simon. 1968. *Toward a Theory of Economic Growth*. New York: W. W. Norton.

Lake, David A., and Matthew A. Baum. 2001. "The Invisible Hand of Democracy: Political Control and Provision of Public Service." *Comparative Politics Studies* 34 (6): 587–621.

Laland, Kevin N., John Odling-Smee, and Marcus W. Feldman. 2000. "Niche Construction, Biological Evolution, and Cultural Change." *Behavioral and Brain Sciences* 23 (1): 131–75.

Laland, Kevin N., John Odling-Smee, and Sean Myles. 2010. "How Culture Shaped the Human Genome: Bringing Genetics and the Human Sciences Together." *Nature Reviews, Genetics* 11 (2): 137–48.

Laland, Kevin N., and Kim Sterelny. 2006. "Seven Reasons (Not) to Neglect Niche Construction." *Evolution* 60 (9): 1751–62.

Land, Kevin, and Jee-Yeon K. Lehmann. 2012. "Racial Discrimination in the Labor Market: Theory and Empirics." *Journal of Economic Literature* 50 (4): 959–1006.

Landes, David S. 1994. "What Room for Accident in History? Explaining Big Changes by Small Events." *Economic History Review* 47 (4): 637–56.

Landes, David S. 1998. *The Wealth and Poverty of Nations: Why Some Are So Rich and Some So Poor*. New York: W. W. Norton.

Landes, David S. 2000. "Culture Makes Almost All the Difference." In *Culture Matters: How Values Shape Human Progress*, edited by Lawrence E. Harrison and Samuel P. Huntington, 2–13. New York: Basic Books.

Langford, Jerome J. [1961] 1992. *Galileo, Science, and the Church*. 3rd ed. Ann Arbor: University of Michigan Press.

Leblang, David A. 1996. "Property Rights, Democracy and Economic Growth." *Political Research Quarterly* 49 (1): 5–26.

Lee, Alexander. 2021. "Does Affirmative Action Work? Evaluating India's Quota System." *Comparative Political Studies* 54 (9): 1534–64.

Lee, Alexander, and Jack Paine. 2019. "British Colonialism and Democracy: Divergent Inheritances and Diminishing Legacies." *Journal of Comparative Economics* 47 (3): 487–503.

Lee, Keun. 2013a. "Capability Failure and Industrial Policy to Move beyond the Middle-Income Trap: From Trade-Based to Technology-Based Specialization." In *The Industrial Policy Revolution I: The Role of Government beyond Ideology*, edited by Joseph E. Stiglitz and Justin Yifu Lin, 247–72. Basingstoke, UK: Palgrave Macmillan.

Lee, Keun. 2013b. *Schumpeterian Analysis of Economic Catch-Up: Knowledge, Path-Creation and the Middle-Income Trap*. Cambridge, UK: Cambridge University Press.

Lee, Melissa M., and Nan Zhang. 2016. "Legibility and the Informational Foundations of State Capacity." *Journal of Politics* 79 (1): 118–32.

Lenski, Gerhard. E. 1966. *Power and Privilege: A Theory of Social Stratification*. New York: McGraw-Hill.

Levi, Margaret. 1988. *Of Rule and Revenue*. Berkeley: University of California Press.

Levi, Margaret. 2002. "The State of the Study of the State." In *Political Science: The State of the Discipline*, edited by Ira Katznelson and Helen Milner, 32–55. New York: W. W. Norton.

Levine, Ross, and David Renelt. 1992. "A Sensitivity Analysis of Cross-Country Growth Regressions." *American Economic Review* 82 (4): 942–63.

Lewis, Peter M. 2007. *Growing Apart: Oil, Politics, and Economic Changes in Indonesia and Nigeria*. Cambridge, UK: Cambridge University Press.

Lewis, W. Arthur. 1955. *The Theory of Economic Growth*. Homewood, IL: Richard D. Irwin.

Lewis, W. Arthur. 1984. "The State of Development Theory." *American Economic Review* 74 (1): 1–10.

Lewontin, Richard C. 1983. "Gene, Organism, and Environment." In *Evolution from Molecules to Man*, edited by D. S. Bendall, 273–85. Cambridge, UK: Cambridge University Press.

Li, Hongyi, and Heng-fu Zou. 1998. "Income Inequality Is Not Harmful for Growth: Theory and Evidence." *Review of Development Economics* 2: 318–34.

Liebenstein, Harvey. 1950. "Bandwagon, Snob, and Veblen Effects in the Theory of Consumers' Demand." *Quarterly Journal of Economics* 64 (2): 183–207.

Lieberman, Robert C. 2002. "Ideas, Institutions, and Political Order: Explaining Political Change." *American Political Science Review* 96 (4): 697–712.

Lin, Justin Yifu. 1989. "An Economic Theory of Institutional Change: Induced and Imposed Change." *Cato Journal* 9 (1): 1–33.

Lin, Justin Yifu. 1995. "The Needham Puzzle: Why the Industrial Revolution Did Not Originate in China." *Economic Development and Cultural Change* 43 (2): 269–92.

Lin, Justin Yifu. 2003. "Development Strategy, Viability, and Economic Convergence." *Economic Development and Cultural Change* 51 (2): 277–308.

Lin, Justin Yifu. 2009. *Economic Development and Transition: Thought, Strategy, and Viability*. Cambridge, UK: Cambridge University Press.

Lin, Justin Yifu. 2012a. *Demystifying the Chinese Economy*. Cambridge, UK: Cambridge University Press.

Lin, Justin Yifu. 2012b. *New Structural Economics: A Framework for Rethinking Development and Policy*. Washington, DC: World Bank.

Lin, Justin Yifu. 2012c. *The Quest for Prosperity: How Developing Economies Can Take Off*. Princeton, NJ: Princeton University Press.

Lin, Justin Yifu, and Jeffrey B. Nugent. 1995. "Institutions and Economic Development." In *Handbook of Development Economics*, vol. 3A, edited by J. Behrman and T. N. Srinivasan, 2301–70. Amsterdam: Elsevier Science.

Lindert, Peter H. 2003. "Voice and Growth: Was Churchill Right?" *Journal of Economic History* 63 (2): 315–50.

Lindert, Peter H. 2004. *Growing Public: Social Spending and Economic Growth since the Eighteenth Century*. 2 vols. Cambridge, UK: Cambridge University Press.

Lindert, Peter. 2011. "Kenneth Sokoloff on Inequality in the Americas." In *Understanding Long-Run Economic Growth*, edited by Dora L. Costa and Naomi R. Lamoreaux, 363–72. Chicago: University of Chicago Press.

Lipset, Seymour M. 1959. "Some Social Requisites of Democracy: Economic Development and Political Legitimacy." *American Political Science Review* 53 (1): 69–105.

List, Friedrich. [1841] 1885. *The National System of Political Economy*. Translated by Sampson Lloyd. London: Longmans, Green & Co.

Lloyd, Peter, and Cassey Lee. 2018. "A Review of the Recent Literature on the Institutional Economics Analysis of the Long-Run Performance of Nations." *Journal of Economic Surveys* 32 (1): 1–22.

Loasby, Brian J. 1999. *Knowledge, Institutions and Evolution in Economics*. London: Routledge.

Lockwood, David. 1957. "Some Remarks on 'The Social System.'" *British Journal of Sociology* 7 (2): 134–46.

Lodder, LeeAnn, Scott McFarland, and Diana White. 2003. *Racial Preference and Suburban Employment Opportunities*. Chicago: Legal Assistance Foundation of Metropolitan Chicago.

Loury, Glenn C. 1998. "Discrimination in the Post–Civil Rights Era: Beyond Market Interactions." *Journal of Economic Perspectives* 12 (2): 117–26.

Lovell, Peggy A., and Charles H. Wood. 1998. "Skin Color, Racial Identities, and Life Chances in Brazil." *Latin American Perspectives* 25 (1): 90–109.

Lucas, Robert E., Jr. 1988. "On the Mechanics of Economic Development." *Journal of Monetary Economics* 22 (1): 3–42.

Lucas, Robert E., Jr. 1993. "The Making of a Miracle." *Econometrica* 61 (2): 251–72.

Lucas, Robert E., Jr. 2002. *Economic Growth*. Cambridge, MA: Harvard University Press.

Lundberg, Mattias, and Lyn Squire. 2003. "The Simultaneous Evolution of Growth and Inequality." *Economic Journal* 113 (487): 326–44.

Luo, Jinfeng, and Yi Wen. 2016. "Institutions Do Not Rule: Reassessing the Driving Forces of Economic Development." Working paper 2015-001, Federal Reserve Bank of St. Louis. https://doi .org/10.20955/wp.2015.001 (accessed January 20, 2018).

Lynch, John, 1992. *Spain 1516–1598: From Nation State to World Empire*. Oxford, UK: Blackwell.

Mackie, Gerry. 2003. *Democracy Defended*. Cambridge, UK: Cambridge University Press.

MacLeod, W. Bentley. 2013. "On Economics: A Review of *Why Nations Fail* by D. Acemoglu and J. Robinson and *Pillars of Prosperity* by T. Besley and T. Persson." *Journal of Economic Literature* 51 (1): 116–43.

Mahoney, James. 2010. *Colonialism and Postcolonial Development: Spanish America in Comparative Perspective*. Cambridge, UK: Cambridge University Press.

Mahoney, James, and Kathleen Thelen. 2010. "A Theory of Gradual Institutional Change." In *Explaining Institutional Change: Ambiguity, Agency, and Power*, edited by James Mahoney and Kathleen Thelen, 1–37. Cambridge, UK: Cambridge University Press.

Maloney, William F., and Gaurav Nayyar. 2018. "Industrial Policy, Information, and Government Capacity." *World Bank Research Observer* 33 (1): 189–217.

Malthus, Thomas R. [1798] 1951. *An Essay on the Principle of Population*. London: Everyman.

Mankiw, N. Gregory, David Romer, and David N. Weil. 1992. "A Contribution to the Empirics of Economic Growth." *Quarterly Journal of Economics* 107 (2): 407–37.

Mann, Michael. [1984] 1988. "The Autonomous Power of the State: Its Origins, Mechanisms, and Results." *European Journal of Sociology* 25 (2): 185–213. Reprinted in Michael Mann, *States, War, and Capitalism: Studies in Political Sociology*, 1–32. New York: Blackwell Publishers.

Mann, Michael. 1986. *The Sources of Social Power*, vol. I of *A History of Power from the Beginning to AD 1760*. Cambridge, UK: Cambridge University Press.

Mann, Michael. 1993. *The Sources of Social Power*, vol. II of *The Rise of Classes and Nation-States, 1760–1914*. Cambridge, UK: Cambridge University Press.

Manski, Charles F. 2000. "Economic Analysis of Social Interactions." *Journal of Economic Perspectives* 14 (3): 115–36.

Mao, Jie, Shiping Tang, Zhiguo Xiao, and Qiang Zhi. 2021. "Industrial Policy Intensity, Technological Change, and Productivity Growth: Evidence from China." *Research Policy* 50 (7):104287. https://doi.org/10.1016/j.respol.2021.104287.

Mao, Tse-tung (Ze-dong). 1927. *Report on an Investigation of the Peasant Movement in Hunan*. www.marxists.org (accessed November 10, 2007).

Marshall, Alfred. [1920] 1982. *Principles of Economics*. Philadelphia, PA: Porcupine Press.

Marx, Karl, and Friedrich Engels. 1848. *The Communist Manifesto*. www.marxists.org (accessed November 2007).

Marx, Karl, and Friedrich Engels. 1932. *The German Ideology*. www.marxists.org (accessed November 2007).

Mason, Roger. 2000. "The Social Significance of Consumption: James Duesenberry's Contribution to Consumer Theory." *Journal of Economic Issues* 34 (3): 553–72.

McCleary, Rachel M., and Robert J. Barro. 2006. "Religion and Economy." *Journal of Economic Perspectives* 20 (2): 49–72.

McClelland, David C., John W. Atkinson, Russell A. Clark, and Edgar L. Lowell. 1976. *The Achievement Motive*. Oxford, UK: Irvington.

McCloskey, Deirdre. 2006. *Bourgeois Virtues: Ethics for an Age of Commerce*. Chicago: University of Chicago Press.

McCloskey, Deirdre. 2010. *Bourgeois Dignity: Why Economics Can't Explain the Modern World.* Chicago: University of Chicago Press.

McGuire, Martin C., and Mancur Olson Jr. 1996. "The Economics of Autocracy and Majority Rule: The Invisible Hand and the Use of Force." *Journal of Economic Literature* 34 (1): 72–96.

McLean, Iain. 2000. "Review Article: The Divided Legacy of Mancur Olson." *British Journal of Political Science* 30 (4): 651–68.

McNeill, William H. [1963] 1991. *The Rise of the West: A History of the Human Community.* Chicago: University of Chicago Press.

Meier, Gerald M. 2001. "The Old Generation of Development Economists and the New." In *Frontiers of Development Economics: The Future in Perspective,* edited by Gerald M. Meier and Joseph E. Stiglitz, 15–50. Oxford, UK: Oxford University Press.

Mendels, Franklin F. 1976. "Social Mobility and Phases of Industrialization." *Journal of Interdisciplinary History* 7 (2): 193–216.

Merton, Robert K. [1938] 1970. *Science, Technology, and Society in the Seventeenth-Century England.* New York: Harper and Row.

Merton, Robert K. 1973. *The Sociology of Science: Theoretical and Empirical Investigations.* Chicago: University of Chicago Press.

Migdal, Joel S. 1988. *Strong Societies and Weak States: State-Society Relations and State Capabilities in the Third World.* Princeton, NJ: Princeton University Press.

Migdal, Joel S. 2001. *State in Society: Studying How States and Societies Transform and Constitute One Another.* Cambridge, UK: Cambridge University Press.

Milgram, Stanley. 1974. *Obedience to Authority: An Experimental View.* New York: Harper Colophon.

Mill, John Stuart. [1871] 2006. *Principles of Political Economy, with Some of Their Applications to Social Philosophy.* Abridged ed. Indianapolis, IN: Hackett Publishing Group.

Miller, Arthur G., Barry E. Collins, and Diana E. Brief. 1995. "Perspectives on Obedience to Authority: The Legacy of the Milgram Experiments." *Journal of Social Issues* 51 (3): 1–19.

Miller, Gary, and Kathleen Cook. 1998. "Leveling and Leadership: Hierarchy and Social Order." In *Institutions and Social Order,* edited by Karol Soltan, Eric M. Uslaner, and Virginia Haufler, 67–100. Ann Arbor: University of Michigan Press.

Miller, Michael K. 2015. "Electoral Authoritarianism and Human Development." *Comparative Political Studies* 48 (12): 1526–62.

Mincer, Jacob. 1958. "Investment in Human Capital and Personal Income Distribution." *Journal of Political Economy* 66 (4): 281–302.

Mises, Ludwig von. [1962] 1996. *Liberalism: The Classical Tradition.* New York: Foundation for Economic Education.

Mo, Di, Hongmei Yi, Linxiu Zhang, Yaojiang Shi, Scott Rozelle, and Alexis Medina. 2012. "Transfer Paths and Academic Performance: The Primary School Merger Program in China." *International Journal of Educational Development* 32 (3): 423–31.

Mobarak, Ahmed Mushfiq. 2005. "Democracy, Volatility, and Economic Development." *Review of Economics and Statistics* 87 (2): 348–61.

Mokyr, Joel. 1990. *The Lever of Riches: Technological Creativity and Economic Progress.* New York: Oxford University Press.

Mokyr, Joel. 1992. "Technological Inertia in Economic History." *Journal of Economic History* 52 (2): 325–38.

Mokyr, Joel. 2002. *The Gifts of Athena: The Historical Origins of the Knowledge Economy.* Princeton, NJ: Princeton University Press.

Mokyr, Joel. 2008. "The Institutional Origins of the Industrial Revolution." In *Institutions and Economic Performance,* edited by Elhanan Helpman, 64–119. Cambridge, MA: Harvard University Press.

Mokyr, Joel. 2014. "Culture, Institutions, and Modern Growth." In *Institutions, Property Rights, and Economic Growth: The Legacy of Douglass North*, edited by Douglass C. North et al., 151–91. Cambridge, UK: Cambridge University Press.

Mokyr, Joel. 2017. *A Culture of Growth*. Princeton, NJ: Princeton University Press.

Montinola, Gabriella, Yingyi Qian, and Barry R. Weingast, 1995. "Federalism, Chinese Style: The Political Basis for Economic Success in China." *World Politics* 48 (1): 50–81.

Moore, Barrington, Jr. 1966. *Social Origins of Dictatorship and Democracy: Lord and Peasants in the Making of the Modern World*. Boston: Beacon Press.

Moore, Barrington, Jr. 1978. *Injustice: The Social Bases of Obedience and Revolt*. New York: M. E. Sharpe.

Morris, Cynthia T., and Irma Adelman. 1989. "Nineteenth-Century Development Experience and Lessons for Today." *World Development* 17 (9): 1417–32.

Moselle, Boaz, and Benjamin Polak. 2001. "A Model of Predatory State." *Journal of Law, Economics, and Organization* 17 (1): 1–33.

Muller, Edward N. 1988. "Democracy, Economic Development, and Income Inequality." *American Sociological Review* 53 (1): 50–68.

Munck, Gerardo L. 2009. *Measuring Democracy: A Bridge between Scholarship and Politics*. Baltimore, MD: Johns Hopkins University Press.

Murphy, Kevin M., Andrei Shleifer, and Robert W. Vishny. 1991. "The Allocation of Talent: Implications for Growth." *Quarterly Journal of Economics* 106 (2): 503–30.

Murtin, Fabrice, and Romain Wacziarg. 2014. "The Democratic Transition." *Journal of Economic Growth* 19 (1): 141–81.

Myrdal, Gunnar. 1957. *Economic Theory and Under-developed Regions*. London: Gerald Duckworth.

Myrdal, Gunnar. 1968. *Asian Drama. An Inquiry into the Poverty of Nations*. New York: Pantheon.

Myrdal, Gunnar. 1974. "What Is Development?" *Journal of Economic Issues* 8 (4): 729–36.

Narizny, Kevin. 2019. "The Political-Economic Foundations of Representative Government." *Perspectives on Politics* 18 (2): 454–69.

Nee, Victor. 2000. "The Role of the State in Making Market." *Journal of Institutional and Theoretical Economics* 156 (1): 64–88.

Nee, Victor. 2001. "Introduction." In *The New Institutionalism in Sociology*, edited by Mary C. Brinton and Victor Nee. Stanford, CA: Stanford University Press.

Needham, Joseph L. 1969. *The Grand Titration: Science and Society in East and West*. Toronto: University of Toronto Press.

Nelson, Richard R. 2006. "Evolutionary Social Sciences and Universal Darwinism." *Journal of Evolutionary Economics* 16 (6): 491–510.

Nelson, Richard R. 2007. "Universal Darwinism and Evolutionary Social Science." *Biology and Philosophy* 22 (1): 73–94.

Nelson, Richard R., and Howard Pack. 1999. "The Asian Miracle and Economic Growth Theory." *Economic Journal* 109 (457): 416–36.

Nelson, Richard R., and Bhaven N. Sampat. 2001. "Making Sense of Institutions as a Factor Shaping Economic Performance." *Journal of Economic Behavior and Organization* 44 (1): 31–54.

Nelson, Richard R., and Sidney G. Winter. 1982. *An Evolutionary Theory of Economic Change*. Cambridge, MA: Harvard University Press.

Nevis, Edwin C., Anthony J. DiBella, and Janet M. Gould. 1995. "Understanding Organizations as Learning Systems." *Sloan Management Review* 36 (2): 73–85.

Ng, Yew-Kwang. 1997. "A Case for Happiness, Cardinalism, and Interpersonal Comparability." *Economic Journal* 107 (445): 1848–58.

North, Douglass C. 1981. *Structure and Change in Economic History*. New York: Norton.

North, Douglass C. 1990. *Institutions, Institutional Change and Economic Performance*. Cambridge, UK: Cambridge University Press.

North, Douglass C. 1994. "Economic Performance through Time." *American Economic Review* 84 (3): 359–68.

North, Douglass C., and Robert P. Thomas. 1973. *The Rise of the Western World: A New Economic History.* Cambridge, UK: Cambridge University Press.

North, Douglass C., John Joseph Wallis, Steven B. Webb, and Barry R. Weingast. 2013. *In the Shadow of Violence: Politics, Economics and the Problems of Development.* Cambridge, UK: Cambridge University Press.

North, Douglass C., John Joseph Wallis, and Barry R. Weingast. 2009. *Violence and Social Orders.* Cambridge, UK: Cambridge University Press.

North, Douglass C., and Barry Weingast. 1989. "Constitutions and Commitment: The Evolution of Institutional Governing Public Choice in Seventeenth-Century England." *Journal of Economic History* 49 (4): 803–32.

Nozick, Robert. 1974. *Anarchy, State, and Utopia.* New York: Basic Books.

Nugent, Jeffrey B., and James A. Robinson. 2010. "Are Factor Endowments Fate?" *Revista de Historia Económica / Journal of Iberian and Latin American Economic History* 28 (1): 45–82.

Nur-tegin, Kanybek. 2014. "Entrenched Autocracy or New Democracy: Which Is Better for Business?" *Kyklos* 67 (3): 398–419.

Ober, Josiah. 2008. *Democracy and Knowledge: Innovation and Learning in Classical Athens.* Princeton, NJ: Princeton University Press.

O'Brien, Michael J., and Kevin N. Laland. 2012. "Genes, Culture and Agriculture: An Example of Human Niche Construction." *Current Anthropology* 53 (4): 434–70.

O'Brien, Patrick. 2000. "The Reconstruction, Rehabilitation, and Reconfiguration of the British Industrial Revolution as a Conjuncture in Global History." *Itinerario* 22 (3/4): 117–34.

O'Brien, Patrick. 2007. "State Formation and the Construction of Institutions for the First Industrial Nation." In *Institutional Change and Economic Development,* edited by H.-J. Chang, 177–97. Tokyo: United Nations University Press.

Odling-Smee, John. 1988. "Niche Constructing Phenotypes." In *The Role of Behavior in Evolution,* edited by Henry C. Plotkin. Cambridge, MA: MIT Press.

Odling-Smee, John. 2010. "Niche Inheritance." In *Evolution: The Extended Synthesis,* edited by Massimo Pigliucci and Gerd B. Müller, 175–207. Cambridge, MA: MIT Press.

Odling-Smee, John, and Kevin N. Laland. 2011. "Ecological Inheritance and Cultural Inheritance: What Are They and How Do They Differ?" *Biological Theory* 6 (3): 220–30.

Odling-Smee, John, Kevin N. Laland, and Marcus W. Feldman. 2003. *Niche Construction: The Neglected Process in Evolution.* Princeton, NJ: Princeton University Press.

Ogilvie, Sheilagh, and A. W. Carus. 2014. "Institutions and Economic Growth in Historical Perspective." In *Handbook of Economic Growth,* vol. 2, edited by Philippe Aghion and Steven Durlauf, 403–513. Amsterdam: Elsevier North-Holland.

Olson, Mancur, Jr. 1963. "Rapid Growth as a Destabilizing Force." *Journal of Economic History* 23 (4): 529–52.

Olson, Mancur, Jr. 1965. *The Logic of Collective Action: Public Goods and the Theory of Groups.* Cambridge, MA: Harvard University Press.

Olson, Mancur, Jr. 1982. *The Rise and Decline of Nations.* New Haven, CT: Yale University Press.

Olson, Mancur, Jr. 1983. "A Less Ideological Way of Deciding How Much Should Be Given to the Poor." *Daedalu* 112 (4): 217–36.

Olson, Mancur, Jr. 1987. "Economic Nationalism and Economic Progress." *World Economy* 10 (3): 241–64.

Olson, Mancur, Jr. 1993. "Dictatorship, Democracy, and Development." *American Political Science Review* 87 (3): 567–76.

Olson, Mancur, Jr. 1996. "Big Bills Left on the Sidewalk: Why Some Nations Are Rich, and Others Poor." *Journal of Economic Perspective* 10 (2): 3–24.

Olson, Mancur, Jr. 2000. *Power and Prosperity: Outgrowing Communist and Capitalist Dictatorships*. New York: Basic Books.

Olsson, Ola. 2009. "On the Democratic Legacy of Colonialism." *Journal of Comparative Economics* 37 (4): 534–51.

Öniş, Ziya. 1991. "The Logic of the Developmental State." *Comparative Politics* 24 (1): 109–26.

Oqubay, Arkebe. 2015. *Made in Africa: Industrial Policy in Ethiopia*. Oxford, UK: Oxford University Press.

Ostrom, Elinor. 1986. "An Agenda for the Study of Institutions." *Public Choice* 48 (1): 3–25.

Ostrom, Elinor. 1990. *Governing the Commons: The Evolution of Institutions for Collective Action*. Cambridge, MA: Cambridge University Press.

Pack, Howard. 1994. "Endogenous Growth Theory: Intellectual Appeal and Empirical Shortcomings." *Journal of Economic Perspectives* 8 (1): 55–72.

Pagano, Ugo. 2003. "Nationalism, Development, and Integration: The Political Economy of Ernest Gellner." *Cambridge Journal of Economics* 27 (5): 623–46.

Papaioannou, Elias, and Gregorios Siourounis. 2008. "Democratisation and Growth." *Economic Journal* 118 (5): 1520–51.

Parente, Stephen L., and Edward C. Prescott. 1999. "Monopoly Rights: A Barrier to Riches." *American Economic Review* 89 (5): 1216–33.

Parente, Stephen L., and José-Víctor Ríos-Rull. 2005. "The Success and Failure of Reforms in Transition Economies." *Journal of Money, Credit and Banking* 37 (1): 23–42.

Peev, Evegeni, and Dennis Mueller. 2012. "Democracy, Economic Freedom and Growth in Transition Economies." *Kyklos* 65 (3): 381–407.

Pepinsky, Thomas A. 2009. *Economic Crises and the Breakdown of Authoritarian Regimes: Indonesia and Malaysia in Comparative Perspective*. Cambridge, UK: Cambridge University Press.

Perotti, Robert. 1996. "Growth, Income Distribution, and Democracy: What the Data Say." *Journal of Economic Growth* 1 (2): 149–87.

Persson, Torsten, and Guido Tabellini. 1994. "Is Inequality Harmful for Growth? Theory and Evidence." *American Economic Review* 84 (2): 600–21.

Persson, Torsten, and Guido Tabellini. 2006. "Democracy and Development: The Devil in the Details." *American Economic Review* 96 (2): 319–24.

Phelps, Edmund. 1968. "Population Increase." *Canadian Journal of Economics* 1 (3): 497–518.

Piketty, Thomas. 2000. "Theories of Persistent Inequality and Intergenerational Mobility." In *Handbook of Income Distribution*, edited by A. B. Atkinson and F. Bourguignon, 429–76. Amsterdam: Elsevier North-Holland.

Piketty, Thomas. 2014. *Capital in the Twenty-First Century*. Translated by Arthur Goldhammer. Cambridge, MA: Harvard University Press.

Pinkovskiy, Maxim, and Xavier Sala-i-Martin. 2016. "Lights, Camera . . . Income! Illuminating the National Accounts-Household Surveys Debate." *Quarterly Journal of Economics* 131 (2): 579–631.

Polanyi, Karl. [1944] 2001. *The Great Transformation: The Political and Economic Origins of Our Time*. Boston: Beacon Press.

Polanyi, Michael. 1941. "The Growth of Thought in Society." *Economica* 8 (32): 428–56.

Polanyi, Michael. 1962. "The Republic of Science: Its Political and Economic Theory." *Minerva* 1: 54–73.

Polanyi, Michael. 1966. *The Tacit Dimension*. Garden City, NY: Doubleday.

Pomeranz, Kenneth. 2000. *The Great Divergence: China, Europe and the Making of the Modern World Economy*. Princeton, NJ: Princeton University Press.

Popper, Karl. [1937] 1959. *The Logic of Scientific Discovery*. London: Routledge.

Popper, Karl. [1945] 1966. *The Open Society and Its Enemies*. 2 vols. Princeton, NJ: Princeton University Press.

Poteete, Amy R. 2009. "Is Development Path Dependent or Political? A Reinterpretation of Mineral-Dependent Development in Botswana." *Journal of Developmental Studies* 45 (4): 544–71.

Pozuelo, Julia Ruiz, Amy Slipowitz, and Guillermo Vuletin. 2016. "Democracy Does Not Cause Growth: The Importance of Endogeneity Arguments." Working paper, Inter-American Development Bank.

Preston, Larry M. 1983. "Freedom and Authority: Beyond the Precepts of Liberalism." *American Political Science Review* 77 (3): 666–74.

Pritchett, Lant. 1997. "Divergence, Big Time." *Journal of Economic Perspectives* 11 (3): 3–17.

Pritchett, Lant. 2000. "Understanding Patterns of Economic Growth: Searching for Hills among Plateaus, Mountains, and Plains." *World Bank Economic Review* 14 (2): 221–50.

Pritchett, Lant. 2003. "A Toy Collection, a Socialist Star, and a Democratic Dud." In *In Search of Prosperity: Analytic Narratives on Economic Growth*, edited by Dani Rodrik, 123–51. Princeton, NJ: Princeton University Press.

Przeworski, Adam. 2004. "Institutions Matter?" *Government and Opposition* 39 (4): 527–40.

Przeworski, Adam, Michael E. Alvarez, Jose Antonio Cheibub, and Fernando Limongi. 2000. *Democracy and Development: Political Institutions and Well-Being in the World, 1950–1990*. Cambridge, MA: Cambridge University Press.

Przeworski, Adam, and Fernando Limongi. 1993. "Political Regimes and Economic Growth." *Journal of Economic Perspectives* 7 (2): 51–69.

Putnam, Robert D. 1993. *Making Democracy Work: Civic Traditions in Modern Italy*. Princeton, NJ: Princeton University Press.

Putterman, Louis, and David N. Weil. 2010. "Post-1500 Population Flows and the Long-Run Determinants of Economic Growth and Inequality." *Quarterly Journal of Economics* 125 (4): 1627–82.

Qian, Yingyi. 2003. "How Reform Worked in China." In *In Search of Prosperity: Analytic Narratives on Economic Growth*, edited by Dani Rodrik, 297–333. Princeton, NJ: Princeton University Press.

Quinn, Dennis P., and John T. Woolley. 2001. "Democracy and National Economic Performance: The Preference for Stability." *American Journal of Political Science* 45 (3): 634–57.

Rabb, Theodore K. 1965. "Religion and the Rise of Modern Science." In *The Intellectual Revolution of the Seventeenth Century*, edited by C. Webster, 262–79. London: Routledge.

Rader, Roy. 1992. "Hierarchy: The Economics of Managing." *Journal of Economic Literature* 30 (3): 1382–415.

Rae, Douglas. 1981. *Equalities*. Cambridge, UK: Cambridge University Press.

Rauch, James E., and Peter Evans. 2000. "Bureaucratic Structure and Bureaucratic Performance in Less Developed Countries." *Journal of Public Economics* 75 (1): 49–71.

Raudenbush, Stephen W., and Robert D. Eschmann. 2015. "Does Schooling Increase or Reduce Social Inequality?" *Annual Review of Sociology* 41 (1): 443–70.

Ravallion, Martin. 2012. "Fighting Poverty One Experiment at a Time: A Review of Abhijit Banerjee and Esther Duflo's *Poor Economics: A Radical Rethinking of the Way to Fight Global Poverty*." *Journal of Economic Literature* 50 (1): 103–14.

Rawls, John. 1999. *A Theory of Justice*. Rev. ed. Cambridge, MA: Harvard University Press.

Ray, James Lee. 2003. "Explaining Interstate Conflict and War: What Should Be Controlled For?" *Conflict Management and Peace Science* 20 (1): 1–29.

Reddy, Sanjay G. 2012. "Randomize This! On Poor Economics." *Review of Agrarian Studies* 2 (2): 61–73.

Redondi, Pietro. [1983] 1987. *Galileo: Heretic.* Translated by Raymond Rosenthal. Princeton, NJ: Princeton University Press.

Reinert, Erik S. 2007. "Institutionalism Ancient, Old, and New: A Historical Perspective on Institutions and Uneven Development." In *Institutional Change and Economic Development*, edited by Ha-Joon Chang, 53–72. Tokyo: United Nations University Press.

Richerson, Peter J., and Robert Boyd. 2005. *Not by Genes Alone: How Culture Transformed Human Evolution.* Chicago: University of Chicago Press.

Rodrik, Dani. 1999. "Where Did All the Growth Go? External Shocks, Social Conflict, and Growth Collapses." *Journal of Economic Growth* 4 (2): 385–412.

Rodrik, Dani. 2000. "Participatory Politics, Social Cooperation, and Economic Stability." *American Economic Review* 90 (2): 140–44.

Rodrik, Dani, ed. 2003a. *In Search of Prosperity: Analytic Narratives on Economic Growth.* Princeton, NJ: Princeton University Press.

Rodrik, Dani. 2003b. "Introduction: What Do We Learn from Country Narratives?" In *In Search of Prosperity: Analytic Narratives on Economic Growth*, edited by Dani Rodrik, 1–19. Princeton, NJ: Princeton University Press.

Rodrik, Dani. 2005. "Growth Strategies." In *Handbook of Economic Growth*, vol. 1A, edited by Philippe Aghion and Steven Durlauf, 967–1014. Amsterdam: Elsevier North-Holland.

Rodrik, Dani. 2007. *One Economics, Many Recipes: Globalization, Institutions, and Economic Growth.* Princeton, NJ: Princeton University Press.

Rodrik, Dani. 2018. "An African Growth Miracle?" *Journal of African Economies* 27 (1): 10–27.

Rodrik, Dani, Arvind Subramanian, and Francesco Trebbi. 2004. "Institutions Rule: The Primacy of Institutions over Geography and Integration in Economic Development." *Journal of Economic Growth* 9 (2): 131–65.

Roemer, John E. 1998. *Equality of Opportunity.* Cambridge, MA: Harvard University Press.

Roemer, John E. 2009. "Equality: Its Justification, Nature, and Domain." In *Oxford Handbook of Economic Inequality*, edited by Wiemer Salverda, Brian Nolan, and Timothy M. Smeeding, 23–39. Oxford, UK: Oxford University Press.

Roemer, John E., and Alain Trannoy. 2015. "Equality of Opportunity." In *Handbook of Income Distribution*, edited by A. B. Atkinson and F. Bourguignon, 217–300. Amsterdam: Elsevier Science.

Roll-Hansen, Nils. 2005. *The Lysenko Effect: The Politics of Science.* Amherst, MA: Humanity Books.

Romer, Paul M. 1989. "Increasing Returns and New Development in the Theory of Growth." Working paper 3098, NBER.

Romer, Paul M. 1990. "Endogenous Technological Change." *Journal of Political Economy* 98: S71–S102.

Rose-Ackerman, Susan. 2003. "Was Mancur a Maoist? An Essay on Kleptocracy and Political Stability." *Economics and Politics* 15 (2): 163–80.

Rosen, Sherwin. 1983. "Specialization and Human Capital." *Journal of Labor Economics* 1 (1): 43–49.

Rosenberg, Nathan. 1982. "Learning by Using." In *Inside the Black Box: Technology and Economics*, edited by Nathan Rosenberg, 120–40. Cambridge, UK: Cambridge University Press.

Rosenberg, Nathan, and L. E. Birdzell, Jr. 1986. *How the West Grew Rich: The Economic Transformation of the Industrial World.* New York: Basic Books.

Rosenthal, Jean-Laurent. 1992. *The Fruits of Revolution.* Cambridge, UK: Cambridge University Press.

Ross, Michael. 2006. "Is Democracy Good for the Poor?" *American Journal of Political Science* 50 (4): 860–74.

Rostow, Walt W. [1960] 1971. *The Stages of Economic Growth: A Non-Communist Manifesto*. 2nd ed. Cambridge, UK: Cambridge University Press.

Rothstein, Bo. 2011. *The Quality of Government: Corruption, Social Trust, and Inequality in International Perspectives*. Chicago: University of Chicago Press.

Rousseau, Jean-Jacques. [1755] 1993. *The Social Contract and Discourses*. Translated by George Douglas Howard Cole. London: Everyman.

Routley, Laura. 2012. "Developmental States: A Review of the Literature." Working paper 3, ESID.

Routley, Laura. 2014. "Developmental States in Africa? A Review of Ongoing Debates and Buzzwords." *Development Policy Review* 32 (2): 159–77.

Ruttan, Vernon W. 1984. "Social Science Knowledge and Institutional Change." *American Journal of Agricultural Economics* 66 (5): 549–59.

Ruttan, Vernon W., and Yujiro Hayami. 1984. "Toward a Theory of Induced Institutional Innovation." *Journal of Development Studies* 20 (4): 203–23.

Sachs, Jeffrey D. 2003. "Institutions Don't Rule: Direct Effects of Geography on Per Capita Income." Working paper 9490, NBER.

Sachs, Jeffrey D. 2012. "Government, Geography, and Growth: The True Drivers of Economic Development." *Foreign Affairs* 91 (5): 142–50.

Sah, Raaj K. 1991. "Fallibility in Human Organizations and Political Systems." *Journal of Economic Perspectives* 5 (2): 67–88.

Sah, Raaj K., and Joseph E. Stiglitz. 1987. "The Architecture of Economic Systems: Hierarchies and Polyarchies." *American Economic Review* 76 (4): 716–27.

Saint-Paul, Gilles, and Thierry Verdier. 1993. "Education, Democracy and Growth." *Journal of Development Economics* 42 (2): 399–407.

Sala-i-Martin, Xavier. 1997. "I Just Ran Four Million Regressions." *American Economic Review* 87 (2): 178–83.

Samuels, Richard J. 2003. *Machiavelli's Children: Leaders and Their Legacies in Italy and Japan*. Ithaca, NY: Cornell University Press.

Sangmpam, S. N. 2007. "Politics Rules: The False Primacy of Institutions in Developing Countries." *Political Studies* 55 (1): 201–24.

Sartori, Giovanni. 1970. "Concept Misformation in Comparative Politics." *American Political Science Review* 64 (5): 1033–53.

Sartori, Giovanni. 1984. "Guidelines for Concept Analysis." In *Social Science Concepts: A Systematic Analysis*, edited by Giovanni Sartori. Beverly Hills, CA: Sage.

Saylor, Ryan. 2013. "Concepts, Measures, and Measuring Well: An Alternative Outlook." *Sociological Methods and Research* 42 (3): 354–91.

Schelling, Thomas C. 1971. "Dynamic Models of Segregation." *Journal of Mathematical Sociology* 1 (2): 143–86.

Schrank, Andrew. 2015. "Toward a New Economic Sociology of Development." *Sociology of Development* 1 (2): 25–50. https://doi.org/10.1525/sod.2015.1.2.233.

Schultz, Theodore W. 1960. "Capital Formation by Education." *Journal of Political Economy* 68 (6): 571–83.

Schultz, Theodore W. 1961. "Investment in Human Capital." *American Economic Review* 51 (1): 1–17.

Schultz, Theodore W. 1981. *Investing in People: The Economics of Population Quality*. Berkeley: University of California Press.

Schultz, Theodore W. 1993. *The Economics of Being Poor*. Cambridge, MA: Blackwell.

Schumpeter, J. A. [1934] 1968. *Theory of Economic Development*. New Brunswick, NJ: Transaction.

Schumpeter, J. A. [1943] 2003. *Capitalism, Socialism, and Democracy*. London: Routledge.

Schumpeter, J. A. 1947. "Theoretical Problems of Economic Growth." *Journal of Economic History* 7 (S1): 1–9.

Schumpeter, J. A. 1949. "The Communist Manifesto in Sociology and Economics." *Journal of Political Economy* 57 (3): 199–212.

Scott, James C. 1995. "State Simplifications: Nature, Space and People." *Journal of Political Philosophy* 3 (3): 191–233.

Sen, Amartya. 1992. *Inequality Re-examined*. Oxford, UK: Oxford University Press.

Sen, Amartya. 2000. *Development as Freedom*. Oxford, UK: Oxford University Press.

Service, Elman R. 1971. *Primitive Social Organization: An Evolutionary Perspective*. 2nd ed. New York: Random House.

Service, Elman R. 1975. *Origins of the State and Civilization: The Process of Cultural Evolution*. New York: W. W. Norton.

Sewell, William H., Jr. 1992. "A Theory of Structure: Duality, Agency, and Transformation." *American Journal of Sociology* 98 (1): 1–29.

Shaver, Robert W. 1989. "Rousseau and Recognition." *Social Theory and Practice* 15 (3): 261–83.

Shi, Xinzheng. 2016. "The Impact of Education Fee Reduction Reform on School Enrollment in Rural China." *Journal of Development Studies* 52 (12): 1791–809.

Shi, Yaojiang et al. 2015. "Dropping Out of Rural China's Secondary Schools: A Mixed-Methods Analysis." *China Quarterly* 224: 1048–69.

Shirley, Mary. 2005. "Institutions and Development." In *Handbook of New Institutional Economics*, edited by Claude Menard and Mary M. Shirley, 611–38. Berlin: Springer.

Shirley, Mary. 2008. *Institutions and Development*. Cheltenham, UK: Edward Elgar.

Shiue, Carol H., and Wolfgang Keller. 2007. "Markets in China and Europe on the Eve of the Industrial Revolution." *American Economic Review* 97 (4): 1189–216.

Si-ma, Guang. [1085] 1935. *Zi-zhi Tong-jian* [The Comprehensive Mirror for Aid in Government]. Shanghai: Zhonghua Shuju.

Simon, Julian. 1981. *The Ultimate Resources*. Princeton, NJ: Princeton University Press.

Singer, H. W. 1995. "*The Economics of Being Poor* by Theodore W. Schultz." *Economic Development and Cultural Change* 43 (4): 889–92.

Sirowy, Larry, and Alex Inkeles. 1990. "The Effects of Democracy on Economic Growth and Inequality: A Review." *Studies in Comparative International Development* 25 (1): 126–57.

Skaaning, Svend-Erik, John Gerring, and Henrikas Bartuševičius. 2015. "A Lexical Index of Electoral Democracy." *Comparative Political Studies* 48 (12): 1491–525.

Skaperdas, S. 2011. "The Costs of Organized Violence: A Review of the Evidence." *Economic Governance* 12 (1): 1–23.

Skocpol, T. 1979. *States and Social Revolutions: A Comparative Analysis of France, Russia, and China*. New York: Cambridge University Press.

Skocpol, T. 1985. "Bringing the State Back In." In *Strategies of Analysis in Current Research*, edited by P. B. Evans, D. Rueschemeyer, and T. Skocpol, 3–43. New York: Cambridge University Press.

Slater, Dan. 2010. *Ordering Power*. Cambridge, UK: Cambridge University Press.

Smith, Adam. [1759] 1979. *The Theory of Moral Sentiments*, edited by D. D. Raphael and A. L. Macfie. Indianapolis, IN: Liberty Press.

Smith, Adam. [1776] 1981. *An Inquiry into the Nature and Causes of the Wealth of Nations*. edited by R. H. Campbell and A. S. Skinner. 2 vols. Indianapolis, IN: Liberty Press.

Smith, Nathan. 2013. "Blog on Acemoglu and Robinson's *Why Nations Fail*." EconBlog, November 13, 2013.

Soifer, Hille. 2008. "State Infrastructural Power: Approaches to Conceptualization and Measurement." *Studies in Comparative International Development* 43 (4): 231–51.

Soifer, Hillel. 2015. *State Building in Latin America*. New York: Cambridge University Press.

Soifer, Hillel, and Matthias vom Hau. 2008. "Unpacking the Strength of the State: The Utility of State Infrastructural Power." *Studies in Comparative International Development* 43 (3/4): 219–30.

Sokoloff, Kenneth L. 1988. "Inventive Activity in Early Industrial America: Evidence from Patent Records, 1790–1846." *Journal of Economic History* 48 (4): 813–50.

Sokoloff, Kenneth L., and Stanley L. Engerman. 2000. "History Lessons: Institutions, Factor Endowments, and Paths of Development in the New World." *Journal of Economic Perspectives* 14 (1): 217–32.

Solow, Robert M. 1956. "A Contribution to the Theory of Economic Growth." *Quarterly Journal of Economics* 70 (1): 65–94.

Solow, Robert M. 1957. "Technical Change and the Aggregate Production Function." *Review of Economics and Statistics* 39 (3): 312–20.

Solow, Robert M. 1994. "Perspectives on Growth Theory." *Journal of Economics Perspectives* 8 (1): 45–54.

Sowell, Thomas. 2004. *Affirmative Action around the World: An Empirical Study.* New Haven, CT: Yale University Press.

Sowell, Thomas. 2018. *Discrimination and Disparity.* New York: Basic Books.

Soyfer, Valery. 1994. *Lysenko and the Tragedy of Soviet Science.* Hermitage, NJ: Rutgers University Press.

Soyfer, Valery. 2001. "The Consequences of Political Dictatorship for Russian Science." *Nature Reviews Genetics* 2 (9): 723–29.

Spaulding, Robert M. 2011. "Revolutionary France and the Transformation of the Rhine." *Central European History* 44 (2): 203–26.

Speller, Jules. 2008. *Galileo's Inquisition Trial Revisited.* Frankfurt, Germany: Peter Lang.

Stephan, Paula E. 1996. "The Economics of Science." *Journal of Economic Literature* 34 (3): 1199–235.

Sterelny, K. 2005. "Made by Each Other: Organisms and Their Environment." *Biology and Philosophy* 20 (1): 21–36.

Stevans, Lonnie K. 2012. "Income Inequality and Economic Incentives: Is There an Equity-Efficiency Tradeoff?" *Research in Economics* 66 (1): 149–60.

Stewart, Frances. 2008. *Horizontal Inequalities and Conflict: Understanding Group Violence in Multiethnic Societies.* New York: Palgrave Macmillan.

Stiglitz, Joseph, and Justin Yifu Lin. 2013. *The Industrial Policy Revolution: The Role of Government beyond Ideology.* New York: Palgrave Macmillan.

Straus, Scott. 2012. "Wars Do End! Changing Patterns of Political Violence in Sub-Saharan Africa." *African Affairs* 111 (443): 179–201.

Subramanian, Arvind, and Devesh Roy 2003. "Who Can Explain the Mauritian Miracle? Meade, Romer, Sachs, or Rodrik." In *In Search of Prosperity: Analytic Narratives on Economic Growth,* edited by Dani Rodrik, 205–43. Princeton, NJ: Princeton University Press.

Swan, T. W. 1956. "Economic Growth and Capital Accumulation." *Economic Record* 32 (2): 334–61.

Sylwester, Kevin. 2000. "Income Inequality, Education Expenditures, and Growth." *Journal of Development Economics* 63 (2): 379–98.

Tabellini, Guido. 2008. "Institutions and Culture." *Journal of the European Economic Association* 6 (2–3): 255–94.

Tabellini, Guido. 2010. "Culture and Institutions: Economic Development in the Regions of Europe." *Journal of the European Economic Association* 8 (4): 677–716.

Tang, Ray, and Shiping Tang. 2018. "Democracy and Growth: A New Institutional Theory and Quantitative Evidences." *Kyklos* 71 (4): 642–66.

Tang, Shiping. 2005. "Knowledge as a Production Factor: Toward a Unified Theory of Economic Growth." Working paper, Institute of Asia-Pacific Studies, Chinese Academy of Social Sciences.

Tang, Shiping. 2010. "The Positional Market and Economic Growth." *Journal of Economic Issues* 44 (4): 915–42.

Tang, Shiping. 2011a. "Foundational Paradigms of Social Sciences." *Philosophy of the Social Sciences* 41 (2): 211–49.

Tang, Shiping. 2011b. *A General Theory of Institutional Change.* London: Routledge.

Tang, Shiping. 2013. *The Social Evolution of International Politics.* Oxford, UK: Oxford University Press.

Tang, Shiping. 2016a. "Eurasia Advantage, Not Genetic Diversity: Against Ashraf and Galor's 'Genetic Diversity' Thesis." *Historical Social Research* 41 (1): 287–327.

Tang, Shiping. 2016b. "Order: A Conceptual Analysis." *Chinese Political Science Review* 1 (1): 30–46.

Tang, Shiping. 2017. "Toward Generalized Evolutionism: Beyond 'Generalized Darwinism' and Its Critics." *Journal of Economic Issues* 51 (3): 588–612.

Tang, Shiping. 2018. "Democracy and Growth: A New Institutional Theory and Qualitative Evidences." www.ssrn.com and www.academia.edu.

Tang, Shiping. 2020. *On Social Evolution: Phenomenon and Paradigm.* London: Routledge.

Tang, Shiping. 2022. "State Capacity: A Conceptual Analysis." Working paper, Fudan University.

Tang, Shiping, and Ming Gao. 2020. "Institution, Knowledge, and Growth: Toward a Unifying Economics of Growth." Unpublished working paper, Fudan University.

Tavares, Jose, and Romain Wacziarg. 2001. "How Democracy Affects Growth?" *European Economic Review* 45 (8): 1341–78.

Tawney, Richard H. 1936. *Religion and the Rise of Capitalism: A Historical Study.* London: John Murray.

Tawney, Richard H. 1941. "The Rise of the Gentry, 1558–1640." *Economic History Review* 11 (1): 1–38.

Temin, Peter. 1997. "Is It Kosher to Talk about Culture?" *Journal of Economic History* 57 (2): 267–87.

Temple, Jonathan. 1999. "The New Growth Evidence." *Journal of Economic Literature* 37 (1): 112–56.

Temple, Jonathan. 2000. "Growth Regressions and What the Textbooks Don't Tell You." *Bulletin of Economic Research* 52 (3): 181–205.

Thaler, Richard H. 2001. "From Homo Economicus to Homo Sapiens." *Journal of Economic Perspectives* 14 (1): 133–41.

Thelen, Kathleen, and Sven Steinmo. 1992. "Historical Institutionalism in Comparative Politics." In *Structuring Politics: Historical Institutionalism in Comparative Analysis*, edited by Sven Steinmo, Kathleen Thelen, and Frank Longstreth, 1–32. Cambridge, UK: Cambridge University Press.

Thomas, M. A. 2010. "What Do the Worldwide Governance Indicators Measure?" *European Journal of Development Research* 22 (1): 31–54.

Tilly, Charles. 1975. "Western State-Making and Theories of Political Transformation." In *The Formation of National States in Western Europe*, edited by Charles Tilly. Princeton, NJ: Princeton University Press.

Tilly, Charles. 1990. *Coercion, Capital, and European States, AD 990–1990.* Malden, MA: Blackwell.

Tilly, Charles. 1998. *Durable Inequality.* Berkeley: University of California Press.

Tilly, Charles. 1999. "A Grand Tour of Exotic Landes." *American Historical Review* 104 (4): 1253–57.

Tilman, Rick. 2006. "Colin Campbell on Thorstein Veblen on Conspicuous Consumption." *Journal of Economic Issues* 40 (1): 97–112.

Tocqueville, Alexis de. [1835] 2004. *Democracy in America.* Translated by Henry Reeve. New York: Random House.

Trigg, Andrew B. 2001. "Veblen, Bourdieu, and Conspicuous Consumption." *Journal of Economic Issues* 35 (1): 99–115.

Truex, Rory. 2017. "The Myth of Democratic Advantage." *Studies in Comparative International Development* 52 (3): 261–77.

Tsai, Lily L. 2007. *Accountability without Democracy: Solidary Groups and Public Goods Provision in Rural China*. New York: Cambridge University Press.

Tumin, Melvin M. 1953. "Some Principles of Stratification: A Critical Analysis." *American Sociological Review* 18 (4): 387–94.

Turner, Adair, et al. 2010. *The Future of Finance: The LSE Report*. London: London School of Economics and Political Science.

Van Arkadie, Brian. 1999. "The State and Economic Change in Africa." In *The Role of State in Economic Change*, edited by Ha-Joon Chang and Robert Rawthorn, 187–211. Oxford, UK: Oxford University Press.

Van de Werfhorst, Herman G., and Jonathan J. B. Mijs. 2010. "Achievement Inequality and the Institutional Structure of Educational Systems: A Comparative Perspective." *Annual Review of Sociology* 36: 407–28.

Veblen, Thorstein. 1898. "Why Is Economics Not an Evolutionary Science?" *Quarterly Journal of Economics* 12 (4): 373–97.

Veblen, Thorstein. [1899] 1967. *The Theory of the Leisure Class: An Economic Analysis of Institutions*. New York: Penguin Press.

Voitchovsky, Sarah. 2009. "Inequality and Economic Growth." In *Oxford Handbook of Economic Inequality*, edited by Wiemer Salverda, Brian Nolan, and Timothy M. Smeeding, 549–74. Oxford, UK: Oxford University Press.

Vu, Tuong. 2010a. *Paths to Development in Asia*. Cambridge, UK: Cambridge University Press.

Vu, Tuong. 2010b. "Studying the State through State Formation." *World Politics* 62 (1): 148–75.

Wacziarg, Romain. 2002. "Review of Easterly's *The Elusive Quest for Growth*." *Journal of Economic Literature* 40 (3): 907–18.

Wade, Robert. 1990. *Governing the Market: Economic Theory and the Role of Government in East Asian Industrialization*. Princeton, NJ: Princeton University Press.

Walder, Andrew G. 1995. "Career Mobility and the Communist Political Order." *American Sociological Review* 60 (3): 309–28.

Walder, Andrew G. 2003. "Elite Opportunity in Transitional Economies." *American Sociological Review* 68 (6): 899–916.

Walder, Andrew G., Bobai Li, and Donald J. Treiman. 2000. "Politics and Life Chances in a State Socialist Regime: Dual Career Paths into the Urban Chinese Elite, 1949 to 1996." *American Sociological Review* 65 (2): 191–209.

Waldner, David. 1999. *State Building and Late Development*. Ithaca, NY: Cornell University Press.

Wallerstein, Immanuel. [1989] 2011. *The Modern World-System III: The Second Era of Great Expansion of the Captialist World-Economy, 1730s–1840s*. Berkeley: University of California Press.

Wang, Erik, and Yiqing Xu. 2018. "Awakening Leviathan: The Effect of Democracy on State Capacity." *Research & Politics*. https://doi.org/10.1177/2053168018772398 (accessed January 20, 2019).

Wang, Gungwu. 1985. "Loving the Ancient in China." In *Who Rules the Past*, edited by Elizabeth McBrady, 175–95. Melbourne: Oxford University Press.

Wang, Gungwu. 2004. "The Fourth Rise of China: Cultural Implications." *China: An International Journal* 2 (2): 311–22.

Weber, Max. 1958. *The Protestant Ethic and the Spirit of Capitalism*. Translated by Talcott Parsons. New York: Charles Scribner & Sons.

Weber, Max. 1978. *Economy and Society*. 2 vols. Translated and edited by Guenther Roth and Claus Wittich. Berkeley: University of California Press.

Weeks, Jessica L. P. 2014. *Dictators at War and Peace*. Ithaca, NY: Cornell University Press.

Weingast, Barry R. 1997. "The Political Foundations of Democracy and Rule of Law." *American Political Science Review* 91 (2): 245–63.

Weingast, Barry R. 2005. "The Constitutional Dilemma of Economic Liberty." *Journal of Economic Perspectives* 19 (3): 89–108.

Wen, Yi. 2015. *The Making of an Economic Superpower: Unlocking China's Secret of Rapid Industrialization.* Singapore: World Scientific.

Wen, Yi. 2016. *The Making of an Economic Superpower.* Singapore: World Scientific.

Wigley, Simon, and Arzu Akkoyunlu-Wigley. 2011. "The Impact of Regime Type on Health: Does Redistribution Explain Everything?" *World Politics* 63 (4): 647–77.

Williamson, Jeffrey G. 2012. "Review of Economic Development in the Americas since 1500: Endowments and Institutions." *Journal of Economic Literature* 50 (3): 809–18.

Williamson, Oliver E. 1975. *Markets and Hierarchies: Analysis and Antitrust Implications.* New York: Free Press.

Williamson, Oliver E. 1985. *The Institutional Foundation of Capitalism.* New York: Free Press.

Williamson, Oliver E. 2000. "The New Institutional Economics: Taking Stock, Looking Ahead." *Journal of Economic Literature* 38 (3): 595–613.

Wintrobe, Ronald. 2001. "Review of *Power and Prosperity: Outgrowing Communist and Capitalist Dictators* by Mancur Olson." *Public Choice* 106 (3/4): 390–95.

Woo-Cumings, Meredith. 1999. *The Development State.* Ithaca, NY: Cornell University Press.

World Bank. 1993. *The East Asian Miracle: Public Policy and Economic Growth.* New York: Oxford University Press.

World Bank. 1997. *World Development Report: The State in a Changing World.* New York: Oxford University Press.

World Bank. 2002. *Building Institutions for Markets.* New York: Oxford University Press.

World Bank. 2005. *Economic Growth in the 1990s: Learning from a Decade of Reform.* Washington, DC: World Bank.

World Bank. 2008. *The Growth Report: Strategies for Sustained Growth and Inclusive Development.* Washington, DC: World Bank.

World Bank. 2017. *World Development Report: Governance and Law.* Washington, DC: World Bank.

Wrong, Dennis H. 1959. "The Functional Theory of Stratification: Some Neglected Considerations." *American Sociological Review* 24 (5): 772–82.

Wu, Chin-en. 2012. "When Is Democracy Better for Economic Performance and When Is It Not: The Interaction between Polity and Structural Factors." *Studies in Comparative International Development* 47 (3): 365–88.

Xu, Chenggang. 2011. "The Fundamental Institutions of China's Reforms and Development." *Journal of Economic Literature* 49 (4): 1076–151.

Yang, Benhua. 2008. "Does Democracy Lower Growth Volatility? A Dynamic Panel Analysis." *Journal of Macroeconomics* 30 (1): 562–74.

Yang, Juan, Terry Sicular, and Desheng Lai. 2014. "The Changing Determinants of High School Attainment in Rural China." *China Economic Review* 30: 551–66.

Yao, Yang. 2014. "The Chinese Growth Miracle." In *Handbook of Economic Growth*, vol. 2, edited by Philippe Aghion and Steven Durlauf, 943–1031. Amsterdam: Elsevier North-Holland.

Yi, Hongmei, et al. 2012. "Dropping Out: Why Are Students Leaving Junior High in China's Poor Rural Areas?" *International Journal of Educational Development* 32 (4): 555–63.

Yi, Hongmei, et al. 2015. "Giving Kids a Head Start: The Impact and Mechanisms of Early Commitment of Financial Aid on Poor Students in Rural China." *Journal of Development Economics* 113 (1): 1–15.

Young, Alwyn. 1995. "The Tyranny of Numbers: Confronting the Statistical Realities of the East Asian Growth Experience." *Quarterly Journal of Economics* 110 (3): 641–80.

Yuan, Cheng, and Lei Zhang. 2015. "Public Education Spending and Private Substitution in Urban China." *Journal of Development Economics* 115: 124–39.

Zak, Paul J., and Stephen Knack. 2001. "Trust and Growth." *Economic Journal* 111 (470): 295–321.

Zeng, Junxia, Xiaopeng Pang, Linxiu Zhang, Alexis Medina, and Scott Rozelle. 2014. "Gender Inequality in Education in China: A Meta-analysis." *Contemporary Economic Policy* 32 (2): 474–91.

Zhang, Yuyan, and Cheng Gao. 2004. "American Bullion and the Rise of the West." *Shehui Kexue Zhanxian* [Frontiers of Social Science] 1: 42–69 (in Chinese).

Zhao, Meng, and Paul Glewwe. 2010. "What Determines Basic School Attainment in Developing Countries? Evidence from Rural China." *Economics of Education Review* 29 (3): 451–60.

Zilsel, Edgar. 1942. "The Sociological Roots of Science." *American Journal of Sociology* 47 (4): 544–62.

Zuo, Xiyin, and Shiping Tang. 2013. "Understanding Strategic Behavior: A Preliminary Analytical Framework." *Social Sciences in China* 34 (2): 68–86.

INDEX

Page numbers in *italics* refer to tables.

A NOTE ON THE TYPE

This book has been composed in Adobe Text and Gotham.
Adobe Text, designed by Robert Slimbach for Adobe,
bridges the gap between fifteenth- and sixteenth-century
calligraphic and eighteenth-century Modern styles.
Gotham, inspired by New York street signs, was designed
by Tobias Frere-Jones for Hoefler & Co.

Milton Keynes UK
Ingram Content Group UK Ltd.
UKHW011832231123
433157UK00003B/91